Microcomputers and mathematics

Microcomputers and mathematics

J. W. BRUCE
Department of Pure Mathematics, University of Liverpool

P. J. GIBLIN
Department of Pure Mathematics, University of Liverpool

P. J. RIPPON
Faculty of Mathematics, The Open University

CAMBRIDGE
UNIVERSITY PRESS

Published by the Press Syndicate of the University of Cambridge
The Pitt Building, Trumpington Street, Cambridge CB2 1RP
40 West 20th Street, New York, NY 10011-4211, USA
10 Stamford Road, Oakleigh, Melbourne 3166, Australia

First published 1990

Reprinted 1993 (with corrections)

British Library cataloguing in publication data
Bruce, J. W.
Microcomputers and mathematics.
1. Mathematics. Applications of microcomputer systems
I. Title   II. Giblin, P. J.   III. Rippon, P. J.
510.285416

Library of Congress cataloguing in publication data
Bruce, J. W. (James William), 1952–
Microcomputers and mathematics / J. W. Bruce, P. J. Giblin, P. J. Rippon.
   p.   cm.
ISBN 0–521–37515–0. – ISBN 0–521–31238–8 (pbk.)
1. Mathematics – Data processing.   2. Microcomputers.
I. Giblin, P. J.   II. Rippon, P. J.   III. Title.
QA76.95.B78   1989
004.16′01′51–dc20   90–31051   CIP

ISBN 0 521 37515 0 hardback
ISBN 0 521 31238 8 paperback

Transferred to digital printing 2003

For   Emily and Isaac,
Stephen and Charlotte,
Stephen, John, Matthew and Kate

Contents

Preface

This book is intended for anyone who has some mathematical knowledge and a little experience with programming a microcomputer in BASIC (or any other language). The book shows how simple programs can be used to do significant mathematics.

To spell out our mathematical prerequisites in more detail, some of the chapters assume no more mathematical knowledge than whole numbers, but for the most part we assume some calculus, and the rudiments of algebra (polynomials, equations) and trigonometry (sines, cosines and tangents). Thus, British readers with A or A/S level in mathematics and American readers with a Freshman calculus course behind them will, we hope, have little difficulty in following most of the mathematics here. We have, naturally, included some material for the more mathematically sophisticated reader: those sections requiring closer inspection are, appropriately, printed in smaller type. (We hope that readers who do not immediately recognise the small type material will be intrigued rather than frightened. Surely one of the charms of mathematics is the glimpses it affords of mysterious and fascinating territory which is for the moment just out of reach.)

As for programming, the knowledge we assume is very small, and most programs are given full listings in the text. It seems to us that a very effective way to learn programming is to use it to solve interesting mathematical problems. We have regarded the mathematics as the pre-eminent interest, and have not tried too hard to make the sample programs beautiful or elegant, or even particularly efficient. It is up to the reader to improve them!

We are not geared to any one machine, but have tried to write the programs in a 'basic BASIC' which will be understood by any microcomputer. (See the 'Note on programs', below, for the exceptions to this which necessarily arise when using graphics.) Thus no software is used, beyond the BASIC language itself. In particular, apart from some work on multi-precision arithmetic in Chapter 4, we do not touch on symbolic manipulation (so we do not say anything about symbolic differentiation, for example). It is worth adding that we make only modest demands on the power of the microcomputers too: virtually any cheap home computer will be adequate for the investigations in this book. Indeed the authors for the most part used only inexpensive home computers when preparing the material.

We have produced the diagrams either by hand or by 'dumping' the screen from a microcomputer, resisting the temptation to use powerful equipment to produce a more polished appearance.

Why use a computer to do mathematics? The fact is that mathematics is, like all the sciences, an experimental subject. Sample computations and extensive calculations form the body of experimental evidence. Sifting through this data, and using his experience and judgement, the mathematician may conjecture a new theorem. Each new example may turn out to be the one which shows the conjecture to be *false*. If no such counterexample is found then eventually enough insight may be gained to write down a formal proof of the theorem. (And if a counterexample *is* found maybe the 'theorem' can be adjusted slightly . . .)

With a microcomputer to hand, we can all be experimenters on a scale which was impossible in the past. Thus we can all discover, and maybe even prove, new results. (We do not have to be the first to discover a result to sense the thrill of discovery!) It is, however, not an easy matter to decide which experiments are worth performing; at the beginning much guidance is needed, and our aim in writing this book is to provide such guidance, in a wide variety of contexts.

We believe that the microcomputer can bring certain parts of mathematics alive in a way that it is not possible for plain text, or even a teacher, to do unaided. This comes about partly because of the possibility of experimentation, but also because facts and relationships can be illustrated swiftly and effectively, either by numerical calculation or through graphics. Because sight is the most refined sense, the pictorial or graphical representation of data, or a problem, or its solution, is without doubt one of the most important paths to understanding. We exploit this in several chapters of the book.

Use of a powerful tool like a microcomputer must always be active, not passive. Passive contemplation of a screen is no more doing mathematics than is passive contemplation of a sheet of paper. It is important to understand the program, study the output carefully, rerun the program with different data, and think about what is happening.

The various chapters of the book are largely independent of one another, in order to provide users (whether students or teachers) with ready-made material for projects or other investigative work and for demonstrations of mathematical ideas. Many exercises and projects are included. The book can also be used as the basis for a course in algorithmic mathematics, at several different levels, depending on the choice of material. All the topics covered should, can and sometimes even do find their way into undergraduate mathematics syllabuses.

Here is a brief run-down of the contents of the book. Each chapter is also provided with an introduction and list of references.

There are two chapters (Chapters 1 and 4) on whole numbers. The topics covered include highest common factors, continued fractions, quadratic residues and prime numbers. Since some of the fascination of number theory results from the contemplation of large numbers, we include (in Chapter 4) a section on manipulation of large numbers by multi-precision arithmetic. But a great deal can be learnt, too, by staying within the ordinary precision of the micro-computer (we do not assume double precision is available).

Solution of equations by approximate means, including the use of approximations to find complex solutions, is the subject of Chapter 2. There is some discussion here of the validity of the Newton–Raphson method of approximation, but we do not venture far, here or elsewhere, into 'numerical analysis'. (The reader will find some material on estimating errors in Chapters 6 and 8.) Chapter 2 is all numerical work, graphs of functions being left to Chapter 3, where there is a section on approximation of functions by polynomials, and a section on two classical constructions from a plane curve, namely parallels and evolutes, which can be appreciated as never before by the use of a microcomputer. Curves continue in Chapter 5, where some harder questions are considered, such as the drawing of contours of a function ($f(x, y) =$ constant) and the drawing of curves traced out by simple linkages.

Chapter 6 is about special numbers such as square roots, e and π. Surely no number has exercised quite such a fascination as π, which is now known to millions of decimal places. Some of the methods used to approximate π are described in this chapter.

Chapter 7 is on differential equations, which are central to so many applications of mathematics to science. The microcomputer is an excellent tool for obtaining approximate graphical solutions, which often reveal a good deal about the physical situation being studied. More precise solutions often require quite sophisticated numerical work, and we do not venture into that difficult territory here.

One of the things the microcomputer can do best is to repeat, over and over, some process which would be extremely tedious to do by hand. But what happens when a simple process is repeated a great many times? Convergence? Divergence? Chaos? This question is studied in some detail in Chapter 8 on iteration of (real) maps. This chapter contains more theoretical material than the others, and also contains a rather detailed account (in Section 9) of quadratic iteration. This section is markedly more difficult than the rest of the book, but we hope that the inclusion of so interesting a topic, so much the subject of current research, will be of value to readers.

We hope that the material in this book conveys the authors' conviction that mathematics is an exciting, beautiful and central subject. Throughout history mathematics has occupied the waking (and no doubt sleeping) hours of very many people, whether as professionals, as scientists trying to use mathematics to solve their problems, or as amateurs interested in the subject for its own sake or as a source of recreation. In this book we have tried to show how a wonder of modern technology, the microcomputer, can be used to illuminate some small parts of this vast living monument to the endeavours of so many men and women, past and present. The great C. F. Gauss, as a schoolboy, calculated the reciprocals of all the integers from 1 to 1000 in order to study the lengths of the decimal periods. He remained an indefatigable calculator all his life. What would he have achieved with a microcomputer?

December, 1988

J. W. BRUCE, P. J. GIBLIN, P. J. RIPPON

Acknowledgements

The second author was, for part of the writing period, a Five Colleges Visiting Professor based at the University of Massachusetts in Amherst. He thanks Five Colleges for hospitality and support, in particular the University of Massachusetts, and Amherst College where his computing was done. The first and third authors were both at University College, Cork, when this book was first mooted. They thank the staff there for all the help and encouragement which they gave to two recent overseas graduates!

Note on programs and machines

The lines printed in UPPERCASE letters are in a form of BASIC which is, we hope, intelligible to most micros and their owners. We have included the (usually) optional words THEN and LET to make the programs easier to read, e.g.

    1ØØ LET X = A + B: LET Y = A * B
    2ØØ IF X < Y THEN GOTO 3ØØ

We have not put 'remark' lines into the programs; instead comments are placed between program lines or at the end of the program, justified to the left margin of the page and printed in ordinary type. They are simply ignored when typing in a program.

Variables which in the text occur with suffices are written in the programs by juxtaposition of characters, thus

x_0 becomes XØ, y_u becomes YU.

We use only uppercase letters for variables in programs; where appropriate these relate to the corresponding lowercase letters in the text.

Given the enormous variety of micros now available it is clearly impossible to write programs even in 'esperanto' BASIC which will run on all machines. This is particularly true of any graphics commands. Lines in programs which are machine dependent are written descriptively and in lowercase letters, e.g.

    1ØØ Draw a line from (a, b) to (c, d).

These must be translated into the particular commands appropriate to the micro you are using.

We do not, however, guarantee that the remaining standard BASIC commands will work on any machine. For example on some machines the standard user defined function instruction DEF FNA ... will not work. On others RND does not generate random numbers between 0 and 1. One particular difficulty concerns natural logarithms, or logs to the base e. On some machines this function is denoted by LN, on others by LOG. In our programs we have always used LN, in accord with the notation used in the text. We are confident, however, that anyone using this book, who has a good understanding of BASIC and their machine, will have no difficulty making the corresponding changes to the listed programs. One further minor point: in Chapter 4, when dealing with large numbers, we shall frequently assume that your micro is capable of *exact* eight digit arithmetic. (That is can add, subtract and multiply numbers with eight or fewer digits *exactly*, i.e. without rounding, provided the result also has at most eight digits.) Some machines (usually the more expensive ones) do *not* have this facility, but this will not prove any real problem.

1

Numbers: Part 1

Numbers, whole positive numbers (or natural numbers as they are usually called) are, of course, in one sense elementary. Basic arithmetic is the first brush we all have with mathematics, and we quickly become adept with the standard arithmetical operations. This is (basically!) the one mathematical talent our micro has, together of course with the extra advantage of speed. Essentially it is the computer's speed which we shall be exploiting in this book, for it makes possible interesting mathematical experiments involving long computations or many computations (or many long computations).

In this chapter we shall certainly spend some of our time using our computer to manipulate large numbers. Very large numbers have a certain fascination and there are some interesting tasks ahead. However, long blind computations are very much *not* the point of this book. Moving away from the mechanical aspects of arithmetic to more general questions one finds that the problems involved become decidedly difficult. In this chapter we hope to introduce you to some of the mysteries of this 'higher arithmetic' and convince you that arithmetic can be fun and extremely difficult.

§1
The Euclidean algorithm

Given two natural numbers a and b how can we find their highest common factor (hcf)? One method of course is to factorize them both as a product of prime numbers and take the product of their common prime factors. Indeed this may well be the method you learnt at school, and for relatively small numbers is quite acceptable. For large numbers, however, it is *very* time consuming (as we shall see later) and unnecessarily inefficient. A far better method, which we now describe, was known to the ancient Greeks.

Let us suppose that $a > b$ (if $b > a$ simply interchange a and b, and of course if $a = b$ there is no need to do any computations anyway). If a is divisible by b clearly the hcf of a and b (which, to save time, we will write hcf(a, b)) is b. Otherwise we can write

$$a = qb + r \qquad (1)$$

where the remainder r satisfies $0 < r < b$. Now using Equation (1) it is

1

clear that any factor of a and b is also a factor of r, since $r = a - qb$, and consequently $hcf(a, b) = hcf(b, r)$. 'Well, so what?' you may ask, we still have to find an hcf, we have simply changed from a and b to b and r. True, *but notice that $b < a$ and $r < b$*: we have a smaller pair of numbers to deal with. If we now carry out the same procedure as above, but with b and r replacing a and b we find that either b is divisible by r, and so $hcf(b, r) = hcf(a, b) = r$ or we can write

$$b = q_1 r + r_1 \qquad (2)$$

where the remainder r_1 satisfies $0 < r_1 < r$.

Of course, just as before, we deduce that $hcf(r, r_1) = hcf(b, r)$ $(= hcf(a, b))$, and we can now replace b and r by r and r_1. Now it is not difficult to see that this process cannot be repeated indefinitely, it *eventually terminates*. Whenever we are designing an algorithm or writing a computer program we must always check that this is so. The reason that it terminates is that the sequence of remainders $r, r_1, r_2, \ldots$ is getting smaller and smaller. However, such a decreasing sequence of positive whole numbers must eventually stop. But if the process terminates then at that stage the larger of the two numbers under consideration is a multiple of the smaller and this smaller number is the required hcf. Here is a program for implementing this Euclidean algorithm with a, b, the input values.

1.1 *Program: Euclid's algorithm*

```
1Ø INPUT A,B
2Ø LET U = A: LET V = B: LET A = B
3Ø LET B = U − INT(U/V)∗V
4Ø IF B < >Ø THEN GOTO 2Ø
5Ø PRINT "HCF IS"; V
```

(As usual with programs you may find it easier to write your own than to decipher somebody else's. The sample programs in this book make no pretence at efficiency; where possible we have opted for clarity in preference. We trust that the reader will incorporate his or her own improvements.)

1.2 *Exercises: More on hcfs and lcms*

(a) You may also recall from your early schoolwork the idea of a lowest common multiple, or lcm, of two numbers; $lcm(a, b)$ denotes the smallest (positive) number which is both a multiple of a and a multiple of b. Write a program for computing the lcm of two numbers a and b. (Hint: $a \cdot b = lcm(a, b)hcf(a, b)$).

(b) The Euclidean algorithm can easily be used to find the hcf of more than two numbers, using the fact that hcf(a, b, c) = hcf(a, hcf(b, c)). We leave its proof, generalization and implementation on your micro to you.

The Euclidean algorithm, as well as producing the hcf of two numbers, actually yields some further interesting information, namely that

$$\text{hcf}(a, b) = ax + by \tag{1}$$

for some *integers x* and *y* (remember integers can be negative). To see this recall our previous discussion. Using Equation (1) of §1 above we had $r = a - qb$, which is in the form (1). Similarly $r_1 = b - q_1 r = b - q_1(a - qb) = -q_1 a + (1 + qq_1)b$ is again of the form (1).

It is now easy to see that all of the remainders generated by the Euclidean algorithm are of the form $ax + by$, in particular this is true for hcf(a, b). How does one compute the corresponding values of x and y in this case? Let us do a certain amount of relabelling: we take $r_1 = a, r_2 = b, r_3 = r, q = q_1$ and rewrite

$$a = bq + r \quad \text{as} \quad r_1 = q_1 r_2 + r_3.$$

At the next stage we replace r_1 by r_2, r_2 by r_3 and write

$$r_2 = q_2 r_3 + r_4$$

the new remainder being denoted by r_4. We continue in this way working our way down the list of rs generating new remainders $r_5, r_6, \ldots$ until at some stage the remainder in question is zero and the Euclidean algorithm terminates. Thus we have

$$r_1 = a, r_2 = b$$

and

$$r_1 = q_1 r_2 + r_3$$
$$r_2 = q_2 r_3 + r_4$$
$$r_3 = q_3 r_4 + r_5$$
$$\vdots$$
$$r_{n-1} = q_{n-1} r_n + r_{n+1}$$
$$r_n = q_n r_{n+1}.$$

Our aim is to write hcf(a, b) = r_{n+1} as $ax + by$; we know that each remainder r_i can be written in this way. Let us write $r_i = x_i a + y_i b = x_i r_1 + y_i r_2$. Then, since $r_{i-1} = q_{i-1} r_i + r_{i+1}$, we deduce that $r_{i+1} = r_{i-1} - q_{i-1} r_i$ and so

$$x_{i+1} = x_{i-1} \cdots q_{i-1} x_i \Big\}$$
$$y_{i+1} = y_{i-1} - q_{i-1} y_i \Big\}. \tag{2}$$

Using these formulae we want to find x_{n+1} and y_{n+1}. Since $r_1 = a$ and $r_2 = b$ clearly $x_1 = 1$, $y_1 = 0$, $x_2 = 0$, $y_2 = 1$, and these two initial sets of values for x and y together with Equations (2) suffice to determine x_{n+1} and y_{n+1}. Here is an implementation of the resulting algorithm. In the program Equation (2) is used in the form

$$x_{\text{new}} = x_{\text{old}} - qx$$
$$y_{\text{new}} = y_{\text{old}} - qy.$$

The qs and rs are determined just as in the Euclidean algorithm itself.

2.1 *Program: Hcf as a linear combination*

```
10  INPUT A,B: LET R = A: LET S = B
20  IF B > A THEN LET C = B: LET B = A: LET A = C
30  LET XOLD = 1: LET YOLD = Ø:
    LET X = Ø: LET Y = 1
40  LET Q = INT(A/B): LET C = A − Q∗B:
    IF C = Ø THEN GOTO 9Ø
50  LET XNEW = XOLD − Q∗X
60  LET YNEW = YOLD − Q∗Y
70  LET XOLD = X: LET YOLD = Y:
    LET X = XNEW: LET Y = YNEW
80  LET A = B: LET B = C: GOTO 4Ø
90  PRINT "HCF IS"; B; " = "; X; "∗"; R; " + "; Y; "∗"; S
```

We shall return to this question of expressing the hcf of two whole numbers as a linear combination of them later in Section 4.7.

2.2 *Exercise: Monkey puzzle*

Here is an old and rather difficult puzzle for you to think about. You may find it impossible to solve at the moment (if you can solve it, well done!) but you should be able to manage it by the time you have finished reading this chapter.

Five sailors were cast away on a desert island. To provide food they collected all the coconuts they could find. During the night one of the sailors awoke divided the nuts into five equal piles and discovered that one nut was left over. This extra one he threw to the monkeys; he then hid his share and went back to sleep. Later a second sailor awoke and did the same as the first. He divided the *remaining* nuts into five equal piles, discovered there was one left over which he threw to the monkeys, and then hid his share. In their turn the three other sailors did the same, each throwing a single coconut to the monkeys.

The next morning the sailors, ignorant of each others' deception, divided the remaining nuts into five equal piles, no nuts being left over this time. The problem is to find the smallest number of nuts in the original pile.

We give two hints for the solution:

(a) Show that the problem reduces to finding a solution of the equation $1024x - 15625y = 8404$ with x and y positive integers and x as small as possible.

(b) First solve the equation $1024x - 15625y = 1$.

2.3 *Exercises*

(a) If the hcf of two numbers a and b is 1 we say that a and b are *coprime*. If this is so then we know that for some integers x and y we have $ax + by = 1$ and consequently any whole number can be written in the form $ax' + by'$ for some integers x' and y'. (There is a moral here for those impressed by the less than scientific evidence put forward for the importance of certain natural biorhythms. If a and b represent the periods, measured in days, of some such fundamental rhythms, then if a and b are coprime any day has some rhythmic significance.)

Conversely if for some integers x and y we have $ax + by = 1$ then clearly hcf$(a, b) = 1$ for this hcf must also divide $ax + by$. Also we might ask to what extent are the numbers x and y here determined by a and b? If $ax + by = 1 = ax_1 + by_1$ then obviously $(x - x_1)a = (y_1 - y)b$. Since a and b have no factors in common a divides $y_1 - y$ and b divides $x - x_1$. Indeed we can write $x - x_1 = rb$, $y_1 - y = ra$ and $x_1 = x - rb$, $y_1 = y + ra$, so $ax_1 + by_1 = ax + by + r(-ab + ba)$, and we see that any two representations $ax + by = 1$ differ in only a rather trivial way. The questions we would like you to think about are the following. The representation $ax + by = 1$ with $x^2 + y^2$ as small as possible is called the minimal one. With the minimal representation how large can x, y (relative to a and b) be? How small can they be? Does the Euclidean algorithm never/ever/always give the minimal representation?

(b) Use your programs for finding hcfs and lcms to write further programs for doing arithmetic with fractions. That is, write programs to add, subtract, multiply and divide fractions. (Note, even multiplication and division are not trivial – no common factors please!)

The Euclidean algorithm can be used to investigate a number of interesting questions. One such is the following: what is the probability that two randomly chosen numbers are coprime, i.e. have no factor greater than 1 in common?

We first have to make precise sense of the question. For a given n we can consider all pairs of numbers a and b with $1 \leq a, b \leq n$; there are clearly n^2 such. Amongst these pairs there will be a certain number $c(n)$ which are coprime. Clearly $c(n)/n^2$ is the probability a randomly chosen pair of numbers between 1 and n are coprime, and the probability we seek, p, is the limit $\lim_{n \to \infty} c(n)/n^2$. We can attempt to find an approximation to p either by computing $c(n)$ exactly for large values of n or by *simulation*. In the former case we observe that we need only consider pairs (a, b) with $1 \leq a < b \leq n$ when running our program. If $d(n)$ is the number of coprime pairs (a, b) as above then $c(n) = 2d(n) + 1$; this observation will halve the running time of your algorithm, and we leave you to write a suitable program. Let us turn to the second suggestion above – what do we mean by simulation? The essential idea here is randomly to select pairs of integers a and b, say m pairs, and record the number of such, say r, which are coprime. In some sense the quotient r/m is an approximation to the required probability p. Since your micro will certainly have a random number generator it is not very difficult to generate your random pairs of integers (a, b). The expression INT$(1 + N*RND)$ will yield a 'random' integer between 1 and n. In practice, of course, we will only randomly select pairs of integers a, b within some specified interval $1 \leq a, b \leq n$, so that the quotient r/m is really an approximation to $c(n)/n^2$. However, if n is large, perhaps so large that it is not feasible to compute $c(n)$ explicitly, r/m should be a good approximation to the required probability p. Here is a program for computing an approximation to p.

3.1 *Program: Coprimality and probability*

```
10 INPUT N,M
20 LET X = 0
30 FOR I = 1 TO M
40 LET A = INT(1 + N*RND):
   LET B = INT(1 + N*RND)
50 LET U = A: LET V = B: LET A = B
60 LET B = U − INT(U/V)*V
70 IF B < >0 THEN GOTO 50
80 IF V = 1 THEN LET X = X + 1
90 NEXT I
```

100 PRINT "PROPORTION OF COPRIME PAIRS IS";
   X/M

Here n determines the interval to which a and b belong while m is the sample size. Clearly the larger n and m are, the better our approximation to the required probability should be. The next section (the first of our mathematical excursions) gives the exact answer.

3.2 *Mathematical excursion*

If you run the above program with fairly large values of n and m the proportion of coprime pairs should be around 0.6. It is a rather startling fact that the correct (precise) answer is $6/\pi^2$: here we have π, which we think of as a geometric quantity, arising as part of the answer to a problem in number theory.

How does one prove this result? Unfortunately the proof is too long and difficult to include here; it would take us through some fascinating topics: the Euler ϕ-function (which we will meet again), Möbius inversion, Riemann's ζ-function and, at the last, the fact that $1 + \frac{1}{4} + \frac{1}{9} + \ldots = \Sigma_{r=1}^{\infty} 1/r^2 = \pi^2/6$. See Rademacher (1964), pp. 105–9. (The authors took $n = 100\,000$, $m = 10\,000$ and obtained $p = 0.6094$ which is a fairly good approximation to $6/\pi^2 = 0.6079\ldots$. The running time was rather long though; definitely the sort of job to start and then leave on its own: take a bath, go for a walk, have a meal $\ldots$.) You should also be warned that the sum $\Sigma_{r=1}^{\infty} 1/r^2$ converges *rather slowly* to $\pi^2/6$, so if you are going to sum it on your micro you will need to add a lot of terms to obtain an accurate result. To obtain the sum correct to just two decimal places requires the first 200 terms, and each additional decimal place needs ten times as many terms as the previous one. By adding the first 100 000 terms for example, and inverting, we obtain $0.6079319\ldots$ as an approximation to $6/\pi^2 = 0.607927\ldots$. See Chapter 6 for further details.

Here is a plausible argument, however, that the probability p *is* $1/\Sigma_{r=1}^{\infty} 1/r^2$. Let m and n be any pair of integers and suppose $\mathrm{hcf}(m, n) = r$. Then clearly m and n are multiples of r and $\mathrm{hcf}(m/r, n/r) = 1$. Consequently the probability that $\mathrm{hcf}(m, n) = r$ is $(1/r)(1/r)p$. (Do you see why? Recall our definition of p.) Given any pair of integers m, n the $\mathrm{hcf}(m, n)$ is *some* positive integer r so the sum $\Sigma_{r=1}^{\infty} p/r^2 = 1$, i.e. $p = 1/(\Sigma_{r=1}^{\infty} 1/r^2)$ as asserted.

3.3 *Exercises: Probabilities*

Investigate the following questions by micro or pen and paper.

(a) What is the probability that two positive integers m, n have $\mathrm{hcf}(m, n) \leq 3$?

(b) What is the average value of $\mathrm{hcf}(m, n)$ for m, n positive integers?

(c) What is the probability that two positive odd integers m and n are coprime?

(*Answers*:

(a) By the argument of the preceding section the probability is

$p(1 + \frac{1}{4} + \frac{1}{9}) = 49/6\pi^2$ which is about 0.83.

(*b*) The probability that hcf$(m, n) = r$ is p/r^2 so the average value of hcf(m, n) is $\sum_{r=1}^{\infty} (p/r^2)r = p \sum_{r=1}^{\infty} 1/r = (6/\pi^2) \sum_{r=1}^{\infty} 1/r$. You may try summing the series $\sum_{r=1}^{\infty} 1/r = 1 + \frac{1}{2} + \frac{1}{3} + \frac{1}{4} + \ldots$, on your micro but round off errors may well blind you to the truth: it simply gets bigger and bigger, i.e. *diverges*. In other words the average value of hcf(m, n) is *infinite*. See Chapter 6 for further details about $\sum_{r=1}^{\infty} 1/r$.

(*c*) Apply the argument used above: let q denote the required probability. If m, n are odd positive integers then hcf$(m, n) = r$ is odd and again hcf$(m/r, n/r) = 1$. Consequently the probability that two odd positive integers m, n have hcf equal to r (also odd) is q/r^2, just as before. It now follows that $q(\frac{1}{1} + \frac{1}{9} + \frac{1}{25} + \frac{1}{49} + \ldots) = q[\sum_{r=1}^{\infty} 1/(2r-1)^2] = 1$, so the required probability, assuming it exists, is given by $q = 1/\sum_{r=1}^{\infty} 1/(2r-1)^2$. Now note that

$$\frac{\pi^2}{6} = 1 + \frac{1}{4} + \frac{1}{9} + \frac{1}{25} + \ldots = \left(1 + \frac{1}{9} + \frac{1}{25} + \frac{1}{49} + \ldots\right)$$

$$+ \left(\frac{1}{4} + \frac{1}{16} + \frac{1}{36} + \ldots\right)$$

$$= \frac{1}{q} + \frac{1}{4}\left(1 + \frac{1}{4} + \frac{1}{9} + \frac{1}{16} + \ldots\right)$$

$$= \frac{1}{q} + \frac{\pi^2}{24},$$

so that $1/q = \pi^2/8$ and $q = 8/\pi^2$, which is 0.81 . . . .)

§4
Continued
fractions

A topic intimately connected with the Euclidean algorithm is that of *continued fractions*, which we now investigate.

We start by applying Euclid's Algorithm to the pair of numbers 67, 28:

$$67 = 2 \times 28 + 11$$
$$28 = 2 \times 11 + 6$$
$$11 = 1 \times 6 + 5$$
$$6 = 1 \times 5 + 1.$$

Naturally the final remainder is 1 since hcf$(67, 28) = 1$. These four equations can be rewritten as

$$\frac{67}{28} = 2 + \frac{11}{28}$$

$$\frac{28}{11} = 2 + \frac{6}{11}$$

$$\frac{11}{6} = 1 + \frac{5}{6}$$

$$\frac{6}{5} = 1 + \frac{1}{5}$$

and you will notice that the last fraction of each line is the reciprocal of the first fraction of the following line. Consequently we can write

$$\frac{6}{5} = 1 + \frac{1}{5} \qquad \text{(from line 4)}$$

$$\frac{11}{6} = 1 + \cfrac{1}{1 + \cfrac{1}{5}} \qquad \text{(substituting the above into line 3)}$$

$$\frac{28}{11} = 2 + \cfrac{1}{1 + \cfrac{1}{1 + \cfrac{1}{5}}} \qquad \text{(using line 2)}$$

and so finally

$$\frac{67}{28} = 2 + \cfrac{1}{2 + \cfrac{1}{1 + \cfrac{1}{1 + \cfrac{1}{5}}}}.$$

This latter expression is called the continued fraction form of 67/28. It is far more convenient to write the above expression as $2 + \frac{1}{2+} \frac{1}{1+} \frac{1}{1+} \frac{1}{5}$ or [2, 2, 1, 1, 5] and we shall use one of these forms from now on.

Clearly every rational number a/b can be expressed in the form of a continued fraction: one simply applies the Euclidean algorithm to obtain an expression

$$\frac{a}{b} = r(1) + \frac{1}{r(2) +} \frac{1}{r(3) +} \frac{1}{r(4) +} \cdots + \frac{1}{r(n)}$$

where the $r(i)$ are natural numbers. For example you can check

$$\frac{53}{11} = 4 + \frac{1}{1+} \frac{1}{4+} \frac{1}{2}.$$

Our first program computes the continued fraction form of any rational number a/b, not necessarily in reduced terms; it prints out the $r(i)$ as a sequence separated by commas. (Note: if $a/b < 1$ the algorithm produces a zero as the first term e.g. $\frac{11}{15} = 0 + \frac{1}{1+} \frac{1}{2+} \frac{1}{1+} \frac{1}{3}$)

4.1 *Program: Continued fractions 1*

```
10 INPUT A,B
20 LET U = A: LET V = B: LET A = B
```

$3\emptyset$ LET B = U − INT(U/V)∗V

$4\emptyset$ PRINT; INT(U/V); ",";

$5\emptyset$ IF B < >$\emptyset$ THEN GOTO $2\emptyset$.

As you will see the program is short and its execution swift. You will also notice, when running this program, that the final term is always an integer greater than 1, for it is the penultimate remainder of Euclid's Algorithm, and consequently cannot equal 1.

Having introduced continued fractions you may well wonder if they are of any use. Clearly an expression like 53/11 is much easier to deal with than $4 + \frac{1}{1+} \frac{1}{4+} \frac{1}{2}$, at least as far as the ordinary arithmetic operations are concerned. In fact, continued fractions are an invaluable tool in number theory; they provide *explicit* solutions to a variety of problems which other methods only solve implicitly.

Before illustrating this point we first consider the converse problem to that studied above: given a continued fraction, find the rational number a/b which it represents. For continued fractions with fewish terms this is not an impossible task by hand of course; e.g.

$$3 + \frac{1}{2+} \frac{1}{4+} \frac{1}{3} = 3 + \frac{1}{2+} \frac{1}{13/3}$$

$$= 3 + \frac{1}{2 + 3/13}$$

$$= 3 + \frac{1}{29/13} = 3\frac{13}{29} = \frac{100}{29}.$$

This rapidly becomes tedious, however, for fractions with a larger number of terms, and the method used is not very easy to implement in a program. A little thought will provide us with a more efficient algorithm and a very elegant program, so let us return for a moment to the general form of a continued fraction

$$r(1) + \frac{1}{r(2) +} \frac{1}{r(3) +} \cdots \frac{1}{r(n-1) +} \frac{1}{r(n)}$$

$$= [r(1), r(2), \ldots, r(n)].$$

A little calculation shows that

$$[r(1)] = \frac{r(1)}{1}, [r(1), r(2)] = \frac{r(1)r(2) + 1}{r(2)},$$

$$[r(1), r(2), r(3)] = \frac{r(1)r(2)r(3) + r(3) + r(1)}{r(2)r(3) + 1},$$

$$[r(1), r(2), r(3), r(4)]$$

$$= \frac{r(1)r(2)r(3)r(4) + r(1)r(2) + r(1)r(4) + r(3)r(4) + 1}{r(2)r(3)r(4) + r(2) + r(4)}.$$

Please do these computations yourself!

Now we make the following observation, which might have occurred to you when doing the above computations. Clearly

$$[r(1), r(2), \ldots, r(n)] = r(1) + \frac{1}{r(2) +} \frac{1}{r(3) +} \cdots \frac{1}{r(n)}$$

$$= r(1) + \frac{1}{[r(2), \ldots, r(n)]},$$

so if

$$[r(2), \ldots, r(n)] = p/q$$

then

$$[r(1), \ldots, r(n)] = r(1) + \frac{q}{p} = \frac{r(1)p + q}{p}.$$

This now gives an inductive method for computing the standard rational representation of a continued fraction. For working backwards through the sequence $r(1), \ldots, r(n)$ we find

$$[r(n)] = r(n) = p \quad (\text{and } q = 1),$$

and

$$[r(n-1), r(n)] = r(n-1) + \frac{q}{p} = \frac{r(n-1)p + q}{p};$$

we now take $r(n-1)p + q$ for our new value of p and p for our new value of q. One step further back we have

$$[r(n-2), r(n-1), r(n)] = r(n-2) + \frac{q}{p} = \frac{r(n-2)p + q}{p};$$

again, we change our running values of p and q, taking our new value of p to be $r(n-2)p + q$, our new value of q to be p. Clearly this provides us with an inductive method of computing $[r(1), \ldots, r(n)]$. Here is this algorithm implemented in a program.

4.2 *Program: Continued fractions 2*

```
1Ø INPUT N
2Ø DIM R(N)
3Ø FOR I = 1 TO N
4Ø INPUT R(I)
```

```
5Ø  NEXT I
6Ø  LET P = 1: LET Q = Ø
7Ø  FOR I = 1 TO N
8Ø  LET U = P: LET V = Q
9Ø  LET P = R(N + 1 − I)∗U + V: LET Q = U
1ØØ NEXT I
11Ø PRINT; "(";
12Ø FOR I = 1 TO N − 1
13Ø PRINT; R(I); ",";
14Ø NEXT I
15Ø PRINT R(N); ") = "; P; "/"; Q
```

The program should be clear. (We have taken greater care with the form of our output here than usual; remember elegance is your responsibility!)

Having written this program we may now investigate the so-called *convergents* of a continued fraction. The convergents are simply the rational numbers or fractions obtained by truncating the continued fraction algorithm at the first, second, third, etc. . . . stages. Thus the convergents of $[r(1), r(2), \ldots, r(n)]$ are $[r(1)]$, $[r(1), r(2)]$, $[r(1), r(2), r(3)]$, ... For example the convergents of 100/29 are 3, 7/2, 31/9, 100/29.

You may combine the preceding two programs to compute the convergents of the continued fraction of any rational number. The problem with this, however, is that Program 4.2 yields the rational representation of a continued fraction starting with its final term $r(n)$ and moving backwards. This will make the obvious algorithm rather inefficient; we want to use the values of earlier convergents to compute those of later ones. The following result provides the required method.

4.3 *Definition of $p(m)$ and $q(m)$*
Define $p(m)$ and $q(m)$ by

$$p(1) = r(1), \; p(2) = r(1)r(2) + 1,$$
$$p(m) = r(m)p(m − 1) + p(m − 2), \; 3 \leqslant m \leqslant n,$$
$$q(1) = 1 \quad, \; q(2) = r(2) \qquad ,$$
$$q(m) = r(m)q(m − 1) + q(m − 2), \; 3 \leqslant m \leqslant n.$$

Then

$$[r(1), r(2), \ldots, r(m)] = p(m)/q(m), \text{ for } 1 \leqslant m \leqslant n.$$

4.4 *Mathematical excursion*
The proof of the above assertion really is not very difficult. We have already seen that it is true for $m = 1$ and 2. We now proceed by induction on m.

Suppose that the assertion is true for all values of $m \leqslant N$. Now $[r(1), r(2), \ldots, r(N), r(N+1)] = [r(1), r(2), \ldots, r(N) + 1/r(N+1)]$ and by induction this latter expression is

$$\frac{(r(N) + 1/r(N+1))p(N-1) + p(N-2)}{(r(N) + 1/r(N+1))q(N-1) + q(N-2)}$$

$$= \frac{r(N+1)(r(N)p(N-1) + p(N-2)) + p(N-1)}{r(N+1)(r(N)q(N-1) + q(N-2)) + q(N-1)}$$

$$= \frac{r(N+1)p(N) + p(N-1)}{r(N+1)q(N) + q(N-1)} = \frac{p(N+1)}{q(N+1)}.$$

The result follows. (The sharp-eyed will have noticed that we have considered a continued fraction above with entries which are rational numbers, not integers. You will easily check though that the reasoning remains valid. Indeed the result is true, and the proof valid, for any real $r(1), \ldots, r(n)$.)

It only remains to implement the resulting algorithm, which we now do.

4.5 *Program: Convergents*
```
10  INPUT A,B
20  PRINT "THE CONVERGENTS FOR";
    A; "/"; B; "ARE";
30  LET P1 = Ø: LET P2 = 1: LET Q1 = 1: LET Q2 = Ø
40  LET U = A: LET V = B: LET A = B
50  LET R = INT(U/V): LET B = U − R∗V
60  LET S = R∗P2 + P1: LET T = R∗Q2 + Q1
70  LET P1 = P2: LET P2 = S: LET Q1 = Q2: LET Q2 = T
80  PRINT; P2; "/"; Q2; ",";
90  IF B < >Ø THEN GOTO 40
```
You should now run this program computing the convergents of various rational numbers.

4.6 *More on convergents*
When you have done this you will doubtless (!) have made the following observations:

(*a*) The functions $p(m)$ and $q(m)$ satisfy

$$\frac{p(m)}{q(m)} - \frac{p(m-1)}{q(m-1)} = \frac{(-1)^{m-1}}{q(m)q(m-1)}$$

$$\frac{p(m)}{q(m)} - \frac{p(m-2)}{q(m-2)} = \frac{(-1)^m r(m)}{q(m)q(m-2)}.$$

(These two results are fairly easily established: clear denominators and use the inductive definitions of $p(m)$ and $q(m)$.)

(b) The even convergents $p(2m)/q(2m)$ increase as m increases, while the odd convergents $p(2m + 1)/q(2m + 1)$ decrease as m increases. These both follow from the second equality of (a), or less directly from the first using the fact that the qs are increasing.

(c) Every odd convergent is greater than any even convergent. This follows from the first equality of (a) and result (b).

(d) Except for the last convergent, which obviously *is* the continued fraction, all odd convergents are greater than the continued fraction while all even convergents are less than the continued fraction. This follows from the previous result.

(e) The convergents $p(m)/q(m)$ are in their lowest terms; i.e. $p(m)$ and $q(m)$ have no common factors. This follows from the first part of (a), for if d divides $p(m)$ and $q(m)$ it also divides $p(m)q(m - 1) - p(m - 1)q(m) = (-1)^{m-1}$. One final interesting feature, to which we will return later, is that the convergents $p(m)/q(m)$ are, for their denominators, excellent approximations to a/b. In fact we have the inequality $|a/b - p(m)/q(m)| < 1/q(m)^2$; which is proved in Hardy and Wright (1975), pp. 136–7. Indeed, the convergents are the 'best possible' approximations to a/b by fractions p/q with $q \leq q(m)$. More precisely any fraction p/q which is nearer to a/b than $p(m)/q(m)$ must have denominator $q > q(m)$. (See Hardy and Wright (1975), pp. 151–2, and Section 5.5 below.)

4.7 *Project: The equation $ax - by = 1$*

We have proved in §2 that if a and b are coprime natural numbers, then for some integers x and y we have $ax - by = 1$. (We *actually* solved $ax + by = 1$, but this is an equivalent equation as can be seen by changing the sign of y.) The equation $ax - by = 1$ is an example of a *Diophantine equation*, named after the ancient mathematician Diophantus of Alexandria. Diophantine equations are polynomial equations (usually) with integral i.e. whole number coefficients like $3x - 7y = 1$ or $x^2 + 2 = y^3$. The key point about the term Diophantine, however, lies not with the equation itself but rather with our demands on its solutions. We seek only integral (whole number) solutions. So $3x - 7y = 1$ is trivially solved, if we only ask that x and

y are real numbers, by taking y to be any number and $x = \frac{1}{3}(1 + 7y)$. This is clearly of no use, however, if we want *integral* solutions. The reader may appreciate that generally solving Diophantine equations can be extremely difficult. (For example, the only solutions of $x^2 + 2 = y^3$ are $y = 3$, $x = \pm 5$ but this is not easy to prove.)

(a) Returning to the equation $ax - by = 1$ you might like to check the following assertion in particular cases by using Program 4.5 with suitable coprime inputs a and b.

If the continued fraction expansion of a/b is $[r(1), \ldots, r(n)]$ with convergents $[r(1), \ldots, r(m)] = p(m)/q(m)$ then, for n odd, $x = q(n - 1)$, $y = p(n - 1)$ solve the equation $ax - by = 1$. If n is even these choices of x and y solve the equation $ax - by = -1$. Replacing x, y by $-x, -y$ we obtain solutions of the original equation, but if we want solutions which are *natural* numbers we can instead take $x = b - q(n - 1)$, $y = a - p(n - 1)$.

(b) Prove the above result (to your own satisfaction at least) by relating the process described in §2 with that of obtaining convergents in the continued fraction form of a/b.

(c) Obtain another proof by noting that the final convergent is, of course, the quotient a/b itself, and using one of the properties of the convergents mentioned in Section 4.6.

(d) Prove that the Diophantine equation $ax - by = c$ has solutions if and only if hcf(a, b) divides c. Show how to use the methods above to solve such an equation.

Later we shall use continued fractions to solve more difficult types of Diophantine equation.

4.8 *Exercise*

Here is a rather tricky problem with a trivial solution. The problem, and its solution, leads us very nicely into our next topic; do not give up too quickly (and do not use your micro!).

The problem is: what is the value of $1 + \frac{1}{1+} \frac{1}{1+} \frac{1}{1+} \ldots$? (The dots indicate that this form repeats itself *ad infinitum*.)

§5
Continued fractions for non-rational numbers

There is another way of viewing the algorithm for computing the continued fraction form of a rational number. Writing $x/y = \text{int}(x/y) + \alpha(1)$ where $0 \leq \alpha(1) < 1$, the first term in the continued fraction expansion of x/y is $r(1) = \text{int}(x/y)$ and clearly $[r(2), \ldots, r(n)] = 1/\alpha(1)$. If we now write

$$1/\alpha(1) = \text{int}(1/\alpha(1)) + \alpha(2),$$

with $0 \leq \alpha(2) < 1$, the same reasoning shows that $r(2) = \text{int}(1/\alpha(1))$

and $[r(3), \ldots, r(n)] = 1/\alpha(2)$. The remaining values $r(3), \ldots, r(n)$ are now found in the same way, the process terminating when some remainder term $\alpha(i) = 0$. Here is a program which implements this algorithm.

5.1 *Program: Continued fractions 3*

```
1Ø  INPUT X,Y
2Ø  PRINT "CONTINUED FRACTION EXPANSION
    OF"; X; "/"; Y; "IS";
3Ø  LET R = X/Y
4Ø  LET S = R − INT(R)
5Ø  IF S = Ø THEN GOTO 9Ø
6Ø  PRINT; INT(R); ",";
7Ø  LET R = 1/S
8Ø  GOTO 4Ø
9Ø  PRINT; INT(R); ")"
```

If you run this program you will find that it has only the one defect – it gives the wrong answers! The problem, of course, lies with line 7Ø. When inverting *s* the computer will naturally have to round off the result: it has no way of storing 1/3 exactly for example. Nevertheless the errors originating from line 7Ø will take a little time to affect the answer so the first few values of the *r*s will be correct, as you can check.

Still if this program gives the wrong answers why introduce it? Well the point of the algorithm is that if we replace the fraction x/y by *any real number c* it will generate a sequence $r(1), r(2), r(3), \ldots$. Of course, one stops short of stating that it will generate a continued fraction; if *c* is not a rational number the above algorithm will *never* terminate (assuming each calculation is done exactly) since any continued fraction clearly is a rational number. What the above algorithm does, for a non-rational real number *c*, is generate an infinite sequence of terms $r(i)$ and the resulting infinite continued fraction

$$r(1) + \cfrac{1}{r(2) +} \cfrac{1}{r(3) +} \cdots \cfrac{1}{r(n) +} \cdots$$

is equal to *c*. Try this program with your computer's approximation to say $\sqrt{2}$, e, π. What do you notice?

Of course, at this stage there are a number of questions to be answered. The most important is undoubtedly: what is an *infinite* continued fraction? What we mean by our statement above is that if we consider the sequence of convergents

$$c(j) = [r(1), r(2), \ldots, r(j)], \quad j \geqslant 1,$$

then the limit as j tends to infinity of the $c(j)$ exists, i.e. as j increases the $c(j)$ settle down to a fixed number, and this limit is c. Of course, this assertion requires proof, but this is not very difficult to supply. See Hardy and Wright (1975) pp. 138, 139. (The fact that the sequence of convergents $c(j)$ converges to some number c already follows from our observations of Section 4.6.)

But what use is a program which (eventually) yields the wrong answers? One reason is outlined in the exercises below. For the second let us suppose that c is a number of the form $a + b\sqrt{m}$ where a, b are rational numbers and m is a positive integer, for example $1 + 3\sqrt{2}$. If we feed this number into Program 5.1 then naturally we shall eventually get the wrong answers for our $r(j)$. However, we can do the inversion step, line 7∅ in our program, *exactly*; for applying the algorithm outlined above we find that $r(1) = 5$ and $\alpha(1) = 3\sqrt{2} - 4$.

Now

$$\frac{1}{\alpha(1)} = \frac{1}{3\sqrt{2} - 4} = \frac{3\sqrt{2} + 4}{(3\sqrt{2} - 4)(3\sqrt{2} + 4)}$$

$$= \frac{3\sqrt{2} + 4}{2} = \frac{3}{2}\sqrt{2} + 2$$

which in turn we can write as $4 + \alpha(2)$, where $0 \leqslant \alpha(2) < 1$. So we take $r(2) = 4$, $\alpha(2) = (3\sqrt{2} - 4)/2$ and again need to invert $\alpha(2)$. This is accomplished by multiplying $2/(3\sqrt{2} - 4)$ top and bottom by $3\sqrt{2} + 4$ to obtain

$$\frac{1}{\alpha(2)} = \frac{2}{(3\sqrt{2} - 4)} \frac{(3\sqrt{2} + 4)}{(3\sqrt{2} + 4)} = \frac{6\sqrt{2} + 8}{2} = 3\sqrt{2} + 4$$

We now write this as $8 + (3\sqrt{2} - 4)$, take $r(3) = 8$, $\alpha(3) = 3\sqrt{2} - 4$. Of course we can continue this process indefinitely. But it is better (and somewhat quicker!) to note that $\alpha(1) = \alpha(3)$. Consequently we can write

$$1 + 3\sqrt{2} = 5 + \alpha = 5 + \cfrac{1}{4 + \cfrac{1}{8 + \alpha}}$$

from which we deduce that

$$\alpha = \cfrac{1}{4 + \cfrac{1}{8 + \alpha}}$$

and so

$$\alpha = \cfrac{1}{4+}\;\cfrac{1}{8+}\;\cfrac{1}{4+}\;\cfrac{1}{8+}\;\cfrac{1}{4+}\;\cfrac{1}{8+}\;\cdots$$

(Check: if

$$\alpha = \cfrac{1}{4+}\;\cfrac{1}{8+\alpha}$$

then

$$\alpha = \cfrac{1}{4+\cfrac{1}{(8+\alpha)}} = \frac{8+\alpha}{33+4\alpha}$$

and hence $4\alpha^2 + 33\alpha = 8 + \alpha$. Consequently α satisfies the quadratic equation $\alpha^2 + 8\alpha - 2 = 0$. But we know that the roots of this equation are $[-8 \pm \sqrt{(64+8)}]/2 = -4 \pm 3\sqrt{2}$. Taking the positive root we do indeed find that $5 + \alpha = 1 + 3\sqrt{2}$.)

We next present a program to compute the terms in the continued fraction expansion of a general real number of the form $a_1/a_2 + (b_1/b_2)\sqrt{m}$ where a_1, a_2, b_1, b_2, m are integers. First we evaluate this expression approximately to determine its integer part, k say. We then consider $a_1/a_2 + (b_1/b_2)\sqrt{m} - k = (a_1 - ka_2)/a_2 + (b_1/b_2)\sqrt{m}$, which corresponds to $\alpha(1)$ above. The key now is to invert this expression *exactly*. Its inverse is

$$\frac{a_2 b_2}{b_2(a_1 - ka_2) + a_2 b_1 \sqrt{m}}$$

$$= \frac{a_2 b_2(b_2(a_1 - ka_2) - a_2 b_1 \sqrt{m})}{(b_2(a_1 - ka_2) + a_2 b_1 \sqrt{m})(b_2(a_1 - ka_2) - a_2 b_1 \sqrt{m})}$$

$$= \frac{a_2 b_2(b_2(a_1 - ka_2) - a_2 b_1 \sqrt{m})}{b_2^2(a_1 - ka_2)^2 - a_2^2 b_1^2 m} = \frac{A_1}{A_2} + \frac{B_1}{B_2}\sqrt{m}$$

where $A_1 = a_2 b_2^2(a_1 - ka_2)$, $B_1 = -a_2^2 b_1 b_2$, $A_2 = B_2 = b_2^2(a_1 - ka_2)^2 - a_2^2 b_1^2 m$. We can now carry out the same process with this new expression, which is *exactly* $1/\alpha(1)$, to generate the next term in the continued fraction expansion. Before writing the program we note that the expressions above for the *a*s and *b*s very rapidly 'blow up'. To circumvent this problem we express A_1/A_2 and B_1/B_2 in lowest terms at each stage. The following program incorporates this step as a subroutine at line 13Ø. (Incidentally this subroutine caused considerable problems on at least one of the machines we used: without the frequent use of the function INT in lines 15Ø and 17Ø this machine produced rounding errors which made the program crash.)

5.2 *Program: Quadratic continued fractions*

```
10 INPUT A1, A2, B1, B2, M
20 LET K = INT(A1/A2 + M↑0.5∗B1/B2)
30 LET Q = B2∗(A1 − K∗A2): LET R = − A2∗A2∗B1
40 LET A1 = A2∗B2∗Q: LET A2 = (ABS(Q))↑2 +
     R∗B1∗M: LET B1 = R∗B2: LET B2 = A2
50 LET X = A1: LET Y = A2
60 GOSUB 130
70 LET A1 = X: LET A2 = Y
80 LET X = B1: LET Y = B2
90 GOSUB 130
100 LET B1 = X: LET B2 = Y
110 PRINT; K; ",";
120 GOTO 20
130 LET S = X: LET T = Y
140 LET X = ABS(X): LET Y = ABS(Y)
150 LET U = X: LET V = Y: LET X = Y:
     LET Y = INT(U − INT(U/V)∗V + 0.5)
160 IF Y < >0 THEN GOTO 150
170 LET X = SGN(S)∗INT(ABS(S/V) + 0.5):
     LET Y = SGN(T)∗INT(ABS(T/V) + 0.5)
180 RETURN
```

Having got this (or your own program) in your micro try running it with $a_1 = 0$, $a_2 = b_1 = b_2 = 1$, and m a non-square between 2 and say 99. In other words compute the continued fraction expansion of $\sqrt{m}$. For example taking $m = 7$ you should get the sequence

$$2, 1, 1, 1, 4, 1, 1, 1, 4, 1, 1, 1, 4, 1, \ldots,$$

or taking $m = 37$ the sequence

$$6, 12, 12, 12, 12, \ldots.$$

In fact for any non-square m you will note that you always obtain a sequence which *eventually* repeats itself. (Purely periodic continued fractions are obtained, for example, by considering the real numbers $1/2 + \sqrt{5}/2$, $1 + \sqrt{2}$, $1 + \sqrt{3}$. Try the program above with e.g. $a_1 = b_1 = 1$, $a_2 = b_2 = 2$, $m = 5$.)

There is a striking general result here due to Lagrange.

5.3 *Lagrange's Theorem*

A real number c has an infinite continued fraction expansion which eventually repeats if and only if c is of the form $(p + q\sqrt{m})/r$ for some *integers p, q, r, m, with m ⩾ 2 a non-square.* Such a number is called a *quadratic irrationality.*

Verify this with some specific examples.

5.4 *Mathematical excursion*

One half of the above assertion is not too difficult to prove. For suppose that c has a continued fraction expansion which repeats

$$c = [R(1), \ldots, R(k), r(1), \ldots, r(n), r(1), \ldots, r(n), r(1), \ldots]$$

Writing $\alpha = [r(1), \ldots, r(n), r(1), \ldots, r(n), r(1), \ldots]$ we note that $\alpha = [r(1), \ldots, r(n), \alpha] = (A\alpha + B)/(C\alpha + D)$ for some integers A, B, C and D. Hence α satisfies the equation $C\alpha^2 + (D - A)\alpha - B = 0$. In turn $c = [R(1), \ldots, R(k), \alpha]$ so that $c = (E\alpha + F)/(G\alpha + H)$ for some integers E, F, G, H. This can be rewritten as $Gac + Hc - E\alpha - F = 0$ or $\alpha = (-Hc + F)/(Gc - E)$. Substituting back into the equation above and clearing denominators, we find that c satisfies a quadratic equation with integer coefficients and consequently is of the form asserted in Section 5.3 above. (Clearly c is a quadratic irrationality if and only if it satisfies such an equation.) The converse is a little harder to prove: see Hardy and Wright (1975) pp. 144–5.

5.5 *Exercises*

(a) Add a few lines to the Program 5.2 so that it will recognise when the continued fraction has repeated itself and stop.

In Section 4.6 we mentioned that the convergents of the continued fraction expansion of a rational number a/b are the *best* approximations to that number amongst those rationals of a fixed 'complexity'. It turns out that the same is true of the convergents of the continued fraction expansion of any real number c. Before discussing this result we make a few observations concerning rational approximations to real numbers.

Let c be a real number, fix a natural number b, and consider all fractions of the form a/b. Clearly for some choice of a we have $|c - a/b| \leqslant 1/2b$. (Taking $b = 100$ this simply asserts that any real number is approximated to within $1/200$ by its decimal expansion rounded to its second decimal place e.g. $|\pi - 3.14| \leqslant 1/200$.) It is a far more remarkable fact that *for certain choices of b* we have the inequality $|c - a/b| \leqslant 1/\sqrt{5}b^2$, and, moreover, if c is not itself a fraction *there are an infinite number of such choices.* The constant $1/\sqrt{5}$ cannot be improved here; it is not this constant but rather the square term $1/b^2$ which is worthy of note, however. One can prove that every third convergent of the continued fraction expansion of c satisfies the above inequality, so we have a constructive method of obtaining these rational approximations.

We would like you to obtain some good rational approximations to π and e by using the continued fraction algorithm. Unfortunately

Program 5.1 produces errors very quickly so we suggest the following alternative.

(*b*) We know for example that $31415/10000 < \pi < 31416/10000$. Compute the continued fraction expansions of the two outside rational numbers. It can be shown that any common convergents of these two rationals will also be a convergent of π. Use Program 4.5 to compute such convergents. (Using the first eight decimal places of π only yields the convergents $22/7 = 3.1428\ldots$, $333/106 = 3.141509\ldots$, $355/133 = 3.1415929\ldots$.) You can try rewriting your programs for continued fractions using multiple precision arithmetic to obtain further convergents (see Chapter 4). You will also need a lengthy decimal expansion of π (see Chapter 6). The situation is much better for e. Here we obtain the convergents 3, $8/3 = 2.66\ldots$, $11/4 = 2.75$, $19/7 = 2.714\ldots$, $387/32 = 2.71875$, $106/39 = 2.7179\ldots$, $193/71 = 2.718309\ldots$, $1264/465 = 2.7182795\ldots$, $1457/536 = 2.7182835\ldots$, $2721/1001 = 2.71828171\ldots$. We hope you will also have noticed that e appears to have a continued fraction expansion

$$2 + \frac{1}{1+} \frac{1}{2+} \frac{1}{1+} \frac{1}{1+} \frac{1}{4+} \frac{1}{1+} \frac{1}{1+} \frac{1}{6+} \frac{1}{1+} \cdots$$

where the numbers 2, 4, 6, ..., are separated by two 1s. This is, in fact, the case – a result due to Euler.

§6
Project on Fibonacci numbers

You have probably already come across the so called *Fibonacci sequence*

$$1, 1, 2, 3, 5, 8, 13, 21, \ldots.$$

This sequence of numbers is obtained by setting the first two terms equal to 1 and taking each consecutive term to be the sum of the two preceding. (Symbolically $u_1 = u_2 = 1$, $u_n = u_{n-1} + u_{n-2}$ for $n \geqslant 3$.) The connection with loose living rabbits is doubtless well known to you: Leonardo of Pisa (also known as Leonardo Fibonacci) posed the following problem in 1202. How many pairs of rabbits can be produced from a single pair in a year's time? If we assume each pair produces a new pair of offspring each month, each new pair becomes fertile after one month, and rabbits never die, some calculation should lead to the Fibonacci series. (Some of the assumptions underlying this model are not *entirely* accurate of course!)

6.1

(*a*) *Prove* the following results direct from the definition of the Fibonacci series.

(i) $u_1 + u_2 + \ldots + u_n = u_{n+2} - 1$.

(ii) $u_1 + u_3 + \ldots + u_{2n-1} = u_{2n}$.

(iii) $u_2 + u_4 + \ldots + u_{2n} = u_{2n+1} - 1$.

(iv) (Harder) $u_n u_{m+1} + u_{n-1} u_m = u_{n+m}$.

(b) Write a program for generating the Fibonacci series. (This should be about the shortest program you will ever write.)

(c) Check the following facts – using your program. (See Hardy and Wright (1975) pp. 148–50 for proofs, and also Knuth (1981) pp. 78–86.)

(i) $\mathrm{hcf}(u_n, u_{n+1}) = 1$ for all n.

(ii) u_n divides u_{rn} for every $r \geqslant 1$.

(iii) If $\mathrm{hcf}(m, n) = d$ then $\mathrm{hcf}(u_m, u_n) = u_d$.

(iv) If $\mathrm{hcf}(m, n) = 1$ then $u_m u_n$ divides u_{mn}.

(v) If p is a prime of the form $5m \pm 1$ then p divides u_{p-1}. If p is a prime of the form $5m \pm 2$ then p divides u_{p+1}.

(vi) Taking $c = (1 + \sqrt{5})/2$, the convergents of the continued fraction expansion of c, $p(n)/q(n)$, are given by $p(n) = u_{n+2}$, $q(n) = u_{n+1}$. You may now deduce that $u_{n+1} u_{n-1} - u_n^2 = (-1)^n$ from previous results concerning convergents (or use (a) (iv)). Property (i) above also follows from this observation and previous results. In fact you might like to prove (i) and (ii) above directly by induction, as well as the next result.

(vii) If c is as in (vi) we have $u_n \leqslant c^{n-1}$.

The Fibonacci numbers enter in the following analysis of the Euclidean algorithm. The basic problem to be studied is: give an upper bound for the number of iterations the Euclidean algorithm, applied to two numbers a, b, performs before terminating. What we will actually prove is the following result of Lamé (1845).

6.2 *Lamé's Theorem*

For $n \geqslant 1$ let a, b be integers with $a > b > 0$ such that Euclid's algorithm applied to a and b requires n iterations before terminating, and suppose a is the smallest integer satisfying this condition. Then $a = u_{n+2}$ and $b = u_{n+1}$.

In other words, in a natural sense, consecutive Fibonacci numbers are the worst inputs for Euclid's Algorithm.

Proof   The key observation is that if the algorithm requires n iterations before terminating the continued fraction expansion of a/b has n terms $[r(1), \ldots, r(n)]$ and $a/b = p(n)/q(n)$, where $p(n)$, $q(n)$ are the integers described in Section 4.3. Moreover $p(n)$ and $q(n)$ are coprime so $a = p(n)d$ and $b = q(n)d$ where $d = \mathrm{hcf}(a, b)$.

Recall that we are attempting to find a *minimum* value for a. The ps are defined inductively by $p(1) = r(1)$, $p(2) = r(1)r(2) + 1$, $p(m) = r(m)p(m-1) + p(m-2)$ for $m \geqslant 3$. If we are to minimise their values clearly we should choose the rs as small as possible. Naturally, then, we choose all of the $r(i) = 1$, except of course for the last, $r(n)$, which we know is $\geqslant 2$, and so we set *equal* to 2. With these choices the definition of the ps becomes

$$p(1) = 1, \; p(2) = 2, \; p(m) = p(m-1) + p(m-2), \; \text{for } m \geqslant 3,$$

so that $p(n) = u_{n+1}$ the $(n+1)$st Fibonacci number. Moreover using the analogous definitions of the qs one easily sees that $q(n) = u_n$. Taking $d = 1$ (we want a minimum value of a) now gives the result.

§7
Pell's equation

As our final use of continued fractions we show how they can be used to produce solutions to the Diophantine equation $x^2 - Ny^2 = 1$ where N is a natural number which is *not* itself a square, e.g. $x^2 - 313y^2 = 1$. This equation, named after Pell (for reasons of mistaken identity) always has integral solutions, indeed an infinite number of them. In this section we shall merely give a description of *how* these can be obtained. Unfortunately a proof that the method, due to Brouncker in 1657, does furnish solutions would take us too far afield. The interested reader is referred to Davenport (1982) pp. 107–11 or Hardy and Wright (1975) pp. 209, 210.

When computing, in §5, the continued fraction expansion of $\sqrt{N} = [r(1), r(2), \ldots, r(j), \ldots]$ we noted that it was, in each case, eventually periodic. In fact, computing this expansion for various values of N provides evidence in support of the fact that it is *purely* periodic if the first term $r(1) = \text{int}(\sqrt{N})$ is discounted. In addition the last term in the periodic part of this expansion turns out to be $2r(1)$, so the expansion is of the form

$$[r(1), r(2), \ldots, r(n), 2r(1), r(2), \ldots, r(n), 2r(1), r(2), \ldots].$$

Let $p(n)/q(n)$ be the nth convergent of this expansion, i.e. $p(n)/q(n) = [r(1), \ldots, r(n)]$. *Then $x = p(n)$, $y = q(n)$ is a solution of the equation*

$$x^2 - Ny^2 = (-1)^{n-1}.$$

In particular if n is odd we have a solution of Pell's equation. For example taking $N = 7$ we have

$$\sqrt{N} = [2, 1, 1, 1, 4, 1, 1, 1, 4, \ldots]$$

and the relevant convergent $p(n)/q(n) = [2, 1, 1, 1] = 8/3$; checking: $8^2 - 7 \times 3^2 = 1$.

If n is even we consider the $2n$th convergent

$$p(2n)/q(2n) = [r(1), \ldots, r(n), 2r(1), \ldots, r(n)].$$

In this case $x = p(2n)$, $y = q(2n)$ provide solutions of $x^2 - Ny^2 = 1$. In fact you can check that if n is odd the convergents corresponding to each multiple of n provide solutions, while if n is even the convergents corresponding to every *second* multiple of n do the trick.

We shall leave you the straightforward task of amalgamating two of the previous programs to obtain a new one which provides solutions of Pell's equations. It turns out that, modulo changes of sign in x and y, the convergents discussed above provide *all* of the solutions to this equation.

7.1 *Exercises: Pell's equation*
(a) Why is Pell's equation, in the case N a perfect square, of no interest?
(b) Let x_1, y_1 be the *first* solution of Pell's equation generated by the above method. Check (experimentally) that all subsequent solutions x, y satisfy

$$x + y\sqrt{N} = (x_1 + y_1\sqrt{N})^r \tag{1}$$

for some $r \geqslant 1$ and conversely any such pair x, y *is* a solution. So for example taking $N = 7$ we note that $(8 + 3\sqrt{7})^2 = 127 + 48\sqrt{7}$ and $(127)^2 - 7 \times (48)^2$ is indeed 1.

The values of x, y generated by the Formula (1) are easily obtained; for writing $(x_1 + y_1\sqrt{N})^r = x_r + y_r\sqrt{N}$ clearly

$$\begin{aligned}
x_{r+1} + y_{r+1}\sqrt{N} &= (x_r + y_r\sqrt{N})(x_1 + y_1\sqrt{N}) \\
&= (x_r x_1 + Ny_1 y_r) + (x_r y_1 + x_1 y_r)\sqrt{N}
\end{aligned}$$

which gives an inductive method of computing the xs and ys that is easily programmed. Note that since

$$\begin{aligned}
x_{r+1}^2 - Ny_{r+1}^2 &= (x_r x_1 + Ny_1 y_r)^2 - N(x_r y_1 + x_1 y_r)^2 \\
&= (x_1^2 - Ny_1^2)(x_r^2 - Ny_r^2)
\end{aligned}$$

this also provides an inductive proof that the pairs x_r, y_r generated in this way *are* solutions.

7.2 *Project*
(Warning: this project requires the use of computer graphics)

The continued fraction expansion of an irrational number has a geometrical interpretation due to Klein in 1895 which we now explain. Consider in the plane all those points whose coordinates are positive integers. These are called *lattice* points. If α is a positive real number then the line $y = \alpha x$ passes through such a point precisely when α is rational. In particular if α is irrational, e.g. $\alpha = \sqrt{N}$ where N is not a square, the line $y = \alpha x$ manages to miss *all* of the infinite number of lattice points.

We now think of the lattice points with integral coordinates as pegs, and the lines $y = \alpha x$ as taut strings of infinite length. Suppose the end of the string at infinity is fixed, and the other end at the origin is pulled to one side or the other. Clearly the string will catch on some pegs. Indeed if the string is pulled taut it will catch on an infinite number of pegs when pulled downwards and an infinite set when pulled up. In fact if $p(n)/q(n)$ are the convergents of the continued fraction expansion of α the coordinates of the relevant pegs are $(q(n), p(n))$ for $n = 1, 2, 3, \ldots$. Write a program to illustrate this fact. Which convergents correspond to the pegs below the line and which above? Do any of the basic results concerning convergents mentioned in Section 4.6 have geometrical interpretations? Does this model explain why the $p(n)/q(n)$ are good rational approximations to α? (See Davenport (1982) pp. 111–13 for further details.)

§8
*Modular
arithmetic*

When doing certain calculations it turns out that the particular value of some integer x is largely irrelevant and what counts is its remainder after division by some other number d. That is any two numbers x and y which differ by some multiple of d will produce the same result. For example the value of $(-1)^n$ depends only on whether n is odd or even, so that any two values of n which differ by a multiple of 2 give the same value. If two numbers x and y differ by some (integral) multiple of d we shall say that x and y are *congruent modulo d* and write

$$x \equiv y \pmod{d}.$$

You can think of this as shorthand notation for '$x - y$ is divisible by d'. Some examples of congruences are $1 \equiv 7 \pmod{2}$, $7^2 \equiv 1 \pmod{12}$, $4^3 \equiv 0 \pmod{8}$. As another example you might note that two integers x and y are congruent modulo 10^n if and only if their last n digits coincide (with the obvious modification if they have less than n digits).

What we wish to do is extract a new type of arithmetic from the concept of congruences, and the key is the not too difficult fact that any pair of congruences, modulo the same integer d, can be added, subtracted or multiplied. More precisely if $a \equiv a_1 \pmod{d}$ and $b \equiv b_1 \pmod{d}$ then we claim that

$$a + b \equiv a_1 + b_1 \pmod{d}$$
$$a - b \equiv a_1 - b_1 \pmod{d}$$
$$ab \equiv a_1 b_1 \pmod{d}.$$

The proof is not very hard. The equation $a \equiv a_1 \pmod{d}$ simply means that for some integer k we have $a - a_1 = kd$; and similarly $b - b_1 = ld$ for some integer l. Now we simply compute away

$$a + b = (a_1 + kd) + (b_1 + ld) = a_1 + b_1 + (k + l)d$$
$$a - b = (a_1 + kd) - (b_1 + ld) = a_1 - b_1 + (k - l)d$$

$$ab = (a_1 + kd)(b_1 + ld) = a_1 b_1 + (kb_1 + la_1)d + kld^2$$

and we see that in each case the results of performing our addition, subtraction or multiplication with a and b or a_1 and b_1 differ by a multiple of d.

8.1 *Arithmetical excursion*

Using these ideas one can derive the standard test for the divisibility of a number by 3. In standard *decimal* (*not* binary) notation any number x is written as a string of digits $x_n x_{n-1} \ldots x_1$ with all of the x_is between 0 and 9 and

$$x = x_1 + x_2 \times 10 + x_3 \times 10^2 + \ldots + x_n \times 10^{n-1}.$$

Now since $10 \equiv 1 \pmod 3$ we have $10^2 \equiv 1 \pmod 3$, $10^3 \equiv 1 \pmod 3$ and so on, and consequently

$$x \equiv x_1 + x_2 + \ldots + x_n \pmod 3.$$

In other words x is divisible by 3 if and only if the sum of its digits is divisible by 3.

The same test works for divisibility by 9 as well; above we only used the fact that $10 \equiv 1 \pmod 3$ and since $10 \equiv 1 \pmod 9$ the same reasoning applies.

Using this method it is very easy to write a program which tests a number $x < 10^9$ for divisibility by 3 or 9. The only slight problem is extracting the individual digits $x_1, \ldots, x_n$ from the input x, and this is easily dealt with by noting that $\text{INT}(X/10\uparrow(N-1))$ is the first digit x_1. To find the second, one forms $x - x_1(10\uparrow(n-1))$ and computes *its* first digit. Why not write a program now of this type? Of course, the method can itself be applied to the sum $x_1 + \ldots + x_n$, and reapplied until eventually the sum of the digits in question lies between 1 and 9. Incorporate this improvement in your program.

8.2 *Program: Divisibility by 3*

```
1Ø  INPUT X
2Ø  LET Y = X
3Ø  LET S = Ø
4Ø  FOR I = 1 TO 9
5Ø  LET R = INT(X/1Ø↑(9 – I))
6Ø  LET S = S + R
7Ø  LET X = INT(X – R*(1Ø↑(9 – I)) + Ø.5)
8Ø  NEXT I
9Ø  LET X = S
1ØØ  IF X ≥ 1Ø THEN GOTO 3Ø
```

110 IF X = 3 OR X = 6 OR X = 9 THEN GOTO 140
120 PRINT Y; "IS NOT DIVISIBLE BY 3"
130 GOTO 150
140 PRINT Y; "IS DIVISIBLE BY 3"
150 END

8.3 *Exercises*

(a) Alter the above program to yield one which tests for divisibility by 9.
(b) Use the observations $10 \equiv -1 \pmod{11}$, $10^2 \equiv 1 \pmod{11}$, $10^3 \equiv -1 \pmod{11}$, ... to obtain a test for divisibility by 11. Write a program which employs this test.
(c) Devise a test for divisibility by 7. See if you can remember it an hour later.

The program above is rather cumbersome and extremely inefficient. The simple question 'is $x = 3\,\mathrm{int}(x/3)$?' is a far more effective way of checking whether or not x is divisible by 3. This does not mean that the tests described above are useless however. As we have observed most micros only have available 8, 9 or 10 digit arithmetic. How then can we test say a 50 digit number for divisibility by 3? Well applying the test above we need only sum the digits (and obtain a number $\leq 50 \times 9 = 450$) and test *that* for divisibility by 3. Indeed this process will work for any number with n digits provided $n \times 9$ can be stored exactly on your micro (i.e. $n \leq 10^8/9$, $10^9/9$ or $10^{10}/9$ depending on your machine). The only problem of course is 'inputting' the number n, but this is easily done as a sequence. Here is a program for testing a number with d digits for divisibility by 3.

8.4 *Program: Divisibility by 3 again*

10 INPUT N: DIM A(N)
20 LET S = 0
30 FOR I = 1 TO N
40 INPUT A(I)
50 LET S = S + A(I)
60 NEXT I
70 IF S = 3 * INT(S/3) THEN GOTO 100
80 PRINT "INTEGER NOT DIVISIBLE BY 3"
90 END
100 PRINT "INTEGER IS DIVISIBLE BY 3"

Actually you may have noted that we have omitted to say whether the digits in your number should be read in from left to right or right to left. Of course you can easily check that the tests discussed above prove that a number is divisible by 3, 9 or 11 if and only if the number obtained by reversing the order of its digits is so divisible.

We shall later, in Chapter 4, spend a considerable amount of time considering the problems of doing arithmetic with very large numbers.

8.5 *Back to congruences*

It is obvious that every integer is congruent modulo *d* to exactly one of the numbers

$$0, 1, 2, \ldots, d - 1.$$

These are, after all, a complete list of the possible remainders after division by *d*. It is often very convenient, when working modulo *d*, to replace each number in some calculation by the corresponding number in this list. In this way we can create an arithmetic from the numbers 0, 1, 2, . . ., *d* − 1 and the operations +, − and ×. A few simple examples should make this clear. Suppose we set *d* = 7 so we are working modulo 7. Then

$$3 + 5 = 8 \equiv 1(\mathrm{mod}\ 7)$$
$$3 - 5 = -2 \equiv 5(\mathrm{mod}\ 7)$$
$$3 \times 5 = 15 \equiv 1(\mathrm{mod}\ 7)$$

and, in general, if we add, subtract or multiply any two integers between 0 and 6 modulo 7 we can arrange for the sum, difference or product to be another such. More generally still, we define addition, subtraction and multiplication operations on the integers 0, 1, . . ., *d* − 1 provided we take congruences modulo *d*. What we shall now do is write programs which will allow us to carry out this modular arithmetic on our computer. First addition.

8.6 *Program: Addition modulo N*

```
1Ø INPUT X, Y, D
2Ø LET S = X + Y
3Ø LET R = INT(S/D)
4Ø LET S = S − R∗D
5Ø PRINT "THE SUM OF"; X; "AND"; Y; "MODULO";
   D; "IS"; S
```

Clearly the same program with *x* + *y* replaced by X ∗ Y in line 2Ø (and sum replaced by product in line 5Ø) will compute products. We do, however, have to be a little careful with differences. Replacing *x* + *y* by *x* − *y* in line 2Ø may sometimes yield the wrong answer, depending on the behaviour of your function 'INT.' It is safer to replace line 2Ø by

$$2\emptyset \quad \text{LET S} = \text{X} - \text{Y} + \text{D}$$

These programs are not very thrilling in themselves; we shall use the idea of congruences later to test some extremely large numbers for primality. While discussing congruences, however, it would be a great shame not to mention two beautiful results: Fermat's (little) Theorem and Wilson's Theorem (apparently neither result was first proved by the person by whose name they are remembered – a not uncommon occurrence in mathematics). We shall describe Fermat's result first.

8.7 *Fermat's Theorem*

Let x be any integer and consider the successive powers x, x^2, x^3, x^4, ... If we consider the list of their remainders after division by some other integer d clearly this list eventually repeats. After all there are only d possible values for the remainders. Moreover, if $x^n \equiv x^m \pmod{d}$ (with say $m > n$) we have $x^n(1 - x^{m-n}) \equiv 0 \pmod{d}$. In particular, when d is prime either x is divisible by d, and so x is divisible by d, or some power of x is congruent to 1 modulo d. Fermat's result states that if d is prime, and x is not divisible by d, then $x^{d-1} \equiv 1 \pmod{d}$. It is not difficult to write a program which verifies this result in particular cases. Better still we can actually write one which computes the *order* of such an x modulo d, that is the *minimal* value of n for which $x^n \equiv 1 \pmod{d}$. You can check that in each case n is a factor of $d - 1$, i.e. $(d - 1) = mn$ for some m. Thus $x^{d-1} = x^{mn} = (x^n)^m \equiv 1^m = 1 \pmod{d}$ as asserted by Fermat. (A little thought should convince you that given Fermat's result the order of x must divide $d - 1$.)

Here is a sample program for computing the order of some natural number x modulo another such d, which need not be prime. Make sure, however, that when d is not prime x and d are *coprime* i.e. have no common factors. Otherwise the program may never reach line 7Ø. (Why? Try $x = 2$, $d = 4$.)

8.8 *Program: Fermat*

```
1Ø  INPUT X,D
2Ø  LET N = 1: LET Y = X
3Ø  IF X = 1 THEN GOTO 7Ø
4Ø  LET X = X * Y
5Ø  LET X = X − D * INT(X/D): LET N = N + 1
```

60 GOTO 30
70 PRINT "THE ORDER OF"; Y; "MODULO";
   D; "IS"; N

8.9 *Mathematical excursion*

The proof of Fermat's Theorem is really quite elementary so we pause to give it here, indeed we give two proofs. Let p be prime and x an integer not divisible by p. We shall now show that $x^p \equiv x \pmod p$, which is clearly equivalent to the required result. Equally clearly we may suppose that $1 \leqslant x \leqslant p - 1$ since we are working modulo p. We may now prove the required result by induction on x. For $1^p \equiv 1 \pmod p$ while

$$\begin{aligned} x^p &= (1 + (x - 1))^p \\ &= 1 + p(x - 1) + \tfrac{1}{2}p(p - 1)(x - 1)^2 \\ &\quad + \ldots + p(x - 1)^{p-1} + (x - 1)^p \end{aligned}$$

by the Binomial Theorem. Since p is prime each of the terms in this expansion other than the first and last is divisible by p so $x^p \equiv 1 + (x - 1)^p$ $\pmod p$. By the inductive hypothesis $(x - 1)^p \equiv (x - 1) \pmod p$ and the result follows. This, the first known proof, is due to Leibniz.

The following alternative proof is due to Ivory. Consider the integers x, $2x, 3x, \ldots, (p - 1)x$. Clearly no two are congruent modulo p, since any such congruence entails a relation $kx \equiv 0 \pmod p$ for some k with $1 \leqslant k \leqslant p - 1$. So this list is congruent in some order to $1, 2, 3, \ldots, p - 1$. Consequently taking products we find that

$$\begin{aligned} 1 \times 2 \times 3 \ldots \times (p - 1) &\equiv x \times 2x \times 3x \times \ldots \times (p - 1)x \pmod p \\ &\equiv x^{p-1} \times 1 \times 2 \times 3 \times \ldots \times (p-1) \pmod p. \end{aligned}$$

Thus $1 \times 2 \times 3 \times \ldots \times (p - 1) \times (x^{p-1} - 1) \equiv 0 \pmod p$ and consequently since the first $p - 1$ factors here are not divisible by p we have $x^{p-1} \equiv 1 \pmod p$ as required.

8.10 *Orders of integers*

Returning to Program 8.8 you might like to investigate, for a given prime p, the list of all possible orders of integers x: obviously one need only compute the orders of the integers $1, 2, 3, \ldots, p - 1$. By replacing lines 10 and 20 of the previous program with

10 INPUT D
15 FOR I = 1 TO D − 1
20 LET X = I: LET Y = X: LET N = 1

and adding a new line

80 NEXT I

you can obtain a list of these orders.

8.11 *Mathematical excursion*

When computing the orders of the integers $1, 2, 3, \ldots, p - 1 \pmod p$ you should observe that there is always some integer x whose order is $p - 1$.

Consequently the powers of x: $x, x^2, \ldots, x^{p-1}$ when reduced modulo p give a list, in some order, of all possible non-zero remainders $1, 2, 3, \ldots, p-1$. In abstract terms the integers $1, 2, 3, \ldots, p-1$ form a *group* under multiplication followed by reduction modulo p, and this group is cyclic. A discussion of these terms would take us too far afield but for those interested we refer to Stewart (1975), Chapter 7, and Budden (1972).

8.12 *Project: Euler's Theorem*

This minor project is concerned with extending Fermat's Theorem to any (not necessarily prime) modulus d. The problem then is as follows. Let x and d be natural numbers with $1 \leqslant x \leqslant d-1$ and consider the powers $x, x^2, x^3, \ldots$ reduced modulo d. Eventually this sequence of powers must repeat itself, so that $x \equiv x^{r+1} \pmod{d}$ for some r; i.e. $x(1 - x^r) \equiv 0 \pmod{d}$. For simplicity's sake we shall further suppose that $\mathrm{hcf}(x, d) = 1$, i.e. x and d are coprime, so that we are really seeking values of r for which $x^r \equiv 1 \pmod{d}$.

(a) Write a program which for a given value of d selects all integers x coprime to d with $1 \leqslant x \leqslant d-1$, and computes their orders.

(b) Let $\phi(d)$ denote the number of integers x with $1 \leqslant x \leqslant d-1$ which are coprime to d; ϕ is the so called Euler ϕ-function. Modify your program to also compute $\phi(d)$. What do you notice about $\phi(d)$ and the orders of the integers computed in (a)?

(c) Suppose $\mathrm{hcf}(x, d) = 1$; use what you have learned from the section on the Euclidean algorithm to show that the equation $xy \equiv 1 \pmod{d}$ has a unique solution y. Conversely show that if this equation has a solution y then x and d are coprime.

(d) Modify Ivory's proof of Fermat's Theorem to prove Euler's Theorem: $x^{\phi(d)} \equiv 1 \pmod{d}$ for any x coprime to d.

(e) Euler's ϕ-function has a number of remarkable properties which you may like to investigate further (see Davenport (1982), pp. 49, 50 for details):

(i) If d_1 and d_2 are coprime then $\phi(d_1 d_2) = \phi(d_1)\phi(d_2)$.

(ii) If p^n is a prime power $\phi(p^n) = p^n - p^{n-1}$ (this is really very easy to prove).

(iii) If d is expressed as a product of distinct prime powers

$$d = p_1^{n_1} p_2^{n_2} \ldots p_r^{n_r}$$

then

$$\phi(d) = (p_1^{n_1} - p_1^{n_1-1})(p_2^{n_2} - p_2^{n_2-1}) \ldots (p_r^{n_r} - p_r^{n_r-1})$$
$$= d(1 - 1/p_1)(1 - 1/p_2) \ldots (1 - 1/p_r).$$

(This clearly follows from (i) and (ii).)

(iv) The sum of the numbers $\phi(x)$, where x is a divisor of d, is equal to d itself. So e.g. taking $d = 18$ we have the divisors 1, 2, 3, 6, 9, 18 and

$$\phi(1) + \phi(2) + \phi(3) + \phi(6) + \phi(9) + \phi(18)$$
$$= 1 + 1 + 2 + 2 + 6 + 6 = 18.$$

Write a program to verify this fact; better still prove it.

8.13 *Wilson's Theorem*

Wilson's Theorem asserts that if p is a prime then $(p - 1)! \equiv -1 \pmod{p}$. Again you can easily write a program to check that this is so.

8.14 *Mathematical excursion*

The following proof of Wilson's Theorem is due to Gauss. Let p be prime. We claim that for any x with $1 \leqslant x \leqslant p - 1$ there is some unique y with $1 \leqslant y \leqslant p - 1$ and $yx \equiv 1 \pmod{p}$. To see this we note, as in Ivory's proof of Fermat's Theorem, that $x, 2x, 3x, \ldots, (p - 1)x$ are congruent modulo p in some order to $1, 2, 3, \ldots, p - 1$. In particular, precisely one of these products is congruent to 1 modulo p. If this unique multiplicative inverse coincides with x we have $x^2 \equiv 1 \pmod{p}$ i.e. $x^2 - 1 = (x + 1)(x - 1)$ is divisible by p, and since $1 \leqslant x \leqslant p - 1$ we have $x = p - 1$ or $x = 1$. Consequently each x with $2 \leqslant x \leqslant p - 2$ is paired with a unique *different inverse* and $(p - 1)! = 1 \times [2 \times 3 \times \ldots \times (p - 2)] \times (p - 1) \equiv 1 \times (p - 1) \pmod{p}$; i.e. $(p - 1)! \equiv -1 \pmod{p}$.

Actually something more is true; if d is any number and $(d - 1)! \equiv -1 \pmod{d}$ then d is prime. In other words the converse of Wilson's Theorem is true. The proof is so obvious that we leave it to you. (Try proving that if d is *not* prime $(d - 1)! \equiv 0 \pmod{d}$.) As a test for the primality of d the converse of Wilson's Theorem is rather ineffective: more on this later, in Chapter 4.

§9
Project on
quadratic residues

One very central topic in number theory is the study of quadratic residues modulo a prime. With the aid of your micro this project should give you an appreciation of some of the results in this area.

In what follows p will be any prime other than 2 (i.e. p is an *odd* prime). If a is any integer we consider the equation

$$x^2 \equiv a \pmod{p}. \tag{1}$$

If this equation has a solution x we shall say that a is a *quadratic residue* of p (i.e. is the remainder left from some square after division by p). So for example 2 is a quadratic residue of 7 since $3^2 \equiv 2 \pmod{7}$. If equation (1) has no solution we shall say that a is a *quadratic non-residue* of p. Taking $p = 7$ you can easily check that 1, 2 and 4 are quadratic residues and 3, 5 and 6 quadratic non-residues. Of course, when determining residues we need only consider values of a between 1 and $p - 1$, and we do so from now on.

(a) Write a program which lists the quadratic residues of any prime p. Use this program in the rest of this project.

(b) Check that there are always $\frac{1}{2}(p - 1)$ residues (and $\frac{1}{2}(p - 1)$ non-residues) for any odd prime p. (Better still prove this by showing that $1^2, 2^2, 3^2, \ldots, \{\frac{1}{2}(p - 1)\}^2$ are all incongruent modulo p, while $(p - r)^2$ and r^2 are congruent modulo p.)

(c) Check that the product of two quadratic residues (qr) is a qr, the product of a qr with a quadratic non-residue (qnr) is a qnr and the product of two qnrs is a qr. (The first assertion is easily proved. The second and third assertions follow from (b) and the fact that for any y which is not divisible by p the products $1 \times y, \ldots, (p-1) \times y$ are all incongruent modulo p. Think about this!)

(d) Define the Legendre symbol (a/p) by

$$\left(\frac{a}{p}\right) = \begin{cases} +1, & \text{if } a \text{ is a qr modulo } p, \\ -1, & \text{if } a \text{ is a qnr modulo } p. \end{cases}$$

So you have just proved that $(a/p)(b/p) = (ab/p)$ (or you have at least verified that this is so in a large number of cases). Check that if p is an odd prime and a is not divisible by p then

$$(p - 1)! \equiv -\left(\frac{a}{p}\right) a^{(p - 1)/2} (\text{mod } p).$$

For example $6! \equiv 5^3 (\text{mod } 7)$. (The proof of this result is not very difficult, you might be able to discover it yourself. If not look at Hardy and Wright (1975) pp. 67, 68.)

(e) From the result stated in (d) you should be able to deduce: (i) Wilson's Theorem; (ii) -1 is a qr of primes of the form $4n + 1$ and a qnr of primes of the form $4n + 3$; (iii) $(a/p) \equiv a^{(p - 1)/2} (\text{mod } p)$. (The second assertion, or at least the part which says that -1 is a qr of primes of the form $4n + 1$ is the key ingredient in Fermat's proof of the Two Squares Theorem: see Hardy and Wright (1975) p. 301 or Davenport (1982) pp. 117–20, as well as §10.)

(f) Check that 2 is a qr of primes of the form $8n \pm 1$ and a qnr of primes of the form $8n \pm 3$.

(g) Check the validity of the following justly famous theorem: *Gauss's Law of Reciprocity. If p and q are odd primes then $(p/q) = (q/p)$ unless p and q are both of the form $4n + 3$, in which case $(p/q) = -(q/p)$.*

This result is *far* from obvious, linking as it does the solvability of the equation $x^2 \equiv p(\text{mod } q)$ with that of $x^2 \equiv q(\text{mod } p)$.

(*h*) The Law of Reciprocity actually allows one to compute Legendre symbols fairly easily. For example

$$\left(\frac{35}{37}\right) = \left(\frac{7}{37}\right)\left(\frac{5}{37}\right) = \left(\frac{37}{7}\right)\left(\frac{37}{5}\right)$$

by (*d*) and (*g*) respectively. Now clearly $(37/7) = (2/7)$, $(37/5) = (2/5)$ so $(35/37) = (2/7)(5/7) = 1 \times (7/5) = 1 \times (2/5) = 1 \times (-1) = -1$, where we have used (*f*) to determine $(2/7)$ and $(2/5)$. Can you write a program which computes (a/q) for q prime by this method?

§10
Sum of squares and Waring's problem

For the final topic of this first chapter we turn to an area of number theory which abounds with beautiful results and provides great opportunities for computer experimentation.

10.1 *Two squares*

We start with the question: which natural numbers can be written as the sum of two squares (of natural numbers)? In other words for which values of m can we solve the Diophantine equation $x^2 + y^2 = m$? Clearly not every value of m will do: consider $m = 3$ or 23.

Our first task is to obtain a list of all such m lying between 1 and some largish number n. The following program produces such a list. (Note we shall allow squares themselves to be considered a sums of two squares: $x^2 = x^2 + 0^2$.)

10.2 *Program: Two squares*

```
1Ø INPUT N: DIM A(N)
2Ø FOR I = 1 TO N
3Ø LET A(I) = Ø
4Ø NEXT I
5Ø FOR X = 1 TO INT(N↑Ø.5)
6Ø FOR Y = Ø TO INT((N − X∗X)↑Ø.5)
7Ø LET A(X∗X + Y∗Y) = 1
8Ø NEXT Y
9Ø NEXT X
1ØØ FOR I = 1 TO N
11Ø IF A(I) = 1 THEN PRINT I; ",";
12Ø NEXT I
```

The list produced by the program above should start 1, 2, 4, 5, 8, 9, 10, ... If you consider this list a number of results become apparent.

10.3 *Results*

(1) If m appears on this list and is odd then on division by 4 we always obtain a remainder of 1, never 3, the other possible remainder.

(2) If m_1, m_2 appear in this list then so does their product $m_1 m_2$. For example 8 and 10 both appear, as does $80 = 8^2 + 4^2$. Of course, it actually follows from this observation that a product of any number of terms of this list is itself listed.

The proof of the first fact is really rather easy. Since m is odd one of x and y is odd and the other is even. (The square of an odd number is odd, the square of an even number is even.) Consequently $m = (2a + 1)^2 + (2b)^2$ for some a and b, and so $m = 4a^2 + 4a + 4b^2 + 1$. Division by 4 clearly leaves a remainder of 1. The second observation has a similarly trivial explanation; trivial to understand, not so trivial to discover. We hope all is made clear with the display of the following algebraic identity:

$$(x^2 + y^2)(X^2 + Y^2) = (xX + yY)^2 + (xY - yX)^2$$

which you can easily check. (This identity is generally attributed to Fibonacci whom we have met elsewhere in this book. Thinking of x, y, X, Y as the real and imaginary parts of complex numbers should furnish an alternative 'proof' of this identity.)

Unfortunately it is not true that every number of the form $4k + 1$ is a sum of two squares; 21 is not for example. You might like to check the following experimentally.

(3) Every prime of the form $4k + 1$ is a sum of two squares. This result, unlike the previous two, is definitely non-trivial. There are four proofs in Hardy and Wright (1975), pp. 297–302; see also Davenport (1982), pp. 117–18. A recent short and elementary argument is given in Zagier (1990).

Finally we ask you to check the validity of the following result.

(4) A number n is the sum of two squares if and only if every prime factor p of the form $4k + 3$ has an even exponent in the prime factorization of n. That is when the number n is written as a product $2^a \times 3^b \times 5^c \times 7^d \times 11^e \times 13^f \times \ldots$ we must have $b, d, e, \ldots$ all even.

Actually it is this more general result which is proved in Hardy and Wright.

10.4 *Exercises*

(*a*) Write a computer program which lists the prime factors of
the form $4k + 3$ (together with their exponents) of integers n
between say 1 and 1000. Check the validity of Result 10.3(4)
for these values of n.

(*b*) Modify Program 10.2 so that it prints both the sums of
squares of non-negative integers and the number of distinct
representations of each such sum. (Naturally we do *not* want
to count $5 = 2^2 + 1^2 = 1^2 + 2^2$ as distinct representations.)

Having done the second exercise above you can now check:

(5) Every prime $p = 4k + 1$ is representable as a sum of two
squares in only one way.

10.5 *Exercise*

Find the number of representations of each integer n, say between 1
and 1000, as a sum of two squares. What can you discover about this
number from texts on number theory? (See Davenport (1982) p. 128
for example.)

Having dealt with sums of two squares it is natural to ask how
many squares are needed to represent *all* numbers? You should be
able to check that three squares are not enough to represent for
example 7. The answer is given by the following result of Legendre.

10.6 *The Four Squares Theorem*

Every natural number can be written as a sum of four squares.

The following program, as well as checking the validity of the
Four Squares Theorem, actually computes the minimum number of
squares needed to represent the integers between 1 and n.

10.7 *Program: Four squares*

```
10 INPUT N: DIM A(N)
20 FOR I = 1 TO N
30 LET A(I) = 5
40 NEXT I
50 FOR R = Ø TO INT(SQRN)
60 FOR S = R TO INT(SQR(N − R ∗ R))
70 FOR T = S TO INT(SQR(N − R ∗ R − S ∗ S))
80 FOR U = T TO INT(SQR(N − R ∗ R − S ∗ S − T ∗ T))
90 LET W = R ∗ R + S ∗ S + T ∗ T + U ∗ U:
   LET V = SGN(R) + SGN(S) + SGN(T) + SGN(U)
100 IF W > N OR W = Ø THEN GOTO 120
110 IF A(W) > V THEN LET A(W) = V
```

```
120 NEXT U
130 NEXT T
140 NEXT S
150 NEXT R
160 FOR I = 1 TO N
170 PRINT I; ","; A(I); ";";
180 NEXT I
```

Here A(I) is the minimum number of squares needed to represent I, and should never take the default value 5.

10.8 *Exercises: Four squares*

(*a*) Check that all integers between 1 and say 5000 can be written as a sum of four squares.

(*b*) Check (by hand!) that

$$(x^2 + y^2 + z^2 + w^2)(X^2 + Y^2 + Z^2 + W^2)$$
$$= (xX + yY + zZ + wW)^2 + (xY - yX - zW + wZ)^2$$
$$+ (xZ + yW - zX - wY)^2 + (xW - yZ + zY - zX)^2.$$

This identity is due to Euler and shows that to prove the Four Squares Theorem one need only establish its validity for primes.

(*c*) Show that no number of the form $8k + 7$ can be written as a sum of three squares.

(*d*) (Harder.) Show that no number of the form $4^r(8k + 7)$ can be written as a sum of three squares.

(*e*) Using Program 10.6 check the following hard result of Legendre, Dirichlet and Gauss: any number *not* of the form $4^r(8k + 7)$ can be written as a sum of three squares.

10.9 *Waring's problem*

Naturally the discussion above is easily generalized. Can every natural number be written as a sum of a *fixed number* of *cubes*? If so how many cubes suffice? The answer here is that every number can be written as a sum of at most nine cubes. You may like to write a program to check that this is so for all integers less than say 1000. (You may run into problems with the natural modification of Program 10.6; this would involve nine FOR–NEXT loops which might well prove too much for your micro.) You should find that 23 and 239 both require the full nine cubes, while any other integer needs at most eight. This raises the interesting question: how many cubes are required to represent all *sufficiently large* integers? The answer is unknown, although it is known that all but a finite number of integers can be written as a sum of seven cubes.

For further information concerning representation of integers as the sum of cubes, fourth, fifth powers etc. the reader is referred to Hardy and Wright (1975) pp. 317–39. The question of how many kth powers are required to represent any integer is known as Waring's problem, for it was Waring who, in 1770, asserted that for every $k \geqslant 2$ there is some fixed s such that every natural number n can be written as a sum of s kth powers. A little thought should convince you that even the existence of s is far from clear. It was eventually established by Hilbert in 1909 that for any k a suitable s does exist. However, its determination is an extremely difficult problem.

As a challenge you might like to use the Four Squares Theorem together with Lucas's Identity:

$$6(w^2 + x^2 + y^2 + z^2)^2 = (w + x)^4 + (w - x)^4 + (w + y)^4$$
$$+ (w - y)^4 + (w + z)^4 + (w - z)^4$$
$$+ (x + y)^4 + (x - y)^4 + (x + z)^4$$
$$+ (x - z)^4 + (y + z)^4 + (y - z)^4$$

to show that every integer is the sum of at most 53 fourth powers. (Hint: write your integer in the form $6m + r$ with $0 \leqslant r \leqslant 5$; write m as $a_1^2 + a_2^2 + a_3^2 + a_4^2$ and each a_i in the form $w^2 + x^2 + y^2 + z^2$.)

10.10 *Project: Finding the squares in the Two Squares Theorem*

Although the Two Squares Theorem, in particular the fact that any prime p of the form $4k + 1$ is a sum of two squares, is very satisfying it *is* a mere existence result. Given such a prime p how does one actually find the two squares involved? Obviously one can do an exhaustive search but this hardly answers the question.

In Davenport (1982) pp. 120–4 there are described four constructive methods of finding the two squares involved. We shall now describe two of these methods; for remarks concerning their justification and the other two algorithms see Davenport and Venkov (1970) pp. 56, 57.

(a) (Gauss's method.) Given p take x to be the integer with $|x| < p$ satisfying $x \equiv (2k)!/(2(k!)^2) \pmod{p}$, and y the integer with $|y| < \frac{1}{2}p$ satisfying $y \equiv (2k)!x \pmod{p}$.

   Check this does give the right answer when $p = 29, 37$. Using your programs from §8 write a new program for constructing x and y from k.

(b) (Serret's method). Find an integer h with $0 < h < \frac{1}{2}p$ satisfying $h^2 + 1 \equiv 0 \pmod{p}$. The continued fraction expansion of p/h then turns out to be of the form $[r(1), r(2), \ldots, r(m), r(m), \ldots, r(2), r(1)]$. (That is, it is symmetrical.) Taking x and y to be numerators of $[r(1), \ldots, r(m)]$, $[r(1), \ldots, r(m-1)]$ respectively now solves the equation $x^2 + y^2 = p$.

Again you can check this does give the right answer by hand for low values of *p*. Writing a program to run through this algorithm involves little more than cobbling together previous ones, and we leave this to you.

References F. J. Budden *The Fascination of Groups*, Cambridge University Press, Cambridge, 1972.

P. M. Cohn *Algebra*, Volume 1, Wiley, London, 1974.

H. Davenport *The Higher Arithmetic*, Cambridge University Press, Cambridge, 5th Edn, 1982.

P. J. Giblin *Primes and Programming*, Cambridge University Press, Cambridge, 1993.

G. H. Hardy and E. M. Wright *An Introduction to the Theory of Numbers*, Oxford University Press, Oxford, 4th Edn, 1975.

D. E. Knuth *The Art of Computer Programming*, Volume 2, *Seminumerical Algorithms*. Addison-Wesley, Reading, Mass., 1981.

H. Rademacher *Lectures on Elementary Number Theory*, Blaisdell Publishing Company, New York, 1964.

I. Stewart *Concepts of Modern Mathematics*, Penguin Books, Harmondsworth, 1975.

B. A. Venkov *Elementary Number Theory*, Wolters-Noordhoff, Groningen, 1970.

D. Zagier 'A one sentence proof that every prime $p \equiv 1 \pmod 4$ is a sum of two squares', *Amer. Math. Monthly*, **97** (1990) 144.

2

Equations

One of the most important and useful ways in which mathematics can help us to solve problems is by the solution of equations. 'Let x be the length of the piece of string; then x satisfies the equation $x^2 - 2x - 3 = 0$ and solving the equation gives $x = 3$.' We are sure that you have solved many problems using equations; unfortunately all but the simplest equations *cannot* be solved exactly.

There are two reasons for this. In the first place even for a quadratic equation, unless the solutions are rational numbers (as in the above example), there is a square root such as $\sqrt{2}$ to be evaluated, and this cannot be done exactly. The decimal expansion does not terminate or recur, so we must be satisfied either with the formal '$\sqrt{2}$' or with an approximation to so-many decimal places.

The second reason is more profound. Exact formulae analogous to the famous quadratic formula do exist for equations of degrees 3 and 4 – of course these formulae involve cube roots and so on, so are open to the same difficulty as we noted above for quadratics. On the other hand no algebraic formula exists at all for equations of degree 5 or more! In a precise sense, the equation $x^5 - 6x + 3 = 0$ cannot be solved algebraically at all. This is a difficult statement and has an even more difficult proof, in which computers won't help in the least. It forms part of the beautiful mathematical subject of Galois Theory, and we must refer you to other books for that. (See for example Stewart (1973), Hadlock (1978) or Birkhoff and MacLane (1965), Chapter 15.)

Even if computers are not so good at proving things are impossible, they are excellent at finding approximate solutions – and approximate here means to eight significant figures if you want that many, or to larger numbers if you are still curious. The subject of solving equations efficiently (i.e. without wasting your and the computer's time), and knowing when your answer is as accurate as you need it to be, forms part of Numerical Analysis. Needless to say, there are plenty of books on that subject, too. See for example Young and Gregory (1972).

We shall not venture far into this difficult territory here. We shall concentrate on the case of *one* equation in *one* unknown (but allow non-algebraic equations such as $x = \tan x$), and present some simple methods for finding approximate solutions, illustrating them with many examples and exercises. Here and there we shall touch on the pitfalls that await the unwary, but for the most part will keep clear of them. We also say something about complex solutions of equations, and in particular about approximating the complex roots of a quadratic equation. (Remember that even the 'exact' formula for the roots involves square roots which need to be approximated!) There is something very orderly about the quadratic case which, as soon as we pass to cubic equations, turns into a state of, literally, chaos. That extraordinary fact is made more explicit in Section 6.10 below.

Nearly all approximation techniques involve *iteration*, which means repetition of some procedure (other than blind guessing!) until sufficient accuracy is obtained. You can read more about iteration in Chapter 8.

§1
Quadratic equations

The equation

$$ax^2 + bx + c = 0 \quad (a \neq 0)$$

has, as is well known, the solutions

$$x = \frac{-b \pm \sqrt{(b^2 - 4ac)}}{2a},$$

which are real if, and only if, $b^2 \geq 4ac$.

1.1 *Exercise*

Write a program which accepts the numbers a, b, c and, provided $a \neq 0$ and $b^2 \geq 4ac$, prints the two values of x (or one value if $b^2 = 4ac$) given by the above formula. Test the program with equations such as $x^2 - 3x + 2 = 0$, solutions $x = 1$ and $x = 2$. Of course, your program will include a call to the square root (or $\frac{1}{2}$ power) function built into your micro; the micro will do the approximation for you. Just for fun, try the equation

$$0.01x^2 + 376854x + 0.1 = 0.$$

The point of this rather outlandish example is that your program will probably give the roots as something like 0.006 ... and $-37\,685\,400$ whereas it is pretty clear that both roots are negative (putting an $x > 0$ in the left-hand side of the equation will always given an answer > 0, not $= 0$). Without dwelling too much on outlandish equations, it is worth pointing out that the trouble arises from the largeness of b^2 compared with $4ac$, which forces the computer to subtract two very nearly equal numbers $\sqrt{(b^2 - 4ac)}$ and b. It isn't possible to keep enough significant figures both before *and* after the decimal point.

1.2 *A remedy*
As it happens, there is an amazingly simple remedy, for, provided $a \neq 0$ and $c \neq 0$,

$$x = \frac{-b \pm \sqrt{(b^2 - 4ac)}}{2a} = \frac{-2c}{b \pm \sqrt{(b^2 - 4ac)}}, \tag{1}$$

the sign, $+$ or $-$, being the same in the two expressions. (Exercise: verify this by cross-multiplying.)

Thus, if $b > 0$ and $4ac$ is much less than b^2, we can use the middle expression for the lower sign and the right-hand expression for the upper sign: the solutions are

$$x = \frac{-b - \sqrt{(b^2 - 4ac)}}{2a}, \quad x = \frac{-2c}{b + \sqrt{(b^2 - 4ac)}}.$$

If $b < 0$ then we reverse and use the middle expression of Equation (1) for the upper sign, the right-hand one for the lower sign.

Using the right-hand expression of Equation (1) for the example of Exercise 1.1 gives roots approximately

$$-0.000\,000\,265 \quad \text{and} \quad 1638.4.$$

This time the second one is nonsense, so we conclude (optimistically) that the actual roots are

$$-0.000\,000\,265\ldots \quad \text{and} \quad -37\,685\,400.$$

1.3 *Exercise*
Write a program to evaluate the right hand expression of Equation (1) (when $b^2 \geqslant 4ac$) and use it to verify the above results. Choose some other equations with b^2 much greater than $4ac$, and compare the results of the two expressions in Equation (1).

One natural place where quadratic equations arise is in the intersection points of a line and a circle (or an ellipse, hyperbola or parabola). Thus we seek the common solutions of

line: $px + qy + r = 0$,   where p, q are not both zero,
circle: $x^2 + y^2 + 2gx + 2fy + c = 0$.

(Or, more generally, $ax^2 + 2hxy + by^2 + 2gx + 2fy + c = 0$, which represents any *conic section*, and in particular any ellipse, hyperbola or parabola. The point is that the variables x and y occur only to degree 2.) Of course we can substitute one equation in the other, eliminating x or y, but that tends to assume $p \neq 0$ or $q \neq 0$, giving two cases. Try the following instead.

1.4 *Exercise*

Since p and q are not both zero,

$$x_0 = -pr/(p^2 + q^2), \quad y_0 = -qr/(p^2 + q^2)$$

always give a point (x_0, y_0) on the line. The general point on the line is then $(x, y) = (x_0 + tq, y_0 - tp)$, where t is any real number. Substitute these x and y in the equation of the circle to obtain

$$t^2(p^2 + q^2) + 2t(gq - fp)$$
$$+ (x_0^2 + y_0^2 + 2gx_0 + 2fy_0 + c) = 0.$$

Note that the coefficient of t^2 is never zero. What does this mean geometrically? What does the form of the constant term tell you?

Write a program which accepts p, q, r, f, g and c as inputs and calculates x_0 and y_0 and hence the coefficients in the quadratic in t. Combine this with the program in Exercise 1.1 so as to solve the quadratic and hence find the intersections of the line and the circle. (Beware of two possible cs, one from the circle and one from the constant term in the quadratic of Exercise 1.1.) (As a harder exercise, do the same for the line and the more general second degree equation $ax^2 + 2hxy + \ldots + c = 0$ above. This time the coefficient of t^2 in the resulting quadratic equation for t could possibly be zero. What does this mean geometrically?)

1.5 *Exercise*

How can the program of Exercise 1.4 be adapted to find the intersections of two circles

$$x^2 + y^2 + 2g_1 x + 2f_1 y + c_1 = 0$$

and

$$x^2 + y^2 + 2g_2 x + 2f_2 y + c_2 = 0?$$

(Hint: subtract these two equations.)

1.6 *Exercise*

A circular object has its centre at $(5, 6)$ and has radius 1 (Fig. 1(*a*)). Missiles travel in straight lines outwards from the origin. When the path of the missile is $y = x \tan t$ for a fixed t, use the program in Exercise 1.4 to determine where, if anywhere, the object is struck. Take $t = 40°$, $45°$, $50°$, $55°$, $60°$ in succession. (You will need to

44   *Equations*

convert these to radians, multiplying by $\pi/180$, before applying the tan function built into your micro.) By taking other values of t determine approximately the coordinates of the points where the *tangents* from (0, 0) to the circle touch the circle.

Check by trigonometry that the corresponding values of t are such that $\tan t = (15 \pm \sqrt{15})/12$ (and t is acute).

1.7 *Exercise*
If you have available a program to find intersections of lines with ellipses, replace the circular object in Exercise 1.6 with an elliptical one centred at (5, 6) with half-axes of lengths 1 parallel to the x-axis and 1.5 parallel to the y-axis.

1.8 *Exercise*
A second circular object moves towards the first one, the radius being also 1 and the centre moving along the line $y = x \tan t$ for a fixed t (Fig. 1(*b*)). Taking the centre at $(s, s \tan t)$ for various values of s, and fixing t at 45° (so the centre moves along the line $y = x$), find the coordinates of the point where the circular objects collide, using the program in Exercise 1.5. Taking other values of t find approximately the smaller value of t for which the objects just touch as the second object moves outwards. Verify by trigonometry that the *larger* angle t with this property is about 65.03°.

1.9 *Exercise: A ladder problem*
A ladder of length l rests as shown in Fig. 2 with its ends on a vertical wall and horizontal ground, just touching a square box of side a. How far is the foot of the ladder from the foot of the wall?

We shall see later that, if the box is rectangular rather than square, then an equation of degree 4 (rather than 2) comes in and it is best to

Fig. 1

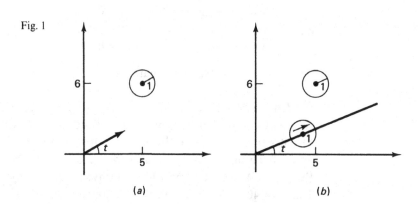

(a)   (b)

use approximation techniques to find the solution. See Section 5.2. Using x and y as in Fig. 2 we have

$$x^2 + y^2 = l^2 \qquad \text{(Pythagoras)}$$

and

$$(y - a)/a = a/(x - a) \qquad \text{(similar triangles)}$$

which gives

$$xy = a(x + y).$$

From these,

$$(x + y)^2 = l^2 + 2xy = l^2 + 2a(x + y),$$

which shows that $x + y$ satisfies a quadratic equation whose coefficients are known once we know l and a. What is the condition for real roots? Using

$$(x - y)^2 = l^2 - 2xy = l^2 - 2a(x + y)$$

we can find $x - y$ from $x + y$, and hence x and y separately. Write a program which accepts l and a as inputs and solves the quadratic equation for $x + y$, then finds $x - y$ and finally finds x and y. Taking $a = 1$, find the solutions, if any, when (a) $l = 4$, (b) $l = 3$, (c) $l = 2.818$, (d) $l = 2$. Which solutions apply to the original problem of the ladder and the box? What is the condition for $l^2 - 2a(x + y) \geq 0$, which guarantees solutions for x and y?

1.10 *Exercise: ladders, continued*
Sketch in the (x, y)-plane the curves $x^2 + y^2 = l^2$ and

Fig. 2

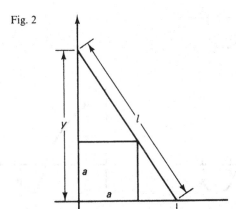

$(x - a)(y - a) = a^2$ (the latter is the curve $xy = a^2$ shifted up and to the right by a). Explain why two solutions for the pair (x, y) will always be real but negative (so no good for the problem) and the other two will be real precisely when $l^2 \geq 8a^2$.

We shall continue with real solutions to equations, and return to quadratics and *complex* solutions later, in §6.

Although methods exist for solving cubic and quartic equations 'exactly' (see for example Boyer (1968), p. 310, Birkhoff and MacLane (1965), p. 105, or Uspensky (1948), Chapter V), it is very doubtful whether they are worth writing programs for. The cubic, in particular, can involve undue difficulties with complex numbers even when the solutions are actually real. We shall concentrate on approximate solutions, and in fact say something about two approximation techniques.

§2
The method of bisection

The simplest approximation technique for finding solutions of an equation $f(x) = 0$ is probably the technique of bisection, which actually looks for *changes of sign* in the function f. (Thus it would be useless for solving, say, $\sin x + 1 = 0$, since $\sin x + 1$ is always ≥ 0.)

The idea is to start with an interval $[a, b]$ (consisting of all x such that $a \leq x \leq b$), and such that $f(a)$ and $f(b)$ have opposite signs, i.e. $f(a)f(b) \leq 0$. (We assume that f is defined on all of the interval and that f is *continuous* there. The Intermediate Value Theorem then applies to f on the interval $[a, b]$. See almost any book on calculus,

Fig. 3

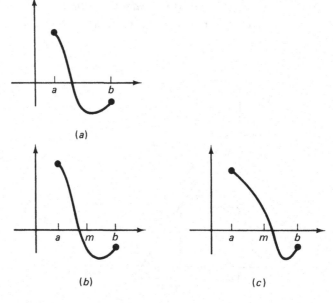

(a)

(b)   (c)

for example Spivak (1980), p. 108.) Thus, as in Fig. 3(*a*), the graph of *f* must cross the axis somewhere between *a* and *b* since it is on opposite sides of the axis at *a* and at *b*. So [*a*, *b*] *contains a solution of* $f(x) = 0$.

Let $m = \frac{1}{2}(a + b)$. Then $f(m)$ cannot have the same sign as both $f(a)$ and $f(b)$, which have opposite signs, so

$$\text{either } f(a)f(m) \leqslant 0 \quad \text{or} \quad f(m)f(b) \leqslant 0 \quad \text{(or both)}.$$

If $f(a)f(m) \leqslant 0$ (Fig. 3(*b*)) then, as before, there is a solution to $f(x) = 0$ somewhere between *a* and *m*, that is in [*a*, *m*]; otherwise there is certainly a solution in [*m*, *b*] (Fig. 3(*c*)). In either case we have narrowed the interval in which we know there to be a solution from [*a*, *b*] to one of half the length: the interval is bisected. Continuing in this way we trap a solution in ever-narrower intervals and so obtain the solution to any desired accuracy. (If there are many solutions with $a \leqslant x \leqslant b$ then we shall only find one of them!)

In fact, after *k* repetitions of the bisection, the solution is known to be inside a particular interval of length $1/2^k$ times the length of the starting interval (*b*–*a* in the above discussion).

Starting with *a* and *b* such that $f(a)f(b) \leqslant 0$ we therefore calculate $m = \frac{1}{2}(a + b)$ and

if $f(a)f(m) \leqslant 0$ we replace *b* by *m*, so [*a*, *b*] becomes [*a*, *m*];
if $f(a)f(m) > 0$ we replace *a* by *m*, so [*a*, *b*] becomes [*m*, *b*];

The following program will do this.

2.1 *Program: Bisection*

```
1Ø  INPUT A,B
2Ø  Calculate c = f(a) and d = f(b) from formula for f
3Ø  IF C*D > Ø THEN GOTO 1Ø
4Ø  LET M = (A + B)/2
5Ø  Calculate e = f(m)
6Ø  IF C*E < = Ø THEN LET B = M ELSE LET A = M
```

If your computer does not have ELSE in its vocabulary, then replace line 6Ø by two lines:

```
6Ø  IF C*E < = Ø THEN LET B = M: GOTO 7Ø
65  LET A = M
```

Now continue:

```
7Ø  PRINT A
8Ø  GOTO 4Ø
```

Ideally, insert a line 75 which causes the program to pause until a key is pressed, otherwise the numbers will flash by rather quickly. At line 7Ø, it does not matter whether a, b or m is printed, since they all converge to the same solution to $f(x) = 0$. It is also possible on some micros to define the function f by a formula in BASIC, e.g.

     5 DEF FNY(X) = whatever formula you want

so that lines 2Ø and 5Ø can be removed, and lines 3Ø and 6Ø become

    3Ø IF FNY(A)*FNY(B) > Ø THEN GOTO 1Ø
    6Ø IF FNY(A)*FNY(M) < = Ø
        THEN LET B = M ELSE LET A = M

with the same change to line 6Ø and addition of line 65 as before, if ELSE is not available to you.

2.2 *Exercise*
Use the program with the function

$$f(x) = x^2 - 1 \quad a = -2, b = 0$$
and $\quad f(x) = x^2 - 1 \quad a = 0, b = 2$

where the numbers printed out should approach -1 (the solution in $[-2, 0]$) and 1 (the solution in $[0, 2]$), respectively.

2.3 *Exercise*
For an original interval of length 1 (i.e. $b = a + 1$), show that 27 repetitions of the bisection are enough to place x in an interval of length less than 10^{-8}. For length 10, show that 30 repetitions are enough.

2.4 *Exercise*
Let $f(x) = \tan x - x$. This has a solution for $f(x) = 0$ in every interval of the form

$$\frac{(2n - 1)\pi}{2} \leqslant x \leqslant \frac{(2n + 1)\pi}{2}$$

($n = 0, \pm 1, \pm 2, \dots$). For $n = 0$ the solution is $x = 0$, for $n = 1$ it is about 4.49341 and for $n = 2$ it is about 7.72525 (all values of x in radians, of course). Don't, however, for $n = 1$ say, put $a = \frac{1}{2}\pi$ and $b = \frac{3}{2}\pi$ since f is actually undefined (infinite) at these values. (All the same, if you ask your computer for $\tan(\frac{1}{2}\pi)$, inserting of course an approximation to π, it will doubtless give you a finite, though rather meaningless, answer.) Something like $a = 1.6$, $b = 4.7$, which are a bit greater than $\frac{1}{2}\pi$ and a bit less than $\frac{3}{2}\pi$, will locate the root between $\frac{1}{2}\pi$ and $\frac{3}{2}\pi$. As n increases, the solution x gets nearer to the right-hand end $(2n + 1)\pi/2$: draw a sketch of $y = \tan x$ and $y = x$ on the same diagram to see why. Thus you need to take b quite close to $(2n + 1)\pi/2$ in order to be sure the solution x satisfies $x \leqslant b < (2n + 1)\pi/2$. (Or: solve $\sin x - x\cos x = 0$!)

2.5 Exercise

Here is a problem where a simple situation leads to a frightful equation: A goat is tethered to a point on the boundary of a circular field; how long should the tethering rope be so that the goat can graze over an area exactly half that of the field? Let the mathematical field have radius 1 unit, let x be the length of the rope and let 2θ be the angle shown (Fig. 4). From the Fig. 4(b), $\frac{1}{2}x = \cos \theta$, so $\theta = \arccos(\frac{1}{2}x)$, which is sometimes written $\cos^{-1}(\frac{1}{2}x)$. Some calculation, which you should try for yourself, shows that the shaded area over which the goat can graze is

$$(x^2 - 2)\theta - x \sin \theta + \pi,$$

where angles are measured in radians. Since we want this to equal $\frac{1}{2}\pi$ ($= \frac{1}{2}$ the area of the circle) we want to solve the equation $f(x) = 0$ where (using $\sin^2(\frac{1}{2}x) + \cos^2(\frac{1}{2}x)^2 = 1$)

$$f(x) = (x^2 - 2)(\arccos(\tfrac{1}{2}x)) - x\sqrt{(1 - x^2/4)} + \tfrac{1}{2}\pi.$$

This is surely a case where only graphical or approximate techniques could reasonably apply. Use the bisection method to show that the solution is about $x = 1.15873$ (clearly it lies between 1 and 2). (If your micro does not know about arc cos, but does know about arc tan, then use the fact that, provided $0 < t \leqslant 1$, $\arccos t = \arctan(\sqrt{(1 - t^2)}/t)$. If $-1 \leqslant t < 0$, then π must be added to the right-hand side of this formula.)

Are there any other solutions to $f(x) = 0$ which do not correspond

Fig. 4

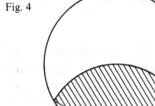

(a)

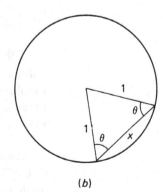

(b)

to the original problem? (Note that $-1 \leq \frac{1}{2}x \leq 1$ since $\frac{1}{2}x = \cos\theta$.) Do such solutions correspond to anything geometrically sensible?

2.6 *Exercise*

One of the problems with the bisection method is knowing when you have all the solutions. An extreme case is $f(x) = \sin(1/x)$, which has a zero (that is a value of x with $f(x) = 0$) for $1/x = n\pi$ and any integer n. Thus there are infinitely many zeros $x = 1/n\pi$. (This function is a favourite in calculus books. See for example Spivak (1980), p. 81.) Suppose we want all solutions > 0.03 of $f(x) = 0$ by the bisection method. Taking $a = 0.03$, $b = 0.04$ gives the solution nearest 0.03, namely $x = 1/10\pi = 0.031831$ approximately. Taking $a = 0.03$, $b = 0.036$ gives $f(a)f(b) > 0$; in fact there are *two* solutions, not none, between 0.03 and 0.036. See if you can find all the solutions > 0.03 by the bisection method.

2.7 *Exercise*

If $f(a)$ happens to be 0 then it's pretty clear that the solution obtained in Program 2.1 will be a itself. What if $f(b) = 0$?

2.8 *Exercise*

Here is an assortment of equations given by polynomials. They arise from a variety of problems which are explained in detail in the next section, which is on the Newton–Raphson method of approximation. Determine (approximately) the roots of these equations using the bisection method

    (a) $x^3 - 2x + 2 = 0$.
    (b) $2x^3 - 9x^2 + 11x - 3 = 0$.
    (c) $x^3 - 9x^2 + x - 1 = 0$.
    (d) $x^3 - 3x + 1 = 0$ (this has three real roots).
    (e) $x^3 - 3x^2 + 3 = 0$ (this has three real roots).
    (f) $4x^3 - 8x^2 + 5x - \frac{1}{2} = 0$ (this has one real root).
    (g) $x^4 - 4x^3 - 71x^2 + 400x - 400 = 0$ (this has four real roots).
    (h) $x^4 - 6x^3 - 75x^2 + 450x - 675 = 0$ (this has two real roots).

2.9 *Exercise*

Solve arc tan $x = 2x/(1 + x^2)$ (compare Exercise 3.2 below). You should find solutions $x = 0$, $x = \pm 1.39175$ approximately. (Can you show by a hand sketch of the two graphs $y = $ arc tan x and $y = 2x/(1 + x^2)$ that these are the *only* solutions?)

2.10 *Exercise: Kepler's equation*

One of Kepler's laws of planetary motion (see almost any book on mechanics, for example Rutherford (1964)) states that, for a planet P

in an elliptical orbit about a sun S, with S at a focus of the ellipse, the line SP sweeps out *area* at a constant rate. That is, in Fig. 5, the area ASP is proportional to the time taken by the planet to travel from the fixed A to the moving P. (You can read more about ellipses in Chapter 3.) Drawing the circle centre C, as shown, touching the ellipse at both ends of the major axis, the point Q directly above P (i.e. with QP perpendicular to CA) gives an angle $x = ACQ$ called the 'eccentric anomaly' of the planet. (Angle ASP is called the 'true anomaly'.) A little knowledge of ellipses is needed to derive from this *Kepler's Equation*:

$$2\pi p = x - e \sin x. \tag{1}$$

Here, p is the fraction of the planet's year which has elapsed between A and P ($p = 0$ means P is at A, and $p = \frac{1}{2}$ that P is at the other end of the major axis). The Equation (1) is derived in Rutherford (1964), p. 73.

The number e is called the *eccentricity* of the ellipse. Taking x and y-axes as usual through C the equation of the ellipse becomes $x^2/a^2 + y^2/b^2 = 1$, where a is the length of CA and $b \leq a$ is the length of the perpendicular half-axis CB. Then you can check that $P = (a \cos x, b \sin x)$. The eccentricity e is then $\sqrt{(a^2 - b^2)}/a$, and S has coordinates $(ae, 0)$. Exercise: prove that the tangent to the ellipse at the point directly below S has slope e. For a long thin ellipse a/b is large, and e is close to 1 (but always $0 \leq e < 1$). For a circle, $a = b$ and $e = 0$, and the tangent just mentioned is horizontal since $S = C$. In the limiting case $e = 1$, b is zero and the 'ellipse' is flat with P moving back and forth along a straight line – and passing periodically through S, which is somewhat unrealistic!

Suppose we are given p (and e); the problem is to find x from Equation (1), i.e., to find the position of the planet at a given moment of its year. Note that we expect just *one* value of x for a

Fig. 5

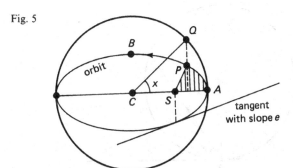

given t. (Does this have something to do with $0 \leqslant e < 1$? Consider $t = 0$.)

If we want to obtain x in *degrees* rather than radians then Equation (1) becomes

$$360p = x - (180/\pi)e \sin (\pi x / 180). \tag{2}$$

Take for example $p = 0.25$ (a quarter of the year has elapsed) and

> $e = 0$ (circle): x should be 90
> $e = 0.017$ (Earth): x should be about 90.974
> $e = 0.206$ (Mercury)
> $e = 0.249$ (Pluto)

Try a *very* long eccentric orbit (such as a comet may have), $e = 0.9$ say. You will find that $x = 129.68$ approximately: the comet is much further than a quarter of the distance round its orbit (which occurs at $x = 90$) on account of its increased speed when near the sun.

2.11 *Exercise*

A planet moves at a constant speed in a *circular* orbit, centre C, and at a point P of the orbit a spaceship leaves the planet and travels at constant speed in a straight line in the plane of the orbit. What should the angle x be in Fig. 6 so that spaceship and planet arrive *simultaneously* at Q? The angle PCQ is $2x$ (can you see why? Remember CP is perpendicular to the tangent line). Let $a = $ (speed of planet)/(speed of spaceship). Then we require (arc PQ) $= a$ (straight line PQ), i.e. $2rx = 2ar \sin x$, where r is the radius of the circle. This gives

$$x = a \sin x, \tag{3}$$

which is equation (1) above for $p = 0$, with a replacing e. Since Equation (1) with $p = 0$ has *only* the solution $x = 0$, there must be a difference! In fact it is that $a > 1$ whereas $e < 1$. (Why

Fig. 6

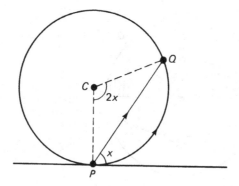

should $a \leqslant 1$ give only $x = 0$ in Equation (3)? Think of the original problem.)

If a is large there will be more than one solution to *Equation* (3) (besides $x = 0$), because the planet can do a complete revolution while the spaceship is on its way. Sketch (by hand!) the graphs $y = \sin x$ and $y = x/a$, and deduce that the *number of solutions $x > 0$ to* Equation (3) *changes from one to two* when the line $y = x/a$, rotating clockwise about $(0, 0)$ as a increases, *touches* the curve $y = \sin x$ for the first time. This happens when $x = \tan x$ and $a = \sec x$ (you can prove this using calculus), and $2\pi < x < 5\pi/2$. Refer back to Exercise 2.4 and show that a is approximately 7.78971. Taking off 2π and converting to degrees, x comes to about 82.62°.

For this value of a, what is the other value of x? (It lies between 90° and 180°.) Any increase in a beyond this value gives *three* solutions for x. At what value of a does this change to four solutions and then five?

2.12 *Exercise*

This problem is very similar to Exercise 2.11. Given the length $2l$ of a circular arc and the length $2d$ of the corresponding chord, determine the height h of the 'arch' (Fig. 7). Writing $2x$ for the angle subtended at the centre of the circle by the arc (or the chord), show that $x/\sin x = l/d$, and that $h = d \tan (\tfrac{1}{2}x)$. Find h when d is one kilometre and l is one metre more. (How about one *centimetre* more?)

§3 The Newton–Raphson method of approximation

In this method for solving the equation $f(x) = 0$ the curve $y = f(x)$ is replaced by its tangent line at a point. Instead of sliding down the *curve* to a solution (where it crosses the x-axis) we slide down the *tangent line* to an approximate solution (x_1 in Fig. 8). Specifically, given a real number x_0, the equation of the tangent line at $(x_0, f(x_0))$ is

$$y - f(x_0) = f'(x_0)(x - x_0), \tag{1}$$

where $f'(x_0)$ is the derivative of f at x_0, i.e. the slope of the tangent line. (In other notation, $f'(x_0) = dy/dx$ at x_0.)

We now solve the linear equation (1) for x when $y = 0$, finding the value x_1 where the tangent line meets the x-axis. Thus

Fig. 7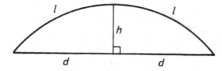

Fig. 8

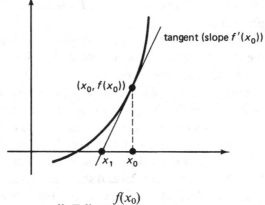

$$x_1 = x_0 - \frac{f(x_0)}{f'(x_0)},$$

so long as $f'(x_0) \neq 0$. (This just says that the tangent isn't parallel to the x-axis. If it is parallel then there is no use looking for its intersection with the x-axis.) The idea is to take x_1 as the 'next approximation' to a root of $f(x) = 0$, thinking of x_0 as the initial guess at a root. We then work out

$$x_2 = x_1 - \frac{f(x_1)}{f'(x_1)},$$

Fig. 9

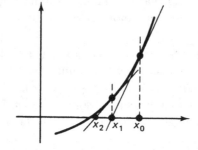

good

(*a*)

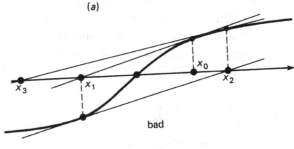

bad

(*b*)

which is the x-coordinate of the point where the tangent line at $(x_1, f(x_1))$ meets the x-axis, regarding x_2 as the next approximation, and so on. See Fig. 9(a). As Fig. 9(b), shows, the process may go badly wrong! We shall not attempt very much theory here (see, however, Sections 3.5–3.9 below), but rather illustrate the method with a variety of examples.

Given f and the initial guess x_0 we define

$$x_{k+1} = x_k - \frac{f(x_k)}{f'(x_k)} \tag{2}$$

for $k = 0, 1, 2, 3, \ldots$, so long as $f'(x_k) \neq 0$ (and it's very unlikely to be *exactly* 0), and consider the sequence of 'approximations', or *iterates* as we shall call them, $x_0, x_1, x_2, \ldots$.

3.1 *Program: Newton–Raphson*

```
10 INPUT XØ
20 LET X = XØ
30 Work out f(x) = a and f'(x) = b from explicit formulae for
   f and its derivative f'
40 LET X = X − A/B
50 PRINT X
60 GOTO 30
```

Ideally insert a line 55 which makes the micro pause before going on to the next iteration. If you can define functions in the program, say FNF(X) for f and FND(X) for f', then you can omit line 3Ø and have

```
5 DEF FNF(X) = formula for f(x)
6 DEF FND(X) = formula for f'(x)
40 LET X = X − FNF(X)/FND(X)
```

3.2 *Exercise*

The graph in Fig. 9(b) may remind you of the inverse tangent graph $y = \arctan x$ (also written $\tan^{-1} x$). For $y = \arctan x$ we have $f'(x) = 1/(1 + x^2)$, so line 4Ø of the program becomes

```
40 LET X = X − (1 + X*X)*ATN(X)
```

Try letting x_0 equal: (a) 1; (b) 2; (c) 1.3; (d) 1.4; (e) 1.391; (f) 1.392. The solution sought is of course $x = 0$. You should find that (a), (c) and (e) are 'good' values for x_0, and do indeed give the solution $x = 0$ after a few iterations, but (b), (d) and (f) are 'bad' values and go off to infinity in the manner of Fig. 9(b).

What is the 'critical' value of x_0 which separates the good from the bad? It is the value of x_0 which makes $x_1 = x_0 - (1 + x_0^2)(\arctan x_0)$

precisely equal to $-x_0$, so that a second iteration merely sends us back to x_0. (Compare Exercise 4.2 below.) That is, the critical value is a solution of arc tan $x = 2x/(1 + x^2)$. Now refer back to Exercise 2.9. (Of course, you could solve *this* equation by Newton–Raphson . . . .)

3.3 *Exercise*

What happens if the Newton–Raphson method is used to seek the root $x = 0$ of $f(x) = 0$ where (a) $f(x) = x^{1/3}$, (b) $f(x) = x^{3/5}$, (c) $f(x) = x^{2/3}$? In each case x_{k+1} can be expressed very simply in terms of x_k, making it relatively easy to spot what will happen. Sketches of the three curves $y = f(x)$ also help.

Note that if, say, $x^{1/3}$ is to be evaluated on the micro we have to do better than writing $X\uparrow(\frac{1}{3})$, for this will be rejected when $x < 0$ (also possibly for $x = 0$). (The micro tries to work out $(\ln x)/3$, and naturally fails because $\ln x$ is undefined for $x \leqslant 0$.) It is necessary to do something like

$$\text{sign } (x) \text{ (abs } (x))^{1/3}$$

where sign(x) is $+1$ for $x > 0$, -1 for $x < 0$ and 0 for $x = 0$, while abs $(x) = |x|$ is the absolute value of x.

Try $f(x) = 1 + x^{2/3}$ (you may be able to write this in BASIC as $1 + (X*X)\uparrow(\frac{1}{3})$, since $x^2 \geqslant 0$), which gives *no* solutions for $f(x) = 0$. You should find that the iterates x_k eventually oscillate between about $x = \pm 5.19615$. Solve $x - f(x)/f'(x) = -x$ to find the exact value!

In this case, $x_{k+1} = -\frac{1}{2}x_k - \frac{3}{2}x_k^{1/3}$. If x_k approaches a limit l as $k \to \infty$, *then* this equation implies $l = -\frac{1}{2}l - \frac{3}{2}l^{1/3}$, which has only the solution $l = 0$. However, as you will discover by taking various values for x_0, there is no starting value x_0 which makes $x_k \to 0$ as $k \to \infty$. (In fact, if $|x_k| < 1$, then $|x_{k+1}| > |x_k|$.)

For $f(x) = 1 + x^p$, where $\frac{1}{2} < p < 1$ and p is a fraction with an odd denominator, the x_k eventually oscillate between $\pm (2p - 1)^{-1/p}$. Try $p = 18/19$.

3.4 *Exercise*

Try seeking the root $x = 0$ of $1 - e^{-x^2} = 0$. Thus x is here replaced by $x - (1 - e^{-x^2})/(2x e^{-x^2})$ in line $4\emptyset$ of Program 3.1. The shape of the graph $y = 1 - e^{-x^2}$ is suggested in Fig. 10. In BASIC, $Y = 1 - \text{EXP}(-X*X)$. Try (a) $x_0 = 1$, (b) $x_0 = 1.6$, (c) $x_0 = 1.528$. Show that the critical value of x_0 separating good values of x_0 (for which $x_k \to 0$) from bad values (for which $x_k \nrightarrow 0$) is a solution of $4x^2 + 1 = e^{x^2}$. Find this critical value using the method of bisection.

Note that if x_0 is much bigger than the critical value (e.g. $x_0 = 2$)

Fig. 10

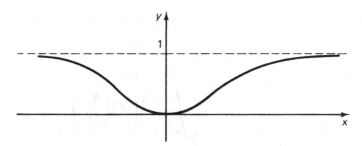

then the Newton–Raphson method gives numbers x_k which are wildly divergent: the iterates tend to infinity so fast that your computer will probably complain about dividing by zero after a couple of iterations. Also the approximations approach zero painfully slowly for say $x_0 = 1.5$. Why is this?

In the next few items we take the opportunity of making some slightly more technical observations on Newton–Raphson, and the limitations of the method.

3.5 *Exercise: Newton–Raphson can deceive us*

Suppose the iterates x_k approach a limit l as $k \to \infty$. Is $f(l) = 0$? If not, we are deceived by the method. Here is a wild example to show that deceit *is* possible. Let

$$f(x) = 1 - 2x \sin (1/x) \quad \text{for } x \neq 0,$$
$$f(0) = 1.$$

See Fig. 11 for a rough sketch. In fact f is continuous for all x, and $f'(x)$ exists for all $x \neq 0$ (compare e.g. Spivak (1980) pp. 80, 146).

Take $x_0 = 1/(2\pi)$, so that $f(x_0) = 1$. Verify that $x_1 = 1/(4\pi)$, $x_2 = 1/(8\pi)$, and in general $x_k = 1/(2^{k+1}\pi)$. Thus certainly $x_k \to 0$, but equally certainly $f(0) \neq 0$. Verify also that $f'(x_k) = 2^{k+2}\pi$, so the derivative $\to \infty$ as $k \to \infty$. Try programming this, and starting with $x_0 = 1/(2\pi)$. Try also $x_0 = 0.5$. Explain what you see.

3.6 *A sufficient condition for Newton–Raphson to work*

Suppose $x_k \to l$ and $|f'(x)| \leqslant M$ for some constant M and all x sufficiently close to l. Then from

$$(x_{k+1} - x_k)f'(x_k) = f(x_k)$$

(which is the definition of x_{k+1} in terms of x_k), it follows that $f(x_k) \to 0$, since the left-hand side $\to 0$. Thus $f(x_k) \to f(l) = 0$ so l *is* a solution to $f(x) = 0$. (Why does this not contradict Exercise 3.5?)

3.7 *Do the x_k approach a limit?*

How can we tell for sure that the iterates x_k are approaching a limit l? The various numbers x_k appearing on the screen stop changing after a while; what guarantee is there that they won't *start* changing again if we wait

Equations

Fig. 11

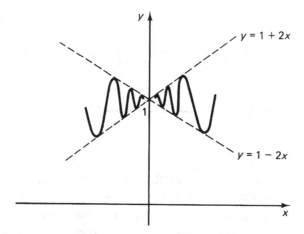

patiently? Actually none at all, though for 'reasonable' functions f this won't happen. What you *can* do is to check on the value of $f(x_k)$ when x_k has stopped changing, to see if it is nearly zero. Or you can evaluate $f(x_k - \epsilon)$ and $f(x_k + \epsilon)$ for ϵ around 10^{-7} to see if there is a change of sign, indicating a solution which will be x_k to six decimal places or so.

Note the contrast with the bisection method, where we can be *certain*, after a definite number of iterations, that we have located a solution to say six decimal places.

3.8 *Another wild example*

This is based on Exercise 3.5, and shows that we can be deceived into believing that $x_k \to l$. We attach a parabola to part of the curve in Exercise 3.5 (Fig. 12). Fix a whole number n and define $\epsilon = 1/(2n + 1)\pi$. Let

$$f(x) = \begin{cases} 1 - 2x \sin{(1/x)} & \text{for } x \geqslant \epsilon \\ a(x^2 + 3x + 2) & \text{for } x < \epsilon \end{cases}$$

where $a = 1/(\epsilon^2 + 3\epsilon + 2)$. Then f is continuous for all x; with more trouble we could make a curve that joined up more smoothly at $x = \epsilon$, but we do not need to do that.

Try $x_0 = 1/2\pi$ ($= 0.15915494 \ldots$), $n = 100\,000$. (You will need to split line 4Ø of the Program 3.1 into two alternatives, according to whether $x < \epsilon$ or $x > \epsilon$.) You should find that the x_k appear to approach 0 but then change their minds and arrive at -1 instead. If n is very large then ϵ will be recorded as 0 by the micro, of course, so we shall never know in that case that the solution is $x = -1$ rather than $x = 0$.

3.9 *When will Newton–Raphson locate a solution?*

Suppose that $f(l) = 0$. What conditions on x_0, l and f will guarantee that $x_k \to l$ as $k \to \infty$? A thorough treatment of this question is to be found in books on Numerical Analysis (for example, Young and Gregory (1972), pp. 132, 146); here we indicate a proof of the following fact: *Suppose that f, f' and f'' ($=$ second derivative of f) are continuous for all x near l, and $f(l) = 0$, $f'(l) \neq 0$. Then, provided x_0 is sufficiently close to l, we have $x_k \to l$ as $k \to \infty$.*

In fact, let $g(x) = x - f(x)/f'(x)$, so $g(x_k) = x_{k+1}$ and $g(l) = l$. We have

$g'(x) = f(x)f''(x)/(f'(x))^2$. Since $f'(l) \neq 0$ and f' is continuous, there exists $c > 0$ with $|f'(x)| \geq c$ for all x sufficiently close to l. Further, for x sufficiently close to l, $|f(x)f''(x)| \leq \frac{1}{2}c^2$, since $f(l) = 0$ and f and f'' are continuous. So $|g'(x)| \leq \frac{1}{2}$ for all x close enough to l. By the Mean Value Theorem (see any book on calculus, e.g. Spivak (1980), p. 179),

$$x_{k+1} - l = g(x_k) - g(l) = (x_k - l)g'(x)$$

for some x between x_k and l. Hence, provided x_0 is close enough to l, $|x_1 - l| \leq \frac{1}{2}|x_0 - l|$, $|x_2 - l| \leq \frac{1}{2}|x_1 - l| \leq \frac{1}{4}|x_0 - l|$, and so on. Generally, $|x_k - l| \leq (1/2^k)|x_0 - l|$, so as $k \to \infty$, we have $x_k \to l$.

The example in Exercise 3.5 above fails because $f''(0)$ does not even exist; also f' is not continuous at $x = 0$.

The above result assumes $f'(l) \neq 0$, i.e. l is a *simple* solution of $f(x) = 0$. See Young and Gregory (1972), p. 146 for further details.

We now turn to examples where the Newton–Raphson method can be (more or less) successfully applied to the solution of equations. For the most part, the examples involve *polynomial* functions f, and the reader may now wish to proceed straight to Exercise 3.12, using a program such as Program 3.1 above. We pause, however, to consider the problem of *efficiently* evaluating a given polynomial.

3.10 *Evaluation of polynomials*

Let $f(x) = a_0 + a_1 x + a_2 x^2 + \ldots + a_n x^n$ ($n \geq 1$) be a polynomial, which we want to evaluate for a given value of x. Thus we want a program which accepts x, n, $a_0, \ldots, a_n$ as inputs and which calculates $f(x)$. The numbers $a_0, \ldots, a_n$ will be stored as an *array*, and because some micros only allow arrays to be indexed from 1 onwards (rather than 0), we write a_j as an array element AA(J + 1) for $j = 0, 1, \ldots, n$. The array AA has dimension $n + 1$, that is contains $n + 1$ entries.

Fig. 12

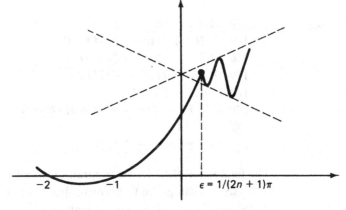

$\epsilon = 1/(2n + 1)\pi$

Brute force will evaluate $f(x)$ by $1 + 2 + \ldots + (n - 1)$ multiplications followed by n additions, a total of $\frac{1}{2}n(n + 1)$ operations. Suppose, however, that we work out in succession

$$b_1 = a_n x, \ b_2 = x(b_1 + a_{n-1}), \ b_3 = x(b_2 + a_{n-2}),$$

and so on, down to $b_n = x(b_{n-1} + a_1)$ and finally $b_{n+1} = b_n + a_0$. Then a little thought will convince you that $b_{n+1} = f(x)$, and working out b_{n+1} involves only n additions and n multiplications, which is a great improvement if n is large.

3.11 *Program: Evaluation*

```
1Ø INPUT N
2Ø DIM AA = N + 1
3Ø FOR J = 1 TO N + 1
4Ø INPUT AA(J)
5Ø NEXT J
6Ø INPUT X
7Ø LET F = AA(N + 1)*X
8Ø IF N = 1 THEN GOTO 12Ø
9Ø FOR J = 1 TO N - 1
1ØØ LET F = X*(F + AA(N - J + 1))
11Ø NEXT J
12Ø LET F = F + AA(1)
13Ø PRINT F
```

The final value of F in the program is $f(x)$.

When both $f(x)$ and $f'(x)$ are needed where

$$f'(x) = a_1 + 2a_2 x + \ldots + na_n x^{n-1},$$

then we could continue:

```
14Ø LET F1 = Ø
15Ø IF N = 1 THEN GOTO 21Ø
16Ø LET F1 = N*AA(N + 1)*X
17Ø IF N = 2 THEN GOTO 21Ø
18Ø FOR J = 1 TO N - 2
19Ø LET F1 = X*(F1 + (N - J)*AA(N - J + 1))
2ØØ NEXT J
21Ø LET F1 = F1 + AA(2)
```

The final value of F1 in the program is then $f'(x)$.

Lastly, we can go on to perform the Newton–Raphson iteration, supposing the x in line 6Ø is the starting value x_0.

```
300 X = X − F/F1
310 PRINT X
320 GOTO 70
```

As usual, a line 315 causing the micro to pause until a key is pressed will make the iteration easier to follow.

At any stage it is possible to check the value of $f(x)$, to see whether it is small, or to check $f(x - \epsilon)$ and $f(x + \epsilon)$ for small ϵ (around 10^{-7}) to see whether there is a change of sign. General theory predicts that once we are close enough to a root iteration will (subject to some mild conditions such as those in Section 3.9) bring us even closer.

3.12 *Exercise: Quadratic equations*
Take $f(x) = x^2 - y$, for various values $y > 0$, to find approximations to $\sqrt{y}$.

Take $f(x) = x^2 - 3x + 2$, with solutions to $f(x) = 0$ given by $x = 1$ and $x = 2$. Check experimentally that, if $x_0 > \frac{3}{2}$ (the half-way point between the roots), then $x_k \to 2$ and, if $x_0 < \frac{3}{2}$, then $x_k \to 1$. What happens if $x_0 = \frac{3}{2}$?

Try some other quadratic equations with real roots and check by experiment that, if x_0 is greater than the average of the two roots (i.e. $x_0 > -b/2$ for $x^2 + bx + c = 0$), then x_k converges to the larger root; if less than the average then x_k converges to the smaller root. Sketch diagrams of quadratic curves and the Newton–Raphson iteration to make this plausible.

3.13 *Exercise: Quadratic equations with complex roots*
Take $x^2 + x + 1 = 0$, which has complex roots. It is hardly likely that x_k will get close to *them*, but try various values of x_0 (not equal to $-\frac{1}{2}$, which makes $f'(x_0) = 0$), and verify experimentally that the numbers $x_1, x_2, x_3, \ldots$ always jump about in a rather random-looking fashion. More of this strange phenomenon later – see §6. Try also $40x^2 - 40x + 11 = 0$.

3.14 *Exercise: Sensitivity to the starting value*
A good example with which to illustrate the sensitivity of the Newton–Raphson method to the starting value x_0 is the equation $2 \sin x - x = 0$, which has two non-zero solutions and the solution $x = 0$. Try various x_0 very close to 1 and on each side of 1 and notice how the iterates may diverge, or converge to any of the three solutions. According to Mackie and Scott (1985) the behaviour of the iterates depends not only on the value of x_0 but also on the machine being used!

4.1 *Exercise: A simple cubic*
Let $f(x) = x(x - 1)(x - 2) = x^3 - 3x^2 + 2x$. Start with various values for x_0 and see when the corresponding approximations x_k approach 0, when 1 and when 2. Is your result reasonable from a diagram?

4.2 *Exercise: Alternating iterates*
Let $f(x) = x^3 - 2x + 2$ and $x_0 = 0$. You should find that the iterates x_k alternate between 0 and 1. Find other cubic equations where the iterates alternate a, b, a, b, ... (Hint: you need $f(a)/f'(a) = -f(b)/f'(b)$ where $f = 0$ is the cubic equation.) Try taking x_0 just > 0 or just < 0 in the above equation.
    Try $2x^3 - 9x^2 + 11x - 3 = 0$, $x_0 = 1$.

4.3 *Exercise: Jumping iterates*
Let $f(x) = x^3 - 9x^2 + x - 1$. With $x_0 = 1$, you will find the iterates jump about near 0. In fact there are two complex roots quite close to 0; there is also a real root around 8.9.

4.4 *A volume problem*
Consider a solid hemisphere, of radius r, and a plane parallel to the base of the hemisphere, at height h above the base (Fig. 13). The volume below the plane is then $\pi r^2 h - \frac{1}{3}\pi h^3$. (If you know how to find volumes by integration, then you can check this.) What must h be in order to cut the hemisphere into two parts of *equal* volume? This requires

$$\pi r^2 h - \tfrac{1}{3}\pi h^3 = \tfrac{1}{4} \text{ (volume of sphere, radius } r)$$
$$= \tfrac{1}{3}\pi r^3.$$

Hence $x = h/r$ satisfies $x^3 - 3x + 1 = 0$. Of course, $0 < x < 1$. In fact, this equation has three real roots; find approximate values for all of them by the Newton–Raphson method.

4.5 *More volume problems*
There are many variants of Section 4.4. For example, if a sphere of radius r stands on a horizontal surface then a horizontal plane at a height h above the surface cuts off a volume $\pi h^2(r - \frac{1}{3}h)$ below itself. (Deduce this from Section 4.4.) Here $0 \leqslant h \leqslant 2r$, of course. What should h be so that, for example, this volume is $\frac{3}{4}$ that of the sphere? This gives $x = h/r$ satisfying $x^3 - 3x^2 + 3 = 0$. Again this equation has three real roots; the answer to the problem is the one satisfying $1 < x < 2$. Find it by means of Program 3.1.
    This also answers the question of the depth h to which a spherical

wooden ball of radius r and specific gravity $\frac{3}{4}$ will sink in water, for by Archimedes' principle the ball sinks until it displaces a volume of water equal to its own weight. What about specific gravity $\frac{2}{3}$, or $\frac{1}{4}$? (Specific gravity s means that a certain volume of the wood weighs s times the weight of the same volume of water.)

Speaking of Archimedes, the kind of volume problem we have been discussing was exactly what led to a very early interest in cubic equations, by Archimedes in about 200 BC (see Boyer (1968), p. 147).

4.6 *A thick cubical box problem*
Consider an open box in the shape of a cube, the outside dimension being c and the thickness of the material being t. What is the net volume of the box, i.e., the volume available for storage? A little thought will show that it is

$$(c - 2t)^3 + (c - 2t)^2 t = c^3 - 5c^2 t + 8ct^2 - 4t^3. \tag{1}$$

(This is the volume of the inner cube plus the volume of the 'plug' at the top since the box is open.) What must $x = t/c$ be so that the volume is *half* that of the outer cube, i.e. half of c^3? This gives the equation

$$4x^3 - 8x^2 + 5x - \tfrac{1}{2} = 0,$$

which in fact has only one real root. Try various values for x_0 and see whether all the sequences x_k converge to the same value (approximately 0.12256). Perhaps this is surprisingly small: t is then about $\frac{1}{8}$ of c for half volume.

4.7 *A spherical shell problem*
A spherical shell with outer and inner radii a and b, respectively, has a volume $\frac{4}{3}\pi(a^3 - b^3)$. For what value of b is this exactly half the volume of a solid sphere of radius a? This gives a rather simple cubic equation for b/a whose solution should be compared with that of Section 4.6.

Fig. 13

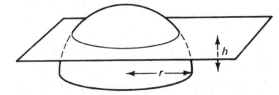

4.8 *Another solid sphere problem*
How can two parallel planes be placed so that they divide a solid sphere into three pieces of equal volume? See Section 4.5.

4.9 *A trisection problem*
The identity $\cos(3\theta) = 4\cos^3\theta - 3\cos\theta$, with $\theta = \pi/9$ radians ($= 20°$), shows that one root of the cubic equation $8x^3 - 6x - 1 = 0$ is $x = \cos(\pi/9)$. What are the other roots? (Given $\cos(3\theta) = \frac{1}{2}$, what are the possible values of θ?) Find $\cos(\pi/9)$ by the Newton–Raphson method.

This cubic equation arises in the proof that certain angles (for example $\pi/3$) cannot be trisected (divided into three equal pieces) using straightedge and compasses alone. The problem as to whether such angles exist goes back to the ancient Greek mathematicians (300 BC or even earlier) and was finally resolved around the beginning of the nineteenth century. (See for example Stewart (1973), p. 57, Courant and Robbins (1947), p. 137, or Hadlock (1978), p. 26.) The crucial fact about the cubic equation is that although its coefficients 8, -6 and -1 are all rational numbers, there are no rational *roots* of the equation. Prove this fact as follows: assume $x = p/q$ is a solution, where p and q are integers and p/q is in its lowest terms. Deduce $8p^3 - 6pq^2 - q^3 = 0$ and from this deduce (i) p is a factor of q, so that $p = 1$, (ii) q is a factor of 8. Now derive a contradiction by examining cases.

It turns out that trisecting the angle $\pi/3$ is equivalent to constructing a length of $\cos(\pi/9)$ given a length of 1. Further, when x satisfies a *cubic* equation with integer coefficients, then x can be constructed from a length of 1 with straightedge and compasses if and only if some root of the cubic equation is rational.

4.10 *A weight suspended by two cables*
Suppose that a weight w is supported by two equal cables, assumed straight and fixed to points $2a$ apart in a horizontal line (Fig. 14), the weight hanging a distance x below this line. Suppose that the cable has a weight of p per unit length. Then it can be shown (do it if you know the principles involved!) that the tension in the cable at the topmost points is

$$T = \frac{w}{2x}\sqrt{(x^2 + a^2)} + \frac{p}{x}(x^2 + a^2).$$

For an x giving *minimum* tension, $dT/dx = 0$, and this comes to

$$wa^2/2p = (x^2 - a^2)\sqrt{(x^2 + a^2)}. \tag{1}$$

(Check this!) Squaring gives a cubic equation in the new variable $u = x^2$. Solve this cubic to find the value of x for minimum tension in the case $w = 5000$ kg, $a = 20$ m, $p = 4$ kg/m. Is there just *one* positive solution for x?

To see theoretically when Equation (1) has one positive solution for x, we write $u = x^2$ as above and sketch in the (u, y)-plane the graph $y = (u - a^2)^2(u + a^2)$ (Fig. 15).

The solutions of Equation (1) then correspond to values $u > 0$ (since $u = x^2$) where the line $y = w^2 a^4/4p^2$ meets the graph. When will there be *one* solution $x > 0$? When two? Are there ever three? Choose values of w, a and p which give two solutions $x > 0$ and find those solutions. When there is a second solution does this give a maximum or a minimum of T? You could decide this by calculating T at this second solution and at nearby values of x (or u) on each side.

4.11 *Number of real roots of a cubic equation*
Given a cubic equation

$$x^3 + ax^2 + bx + c = 0 \qquad (2)$$

how can we tell whether it has one real root or three (or one real root and another 'repeated' root)? Substituting $x = y - a/3$ turns the equation (2) into

$$y^3 + py + q = 0 \qquad (3)$$

where $p = (3b - a^2)/3$ and $q = (2a^3 - 9ab + 27c)/27$. It is not hard to determine when Equation (3) has just one real root, for example by writing down the condition that the curve $z = y^3 + py + q$ has either no turning point, or two with the minimum *above* the horizontal (y-) axis, or one inflexional turning point not on the axis. See Fig. 16. Check that all these conditions can be combined in

$$4p^3 + 27q^2 > 0 \qquad (4)$$

Fig. 14

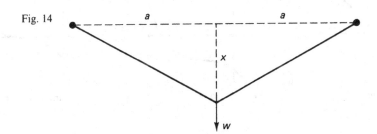

which is the necessary and sufficient condition for one real root of Equation (3). With $<$ in Equation (4) there are three real roots and with $=$ in Equation (4) there is a coincidence of two or more roots (the graph touches the horizontal axis). This means that Equation (2) has one real root if and only if

$$4(3b - a^2)^3 + (2a^3 - 9ab + 27c)^2 > 0. \tag{5}$$

Fig. 15

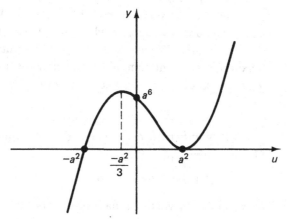

Fig. 16

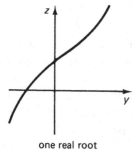

one real root

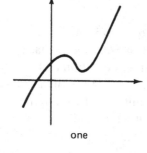

one

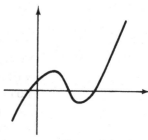

three

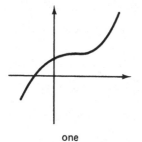

one

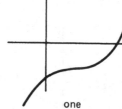

one

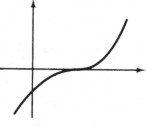

three coincident

Use Equation (5) to check the number of real roots in the cubic equations of Sections 4.1–4.10 above.

The expression on the left-hand side of Equations (4) or (5) is called the *discriminant* of the cubic equation (Equations (3) or (2) respectively). Note that in the (p, q)-plane, the equation $4p^3 + 27q^2 = 0$ is a cusped curve, as in Fig. 17. This curve separates those pairs (p, q) for which Equation (3) has one real root from those for which Equation (3) has three real roots – see Fig. 17.

For a quartic equation in which the cubic term has been removed by a trick similar to that above,

$$y^4 + py^2 + qy + r = 0,$$

the discriminant is obtained by writing down the condition for coincident roots, which is a matter of eliminating y between the equation and its derivative $4y^3 + 2py + q = 0$. This is not easy! The discriminant is a polynomial in p, q and r which in (p, q, r)-space represents a surface known as the *swallowtail* surface. A little will be said about that surface in Section 4.14 of Chapter 3.

There is a wonderful numerical method for finding the number of solutions of a polynomial equation, not just on the whole real line but between any two given numbers. This is called Sturm's Theorem, and you can read about it in books on the theory of equations, for example Turnbull (1952), p. 103 or Uspensky (1948), p. 138. Sturm's Theorem, which dates from 1829, is a considerable amount of trouble to program. See Section 7.2 below.

§5
Some quartic equations to solve

5.1 *A simple quartic*

Let $f(x) = x(x - 1)(x - 2)(x - 3)$; use Newton–Raphson to solve $f(x) = 0$, i.e. $x^4 - 6x^3 + 11x^2 - 6x = 0$, verifying that the iterates x_k do always approach 0, 1, 2 or 3. For $x_0 < 0$ they should approach 0 and for $x_0 > 3$ they should approach 3, but in between it's anybody's guess. Try $x_0 = 1.6$, then $x_0 = 1.7$. Try also $x^4 = 0$ with $x_0 = 1$ (or, come to that, $x^{10} = 0$ with $x_0 = 1$). What do you notice about the rate

Fig. 17

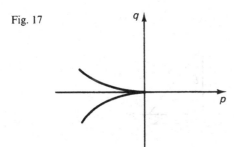

of approach of the x_k to the solution $x = 0$? Explain your observation by calculating the x_k explicitly in this case.

5.2 *A harder ladder problem*

In Exercise 1.9 a ladder was touching a square box; here we make it rectangular with sides a and b, as in Fig. 18. Using the notation in the figure, we have

$$x^2 + y^2 = l^2 \tag{1}$$

and $(y - b)/a = b/(x - a)$, which gives $(x - a)(y - b) = ab$, or

$$xy = bx + ay. \tag{2}$$

Eliminating y between Equations (1) and (2) gives

$$x^4 - 2ax^3 + (a^2 + b^2 - l^2)x^2 + 2al^2 x - a^2 l^2 = 0. \tag{3}$$

Take $l = 10$ and $a = 2$. Verify experimentally that $b = 5$ allows a physically possible solution for x, but $b = 6$ does not.

Take $a = 2$, $b = 5$ and verify that no physically possible solutions appear when $l = 9$. Find the solutions when $l = 20$.

Take $a = 2$, $b = 5$, $l = 9.582299$. In this case there are two very nearly equal (and physically possible) solutions. Note the slowness with which the Newton–Raphson method converges – in fact the x_k appear to jiggle about very slightly after even quite a few steps (i.e. for large k). Decreasing l a tiny bit makes the solutions disappear.

To find the condition on l, a and b for real solutions which are physically possible, we need to do a little mathematics! The two curves (1) and (2) in the (x, y)-plane are a circle and rectangular

Fig. 18

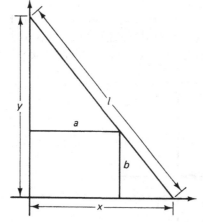

hyperbola respectively, and look like Fig. 19. Thus there are always two real but irrelevant values of x, given by the x-coordinates of the points A and B in the figure, and there *may* be two real and relevant ones (C and D) which are the intersection points of the curves to the right of $x = a$. (Incidentally, when $a = b$, the quartic Equation (3) reduces to two quadratics; compare Exercise 1.9. If you consider $(x^2 - ax + a^2)^2$ you may be able to reduce Equation (3) to a product of two quadratics directly, when $a = b$.)

The condition for the points C and D in Fig. 19 to exist turns out to be

$$a^{2/3} + b^{2/3} \leq l^{2/3} \tag{4}$$

(when $a = b$ this becomes $8a^2 \leq l^2$; compare Exercise 1.9 again). One way to see that (4) is the condition is to imagine the ladder sliding down the wall, keeping in a vertical plane (a frightening possibility, admittedly). All positions of the ladder touch the 'astroid' curve $X^{2/3} + Y^{2/3} = l^{2/3}$, where X and Y are axes along ground and wall respectively (Fig. 20). The boxes that *just fit* under this curve are the biggest that allow the ladder to be placed in position, and so $a^{2/3} + b^{2/3} = l^{2/3}$ for these boxes, and an l satisfying this is the shortest which allows real solutions for given a and b.

It is also possible to argue from the geometrical idea of Exercise 1.9, where we now want the circle (Equation (1)) to touch the hyperbola (Equation (2)) for a shortest possible l with given a and b. Writing $x = l \cos u$, $y = l \sin u$ it turns out that for touching we have $l \cos^3 u = a$ and $l \sin^3 u = b$.

Fig. 19

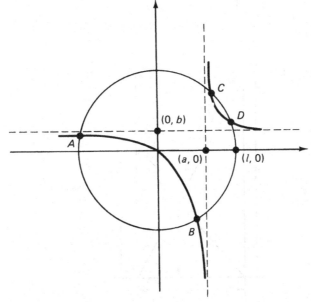

5.3 *Two ladders this time*

Two ladders in an alley way between vertical walls (and on horizontal ground) meet at a height c above the ground. Given the lengths, a and b, of the ladders, the problem is to calculate the width w of the alley. See Fig. 21. It is clearly enough to calculate either of the lengths x or y in the figure.

Fig. 20

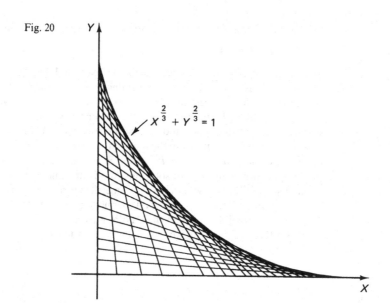

$$X^{\frac{2}{3}} + Y^{\frac{2}{3}} = 1$$

Fig. 21

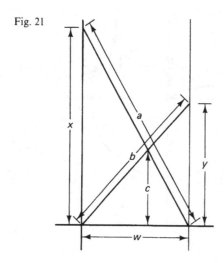

In fact $x^2 + w^2 = a^2$, $y^2 + w^2 = b^2$ gives

$$x^2 - y^2 = a^2 - b^2 \tag{5}$$

(and we shall take $a \geqslant b$). Also, by splitting the width w into two parts and using similar triangles, we find

$$\frac{1}{x} + \frac{1}{y} = \frac{1}{c}$$

which gives

$$xy = c(x + y). \tag{6}$$

Note the similarity with Exercise 1.9, where $x^2 + y^2$ appears instead of $x^2 - y^2$. Each example involves finding the intersection points of two curves of degree two in the (x, y)-plane, but by a fluke (or is it?) the example of Exercise 1.9 reduced to two quadratic equations.

There are various ways of solving Equations (5) and (6). We can eliminate y to give

$$x^4 - 2cx^3 - (a^2 - b^2)x^2 + 2c(a^2 - b^2)x - (a^2 - b^2)c^2 = 0. \tag{7}$$

Alternatively, let $u = x + y$; then $(x - y)^2 = (x + y)^2 - 4xy = u^2 - 4uc$, so that

$$(a^2 - b^2)^2 = (x^2 - y^2)^2 = (x - y)^2(x + y)^2 = (u^2 - 4uc)u^2.$$

Thus

$$u^4 - 4u^3 c - (a^2 - b^2)^2 = 0,$$

and x and y can be found from this and $x - y = (a^2 - b^2)/u$, namely $x = \frac{1}{2}(u + (a^2 - b^2)/u)$, $y = \frac{1}{2}(u - (a^2 - b^2)/u)$.

In this example, the only solutions of interest satisfy $0 \leqslant x \leqslant a$ and $0 \leqslant y \leqslant b$. Note that from Equation (5), $x = a$ just when $y = b$ (what does this mean geometrically?), and, from Equation (6), this happens when $ab = c(a + b)$. So we need

$$0 \leqslant c \leqslant ab/(a + b). \tag{8}$$

Try $a = 10$, $b = 5$, $c = 3$ and various values for x_0 in the iteration to solve Equation (7). You should discover two real roots for Equation (7), approximately 9.689 and -8.947.

What if $a = 10$, $b = 5$, $c = 4$, which violates (8)?

Do you always find two real solutions for Equation (7)? Try sketching the curves of Equations (5) and (6) in the (x, y)-plane to explain in general terms what solutions can be expected. (You can sketch with pencil and paper (that is preferable!) or, using the techniques of Chapter 3, with the micro itself, although that necessarily restricts you to definite choices for *a*, *b* and *c*.)

§6
Complex solutions

We shall now consider the problem of finding *complex* solutions of some equations, so to read this section you will need to know a very little about complex numbers – how to add, subtract, multiply and divide them. The only extra problem that presents itself is that your micro must be told how to perform these operations, since it is no good just writing

$$\text{PRINT}(1 + \text{I}) * (1 - \text{I})$$

and expecting the answer 2. (Mind you, if you are a very sophisticated programmer, then you could educate your micro to understand statements involving i. We shall attempt no such thing here.)

It is, of course, possible to do all the calculations explicitly in real and imaginary parts, calculating sums, products, etc., as formulae and inserting them as required in the programs. It is much more convenient, however, to write *subroutines*, or, even better, *procedures* (if your micro allows them) for multiplication and division. Write $x_1 + iy_1$ and $x_2 + iy_2$ for two complex numbers; then from the data x_1, y_1, x_2 and y_2 we want to calculate the real and imaginary parts of

$$(x_1 + iy_1)(x_2 + iy_2)$$

and

$$(x_1 + iy_1)/(x_2 + iy_2) = (x_1 + iy_1)(x_2 - iy_2)/(x_2^2 + y_2^2).$$

Both subroutines or procedures must accept data x_1, y_1, x_2, y_2 and pass the answers back to the main calculation.

6.1 *Procedures or subroutines for multiplication and division*
1000 PROCMULT (X1, Y1, X2, Y2)

For a subroutine, line 1000 is omitted and GOSUB 1010 is the command needed in the program

```
1010  LET XP = X1 * X2 - Y1 * Y2
1020  LET YP = X1 * Y2 + Y1 * X2
1030  ENDPROC (or RETURN for a subroutine)

2000  PROCDIV (X1, Y1, X2, Y2)
```

For a subroutine, line 2000 is omitted and GOSUB 2010 is the command needed in the program.

```
2010 LET Z = X2 * X2 + Y2 * Y2
2020 LET XQ = (X1 * X2 + Y1 * Y2)/Z
2030 LET YQ = (−X1 * Y2 + Y1 * X2)/Z
2040 ENDPROC (or RETURN for a subroutine)
```

Thus XP, YP are the real and imaginary parts of the product and XQ, YQ the real and imaginary parts of the quotient of the complex numbers.

6.2 *Square roots of complex numbers*

Let $a + ib$ be a given complex number. How are we to calculate $\sqrt{(a + ib)}$? We require a complex number $x + iy$ such that $(x + iy)^2 = a + ib$. We have, on comparing real and imaginary parts,

$$x^2 - y^2 = a \quad \text{and} \quad 2xy = b.$$

Hence

$$(x^2 + y^2)^2 = (x^2 - y^2)^2 + 4x^2 y^2 = a^2 + b^2.$$

It follows that $x^2 - y^2 = a$ and $x^2 + y^2 = \sqrt{(a^2 + b^2)}$, so that $x^2 = \frac{1}{2}(a + \sqrt{(a^2 + b^2)})$, $y^2 = \frac{1}{2}(-a + \sqrt{(a^2 + b^2)})$. Let us take $x = + \sqrt{(\frac{1}{2}(a + \sqrt{(a^2 + b^2)}))} \geq 0$, so that, if $b \neq 0$, the equation $2xy = b$ tells us that $y = b/2x$. (Alternatively, $y = (\text{sign of } b) \sqrt{(\frac{1}{2}(-a + \sqrt{(a^2 + b^2)}))}$.) If $b = 0$ then

for $a \geq 0$ we have $x = \sqrt{a}$, $y = 0$
for $a < 0$ we have $x = 0$, $y = \sqrt{(-a)}$.

6.3 *Exercise*

Write a program which accepts a and b as inputs and calculates the square root of $a + ib$ found above, using the built-in square root function for real numbers to find $\sqrt{(a^2 + b^2)}$, etc. Use the program to find $\sqrt{1}$, $\sqrt{(-4)}$, $\sqrt{(-2i)}$, $\sqrt{(-3 + 4i)}$ and $\sqrt{(408 + 506i)}$. A harder exercise is to use the above to write a program for solving the quadratic equation

$$(a_2 + ib_2)z^2 + (a_1 + ib_1)z + (a_0 + ib_0) = 0,$$

where the as and bs are real, for the unknown $z = x + iy$. Test such a program with $z^2 - (3 + 4i)z + (-1 + 5i) = 0$, which has roots $z = 1 + i$ and $z = 2 + 3i$.

6.4 *Complex square roots by Newton–Raphson iteration*
For *real* numbers, the Newton–Raphson iteration for $f(x) = x^2 - a$,

$$x_{k+1} = x_k - (x_k^2 - a)/2x_k = (x_k^2 + a)/2x_k,$$

starting from $x_0 = 1$, always converges to $\sqrt{a}$, provided $a > 0$ (compare Sections 3.6 and 3.9 above). Here is a program which performs exactly the same iteration for a given complex number $a + ib$, the iterates being say $z_k = x_k + iy_k$. It is written in terms of subroutines for multiplication and division as in Section 6.1; only small changes are needed to use procedures instead.

```
    Program: Squareroot
10  INPUT A,B,XØ,YØ
20  LET X = XØ: LET Y = YØ
30  LET X1 = X: LET Y1 = Y: LET X2 = X: LET Y2 = Y
40  GOSUB 1Ø1Ø
```

The numbers XP and YP (see Section 6.1) are now the real and imaginary parts of $(x + iy)^2$.

```
50  LET X1 = XP + A: LET Y1 = YP + B: LET X2 = 2*XP:
    LET Y2 = 2*YP
60  GOSUB 2Ø1Ø
```

The numbers XQ, YQ are now the real and imaginary parts of $((x + iy)^2 + (a + ib))/2(x + iy)$.

```
70  LET X = XQ: LET Y = YQ
80  PRINT X; " + i("; Y; ")"
```

This prints out the current iterate $x_k + iy_k$, starting at $k = 1$

```
90  GOTO 3Ø
```

As usual, a line 85 halting the program until a key is pressed will greatly facilitate the reading of iterates from the screen.
  Try this out on the square roots in Exercise 6.3, for various starting points $x_0 + iy_0$:
  (a) For $\sqrt{1}$ verify that if $x_0 > 0$ then the iterates $\rightarrow 1 + 0i$ and if $x_0 < 0$ then the iterates $\rightarrow -1 + 0i$.
  (b) For $\sqrt{(-4)}$ verify that if $y_0 > 0$ then the iterates $\rightarrow 2i$ and if $y_0 < 0$ then the iterates $\rightarrow -2i$.
  (c) For $\sqrt{(-2i)}$ verify that if $x_0 > y_0$ then the iterates $\rightarrow 1 - i$ and if $x_0 < y_0$ then the iterates $\rightarrow -1 + i$.

(*d*) For $\sqrt{(-3 + 4i)}$ verify that if $x_0 + 2y_0 > 0$ then the iterates $\rightarrow 1 + 2i$ and if $x_0 + 2y_0 < 0$ then the iterates $\rightarrow -1 - 2i$.

Do you have any conjectures about the general rules governing (*a*)–(*d*)? Try making sketches on an Argand diagram of the complex numbers. What do you observe if $x_0 = 0$ in (*a*), $y_0 = 0$ in (*b*), and so on? See Section 6.10 below for more detail on this.

6.5 *The complex Newton–Raphson iteration*

The idea here is perfectly simple: we use the same formula as before (Equation (2) in §3), but allow *complex* values z_0 for the initial 'guess'. The diagram (Fig. 8) makes little sense now, but the same mathematical *idea* works. For we replace $f(z)$ by the linear function

$$f(z_0) + (z - z_0)f'(z_0)$$

which is, as in the real case, the best linear approximation to f near z_0. Thus we put this expression equal to 0 and solve for z, taking this as an 'approximate' way of solving $f(z) = 0$. We obtain $z = z_0 - f(z_0)/f'(z_0)$, and use this as the next iterate z_1. Thus, as before

$$z_{k+1} = z_k - f(z_k)/f'(z_k)$$

for $k = 0, 1, 2, \ldots$.

The examples below are of polynomial equations $f(z) = 0$ where

$$f(z) = a_0 + a_1 z + a_2 z^2 + \ldots + a_n z^n$$

and the a_j are all *real* numbers. Thus we need only evaluate $f(z_k)$ and $f'(z_k)$ on this understanding; the modifications needed to deal with $a_j = b_j + ic_j$ are not hard to supply.

We assume, then, that $n, a_0, \ldots, a_n$ are known to the computer (as N, AA(1), ..., AA(N + 1); compare Section 3.10), and that $z = x + iy$ where x and y are known real numbers. Then we use the method of Section 3.10 to evaluate $f(x + iy)$, calling the answer $r + is$.

Program: Complex

```
1Ø INPUT N
2Ø DIM AA = N + 1
3Ø FOR J = Ø TO N
4Ø INPUT AA(J + 1)
5Ø NEXT J
6Ø INPUT XØ, YØ
```

```
 70  LET X = XØ: LET Y = YØ
 80  LET R = AA(N + 1)*X: LET S = AA(N + 1)*Y
 90  IF N = 1 THEN GOTO 150
100  FOR J = 1 TO N – 1
110  LET X1 = R + AA(N – J + 1): LET Y1 = S: LET X2 = X:
     LET Y2 = Y
120  GOSUB 1010
130  LET R = XP: LET S = YP
140  NEXT J
150  LET R = R + AA(1)
```

The final value of $r + is$ is then $f(x + iy)$

```
200  LET R1 = Ø: LET S1 = Ø
210  IF N = 1 THEN GOTO 290
220  LET R1 = N*AA(N + 1)*X:
     LET S1 = N*AA(N + 1)*Y
230  IF N = 2 THEN GOTO 290
240  FOR J = 1 TO N – 2
250  LET X1 = R1 + (N + J)*AA(N – J + 1): LET Y1 = S1:
     LET X2 = X: LET Y2 = Y
260  GOSUB 1010
270  LET R1 = XP: LET S1 = YP
280  NEXT J
290  LET R1 = R1 + AA(2)
```

The final value of $r_1 + is_1$ is $f'(x + iy)$

```
300  LET X1 = R: LET Y1 = S: LET X2 = R1: LET Y2 = S1
310  GOSUB 2010
320  LET X = X – XQ: LET Y = Y – YQ
330  PRINT X; "+i("; Y; ")"
340  GOTO 80
```

(see Section 6.1 for subroutines.) As usual, a pause after line 33Ø will facilitate reading the numbers from the screen.

6.6 *Square roots by Newton–Raphson again*

If you have not already done so, in Section 6.4 above, use the complex version of Newton–Raphson to approximate solutions of $z^2 - a = 0$ where, with the program in Section 6.5, a is *real*. For $a > 0$ the iterates should approach $\sqrt{a}$ or $\sqrt{(-a)}$ according as $x_0 > 0$ or $x_0 < 0$; for $a < 0$ they should approach $i\sqrt{(-a)}$ or $-i\sqrt{(-a)}$ according as $y_0 > 0$ or $y_0 < 0$. So in each case there is a *dividing line L* (the y-axis for $a > 0$, the x-axis for $a < 0$) separating those z_0 with z_k tending to one root from those z_0 with z_k tending to the other root of $z^2 - a = 0$. See Fig. 22. What if $a = 0$?

6.7 *Other quadratic equations*

For $f(z) = 0$ where $f(z) = z^2 - 3z + 2$ the dividing line separating points $z_0 = x_0 + iy_0$ giving iterates z_k approaching 1 from those giving iterates approaching 2 is the line $x_0 = \frac{3}{2}$. Verify this for several choices of z_0. What happens if z_0 is *on* the line $x_0 = \frac{3}{2}$?

What happens in the case of the equation $z^2 - 2z + 1 = 0$, where the roots coincide?

Do you have any conjectures on the position of the dividing line L based on the evidence of Sections 6.6 and 6.7? What seems to happen when z_0 is chosen *on* the line L?

6.8 *Some equations of higher degree*

Find the complex roots of the equation in Section 4.6: $4z^3 - 8z^2 + 5z - \frac{1}{2} = 0$. They should come to about $0.9387 \pm 0.3724i$. Also the equation of Exercise 4.3: they come to about $0.04987 \pm 0.331i$. Can you see any connexion between your starting guess z_0 and finishing point (one of the four roots) in these examples?

Find the complex roots of the quartic equation of Section 5.2 when $l = 0$, $a = 2$ and $b = 5$; also when $l = 20$, $a = 2$, $b = 5$.

6.9 *A variant on the two-ladders quartic*

The quartic equation of Section 5.3 provides other examples to solve, of course. Here is a different quartic which comes out of the

Fig. 22

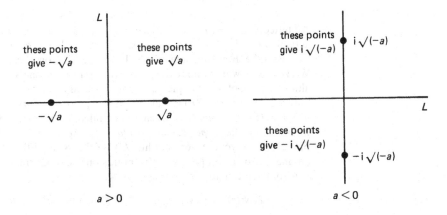

same problem. Write $x = c + ct$, $y = c + c/t$, which is the general solution of Equation (6) in Section 5.3. Then substitution in Equation (5) in Section 5.3 gives

$$(t^2 - 1)(t + 1)^2 = dt^2$$

where $d = (a^2 - b^2)/c^2$. This is

$$t^4 + 2t^3 - dt^2 - 2t - 1 = 0.$$

Now find all the roots of this quartic equation for $a = 10$, $b = 5$, $c = 3$ (thus $d = 25/3$) and compare the solution for $x = c + ct$ with that obtained in Section 5.3. Notice that, if a starting value t_0 for t leads to a certain solution, then the conjugate value $\bar{t}_0$ leads to the conjugate solution. Why is this? Is it a general phenomenon?

6.10 *Complex Newton–Raphson for quadratic equations and beyond*

The following argument shows why, in the examples of Sections 6.6 and 6.7, *there is a line L dividing those z_0 which give iterates z_k converging to one root from those which give iterates converging to the other root, assuming the roots are distinct.*

Consider the quadratic equation $z^2 + az + b = 0$ and let α, β be the roots of the equation (given by the usual formula as in §1). Let N (for Newton) be defined by

$$N(z) = z - \frac{z^2 + az + b}{2z + a} = \frac{z^2 - b}{2z + a}.$$

When $\alpha \neq \beta$, let T (for transformation) be

$$T(z) = \frac{z - \alpha}{z - \beta}.$$

We leave it to you to verify the remarkable fact that, for all z,

$$T(N(z)) = (T(z))^2. \tag{1}$$

Admittedly $z = -\frac{1}{2}a$, $z = \beta$ make one or other denominator zero, but actually Equation (1) still makes sense for these values provided z is assumed to live on the 'Riemann sphere' which includes the complex number $z = \infty$. We shall not worry about this point (in more than one sense!) here. See almost any book on complex analysis, for example Ahlfors (1953), p. 21. Suffice it to say that $T(\alpha) = 0$ and $T(\beta) = \infty$; also $N(-\frac{1}{2}a) = \infty$.

Now $|T(z)| = 1$ precisely when z is equidistant from α and from β, i.e. when z is on the *perpendicular bisector L of the line joining the roots*. See Fig. 23. (Keep your eye on that line L!) It follows that $|T(z)| > 1$ for points on one side of L and $|T(z)| < 1$ for points on the other side.

Also, from Equation (1), we get

$$T(N^2(z)) = T(N(N(z))) = (T(N(z)))^2 = (T(z))^4$$

and, more generally,

$$T(N^k(z)) = (T(z))^{2^k} \tag{2}$$

where $N_k(z) = N(N(\ldots(z)\ldots))$, the kth iterate of N operating on z. Thus $N^k(z)$ is the kth iterate under the Newton–Raphson iteration, starting with z as the first guess at a solution.

Now if $|T(z)| < 1$ then powers of $T(z)$ approach 0 as the powers get higher (since $|T(z)|^m \to 0$ as $m \to \infty$), while, if $|T(z)| > 1$, powers of $T(z)$ go off to infinity as the powers get higher. It follows from Equation (2) that, when $|T(z)| < 1$ (i.e. z is on one side of L), $N^k(z)$ approaches a point which T takes to 0. Hence:

$$N^k(z) \to \alpha \quad \text{as } k \to \infty \text{ if } |T(z)| < 1.$$

Similarly

$$N^k(z) \to \beta \quad \text{as } k \to \infty \text{ if } |T(z)| > 1.$$

This is the required result.

Note that, if $|T(z)| = 1$ then $|T(N^k(z))| = 1$ for all k so $N^k(z)$ remains on the line L if z is on L. The dividing line is precisely L. When the roots are *real*, L is vertical (parallel to the imaginary axis) and when the roots are *conjugate complex numbers*, L is the x-axis. The above argument does *not* assume (as we did in Section 6.5) that the coefficients a and b are real numbers.

The dividing line L is, by the above argument, *the perpendicular bisector of the line joining the roots of the quadratic equation*, in the plane of complex numbers z. Put another way, L is the line through $-\frac{1}{2}a$ and $-\frac{1}{2}a + \frac{1}{2}i\sqrt{(a^2 - 4b)}$. If $a^2 = 4b$ then the roots of the quadratic equation coincide so there is no line L. In fact in this case *every starting value z gives iterates which approach the single root of the quadratic equation*. (You can prove this by redefining

Fig. 23

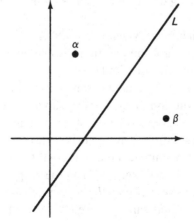

$T(z) = z - \alpha$, and using the resulting identity $T(N(z)) = \frac{1}{2}T(z)$, which replaces Equation (1).)

A little experimentation with cubic equations such as those in §4 will convince you that, if there is a rule for deciding which starting points yield which roots, it is more obscure than is the case for quadratic equations. That is actually putting it very mildly.

The argument for quadratic equations depended on 'reducing' the Newton map N to the map $z \mapsto z^2$ via the transformation T (that is exactly the content of Equation (1)). If we consider instead the simple cubic equation $z^3 - 1 = 0$ (whose solutions are $z = 1$, $e^{2\pi i/3}$, $e^{-2\pi i/3}$), then the corresponding Newton map is

$$N(z) = z - \frac{z^3 - 1}{3z^2} = \frac{2z^3 + 1}{3z^2}.$$

This *rational map* does not 'reduce' to anything simple, and the region consisting of those z which, under repeated application of N, approach a chosen one of the three solutions of $z^3 - 1 = 0$, is exceedingly complicated. The *three* regions, corresponding to solutions $z = 1$, $z = e^{2\pi i/3}$ and $z = e^{-2\pi i/3}$, have *the same boundary*, which is called the *Julia set* of N. (It is almost impossible, isn't it, to imagine three regions in the plane which share exactly the same boundary?) For z *on* the Julia set, repeated application of N does not produce points approaching *any* of the three solutions, so the Julia set corresponds to the line L in the case of quadratic equations. But far from being a nice straight line, the Julia set of the above N is infinitely complicated, that is to say the complication is not in any way diminished by magnifying the set to look at it more closely. You can read about this extraordinary phenomenon in e.g. Peitgen, Saupe and v. Haeseler (1984) and Devlin (1988), Chapter 4. The subject of rational maps and their Julia sets is one where much work is currently being done, and much remains to be discovered.

§7 Projects

7.1 *A variant of Newton–Raphson*

In the Newton–Raphson iteration a single sequence $x_1, x_2, x_3, \ldots$ of iterates is produced, with limit (usually) an x with $f(x) = 0$. When the second derivative f'' has the same sign throughout an interval containing a solution to $f(x) = 0$ (say, an interval on which f changes sign), there is a simple method of producing *two* sequences which approach the solution from opposite sides.

Suppose for definiteness that $f''(x) > 0$ for all x in $[a, b]$ and that $f(a) < 0$, $f(b) > 0$ – see Fig. 24. Then the graph of f lies below any of its chords and there is *exactly one* value of x in $[a, b]$ for which $f(x) = 0$. (These facts can be proved by 'elementary analysis' such as one finds in Spivak (1980). The first fact is often stated as 'the graph is concave upwards'.)

Let a_1 be the point where the chord joining $(a, f(a))$ to $(b, f(b))$ meets the x-axis. Since the graph lies below its chords, $f(a_1) < 0$ and a_1 is to the *left* of the solution. Verify that

$$a_1 = a - f(a) \left(\frac{b - a}{f(b) - f(a)} \right). \tag{1}$$

The graph of f will also lie above the tangent at $(b, f(b))$, so the point x_1 where the tangent meets the x-axis is to the *right* of the solution. As in §3,

$$x_1 = b - f(b)/f'(b).$$

Now a sequence $x_1, x_2, x_3, \ldots$ of values of x approaching the solution from the right can be created by the usual Newton–Raphson iteration. A sequence $a_1, a_2, a_3, \ldots$ approaching the solution from the left can be created too. For a_2 replace a by a_1, and a_1 by a_2, in Equation (1); you can also replace b by x_1. The subsequent numbers $a_3, a_4, \ldots$ are obtained in the same way.

What happens if $f'' > 0$ on $[a, b]$ but $f(a) > 0$, $f(b) < 0$? What if $f'' < 0$ on $[a, b]$?

Write a program to implement this method (granted say that you can determine an interval $[a, b]$ on which f'' does not change sign). Apply the method to appropriate examples from this chapter.

7.2 *Sturm's Theorem* (See Turnbull (1952), p. 103, Uspensky (1948), p. 138, or Childs (1983), p. 161.)

This is an ambitious project that will require quite a lot of programming in order to manipulate polynomials.

Let $f = f_0$ be a polynomial (all coefficients and values of the variable will be real here) and let $f' = f_1$ be its derivative. Then successive division produces polynomials $f_2, f_3, \ldots f_k$ as follows:

$$f_0 = f_1 q_1 - f_2 \quad \text{where degree } f_2 < \text{degree } f_1$$
$$f_1 = f_2 q_2 - f_3 \quad \text{where degree } f_3 < \text{degree } f_2,$$

Fig. 24

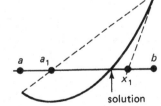

and so on. The q_i are the quotients in the division and the $-f_{i+1}$ are
the remainders. (Compare the Euclidean algorithm in Chapter 1.)

Sturm's Theorem is then as follows: For $j = 1$, 2 let n_j be the
number of *changes of sign* in the sequence

$$f_0(x_j), f_1(x_j), f_2(x_j), \ldots, f_k(x_j).$$

Here $x_1 < x_2$ are chosen real numbers and f_k is the last polynomial f_i
produced by the successive division process which has degree > 0.
(Since the degrees go down, there must be such an f_k.) A change of
sign is said to occur when one term of the sequence is > 0 and, *apart
from zero terms*, the next is < 0, or else the same happens with > 0
and < 0 interchanged. So zero terms are ignored for the purpose of
counting sign changes. Then *the number of distinct roots x of $f(x) = 0$
satisfying $x_1 \leqslant x \leqslant x_2$ is precisely $n_1 - n_2$.*

In order to program Sturm's Theorem you will need to write
subroutine (or procedure) programs which divide one polynomial by
another, when the coefficients of the two polynomials are input to
the computer. It is also necessary to count the number of sign
changes in a known sequence of real numbers.

When applying Sturm's Theorem it is useful to have available a
simple estimate for the approximate location of the zeros of a given
polynomial. The following result (due to the nineteenth Century
French mathematician Cauchy) is easy to apply (and easy to
remember!). We suppose that p is a polynomial of the form

$$p(x) = x^n + a_{n-1}x^{n-1} + \ldots + a_1 x + a_0,$$

so that the coefficient of the highest power of x is 1, and calculate

$$M = 1 + max\{|a_0|, |a_1|, \ldots, |a_{n-1}|\}.$$

Cauchy's Theorem   All of the real zeros of p (if there are any)
must lie in the interval $-M < x < M$.

Proof   First write p in the form

$$p(x) = x^n(1 + r(x)). \tag{*}$$

Now, for $x \neq 0, \pm 1$ we have

$$
\begin{aligned}
|r(x)| &= |a_{n-1}x^{-1} + a_{n-2}x^{-2} + \ldots + a_0 x^{-n}| \\
&\leqslant |a_{n-1}x^{-1}| + |a_{n-2}x^{-2}| + \ldots + |a_0 x^{-n}| \\
&\leqslant max\{|a_0|, |a_1|, \ldots, |a_{n-1}|\}(|x|^{-1} + |x|^{-2} + \ldots + |x|^{-n}) \\
&= \frac{(M-1)(1 - |x|^{-n})}{|x| - 1}
\end{aligned}
$$

using the triangle inequality and the formula for summing a geometric progression. So if $|x| \geq M$ we have $|r(x)| \leq (1 - |x|^{-n})$ < 1, and by (*) above $p(x)$ is non-zero, the required result.

References   L. V. Ahlfors *Complex Analysis*, McGraw-Hill, New York, 1953.

G. Birkhoff and S. MacLane *A Survey of Modern Algebra*, Macmillan, New York, 3rd edn, 1965.

C. B. Boyer *A History of Mathematics*, Wiley, New York, 1968.

L. Childs *A Concrete Introduction to Higher Algebra*, Springer-Verlag, New York, 1983.

R. Courant and H. Robbins *What is Mathematics?*, Oxford University Press, Oxford, 4th Edn, 1947: (Paperback 1978).

K. Devlin *Mathematics: The New Golden Age*, Penguin, London, 1988.

C. Hadlock *Field Theory and its Classical Problems*, Carus Mathematical Monographs, 19, Mathematical Association of America, Washington DC, 1978.

D. Mackie and T. Scott 'Pitfalls in the use of computers for the Newton–Raphson method', *Mathematical Gazette* **69** (1985), 252–7.

H. O. Peitgen, D. Saupe and F. v. Haeseler 'Cayley's problem and Julia sets, *Mathematical Intelligencer*, **6** (1984), 11–20.

D. E. Rutherford *Classical Mechanics*, Oliver and Boyd, Edinburgh, 1964.

M. Spivak *Calculus*, Publish or Perish, Boston, 2nd Edn, 1980.

I. Stewart *Galois Theory*, Chapman and Hall, London, 1973.

H.W. Turnbull *Theory of Equations*, Oliver and Boyd, Edinburgh, 5th Edn, 1952.

J. V. Uspensky *Theory of Equations*, McGraw-Hill, New York, 1948.

D. M. Young and R. T. Gregory *A Survey of Numerical Mathematics* Volume 1, Addison-Wesley, Reading, Mass., 1972.

3

Curves: Part 1

In this chapter and in Chapter 5 we shall present many mathematical applications of computer graphics. In order to draw the line somewhere (pardon the pun) we shall restrict ourselves to the mathematics associated with the plane and in particular with curves in the plane. There is a whole other realm, just as fascinating, connected with objects, such as curves, polyhedra and surfaces, in three-dimensional space. Nevertheless what the computer actually draws is, in these cases too, a curve or system of curves in the plane – that of the screen. The extra complications come from taking a three-dimensional object and associating with it a curve or system of curves – for example its outline when seen from a distance, or a sequence of such outlines or a sequence of plane sections of the object. We touch on this in a discussion of the swallowtail surface in Section 4.14.

The computer can (with our help) draw curves and collections of curves which are just too complicated to attempt by hand. For some purposes a rough sketch of a curve does very well – you will probably have drawn many such sketches by hand, and we are certain that the art of curve-sketching by hand is still an art well worth acquiring. However, for some other purposes, such as the illustration or discovery of facts connected with the differential geometry of curves and families of curves (not to mention surfaces), accurate drawings are essential. They can also be extremely useful, for example, in judging the number of solutions of an equation $f(x) = 0$, and their approximate positions, from the graph of f.

In order to draw curves or anything else on the screen you must, of course, be able to use the graphical facilities of your micro. We have done our best to make it easy for you, once you have a little familiarity with those features, to proceed quickly to interesting and challenging mathematics.

In §1 we give an introduction to the drawing of curves on the screen, and in §2 and §4 we apply this to the drawing of graphs $y = f(x)$ and parametrised curves, where x and y are each a function of the parameter t. The graph of a function f provides a good first approximation to the solutions of $f(x) = 0$ and we refer back to several of the equations encountered in Chapter 2. In §3 we consider polynomial approximations to functions – the Taylor series approximations – and use the graph-drawing facility to compare the actual function with its various approximating polynomials. This kind of comparison is very striking and scarcely possible without a fast and accurate graph plotter. Parametrised curves can often be defined dynamically (think of the parameter t as time and the curve defined by a *moving* point), and we give several such curves in §4 – Lissajous figures, spirographs and rose curves for example. We also consider briefly curves which arise as the intersections of a surface with a plane.

In §5 we continue to investigate parametrised curves, but now consider *parallels*, which arise in the same way that waves emanate from a disturbance on the surface of a pond and for that reason are also called wavefronts. §6 is devoted to evolutes, which are intimately connected with parallels: the evolute of a curve is swept out by the 'singularities' of its associated parallel curves.

There is another way to define curves, namely 'implicitly' by an equation $f(x, y) = 0$. We postpone consideration of this until Chapter 5.

Finally, we mention that there are many applications of computer graphics to mathematics, different from those presented here, in the book by Abelson and diSessa (1980).

§1

An introduction to curve drawing on the micro

In all the sections of this chapter we shall be concerned with drawing curves on the screen – sometimes singly, sometimes several one after the other, sometimes several simultaneously (or nearly so) – and we begin by some general remarks on the joys and sorrows of curve drawing. As always in this book we regard the mathematical problems being tackled as of first importance, and the computational difficulties which they inevitably raise as interesting, but secondary to the mathematics. Nevertheless there are a few computational pitfalls which certainly have to be avoided if chaos (of a rather uninteresting kind) is not to result.

Whenever a curve is to be drawn, there will be points found on the curve, one after another. There are then two ways to exhibit the curve on the screen:

(i) by putting a dot at the position on the screen corresponding to each calculated point – this we call *dots-only*;

(ii) by joining consecutive dots with straight segments – this we call *join-the-dots*.

(Large computers often have more sophisticated ways of doing (ii) by joining up in a 'smooth' way.)

Now dots-only is much easier to implement than join-the-dots, especially for curves which go out of sight off the screen and return. For the applications in this chapter, dots-only is perfectly adequate, and we shall assume the reader is using this method. In the appendix there is a discussion of the extra precautions and tricks needed for join-the-dots.

1.1 *Coordinates*

We shall draw curves which have their mathematical existence in the (x, y)-plane, and the part of the plane represented on the computer screen will be a rectangle which we refer to as the *plotting rectangle*. Let this consist of points (x, y) with

$$x_\ell \leqslant x \leqslant x_u \quad \text{and} \quad y_\ell \leqslant y \leqslant y_u.$$

Thus ℓ = 'lower' and u = 'upper'; x_ℓ for example can be conveniently written XL in programs. See Fig. 1, left.

Micros work with screen coordinates, (u, v) say, with an origin either at bottom left as in (a) of Fig. 1, or at top left, as in (b), where the second coordinate v increases downwards in this case.

Thus a transformation is necessary from (x, y)-coordinates of points in the mathematical plane, which contains the plotting rectangle, to (u, v)-coordinates on the screen. The maximum values u_{max} and v_{max} of u and v will be in the users' handbook for the particular micro you are using. In all cases u and v have smallest value 0. Thus, in case (a) we want $x = x_\ell$ to correspond to $u = 0$, $y = y_\ell$ to $v = 0$, $x = x_u$ to $u = u_{max}$ and $y = y_u$ to $v = v_{max}$. In case (b), $y = y_\ell$ corresponds to $v = v_{max}$ and $y = y_u$ to $v = 0$. The resulting transformations we call the *arbitrary scales equations* since they do not assume that the *shape* of the plotting rectangle is the same as that of the screen. They are

$$u = x_s(x - x_\ell), \quad v = y_s(y - y_\ell) \tag{1a}$$

Fig. 1

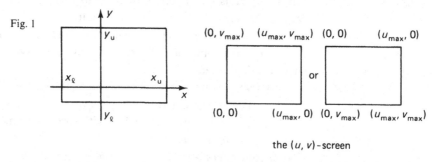

plotting rectangle   (*a*) origin at   (*b*) origin at
in (x, y)-plane   bottom left   top left

or

$$u = x_s(x - x_\ell), \quad v = y_s(y_u - y) \tag{1b}$$

where $x_s = u_{max}/(x_u - x_\ell)$ and $y_s = v_{max}/(y_u - y_\ell)$. The constants x_s and y_s we shall call scaling factors.

Some micros have a WINDOW command, or an equivalent command, which does the conversion from mathematical co-ordinates (x, y) to screen coordinates (u, v) automatically. Typically you type

WINDOW (XL, YL) – (XU, YU).

Then the rectangle $x_\ell \leqslant x \leqslant x_u, y_\ell \leqslant y \leqslant y_u$ is displayed on the screen, and the command to plot a point (x, y) results automatically in the corresponding point (u, v), as in Equations (1a) or (1b), appearing on the screen. This is a great convenience, but you must still be prepared to adjust the ratio of $x_u - x_\ell$ to $y_u - y_\ell$ to the aspect ratio of the screen (see below) if you want equal scales.

If we want *shapes* to be accurately represented on the screen – if, for example, we want squares to look square and circles circular – then we are not free to choose the sides of the plotting rectangle independently. In fact their ratio, namely $(x_u - x_\ell)/(y_u - y_\ell)$, must equal the *aspect ratio* of the screen, that is the ratio of sides of that part of the screen on which graphics are drawn. As a rule with micros the whole screen is used for graphics, so the aspect ratio is about $\frac{4}{3}$:

$$(x_u - x_\ell)/(y_u - y_\ell) = \text{aspect ratio} \doteq \tfrac{4}{3}.$$

This value will give perfectly acceptable pictures, but you can adjust it slightly if you need to: see Section 1.2 below. We shall use $\frac{4}{3}$ in what follows. (Note that this is not necessarily the same as u_{max}/v_{max}. See Section 1.3 below.)

Rather than choosing three of x_ℓ, x_u, y_ℓ, y_u and then calculating the fourth from the aspect ratio, we shall choose x_ℓ, x_u and the *central value* of y, i.e. the value it takes along the horizontal centre line of the screen, namely $y_c = \frac{1}{2}(y_\ell + y_u)$.

Assume, then, that x_ℓ, x_u and y_c are input to the program and u_{max}, v_{max} are known (from the users' handbook). The *equal scales* equations, for preserving shape, are as follows:

$$u = x_s(x - x_\ell) \quad v = y_s(y - y_\ell) \tag{2a}$$

if the origin is at bottom left of the screen; or

$$u = x_s(x - x_\ell) \quad v = y_s(y_u - y) \tag{2b}$$

if the origin is at top left of the screen, where

$$y_\ell = y_c - \tfrac{3}{8}(x_u - x_\ell), \quad y_u = y_c + \tfrac{3}{8}(x_u - x_\ell)$$

and, as before,

$$x_s = u_{max}/(x_u - x_\ell), \quad y_s = v_{max}/(y_u - y_\ell).$$

(These formulae for y_ℓ and y_u follow from the aspect ratio equation and $2y_c = y_\ell + y_u$.)

1.2 *Remark on the aspect ratio*

It is possible that the factor $\tfrac{3}{8}$ in the above equations does not make squares look *exactly* square. You can determine this for yourself by a test program along the following lines:

```
10  LET XL = − Ø.5: LET XU = 1.5: LET YC = Ø.5
20  LET YL = YC − 3*(XU − XL)/8:
    LET YU = YC + 3*(XU − XL)/8
30  LET XS = UMAX/(XU − XL):
    LET YS = VMAX/(YU − YL)
40  LET UØ = − XS*XL: LET U1 = XS*(1 − XL)
```
(a) `50  LET VØ = − YS*YL: LET V1 = YS*(1 − YL)`
(b) `50  LET VØ = YS*YU: V1 = LET YS*(YU − 1)`

Thus $u = u_0$ corresponds to $x = 0$, $u = u_1$ to $x = 1$, $v = v_0$ to $y = 0$ and $v = v_1$ to $y = 1$.

```
60   Move the cursor to (u₀, v₀)
70   Draw a line to (u₁, v₀)
80   Draw a line to (u₁, v₁)
90   Draw a line to (u₀, v₁)
100  Draw a line to (u₀, v₀)
```

This draws the four sides of the square whose corners in the plotting rectangle in the (x, y)-plane are $(0, 0)$, $(1, 0)$, $(1, 1)$, $(0, 1)$. See Fig. 2. Now *measure* the image on the screen with a ruler. Are the sides equal? If they are nearly so, that is good enough, but otherwise you can try adjusting the ratio $\tfrac{3}{8}$ in line $2Ø$ a little bit. Or perhaps, even better, you can measure and then *calculate* the correct factor!

Fig. 2

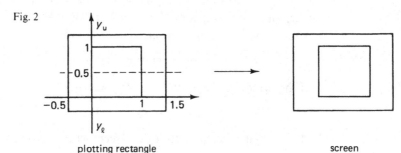

plotting rectangle   screen

In the graphics programs below we shall adopt the format of the above program, putting lines such as 6∅–1∅∅ in lower case, to remind you that they must be translated into the simple commands appropriate to your micro.

We shall also assume, unless otherwise stated, that the equal scales equations, Equations (2a) or (2b), are being used. It is indeed useful or necessary on occasion to use unequal scales, for example to get all of a graph on the screen, and then we use Equations (1a) or (1b) with all of x_ℓ, x_u, y_ℓ, y_u input at the beginning of the program. See especially §2 below.

1.3 *Screen equations*

Here we consider briefly the *equations* of some curves expressed in the (u, v) coordinates on the screen. There is a snag: very likely the scales along the u and v axes on the screen are *unequal*, i.e. the horizontal distance from $u = 0$ to $u = 1$ (say) may not equal the vertical distance from $v = 0$ to $v = 1$. (See Fig. 3, where we place $(0, 0)$ at bottom left.) Another way of putting this is that for most microcomputers

$$u_{max}/v_{max} \neq \text{aspect ratio (which we take as } \tfrac{4}{3}\text{)}.$$

This implies that, for example, the equation of a curve which *looks* circular on the screen will not usually have the familiar form of the equation of a circle, namely $(u - a)^2 + (v - b)^2 = r^2$, for constants a, b and r. This can be remedied by changing scale on, say, the u-axis. Write

$$\bar{u} = \lambda u, \quad \text{where} \quad \lambda = \tfrac{4}{3} u_{max}/v_{max},$$

taking the aspect ratio to be $\tfrac{4}{3}$. Then $\bar{u}_{max}/v_{max} = \tfrac{4}{3}$ and with $(\bar{u}, v)$-coordinates on the screen, scales are equal. The following exercises will illustrate this point.

Fig. 3

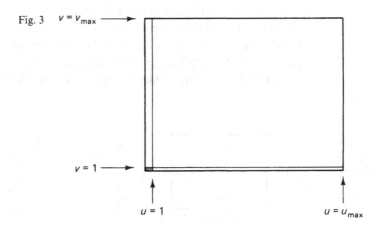

the shaded region on the screen
may not be square

1.4 *Exercise*

Show that, for arbitrary scales (Equations (1a) or (1b)),

$$x = au + b, \quad y = cv + d$$

for constants a, b, c and d, and

$$x = \bar{a}\bar{u} + b$$

where $\bar{a} = a/\lambda$. Show that, for equal scales (Equations (2a) or (2b)), $\bar{a} = c$ (i.e. $a = \lambda c$).

1.5 *Exercise*

Suppose that $px + qy = r$ for constants p, q and r, so that (x, y) lies on a certain straight line. Show, using Exercise 1.4, that u and v are connected by a linear equation, and also $\bar{u}$ and v are so connected. This shows that, for arbitrary (or equal) scales, straight lines in the (x, y)-plane are always represented by straight lines on the screen. (Mind you, they may look a bit jagged on the screen, but the computer is doing its best to make them look straight!)

Suppose instead that $(x - p)^2 + (y - q)^2 = r^2$ for constants p, q and r, so that (x, y) lies on a circle, centre (p, q) and radius r. Show from Exercise 1.4 that, with arbitrary scales, $(\bar{u}, v)$ satisfies an equation of the form

$$\frac{(\bar{u} - P)^2}{(1/\bar{a})^2} + \frac{(v - Q)^2}{(1/c)^2} = r^2$$

where (P, Q) is the point in $(\bar{u}, v)$-coordinates corresponding to $(x, y) = (p, q)$.

For equal scales (i.e. $\bar{a} = c$) this is a *circle* centre (P, Q): circles go to circles, and centres to centres. For arbitrary scales it is an *ellipse*, also with centre (P, Q): circles go to ellipses. Show that the horizontal axis of the ellipse has length $2r/\bar{a}$ and the vertical axis has length $2r/c$. See Fig. 4.

1.6 *Avoiding chaos in dots-only programs*

A computational problem arises when the computer is presented with a very large value for one of the screen coordinates (u, v). This is simply because, of the binary digits used to represent the coordinate, one (the 'largest', or 'most significant digit') is actually used to store the *sign* of the coordinate. Thus a '1' in this position will be read as a

Fig. 4

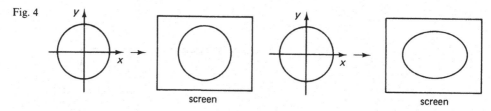

equal scales   arbitrary (unequal) scales

'minus' when, in fact, from the calculation of the coordinate, it means some high power of 2 ($2^{15} = 32768$ for a 16-bit micro).

Try the following program:

```
10 LET XL = - 10: LET XU = 10: LET YC = 0
20 LET YL = YC - 3*(XU - XL)/8:
   LET YU = YC + 3*(XU - XL)/8
30 LET XS = UMAX/(XU - XL):
   LET YS = VMAX/(YU - YL)
```

These are absolutely standard lines, to calculate y_ℓ, y_u, x_s, y_s in the equal scales context. Adjust the factor $\frac{3}{8}$ in line 20 if you need to (see Section 1.2).

```
    40 FOR I = 1 TO 200
    50 LET X = - 10 + I/10
    60 LET Y = X*X*X*X*X
(a) 70 LET U = XS*(X - XL): LET V = YS*(Y - YL)
(b) 70 LET U = XS*(X - XL): LET V = YS*(YU - Y)
```

Again this is a standard line, coming from Equations (2a) or (2b) for equal scales, or (the same line) from Equations (1a) or (1b) for arbitrary scales. We shall usually just say 'convert to screen co-ordinates (u, v)' in later programs.

```
    80 Put a dot at the point with screen coordinates (u, v)
```

The precise directions for this will be in the users' handbook.

```
    90 NEXT I
```

The program plots the graph of $y = x^5$ for $-10 \leqslant x \leqslant 10$, but with a lot of the graph off the screen. In fact, if $|x|^5 > 10$, i.e. $|x| > 10^{1/5} = 1.58$, the calculated point (x, x^5) will certainly be off the screen. Most computers do not mind being given such points: they merely ignore line 80 in the program. But on account of the problem mentioned above there is likely to be a random-looking scattering of dots on the screen away from the obviously correct part of the curve shown in Fig. 5.

The remedy for the dots-only drawing above is very simple and obvious: tell the computer to disregard any calculated points which lie off the screen, by inserting

```
    65 IF Y < YL OR Y > YU THEN GOTO 90
```

There are some circumstances where the appropriate line is

```
    IF X < XL OR X > XU OR Y < YL OR Y > YU THEN
                                            GOTO -
```

Fig. 5

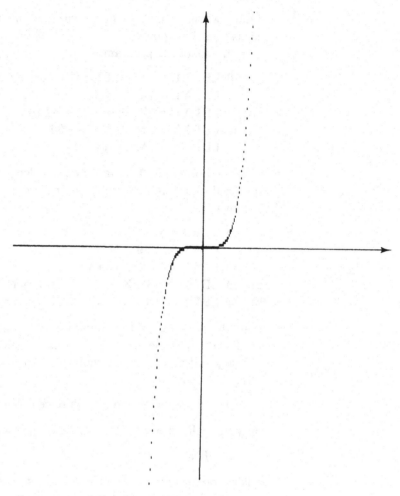

where — stands for the terminating line of a plotting loop. But in the present program x is restricted by line 5Ø to be within the range $x_\ell \leq x \leq x_u$.

With join-the-dots programs a little more subtlety is needed. See the appendix.

1.7 Summary of standard lines in all graphics programs
Arbitrary scales

```
INPUT XL, XU, YL, YU
LET XS = UMAX/(XU – XL):
LET YS = VMAX/(YU – YL)
```

Substitute the values of **UMAX** and **VMAX** for your micro.

When a point (x, y) is to be plotted (using dots-only), first reject it if it lies outside the plotting rectangle (see Section 1.6):

IF X < XL OR X > XU OR Y < YL OR Y > YU THEN GOTO —

where — stands for the terminating line of the plotting loop (or some appropriate later line in the program).

Then convert to screen coordinates by

(*a*) LET U = XS*(X − XL): LET V = YS*(Y − YL) (origin at bottom left)

(*b*) LET U = XS*(X − XL): LET V = YS*(YU − Y) (origin at top left).

Equal scales
INPUT XL, XU, YC
LET YL = YC − 3*(XU − XL)/8:
LET YU = YC + 3*(XU − XL)/8

(see Section 1.2 for remarks on $\frac{3}{8}$).

LET XS = UMAX/(XU − XL): LET YS = VMAX/(YU − YL)

Substitute the values of UMAX and VMAX for your micro.

When a point (*x*, *y*) is to be plotted (using dots-only), reject it if it lies outside the plotting rectangle (see Section 1.6):

IF X < XL OR X > XU OR Y < YL OR Y > YU THEN GOTO —

where — stands for the terminating line of the plotting loop (or some appropriate later line in the program).

Then convert to screen coordinates by

(*a*) LET U = XS*(X − XL): LET V = YS*(Y − YL) (origin at bottom left)

(*b*) LET U = XS*(X − XL): LET V = YS*(YU − Y) (origin at top left).

For both equal and arbitrary scales with join-the-dots, see the appendix. Note that in Chapter 8 an abbreviated form is adopted in the graphics programs. See Program 3.1 in Chapter 8.

§2
Graphs of functions
Suppose that the function $y = f(x)$ is to be plotted over a range of values $x_\ell \leqslant x \leqslant x_u$. Choose a number *n*, where $n = 100$ or $n = 200$ is usually enough, and plot the point $(x, f(x))$ for *n* equally spaced values of *x* between x_ℓ and x_u, namely $x = x_\ell + i(x_u - x_\ell)/n$, where $i = 1, 2, 3, \ldots, n$. (This list of values of *x* starts just to the right of x_ℓ; this does not matter.) Occasionally it is necessary to omit some values of *x* (where *f* is undefined, perhaps); see e.g. Exercise 2.11 below. The general program required, which will need occasional modification, is as follows.

2.1 *Program: Graph*

```
      10 INPUT N, XL, XU, YC (equal scales)
or    10 INPUT N, XL, XU, YL, YU (arbitrary scales)
      20 Equal scales only: calculate YL, YU as in Section 1.7
      30 Calculate scaling factors XS, YS as in Section 1.7
      40 FOR I = 1 TO N
      50 LET X = XL + I*(XU − XL)/N
      60 Calculate y = f(x) for the chosen function f
      70 IF Y < YL OR Y > YU THEN GOTO 100
      80 Convert to screen coordinates (u, v) as in Section 1.7
      90 Put a dot at screen point (u, v)
      100 NEXT I
```

Note that in line 70 there is no need to include $X < XL$ OR $X > XU$ (see Section 1.7) as this can never happen from line 50.

Sometimes it is useful to put one or both axes in the picture. To put the *x*-axis in we do as follows, assuming that the *x*-axis does meet the plotting rectangle, i.e. that $y_\ell \leqslant 0 \leqslant y_u$:

```
      110 LET X = XL: LET Y = 0
      120 Convert to screen coordinates (u, v) as in Section 1.7
      130 Move the cursor to screen point (u, v)
      140 LET X = XU: LET Y = 0
      150 Convert to screen coordinates (u, v) as in Section 1.7
      160 Draw a line to screen point (u, v)
```

The *y*-axis is drawn similarly, by joining the screen points corresponding with $(0, y_\ell)$ and $(0, y_u)$, assuming that the *y*-axis does meet the plotting rectangle, i.e. $x_\ell \leqslant 0 \leqslant x_u$.

An alternative to line 50 is to declare a starting value and an increment for *x*:

```
      35 LET X = XL: LET DX = (XU − XL)/N
```

and to replace line 50 by

```
      50 LET X = X + DX
```

2.2 *Exercise: Powers of x*

Take $f(x) = x^k$ for $k = 2, 3, 4, 5$ in succession, with $x_\ell = -1$, $x_u = 1$, $y_c = 0$ (and equal scales). Here, $n = 100$ should be sufficient. Notice how *flat* the curve is near $x = 0$ for $k = 4$ or 5. Of course, $k = 2$ gives a *parabola*.

2.3 *Exercise: Cubic polynomials*

Let

$$y = f(x) = x^3 + ax^2 + bx + c.$$

Show that, replacing x by $x + \alpha$, y by $y + \beta$ and choosing α and β suitably, the equation reduces to the form

$$y = x^3 + px. \tag{1}$$

(Compare Section 4.11 of Chapter 2.) This says that by translation of the graph (α to the left and β down), the original cubic simplifies to Equation (1).

Study the shape of the graph of Equation (1) for various values of p between -1 and 1. (Take $x_\ell = -1.5$, $x_u = 1.5$, $y_c = 0$ and equal scales.) How does the shape change?

2.4 *Exercise: The goat problem*

Plot the graph of the function in Exercise 2.5 of Chapter 2,

$$f(x) = (x^2 - 2)(\text{arc } \cos(\tfrac{1}{2}x)) - x \sqrt{(1 - x^2/4)} + \tfrac{1}{2}\pi,$$

taking $x_\ell = -1.99$, $x_u = 1.99$ (to avoid any possible trouble near $x = \pm 2$), $y_\ell = -2$, $y_u = 8$ (so the scales are unequal and the arbitrary scales equations are used), and drawing also the axes. (If your micro does not know about arc cos then use

$$\text{arc } \cos t = \begin{cases} z & \text{if} \quad 0 < t \leqslant 1, \\ z + \pi & \text{if} \quad -1 \leqslant t < 0, \end{cases}$$

where

$$z = \text{arc } \tan \left(\frac{\sqrt{(1 - t^2)}}{t} \right).$$

Note $t = 0$ must be avoided.)

Confirm that the graph crosses the x-axis twice only, once for $x < 0$ and once for $x > 0$. (Fig. 6.)

From the graph, pick out the range of values of c for which $f(x) = c$ has (a) two solutions, (b) one solution. Compare with the original goat problem (Chapter 2, Exercise 2.5).

2.5 *Exercise*

Let $f(x) = \text{arc } \tan x - 2x/(1 + x^2)$ (compare Exercises 2.9 and 3.2 of Chapter 2), with $x_\ell = -3$, $x_u = 3$, $y_\ell = -1$, $y_u = 1$. Confirm that there are three solutions only to $f(x) = 0$ by drawing the axes.

Fig. 6

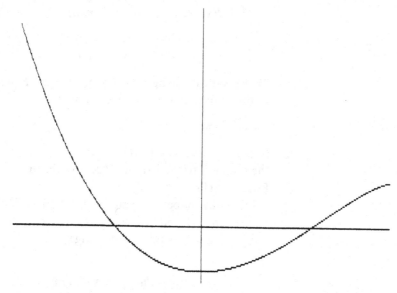

2.6 *Exercise: More cubics*

Let $f(x) = x^3 - 2x + 2$ (compare Exercise 4.2 of Chapter 2), with $x_\ell = -2$, $x_u = 2$, $y_\ell = -3$, $y_u = 6$. How many real roots does the cubic have? Try other cubics from §4 of Chapter 2, finding suitable ranges of values of x and y by trial. Compare Section 4.11 of Chapter 2.

2.7 *Exercise: Two quartics*

Let

$$f(x) = x^4 - 4x^3 - 71x^2 + 400x - 400$$

(Section 5.2 of Chapter 2, with $a = 2$, $b = 5$, $l = 10$), and $x_\ell = -12$, $x_u = 12$, $y_\ell = -1000$, $y_u = 1000$ (arbitrary scales again!), $n = 500$. How many (real) roots are there?

For

$$f(x) = x^4 - 6x^3 - 75x^2 + 450x - 675$$

(i.e. $a = 10$, $b = 5$, $c = 3$ in Section 5.3 of Chapter 2), try initially $x_\ell = -10$, $x_u = 10$, $y_\ell = -10$, $y_u = 10$, $n = 100$. Is anything at all drawn of the curve? Are you surprised, bearing in mind that $f(x) = 0$ has solutions around 9.7 and -8.9? Now try $x_\ell = -10$, $x_u = 10$, $y_\ell = -1000$, $y_u = 1000$, $n = 100$ (or $n = 500$ even). From the picture, explain the previous failure. (If you are using a join-the-dots plotting program then you may not have failed so badly the first time!) Note how essential it is to use *unequal* scales in a problem like this.

2.8 *Exercise: Kepler's equation*

Let

$$f(x) = x - (180/\pi)e \sin(\pi x/180) - 360p$$

(compare Exercise 2.10 of Chapter 2, especially equation (2)), for $p = 0.25$, $e = 0.017$, and confirm that $f(x) = 0$ has only one solution (take $x_\ell = -180$, $x_u = 180$, $y_\ell = -300$, $y_u = 300$). Does the graph resemble a straight line? Why? Try some other values of e (or indeed p); see Exercise 2.10 of Chapter 2.

2.9 *Exercise: General quartics*

Show that replacing x by $x + \alpha$, y by $y + \beta$ and choosing α and β suitably turns the quartic polynomial

$$y = x^4 + ax^3 + bx^2 + cx + d$$

into the form

$$y = x^4 + px^2 + qx. \tag{2}$$

Investigate the shape of the graph of Equation (2) for various values of p and q (say, with $-2 \le p \le 2$, $-2 \le q \le 2$), paying particular attention to the number of turning points (where $dy/dx = 0$) on the graph and whether there are two turning points at the same *level*, i.e. giving the same value of y. For $p = -1$, verify that, as q increases from 0 to 1, a change of shape takes place where two turning points coalesce (Fig. 7) at around $q = 0.54$, giving a *horizontal inflexion* on the graph. You can check this result by calculus.

Given that the condition for two turning points to coalesce at x is that $y' = dy/dx$ and $y'' = d^2y/dx^2$ both equal zero at x, show that the graph of Equation (2) has two coalescing turning points at x just when $p = -6x^2$ and $q = 8x^3$. Eliminate x between these equations to show that this phenomenon occurs for *some* x precisely when $8p^3 + 27q^2 = 0$. (Thus $p = -1$ as above requires $q = \pm\sqrt{(8/27)} = \pm 0.54433\ldots$) In the plane with coordinates (p, q) what does the curve $8p^3 + 27q^2 = 0$ look like? (Compare Fig. 17 in Chapter 2.)

On a piece of paper representing the (p, q)-plane sketch the curve and, at various positions (p, q) on the paper for which you have drawn the graph of Equation (2) with those values of p and q, draw in a little sketch of the shape of the graph of Equation (2).

Verify, and check by calculus, that the condition for two turning points at the same level (i.e. $y'(x_1) = y'(x_2) = 0$, $y(x_1) = y(x_2)$ for some x_1 and x_2 with $x_1 \ne x_2$) is $q = 0$, $p < 0$.

Fig. 7

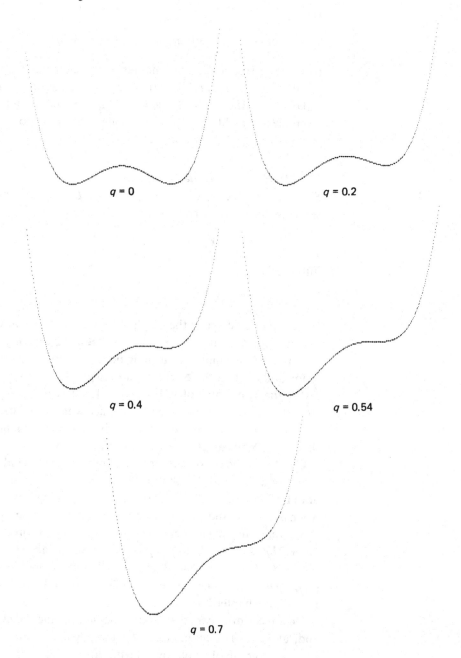

$q = 0$

$q = 0.2$

$q = 0.4$

$q = 0.54$

$q = 0.7$

2.10 *Exercise: Exponential functions*

Plot the graph of $f(x) = e^x$, taking say $x_\ell = -1$, $x_u = 10$, $y_\ell = 0$, $y_u = 25\,000$ (arbitrary scales equations again). Note the steep rise in the curve! (In BASIC, Y = EXP(X).)

Plot the graph of $f(x) = x^{10}/e^x$ for $x_\ell = 0$, $x_u = 30$, $y_\ell = 0$, $y_u = 500\,000$. Note again how the curve rises slowly, then steeply (as x^{10} gets big), then falls again as e^x swamps even the very large function x^{10}. Show by calculus that the maximum value occurs at $x = 10$, and is about 454 000. Note that the function $f(x)$ becomes *very* small on the above scale by about $x = 30$. How small? How about $x = 50$?

For $f(x) = x^k/e^x$ show by calculus that the maximum is reached at $x = k$.

2.11 *Exercise: Functions with restricted domains*

For $f(x) = 1/x$ we must naturally avoid $x = 0$. Either add a line 55 in Program 2.1,

> 55 IF X = $\emptyset$ THEN GOTO 1$\emptyset\emptyset$

or else cunningly choose x_ℓ, x_u and n so that $x = 0$ is avoided, say $x_\ell = -1$, $x_u = 1$, $n = 101$. Try also

$$f(x) = 1/(x(x-1)), f(x) = x/(x-1), f(x) = 1/(x(x^2-1)).$$

(If you use join-the-dots then beware of 'asymptotes'. See Appendix A2.)

The graph $y = \sin(1/x)$ goes berserk at $x = 0$ since it crosses the x-axis at $x = 1/n\pi$ for every integer n (compare Exercise 2.6 in Chapter 2). Get some idea of the shape of the graph for say $0.05 \le x \le 1$.

For $f(x) = \sqrt{(1-x^2)}$ the largest possible range of values of x is $-1 \le x \le 1$. Try $x_\ell = -1$ (or -0.999?), $x_u = 1$ (or 0.999?), $y_c = 0.5$ and equal scales. Try fairly small values of n such as $n = 50$, and note that the points on the semi-circular graph, drawn with dots-only so you can see the individual points, are not at all equally spaced. See §4 below for a different approach to drawing this graph.

§3
Taylor polynomials

Functions can often be usefully approximated by polynomials, and on the micro screen we can visually demonstrate how good (or bad) the approximation is. Take for example $f(x) = \sin x$. Then

$$x - \frac{1}{3!} x^3 + \frac{1}{5!} x^5 - \frac{1}{7!} x^7 + \ldots,$$

stopped after say k terms, is a polynomial of degree $2k - 1$ which approximates $\sin x$ very well provided x is not too large. It is the *Taylor polynomial* of $\sin x$, and comes from the Taylor series of $\sin x$, truncated to degree $2k - 1$. (Strictly, the Taylor series based at 0, or the Maclaurin series, of $\sin x$. See below and almost any book on calculus, for example Spivak (1980), Chapter 19.)

It is not difficult to write a program which, for a selected k, will plot the graph of the Taylor polynomial with k terms. It is very instructive to go on to plot (perhaps in a different colour) the graph of the original function $\sin x$, for comparison. Here is a suggestion, where we assume $k \geqslant 2$.

3.1 *Program: Taylorsine*
```
10 INPUT XL, XU, N, K
20 LET YL = − 2: LET YU = 2
```

This range of values of y will be suitable for all the cases treated below.

```
30 LET XS = UMAX/(XU − XL):
   LET YS = VMAX/(YU − YL)
```

This is the usual calculation of scale factors: see Section 1.7.

```
40 FOR I = 1 TO N
50 LET X = XL + I*(XU − XL)/N
60 LET Y = X: LET S = − 1: LET W = X
70 FOR J = 1 TO K − 1
80 LET W = W*X*X/(2*J*(2*J + 1))
90 LET Y = Y + S*W
100 LET S = − S
110 NEXT J
```

The purpose of s is to put an alternating sign in front of $w = x^{2j+1}/(2j+1)!$. The final value of y is then the value of the Taylor polynomial of degree $2k − 1$, at the chosen x. Because of the very special nature of this polynomial it is probably *not* an advantage to use the polynomial evaluation scheme of Section 3.10 in Chapter 2.

```
120 Calculate screen coordinates (u, v) as in Section 1.7
130 Put a dot at screen point (u, v)
140 NEXT I
```

You can now, if you wish, change colour and plot the graph of $y = \sin x$ in the usual way (as in Program 2.1).

Try $x_\ell = 0$, $x_u = 10$, $n = 100$ and values of k from 2 up to say 10. Notice how the approximation is very good up to a certain value of x and then, as the highest power x^{2k+1} begins to dominate the other terms, the approximation goes completely wrong. See Fig. 8.

3.2 *Some theory of Taylor polynomials*
Given a smooth function f (i.e. a function all of whose derivatives exist, at

any rate for values of x which are relevant), and a number a, the *Taylor polynomial of f of degree r*, for any integer $r \geqslant 0$ is

$$P_r(x) = f(a) + (x - a)f'(a) + \frac{1}{2!}(x - a)^2 f''(a) + \ldots + \frac{1}{r!}(x - a)^r f^{(r)}(a),$$

where $f', f'', \ldots, f^{(r)}$ are the first, second, $\ldots$, rth derivatives of f. For example, $a = 0$ and $f(x) = \sin x$, with $r = 2k - 1$, gives the polynomial above for $\sin x$.

Note that $y = P_1(x)$ is the equation of the *tangent line* to the graph $y = f(x)$ at $x = a$.

For many functions f, the polynomial P_r is, at any rate for large enough r, a *very good approximation* to f, for values of x fairly close to a. It is this fact that is being illustrated by the examples of this section, where the graphs of $y = P_1(x), y = P_2(x), y = P_3(x)$ and so on are being compared with the graph of $y = f(x)$ itself. For simplicity we take $a = 0$ and refer to the Taylor polynomial of f at 0 as just the Taylor polynomial of f.

To say that P_r is a good approximation to f is to say that $f - P_r$ is small. There are many expressions for the *remainder term* $R_r = f - P_r$, and often one can prove that, for some range of values of x, the remainder $R_r(x)$ tends to zero as $r \to \infty$. This shows that we can approximate $f(x)$ as closely as we please, for the appropriate range of values of x, by taking $P_r(x)$ with r large enough. (But the number r needed to approximate $f(x)$ to within say 10^{-8} will in general depend on x, being generally larger as x goes further from a.)

It is not hard to check that the Taylor polynomial of degree r is the unique polynomial of degree r whose value and derivatives, at the single point $x = a$, agree with those of f, up to and including the rth derivative. For example, the tangent line ($r = 1$) is the unique straight line which agrees with f at $x = a$ so far as the value at a and the derivative at a are concerned.

For $f(x) = \sin x$ or $\cos x$ or e^x it can be shown that the remainder term

$k = 3$ $k = 7$

Fig. 8

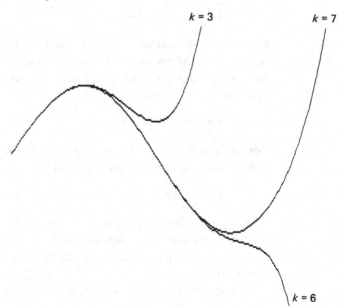

$k = 6$

$R_r(x)$ tends to zero as $r \to \infty$, for every real number x. However, as the example above of $f(x) = \sin x$ confirms, to approximate $f(x)$ well near $x = 10$ needs a much bigger value of r than to approximate it well near $x = 1$.

See, for example, Spivak (1980), Chapter 19, for more information.

3.3 *Exercise: Cosine and exponential functions*

Adapt Program 3.1 to $f(x) = \cos x$, which has Taylor polynomial

$$1 - \frac{1}{2!} x^2 + \frac{1}{4!} x^4 - \frac{1}{6!} x^6 + \ldots$$

stopped after k terms (so that the degree r is $2k - 2$).

Adapt Program 3.1 to $f(x) = e^x$, with Taylor polynomial

$$1 + x + \frac{1}{2!} x^2 + \frac{1}{3!} x^3 + \ldots$$

stopped after k terms (so here the degree r is $k - 1$). Try ranges $x_\ell = 0$, $x_u = 4$, $y_\ell = 0$, $y_u = 60$ and various k. For which k are the graphs of the polynomial and of e^x more or less indistinguishable over this range of values of x? Try $x_\ell = 0$, $x_u = 10$ or even 20, and suitable ranges for y. (See Chapter 6 for more on e^x.)

3.4 *Exercise: A geometric series*

Let $f(x) = 1/(1 - x)$, which has Taylor polynomial of degree r equal to

$$1 + x + x^2 + x^3 + \ldots + x^r, \tag{1}$$

which is called geometric because each term is the same multiple (namely x) of the one before. (Here k = number of terms = $r + 1$.) In fact the Taylor polynomial itself can here be written in 'closed form' (without any . . .), namely

$$1 + x + x^2 + \ldots + x^r = (1 - x^{r+1})/(1 - x).$$

You can prove this by cross-multiplying. The *remainder*, that is the difference between the polynomial and $f(x)$, is here

$$R_r(x) = 1/(1 - x) - (1 + x + x^2 + \ldots + x^r) = x^{r+1}/(1 - x).$$

If $-1 < x < 1$ then $x^{r+1} \to 0$ as $r \to \infty$, so for such x the Taylor polynomial of degree r approximates f better and better as $r \to \infty$. If $|x| > 1$ then $|R_r(x)| \to \infty$ as $r \to \infty$, so the approximation gets *worse* as $r \to \infty$!

Thus we must certainly restrict to $-1 < x < 1$ if we are to use Equation (1) as the approximation to $1/(1 - x)$. Confirm by plotting the Taylor polynomial given by Equation (1) and the function $1/(1 - x)$ that this is so.

Note that

$$\frac{1}{1 - x} = -\frac{1}{x}\,\frac{1}{(1 - 1/x)}.$$

so that, if $x > 1$, then $1/x < 1$ and using the approximation of Equation (1) for $1 - 1/x$ (replacing x by $1/x$ in Equation (1)), we obtain

$$\frac{1}{1 - x} \approx -\frac{1}{x} - \frac{1}{x^2} - \frac{1}{x^3} \cdots - \frac{1}{x^r}.$$

Try comparing the graph of the two sides of this, for $x > 1$ and values of r around 10.

3.5 *Exercise: The logarithm*

The function $f(x) = \ln(1 + x)$ (where ln here means 'natural logarithm') has Taylor polynomial

$$x - \frac{1}{2}x^2 + \frac{1}{3}x^3 - \ldots \pm \frac{1}{r}x^r,$$

where the number of terms is here $k = r$. Here again only a limited range of values of x is appropriate; in fact it is $-1 < x \leqslant 1$. (See for example Spivak (1980), p. 391.) Of course, x has to be > -1 for the ln of $x + 1$ to exist. Try plotting this Taylor series and the function $\ln(1 + x)$.

§4
Parametrised curves

Instead of writing y as a function of x, as in §2 above, we can write *both* x and y as functions of another variable (or *parameter*) t. For example if

$$x = \cos t, \quad y = \sin t$$

then $x^2 + y^2 = 1$. Conversely if x and y are real numbers with $x^2 + y^2 = 1$ then there exists t such that $x = \cos t$ and $y = \sin t$. (Indeed there are many such t, obtained from one another by adding multiples of 2π.) Thus the circle with equation $x^2 + y^2 = 1$ is *parametrised* by $x = \cos t$, $y = \sin t$, and we get the whole circle by taking $0 \leqslant t \leqslant 2\pi$.

When plotting parametrised curves we need, in addition to setting the bounds of x and y defining the plotting rectangle in the (x, y)-plane, to set the bounds of the parameter t, say $t_\ell \leqslant t \leqslant t_u$. We can then take n equally spaced values of t between t_ℓ and t_u, find x and y for these t and plot these n points.

In most of the exercises below, the idea is to draw a *closed* curve for which the parameter t goes (as a rule) between 0 and 2π. Thus the program Graph of Section 2.1 need only be amended as follows.

4.1 *Program: Curve*

       10 INPUT N, XL, XU, YC, TL, TU (equal scales)
or   10 INPUT N, XL, XU, YL, YU, TL, TU (arbitrary scales)
       20 Equal scales only: calculate YL and YU as in Section 1.7
       30 Calculate scaling factors XS, YS as in Section 1.7
       40 FOR I = 1 TO N
       50 LET T = TL + I*(TU − TL)/N
       55 Calculate x for this value of t
       60 Calculate y for this value of t
       70 IF X < XL OR X > XU OR Y < YL OR Y > YU THEN
            GOTO 100
       80 Convert to screen coordinates (u, v) as in Section 1.7
       90 Put a dot at screen point (u, v)
     100 NEXT I

Note that in line 70 we do now need to warn the computer to ignore x-values outside the range $x_\ell \leqslant x \leqslant x_u$, as well as y-values outside the range $y_\ell \leqslant y \leqslant y_u$. Note also that if you are using join-the-dots and want to draw a closed curve, then it is better to replace line 50 by

    50 LET T = TL + (I − 1)*(TU − TL)/(N − 1).

Can you see why?

As with graphs, it is sometimes a help to put the axes on the picture; see Program 2.1.

Note   Strictly speaking, in mathematical arguments we should recognise the fact that x and y are functions of the parameter t by writing $x(t)$, $y(t)$, and similarly $x'(t)$, $y'(t)$ for their derivatives

Fig. 9

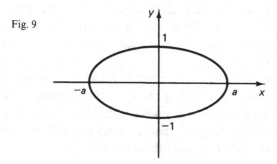

$(x'(t) = \mathrm{d}x/\mathrm{d}t$, etc.). But we shall as a rule write simply x, y, x', y' in order to simplify the appearance of formulae. We trust this will cause no dismay.

4.2 *Exercise: Ellipses*

For a chosen value of the constant a, let $x = a \cos t$, $y = \sin t$, so that $(x/a)^2 + y^2 = 1$. (Also conversely: if (x, y) satisfies this equation, then there is a value of t (indeed many values) with $x = a \cos t$, $y = \sin t$.) This is an ellipse, centre $(0, 0)$, with axes of lengths $2a$ and 2 (Fig. 9). Try plotting this with equal scales, setting $t_\ell = 0$, $t_u = 2\pi$, $y_c = 0$ (so the x-axis is across the middle of the screen), and

$$a = 2, \quad x_\ell = -2.5, \quad x_u = 2.5;$$
$$a = 3, \quad x_\ell = -3.5, \quad x_u = 3.5.$$

We shall meet ellipses again in various contexts. What are the eccentricities of these ellipses? (See Exercise 2.10 of Chapter 2.) If e is the eccentricity, then the *foci* are at $(\pm ae, 0)$. Mark these points with a dot on the screen.

If you read Section 1.3 on screen equations, consider how you could use arbitrary scales to make the ellipse with $a = 2$ appear circular on the screen. How could you make a circle appear on the screen in the shape of an ellipse in which the horizontal axis is twice the vertical axis (i.e. in the shape of the $a = 2$ ellipse)?

4.3 *Exercise: A singular curve*

Let $x = t^2$, $y = t^3$ and $t_\ell = -1$, $t_u = 1$, $x_\ell = -1$, $x_u = 2$, $y_c = 0$ (equal scales). This curve has a *cusp* at $(0, 0)$, given by $t = 0$. Compare Chapter 2, Fig. 17. At a cusp the plotting slows down (the dots move more slowly across the screen), and in fact momentarily stops, before the direction of the curve completely reverses. Try also $x = t^2$, $y = t^5$, and $x = t^3$, $y = t^4$. Does the last curve have a cusp?

In all these three cases, $t = 0$ gives $x' = y' = 0$: both derivatives vanish at $t = 0$. This says that the *speed* of the curve, which is a measure of how fast the point (x, y) is moving as t increases, is zero at $t = 0$. The speed is $\sqrt{(x'^2 + y'^2)}$. See, e.g., Bruce and Giblin (1984), p. 15. Whenever a parametrised curve has a point where $x' = y' = 0$ we call that point a *singular point* of the parametrised curve. For $x = t^3$, $y = t^4$ the singular point is less noticeable on the curve than it is for the other two examples above, as you will see from the picture. Try also $x = t^2$, $y = t^4$ and explain what you see.

When $x' = 0$, $y' \neq 0$, the curve is 'vertical': the tangent is parallel to the y-axis; when $x' \neq 0$, $y' = 0$, the curve is 'horizontal': tangent parallel to the x-axis.

4.4 *Exercise: Limaçon*

Let

$$x = a \cos t + \cos(2t), \quad y = a \sin t + \sin(2t),$$

where a is constant. Taking $a > 0$ it is certainly true that

$$-(a+1) \leqslant x \leqslant a+1, \quad -(a+1) \leqslant y \leqslant a+1$$

(since sines and cosines are always between -1 and $+1$), so for a start take $x_\ell = -(a+1)$, $x_u = a+1$, $y_c = 0$ and equal scales. As with the ellipse, take $t_\ell = 0$ and $t_u = 2\pi$. Try in succession the values $a = 1, 2, 3, 4$ and 5, and describe how the shape changes, adjusting x_ℓ and x_u to get a good picture (keeping $y_c = 0$ since the curve is symmetrical about the x-axis). (Compare Bruce and Giblin (1984), p. 21.) Are there any values of a for which the limaçon has a cusp (where $x' = y' = 0$ for some value of t)? Check this by calculus.

4.5 *Exercise: A cubic oval*

We wish to plot the cubic oval with equation

$$y^2 = a^2(x - x^3),$$

where a is constant, $a > 0$. The oval lies entirely in the region $0 \leqslant x \leqslant 1$ and is (because of the y^2) symmetrical about the x-axis: if (x, y) lies on the curve, so does $(x, -y)$. Of course, we can write

$$y = \pm a\sqrt{(x - x^3)} \tag{1}$$

and plot this as two separate *graphs*, one for the $+$ sign and one for the $-$ sign. Take $a = 1$ and try this method. Is there any more to the curve outside the strip $0 \leqslant x \leqslant 1$? Beware that $x - x^3 \geqslant 0$ for real y; show that this requires $0 \leqslant x \leqslant 1$ or $x \leqslant -1$.

Here is another parametrisation of the oval. Consider a circle, as in Fig. 10(a) centred at $(\frac{1}{2}, 0)$ and of radius $\frac{1}{2}$. Parametrising the *circle* by the angle t as shown, the x-coordinate of a point on the circle is $\frac{1}{2} + \frac{1}{2} \cos t$. Now use *these* values of x and the Formula (1) to obtain points on the oval. Thus, say $n = 200$, $t = \pi i/100$ for $i = 1, \ldots, 100$, $x = \frac{1}{2} + \frac{1}{2} \cos t$ and $y = a\sqrt{(x - x^3)}$ gives one half of the oval, while $y = -a\sqrt{(x - x^3)}$, for $i = 101, \ldots, 200$ gives the other half. Doing things this way has the effect of producing points which are much more evenly spaced round the oval than using x-values equally spaced between 0 and 1. Can you see why?

Taking equal scales, starting with $x_\ell = -0.5$, $x_u = 1.5$, and using

Fig. 10

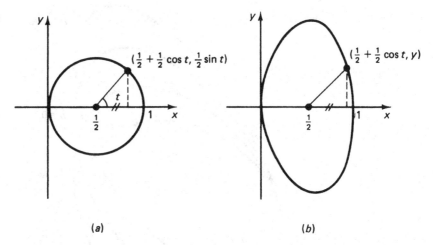

(a) (b)

the second parametrisation above, investigate how the shape of the oval is influenced by the value of a.

Here is an even better plotting method for this oval. Show that, for $0 \leqslant t \leqslant 2\pi$, the formulae

$$x = \tfrac{1}{2} + \tfrac{1}{2} \cos t, \quad y = \tfrac{1}{4}a(\sin t)\sqrt{(6 + 2 \cos t)}$$

give the whole oval, without having to change formulae in mid-stream. Thus with this parametrisation you can take say $n = 200$, $t = \pi i/100$ for $i = 1, \ldots, 200$, and do not need to change at $i = 100$ this time. Try this method of plotting.

A larger family of ovals has the equation

$$(y - bx)^2 = a^2(x - x^3),$$

where a and b are both constants. This can be parametrised in a way analogous to the last method above:

$$x = \tfrac{1}{2} + \tfrac{1}{2} \cos t, \quad y = \tfrac{1}{4}a(\sin t)\sqrt{(6 + 2 \cos t)} + \tfrac{1}{2}b(1 + \cos t).$$

Verify this, and also that the oval still lies in the strip $0 \leqslant x \leqslant 1$. Take say $a = 0.8$ and see the effect of changing b on the shape and position of the oval. (See Fig. 11.)

4.6 *Rational curves*

Many of the parametrisations we shall meet are *rational*, in the sense that x and y are expressed, or can be readily reexpressed, as rational functions of the parameter. (A rational function is one of the form f/g where f and g are polynomials.)

The singular curves in Exercise 4.3 are certainly of this form, while circle, ellipse and limaçon can all be turned into this form by the famous substitution $s = \tan(\tfrac{1}{2}t)$. (At present they contain sines and cosines, so are not rational functions of t.) With this formula for s, we have

Fig. 11

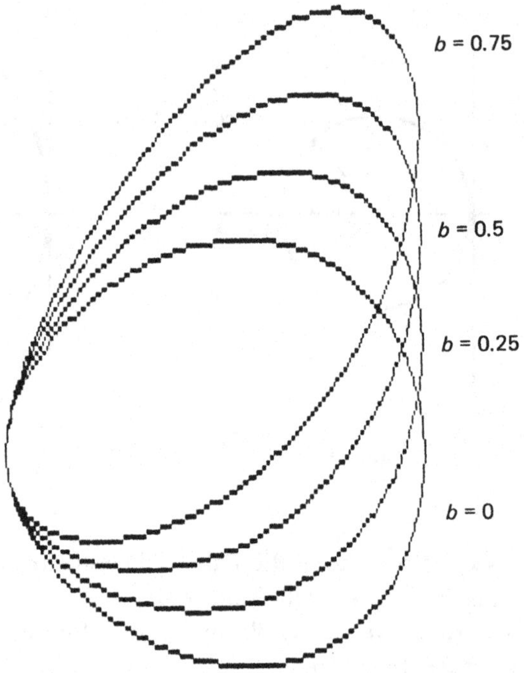

b = 0.75

b = 0.5

b = 0.25

b = 0

$$\tan t = 2s/(1 - s^2), \quad \sin t = 2s/(1 + s^2), \quad \cos t = (1 - s^2)/(1 + s^2),$$

using standard trigonometrical formulae. (These formulae are often used in evaluating integrals by substitution.)

For the ellipse (Exercise 4.2) this gives

$$x = a(1 - s^2)/(1 + s^2), \quad y = 2s/(1 + s^2).$$

Here, as s increases through all the real numbers, the point (x, y) travels anticlockwise from very close to $(-a, 0)$ when s is very large and negative, round to $(0, -1)$ when $s = -1$, then to $(a, 0)$ when $s = 0$, to $(0, 1)$ when $s = 1$ and very close to $(-a, 0)$ as $s \to \infty$ (Fig. 12(a)). The point $(-a, 0)$ on the ellipse is not taken at all, but it would not be unreasonable to say that it

Fig. 12

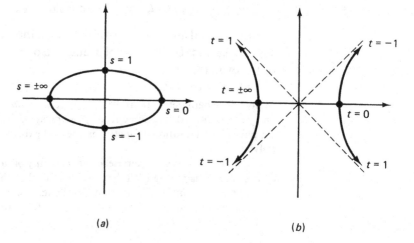

(a)   (b)

was given by $s = \infty$, or indeed by $s = -\infty$. To make precise sense of this we have to use 'homogeneous coordinates' and consider curves in the 'projective plane'. See, for example, Coxeter (1964), Chapter 12, Coxeter (1969), Chapter 14, or Rees (1983), Part II. Note that compared with the trigonometric parametrisation in Exercise 4.2 the above rational parametrisation is very inconvenient for plotting purposes!

A *rational curve* is, roughly speaking, a curve that can be parametrised with x and y as rational functions of the parameter. But, as above, there may be a point missing, corresponding to the 'infinite' value of the parameter. (*The* infinite value because rational functions have the same limit when the variable tends to $+\infty$ as they do when it tends to $-\infty$, so it is convenient to regard $+\infty$ and $-\infty$ as the same value of the parameter. In fact, it is best to regard the parameter values as lying on a circle, closing up the real line by identifying the two 'ends' together. This is called a 'projective line'.)

Also certain finite values of the parameter might give points 'at infinity' on the curve. For example,

$$x = (1 + t^2)/(1 - t^2), \quad y = 2t/(1 - t^2)$$

is a parametrisation of the hyperbola $x^2 - y^2 = 1$ (Fig. 12(*b*)). Here, $t = \pm 1$ give 'infinite' values of x and y. We could do slightly better with

$$x = (s^2 + 1)/2s, \quad y = (s^2 - 1)/2s,$$

where now $s = 0$ and $s = \infty$ give the infinite points of $x^2 - y^2 = 1$. Note that $s > 0$ gives one branch and $s < 0$ the other branch.

The trigonometric parametrisations of cubic ovals in Exercise 4.5 are *not* rational, even after substituting $s = \tan(\frac{1}{2}t)$, because of the square roots. In fact it can be shown that these ovals cannot be parametrised by rational functions at all: the curves are *not* rational. Questions of this kind form the subject matter of algebraic geometry. For an introduction to this subject (which is relatively technical and abstract) see e.g. Shafarevich (1974), Chapter I.

The next few exercises give more examples of rational curves.

4.7 *Exercise: Nodal cubic*

Show that, if $b > 0$, the parametrisation $x = t^2 - b$, $y = t(t^2 - b)$ gives all the points of the curve with equation $y^2 = x^2(x + b)$. It is easy to prove that, for all t, the given x and y satisfy this equation, but you should also show that, *if* x and y satisfy $y^2 = x^2(x + b)$, *then* there exists t with x and y expressed as above in terms of t. That is where $b > 0$ comes in, for if $b < 0$ then you find that there is no value of t which gives $x = y = 0$. This very odd situation is explained by the fact that $(0, 0)$ is an *isolated* point on the curve with equation $y^2 = x^2(x + b)$, when $b < 0$. (For $b = 0$ see Exercise 4.3 above.)

Plot the curve by means of the parametrisation, both for $b > 0$ and for $b < 0$ (where you could put a single dot at $(0, 0)$ to finish if off!). For $b > 0$ there is a crossing (also called a *node*) at $(0, 0)$.

The parametrisation above can be found from the equation by substituting $y = tx$ and cancelling t^2. This amounts to finding the point, other than $(0, 0)$, where the line $y = tx$ meets the curve (Fig. 13.).

Fig. 13

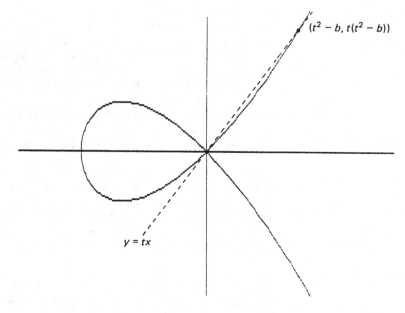

$(t^2 - b, t(t^2 - b))$

$y = tx$

4.8 *Exercise: Two more rational curves*
Substitute $y = tx$ into the equation

$$(x^2 + y^2)^2 = y(3x^2 - y^2)$$

and so parametrise the curve. Plot the curve using this parametrisation. (In polar coordinates the equation is $r = \sin(3\theta)$; compare Section 4.13 below.)

Substitute $y = tx$ into

$$x(x + y)(x + 2y)(x + 3y) = y^5$$

and so parametrise the curve. How many branches do you think will cross at the origin? Plot the curve to test your answer.

Find and plot a curve which has any given number (such as 6 or 10) branches crossing at the origin.

4.9 *Exercise: Lemniscate of Bernoulli*
This has the equation

$$(x^2 + y^2)^2 = a(x^2 - y^2),$$

for a constant $a > 0$. It is rather harder to parametrise this curve than those in Exercise 4.8 (though its polar equation is simple: $r^2 = a \cos(2\theta)$). Substitute $x^2 + y^2 = t(x - y)$ to find the parametrisation

$$x = at(t^2 + a)/(t^4 + a^2), \quad y = at(t^2 - a)/(t^4 + a^2).$$

Plot the curve; note that it has a crossing (node) at $(0, 0)$, given by $t = 0$ and by the limit as $t \to \pm \infty$ (so you will need to take a fairly big range of t to get most of the curve). See Fig. 14

Can you think of a geometrical interpretation for the substitution used here, analogous to that for the substitution $y = tx$ in Fig. 13?

4.10 *Exercise: Lissajous figures*

These are also called Bowditch curves, and are particular cases of curves produced by a simple harmonograph – see e.g. Cundy and Rollett (1961), p. 244. The ellipse in Exercise 4.2 above results from two *oscillatory* motions: $x = a \cos t$ makes x go back and forth between $-a$ and $+a$ while $y = \sin t$ makes y go back and forth between -1 and $+1$. Furthermore both return to their starting values at the same instant, when t reaches 2π.

We can make more complicated curves by having

$$x = a \cos(bt + c), \quad y = \sin t$$

for constants a, b and c. These are Lissajous figures.

Notice that x still oscillates between $-a$ and $+a$ but now it returns to its initial value (namely $a \cos c$, when $t = 0$) when $t = 2\pi/b$: the *period* of x is $2\pi/b$ (its *frequency* is $b/2\pi$). On the other hand, y still has period 2π. For example, if $b = p/q$ is a fraction in its lowest terms, then between $t = 0$ and $t = 2\pi q$, x will complete p oscillations and y will complete q oscillations. Furthermore, $t = 2\pi q$ is the smallest value of t which makes x and y both complete a whole number of oscillations (why is this?). For $t > 2\pi q$, precisely the same curve is drawn all over again.

We suggest that you put $a = 1$, input p, q and c, and take $b = p/q$,

Fig. 14

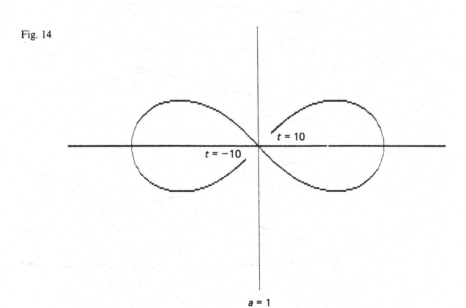

$a = 1$

$x_\ell = -1$, $x_u = 1$, $y_\ell = -1$, $y_u = 1$ and $n = 50q$. Then take for values of t, $t = i\pi/25$ for $i = 1, 2, 3, \ldots, 50q$. Try the following:

$p = q = 1$, $c = 0$:   this gives a circle;

$p = q = 1$, $c = \frac{1}{2}\pi$:   this gives a straight line (which straight line?);

$p = 2$, $q = 1$, $c = 0$;

$p = 3$, $q = 1$, $c = \frac{1}{2}\pi$.

In the last two cases, are there values of t which make $x' = y' = 0$? In the first of the two, what is the *equation* of the (x, y) curve? Notice that the curve does *not* have cusps at the singular points (compare Exercise 4.3 above). Find other values of b and c for which $x' = y' = 0$ is possible.

Try $p = 3$, $q = 1$, $c = 0$ (Fig. 15), and also other odd values of p, with $c = 0$. Are there any values of t here where $x' = y' = 0$? Look first at the curve and then check by calculation.

Try $p = 3$, $q = 2$, $c = 0$. Is this curve symmetrical about the origin? (That is, does $(-x, -y)$ lie on the curve whenever (x, y) does?) Perhaps you can find other values of p, q and c for which there is some symmetry.

4.11 *Exercise: Cycloids*

A dab of paint on a train wheel describes a *cycloid* as the train moves. Consider a circle, radius 1 say, rolling along a horizontal line, and a

Fig. 15

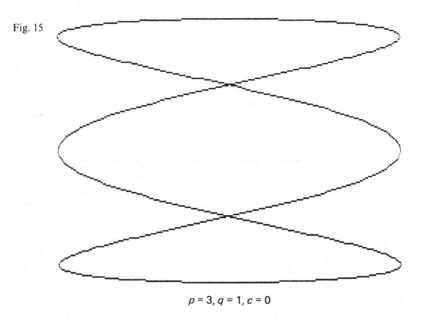

$p = 3, q = 1, c = 0$

point P on a radius CQ, fixed to the circle, with $CP = d$, as in Fig. 16. With the point of contact R initially at the origin, the *rolling condition* is $OR = $ arc RQ, i.e. with $t = $ angle RCQ, the point R has coordinates $(t, 0)$. We shall measure t in radians. Thus P is the point (x, y), where

$$x = t - d \sin t, \quad y = 1 - d \cos t.$$

(Check this from the diagram and a little trigonometry.)

A complete cycle, after which the curve repeats but is displaced a distance 2π to the right, is given by $0 \leq t \leq 2\pi$. You might want to draw the curve for $0 \leq t \leq 4\pi$; this gives two copies of the basic shape. Thus try equal scales (so that you get more of the feeling of a *circle rolling!*), with $x_\ell = 0$, $x_u = 4\pi$, $y_c = 0$, and say $n = 200$, $t = \pi i/50$ for $i = 1, 2, \ldots, 200$. Try the values $d = \frac{1}{2}$, then $d = 1$ and $d = \frac{3}{2}$. Check that, for $d = 1$, there are values of t (namely $t = 0, 2\pi, 4\pi, \ldots$) where $x' = y' = 0$, whereas for other positive values of d there are no such values of t. What do you see on the cycloid $d = 1$ at $t = 2\pi$?

This example can be used also to illustrate the idea of 'unit speed' parametrisations. Take $d = 1$ (the dab of paint P is on the rim of the wheel). Then the arclength of the cycloid curve from the origin to the point $(t - \sin t, 1 - \cos t)$ is $s = 4(1 - \cos(\frac{1}{2}t))$, provided $0 \leq t \leq 2\pi$. Arclengths are calculated by the formula $s' = \sqrt{(x'^2 + y'^2)} = \sqrt{(2(1 - \cos t))} = \sqrt{(4sin^2(\frac{1}{2}t))} = 2 \sin(\frac{1}{2}t)$ provided $\sin(\frac{1}{2}t) \geq 0$, which is true for $0 \leq t \leq 2\pi$. Of course $s = 0$ when $t = 0$ since we are measuring arclength from the origin, where $t = 0$. (See any book on calculus for an intuitive explanation of the arclength formula; for more detail see Courant (1937), p. 276, Courant and Robbins (1947), p. 466, or Apostol (1967), p. 529.)

As t goes from 0 to 2π so s goes from 0 to 8; thus the length of one arch of the cycloid is exactly eight times the radius of the rolling circle. Suppose we divide this length into say 100 equal pieces (of length 0.08 each), calculate $t = 2 \arccos(1 - \frac{1}{4}s)$ for $s = 0, 0.08, 0.16,$

Fig. 16

0.24, . . ., 8, and then use *these* values of t to plot the curve? The resulting dots will be *equally spaced* along the cycloid; i.e. the curve will be drawn at *constant speed*. (In fact *unit speed*, since when $s = 1$ the distance travelled is 1.)

Try plotting the curve in the above way, so that for each of the equally spaced values of s you calculate first t by the formula above, then $x = t - \sin t$, $y = 1 - \cos t$. You will find that the speed of drawing is perfectly even, whereas plotting by equal increments of t the drawing speeds up as t leaves 0 and then slows down as t approaches 2π.

The cycloid with $d = 1$ has many interesting properties. For example, its evolute (see §6 below) is an equal cycloid (see Exercise 6.5). If the cycloid is turned upside-down to make a bowl instead of an arch, particles can be slid down the bowl under gravity (but no friction!). The cycloid is then the curve which gives the fastest time of descent between two points, and is called the 'brachistochrone' for that reason. For a given cycloid, the time of descent to the bottom of the bowl is also the same for any starting position up the side of the bowl, a property which earns the cycloid the name 'tautochrone'. See for example Yates (1974), pp. 65–70, or Lockwood (1967), p. 80.

4.12 *Spirographs*

Instead of rolling a wheel on a horizontal track as in Exercise 4.11 we can roll it along the circumference of another wheel. In fact, a circle can be rolled round the outside or the inside of a second circle. The locus of a point fixed to the rolling circle is then called an *epicycloid*

Fig. 17

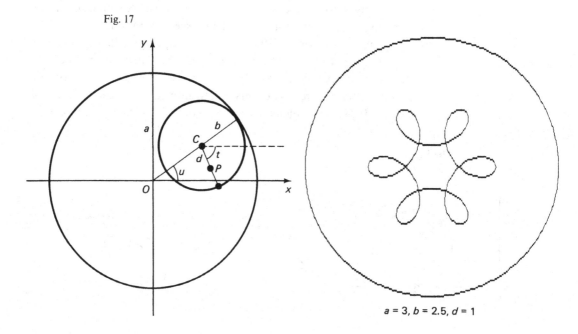

$a = 3, b = 2.5, d = 1$

(rolling outside) or a *hypocycloid* (rolling inside). Collectively these curves are also known as *cycloids* or *spirographs*. Another name in the literature is *trochoids* (epi- and hypo- as before); in this terminology the word 'cycloid' refers only to the case where the moving point is located on the circumference of the rolling circle ($d = 1$ below).

In the hypo- case, with a circle of radius b rolling *inside* a circle of radius $a > b$, we take a point P fixed on a radius of the smaller circle, P being a distance d from the centre C of this circle. Taking axes through the centre of the larger circle, supposing CP horizontal at the start and pointing along the positive x-axis, write t for the angle turned through by CP at any later time (Fig. 17).

4.12.1 *Exercise*   Use the rolling condition to deduce that the angle u turned through by OC is $u = bt/(a - b)$. Hence show that the (x, y)-coordinates of P are (for the hypocycloid):

$$x = (a - b)\cos(bt/(a - b)) + d\cos t, \atop y = (a - b)\sin(bt/(a - b)) - d\sin t. \tag{2}$$

Take $b = 1$, $d = 1$ and, in succession, the values $a = 2, 3$ and 4. Take equal scales and plot the hypocycloid with $y_c = 0$, $x_\ell = -3a/2$, $x_u = 3a/2$. Explain what you see for $a = 2$. If a is a whole number and $b = 1$ show that the curve closes when $t = 2(a - 1)\pi$. What happens if $b = 1$ and $a = p/q$, a fraction in its lowest terms (with $p > q$)? What happens with $b = d = 1$ as $a \to \infty$?

Fig. 18

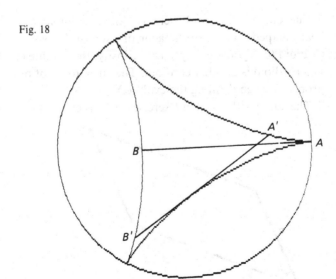

The hypocycloid with $a = 3b$ (e.g. $b = 1$, $a = 3$ as above), and $d = 1$, is called a *deltoid* because of its three-pointed shape. This curve has a very interesting property, illustrated in Fig. 18. The length of the tangent $A'B'$ to the deltoid, measured between the points of intersection with the deltoid itself, is *the same* for all tangents. Taking a limiting case, these lengths all equal that of the cuspidal tangent AB. Mathematical exercise: prove this result by calculus.

This means that a segment of length AB can be moved so as to completely reverse in direction (finishing with A and B interchanged), and keeping inside the deltoid at all times. (Perhaps you can even write a program to show the segment moving.) Here is another exercise: the area of the deltoid is $\pi(AB)^2/8$; notice that this is *half* the area of a circle with diameter AB. Clearly the segment can be reversed while keeping inside a circle of diameter AB so the deltoid is a more economical curve in this respect. It was conjectured by S. Kakeya in 1917 that the deltoid was the curve of *smallest* area inside which a segment (of length AB as above) can be reversed. Alas, A. S. Besicovitch proved in 1928 that there are curves of *arbitrarily small* area inside which a segment of a given length can be reversed! See Schoenberg (1982), Chapter 3.

4.12.2 *Exercise*   Show that the epicycloid, where the circle of radius b rolls *outside* the fixed circle of radius a, and where CP starts out pointing along the positive x-axis with $C = (a + b, 0)$, $P = (a + b + d, 0)$, has a parametrisation

$$\left. \begin{array}{l} x = (a + b)\cos(bt/(a + b)) + d \cos t, \\ y = (a + b)\sin(bt/(a + b)) + d \sin t. \end{array} \right\} \tag{3}$$

The angle u turned through by OC is related to the angle t turned through by CP by $u = bt/(a + b)$.

Plot this curve for $b = 1$, $d = 1$, and the values $a = 1, 2, 3, 4$ in succession, taking equal scales, $y_c = 0$ and appropriate x_ℓ and x_u.

The curve with $a = 1$ here is called a *cardioid*, because it is heart-shaped. In fact, the limaçon of Exercise 4.4 with $a = 2$ is also a cardioid (can you see why?). (A curiosity: the evolute (see §6 below) of a cardioid is another cardioid. The cusp does not present serious problems when defining the evolute.)

The curve with $a = 2$ in Exercise 4.12.2 is called a *nephroid* and is,

Fig. 19

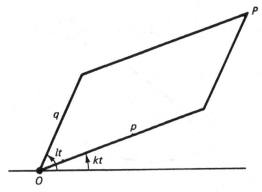

in fact, the caustic by reflexion of a circle with light source at infinity; compare Exercise 1.13 and Fig. 8 of Chapter 5 below.

4.12.3 *Exercise*   Let $b = 1$, $d = a - 1$, so d is the difference between the radii, in the hypocycloid case. Particularly pleasant curves are obtained by taking $a = 2m/(m + 1)$ for m a whole number (giving $d = (m - 1)/(m + 1)$). These curves are called *rose curves*. See also Section 4.13 below. Try plotting some rose curves. In terms of m, how many petals does the curve have?

Notice that both epicycloids and hypocycloids have the form

$$x = p \cos(kt) + q \cos(lt), \\ y = p \sin(kt) + q \sin(lt), \tag{4}$$

for constants p, q, k and l. For example the hypocycloid (Equation (2)) has $p = a - b$, $k = b/(a - b)$, $q = d$, $l = -1$. The curve of Equation (4) has a different dynamic interpretation (Fig. 19). Consider arms of lengths p and q rotating about O at angular velocities in the ratio $k:l$. Thus the angles of rotation can be written kt and lt for $t \geqslant 0$, if both arms start out ($t = 0$) horizontal and pointing the same way. The fourth vertex P of the parallelogram in Fig. 19 then has coordinates given by Equation (4).

4.12.4 *Exercise*   Is a curve of the form of Equation (4) always a hypocycloid or epicycloid as in Equations (2) or (3)? Notice that, choosing new values p', q', k', l' for p, q, k, l in Equation (4) we shall obtain the *same set of points* (x, y) if $p' = q$, $q' = p$ and $k'/l' = l/k$. Apply this to the hypocycloid (Equation (2)) to show that the *same curve* as Equation (2), but differently parametrised, results if we choose new values

$$a' = da/b, \quad b' = d(a - b)/b, \quad d' = a - b$$

for the 'fixed' radius, the 'rolling' radius and the 'arm' respectively. Take some of the examples already considered and plot the curve with these new values (thus $b = d = 1$, $a = 3$ gives new values $a' = 3$, $b' = 2$, $d' = 2$, for example) to check that the curve still looks the same.

4.13 *Polar coordinates*

A curve can be specified by the relationship between the radius r and the angle t as in Fig. 20. (The angle t is more usually called θ, but we obviously want to avoid Greek letters in programs!) Clearly

$$x = r \cos t, \quad y = r \sin t,$$

so if r is specified as a function of t then it is a simple matter to work out x and y as functions of t and go on to plot the curve as in Program 4.1.

Fig. 20

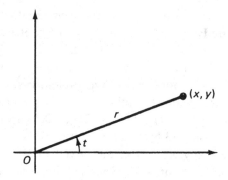

Try $r = at$ for various constants a, and say $0 \leqslant t \leqslant 2\pi$, which gives an *Archimedean spiral*.

Take $r = 2 \cos t + a$, where a is constant. In fact this gives a limaçon; can you connect the polar equation with Exercise 4.4 above? Hint: consider $x = a \cos t + \cos 2t + 1$ rather than the x of Exercise 4.4.

Take $r = c \cos(mt)$ for c constant and m a fixed whole number. These are *rose curves*, as in Exercise 4.12.3 above. To relate the two definitions, use x- and y-axes as in Fig. 17, and take $b = 1$. Thus, with $u = bt/(a-1)$ (see Exercise 4.12.1), we have

$$x = (a-1)\cos u + d \cos((a-1)u),$$
$$y = (a-1)\sin u - d \sin((a-1)u). \tag{5}$$

From now on ignore the t in Exercise 4.12.1 for it is *not* the same as the t in $r = c \cos(mt)$. Use $x = r \cos t$, $y = r \sin t$ and the formula for r to show that the curve $r = c \cos(mt)$ coincides with the curve given by Equation (5) when $d = a - 1$ and $a = 2m/(m+1)$, $c = 2(a-1) = 2(m-1)/(m+1)$. Try plotting $r = c \cos(mt)$ for $m = 2, 3, 4$ and 5 in succession, using this value of c (though changing c merely scales the picture up or down).

You should find that the number of petals is $2m$ when m is even but is only m when m is odd. Perhaps the easiest way to check this directly from $r = c \cos(mt)$ is to ask: (*a*) What is the smallest value of $t > 0$ for which the curve, starting at $t = 0$, closes up? (*b*) How many times does the curve pass through the origin before it closes? For (*a*), note that $t = 2\pi$ certainly gives the same point as $t = 0$, but, in fact, if m is *odd*, then $t = \pi$ gives the same point as $t = 0$. This is because, in polar coordinates, the point (r, t) is the same as the point $(-r, t + \pi)$. With this hint, you should be able to check that the answer to (*b*) is $2m$ when m is even and m when m is odd.

4.14 *The swallowtail surface*

Here is one of a wide class of examples where the object of study is a *surface* in three-dimensional space and we study this surface by drawing plane sections of it. That is, we take a whole family of parallel planes and draw the curves in which these planes cut the surface; the whole surface is obtained by assembling the plane sections.

Consider a quartic equation from which the cubic term has been eliminated (compare Exercise 2.9, and note that we leave the constant term in now):

$$x + yt + zt^2 + t^4 = 0. \tag{6}$$

The variable (unknown) here is t and we use, suggestively, x, y and z as the coefficients. Thus each point (x, y, z) of three-dimensional space corresponds to an *equation* (6). The condition on Equation (6) that it should have a repeated real root (i.e. for $(t - a)^2$ to be a factor of the left-hand side, for some real number a) is that the derivative with respect to t should be zero:

$$y + 2zt + 4t^3 = 0. \tag{7}$$

Only certain equations of the form (6) will have a repeated real root, namely those for which Equations (6) and (7) hold simultaneously for some real number t. Which points (x, y, z) correspond to these equations?

From Equation (7), $y = -2zt - 4t^3$ and then, from Equation (6), $x = 3t^4 + zt^2$. As z and t vary, the point

$$(x, y, z) = (3t^4 + zt^2, -2zt - 4t^3, z) \tag{8}$$

then fills up a *surface* in three-dimensional space representing these special quartic equations (Equation (6)) which have a repeated root. The surface is called the *discriminant surface* of Equation (6). (Compare Section 4.11 in Chapter 2.)

Let us fix z and let t vary in Equation (8). Then in the plane $z = $ constant we obtain a curve, where the surface cuts that plane. For example, let $z = -1$. Then we are talking about the curve of points

$$(3t^4 - t^2, 2t - 4t^3, -1)$$

lying in the plane $z = -1$. Drawing the curve in the (x, y)-plane given by

$$x = 3t^4 - t^2, \quad y = 2t - 4t^3$$

tells us what the section of the surface by the plane $z = -1$ looks like.

Try drawing this curve, taking $x_\ell = -1$, $x_u = 1$, $y_c = 0$ (equal scales), and t from -1 to 1; $n = 100$ is perfectly adequate. Draw also the sections corresponding to $z = 0$ and $z = 1$, and perhaps some

Fig. 21

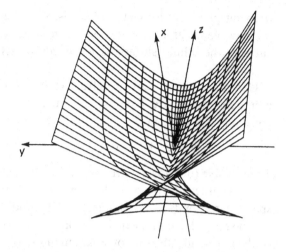

intermediate values too. The whole surface is shown in Fig. 21, and is called a *swallowtail* surface. See for example Bruce and Giblin (1984), p. 98.

4.15 *Another family of curves*
For each fixed *a*, the equations

$$x^2 = a + t^2, \ y = t^3$$

determine a curve in the plane of x and y, as t varies. Plot this curve for various negative and positive values of a, and so describe the *transition* which occurs as a passes through 0. What if $x^2 = a - t^2$, $y = t^3$?

§5
Parallels
(wavefronts)

If you drop a stone into a pond the waves spread out in all directions, the leading edge of the waves, called the *wavefront*, being at any moment a circle. All the points of the wavefront are the *same distance* from the centre where the stone was dropped, and the longer you wait the bigger will be the distance. (There is an additional and very interesting complication for real water waves: the speed of the waves over the surface is greater, the greater the wavelength. So little ripples travel more slowly than rollers. We do not consider this here: all our imaginary waves are travelling at the same speed.)

If the initial disturbance takes place along a straight line (a long rod rather than a stone), then the wavefront is at any later moment along two parallel straight lines with the initial line half-way between them. (We assume here that the rod is *very* long, so 'end effects' do not enter the picture.) All the points of the wavefront are at the *same distance* from the initial line (Fig. 22).

What if the initial disturbance is along a *curve C*? We want to find

Fig. 22

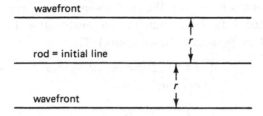

the wavefronts, one on each side of C, and at a particular 'distance' from C, the distance increasing proportionally to the time elapsed. We do this as follows (Fig. 23).

At each point P of C take the *normal* line (i.e. the straight line through P perpendicular to the tangent at P) and measure a distance r down the normal from P, arriving at Q say. As P moves on C, so Q moves on a curve which is exactly the wavefront at distance r on one side of C. There is, of course, a wavefront on the other side of C too, namely the locus of points Q' in Fig. 23.

The geometry of these wavefronts (which applies to electromagnetic or light waves, too) is the subject of this section. We shall adapt the geometrical term *parallel*: the locus of points Q is a curve *parallel* to C at distance r, or, using 'parallel' as a noun, the locus Q is a *parallel* to C at distance r. In order to *draw* parallels, all you need to know is the Formula (1) below, so you could try some of the exercises straight away.

5.1 *The formula for parallels*
As in the section on parametrised curves (§4), we suppose that x and y are functions of a parameter t. As t increases, the point $P = (x, y)$ moves in a definite direction, or *orientation* along C, indicated by an

Fig. 23

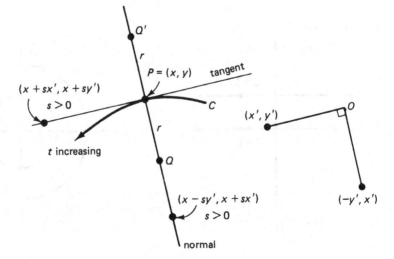

arrow in Fig. 23. We shall assume that x' and y' are never zero for the same t, i.e. that the parametrisation has no singular points (compare Exercise 4.3 above). Then:

> *The point Q on one of the parallels to C at distance r has coordinates*

$$Q = \left(x - \frac{ry'}{\sqrt{(x'^2 + y'^2)}}, \quad y + \frac{rx'}{\sqrt{(x'^2 + y'^2)}} \right). \tag{1}$$

Note   We call the locus of Q *the* parallel C_r at distance r; Q' is obtained by replacing r by $-r$ in Equation (1) and we call the locus of Q' *the* parallel C_{-r} at distance $-r$.

Proof of Equation (1):   Because the direction of the tangent line is given by (x', y'), every point on this tangent line at P has the form

$$(x + sx', \; y + sy')$$

for some real number s. The direction of the *normal* line at P is $(-y', x')$: this is the direction (x', y') turned anti-clockwise through a right angle. The points on the normal line have the form

$$(x - sy', \; y + sx')$$

for real s. The condition that the latter point should be a distance r from (x, y) is

$$s^2(x'^2 + y'^2) = r^2.$$

Choosing the value $s = r/\sqrt{(x'^2 + y'^2)}$ gives the point Q in the statement above.

Fig. 24

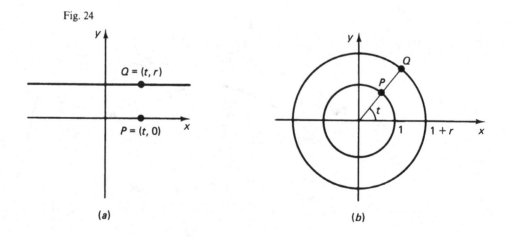

(a)   (b)

Thus $r > 0$ gives points Q on the 'left' of the curve, when you face in the direction in which the curve is oriented by increasing values of t.

When the curve C is the x-axis (admittedly not a very curved curve!) given by $x = t$, $y = 0$, we have $x' = 1$, $y' = 0$ for all t so $Q = (t, r)$ and, as P moves along C, so Q moves along the parallel line at height r (Fig. 24(a)). For $C =$ unit circle, with $x = \cos t$, $y = \sin t$, we have

$$Q = ((r + 1)\cos t, \ (r + 1)\sin t),$$

so the parallel curve is a circle of radius $r + 1$ (Fig. 24(b)). (To allow for $r < -1$ we could write the radius as $|r + 1|$.) Compare the introductory remarks concerning stones on ponds.

How dull! Perhaps parallel curves are always the same 'shape' as the original curve C. Wait and see!

5.2 *The parallels program*
In order to draw parallels to C you need:

  the functions x and y which parametrise C;

  their derivatives x' and y';

  the number r, when drawing the parallel at distance r.

In addition, you need the usual x_ℓ, x_u etc. We shall take *equal scales* in order to preserve shapes (so circles are circular, and so on). The following program draws a sequence of m parallels to a curve, for values of r which are input just before each parallel is drawn. For convenience we take 100 points on each parallel ($n = 100$ in earlier notation). The parameter is t, with lower and upper values t_ℓ, t_u.

Program: Parallels

```
10 INPUT XL, XU, YL, YU, TL, TU, M
20 Calculate yℓ and yu as in Section 1.7
30 Calculate scaling factors xs, ys as in Section 1.7
40 FOR J = 1 TO M
50 INPUT R
60 FOR I = 1 TO 100
70 LET T = TL + I*(TU − TL)/100
80 Calculate x and y for this t
90 Calculate x' and y' for this t
```

We shall write X1 and Y1 for the values of x' and y'.

```
100 LET W = SQR(X1*X1 + Y1*Y1)
110 LET X = X − R*Y1/W: LET Y = Y + R*X1/W
120 Convert to screen coordinates (u, v) as in Section 1.7
130 Put a dot at screen point (u,v)
```

140 NEXT I
150 NEXT J

By starting with $r = 0$, you could draw the curve itself to begin with –
and you could change colour after $J = 1$ so that the curve is in one
colour and the parallels in another.

5.3 *Exercise: Parabola*

Here $x = t$, $y = t^2$ (there are no new phenomena if we take the more
general $y = at^2$), so $x' = 1$, $y' = 2t$. Take $t_1 = -2$, $t_u = 2$, $x_\ell = -2$,
$x_u = 2$, $y_c = 1.6$ and plot the parallels for $r = 0, 0.1, 0.2, \ldots, 1.0$. You
should find that for $r < 0.5$ the parallels keep more or less the same
shape as the original parabola, but at $r = 0.5$ a striking change
occurs and thereafter the shape is quite different.

Try also some values $r < 0$, for which you will need to adjust x_ℓ, x_u
and y_c. The general shape of these parallels should resemble that of
the original parabola.

5.4 *Swallowtail transitions*

The transition which occurs at $r = 0.5$ for the parabola of Exercise
5.3 is called a *swallowtail* transition since it resembles the sections of
the swallowtail surface (compare Section 4.14). See Fig. 25, which
shows a sketch of two cusps (sharp points on the curve) being
created from left to right; that is what happens to the parallels as the
distance r increases from 0 through $\frac{1}{2}$ to 1.

As a mathematical exercise, you could take the parametrisation of
the parallel at distance r, namely

$$x = t - 2tr/\sqrt{(1 + 4t^2)}, \quad y = t^2 + r/\sqrt{(1 + 4t^2)},$$

and check that for $r < \frac{1}{2}$ there are no values of t for which $x' = y' = 0$
($x' = dx/dt$, as usual), while for $r > \frac{1}{2}$ there are two such values of t.

Generally speaking, the swallowtail transition is the only one to
occur on evolving parallels of plane curves. See Bruce and Giblin
(1984), pp. 33, 90, for more details of parallels.

Fig. 25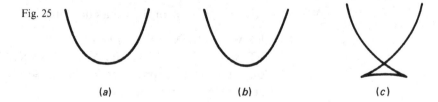

(a)   (b)   (c)

5.5 *Exercise: Ellipse*

Here $x = a \cos t$, $y = \sin t$ as in Exercise 4.2. Take $a = 1.5$, $t_\ell = 0$, $t_u = 2\pi$, $x_\ell = -2$, $x_u = 2$, $y_c = 0$ and parallels at distances $r = 0.3$, 0.6, 0.6667, 0.85, 1.0, 1.5, 2.0, 2.25 and 2.5. You should observe two swallowtail transitions of the kind described above occurring simultaneously between $r = 0.6$ and $r = 0.85$, and another two between $r = 2.0$ and $r = 2.5$. For $r < \frac{2}{3}$ and $r > \frac{9}{4}$ there are *no* cusps on the parallels; in particular this includes all negative values of r, for which the parallel is 'outside' the ellipse. See Fig. 26.

Some of the parallels have self-crossings, created in a swallowtail transition, and as the parallels evolve these self-crossings trace out a certain locus in the plane. Can you tell what it is? What about the locus of cusps on the parallels? See Section 5.10 below.

5.6 *Exercise: Cubic oval*

Here (compare Exercise 4.5) we have, for constants a and b,

$$x = \tfrac{1}{2}(1 + \cos t), \quad y = \tfrac{1}{4}a(\sin t)\sqrt{(6 + 2\cos t)} + \tfrac{1}{2}b(1 + \cos t),$$

so that

$$x' = -\tfrac{1}{2}\sin t,$$
$$y' = \tfrac{1}{4}a(3\cos^2 t + 6\cos t - 1)/\sqrt{(6 + 2\cos t)} - \tfrac{1}{2}b\sin t.$$

Start with $a = 1$, $b = 0$ and examine the evolution of the parallels as r increases from 0 to 2. (Take $x_\ell = -1$, $x_u = 2$, $y_c = 0$ to begin with.) Try $a = 0.8$, $b = 0.17$ and r increasing from 0.5 to 1. What do you observe?

Fig. 26

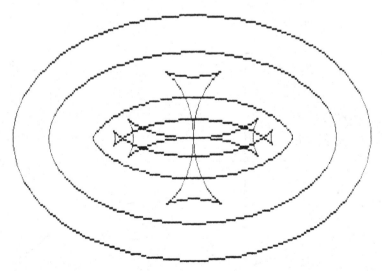

parallels at distances 0.3, 0.6667, 0.85, 1 and 1.5

5.7 *Exercise: More examples*

Try drawing the parallels to the curve $y = x^3$ (so $x = t$, $y = t^3$ is a parametrisation) and $y = x^4$ ($x = t$, $y = t^4$). The latter example is rather different from the ones given so far. Try also the limaçons of Exercise 4.4.

Here is a more risky example. Consider C, given by $x^{3/2} + y^{3/2} = 1$, where x and y are ≥ 0. This is parametrised by

$$x = (\cos t)^{4/3}, \quad y = (\sin t)^{4/3},$$

where $0 \leq t \leq \frac{1}{2}\pi$, so $x' = -\frac{4}{3}(\cos t)^{1/3} \sin t$, $y' = \frac{4}{3}(\sin t)^{1/3} \cos t$. Thus $x' = y' = 0$ at $t = 0$ and at $t = \frac{1}{2}\pi$, which is unfortunate! However, writing down the formula, as in Section 5.1, for the parallel and multiplying the fractions top and bottom by $(\cos t)^{-1/3}(\sin t)^{-1/3}$ gives the point

$$\left((\cos t)^{4/3} - \frac{r(\cos t)^{2/3}}{p}, \ (\sin t)^{4/3} - \frac{r(\sin t)^{2/3}}{p} \right)$$

where $p = \sqrt{((\sin t)^{4/3} + (\cos t)^{4/3})}$. This can be used to plot parallels. Very beautiful curves are obtained by plotting C and completing an oval by symmetry (Fig. 27). This is done by plotting also the curves $(-x, y)$, $(-x, -y)$ and $(x, -y)$. You can, of course, do the same for the parallels, so that they join up to form closed curves. (The equation of the oval obtained in this way from C is $|x|^{3/2} + |y|^{3/2} = 1$.)

Fig. 27

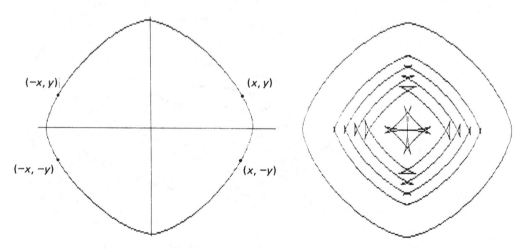

parallels at distances 0.3, 0.4, 0.5, 0.6 and 1

5.8 *Parallels of parallels*

Suppose you drew the parallels of a curve C_r which is a parallel of C. Would these just be parallels of C?

5.9 *Self-crossing of parallels*

As the above examples show, parallels tend to acquire cusps and self-crossings as the distance from the parent curve C increases. What is the significance of these? The easier one to interpret is the self-crossing, for this simply means that there is a point P whose distances from two points A and B of C, measured along the normal lines at A and B, are both equal to r. There is then a circle of radius r touching C at both A and B, i.e. *bitangent to C*. Momentarily, C is symmetric about a line through P, as in Fig. 28, which shows the general setup and the special case of a parabola. As r increases the self-crossings on the parallels travel on a set known as the *symmetry set* of C (see Giblin and Brassett (1985) and Bruce and Giblin (1984), p. 137). This is therefore the locus of centres of circles which are bitangent to C. By studying the parallels of parabola and ellipse, can you guess what the symmetry sets of these curves are? In general, it is hard to plot symmetry sets, but the problem has interest in pattern recognition and theoretical biology.

5.10 *Cusps of parallels*

The locus traced out by the cusps on the parallels of a given curve C is obtained by differentiating the parametrisation (Equation (1)) in Section 5.1. For whenever a cusp occurs on a parametrised curve the speed of the curve slows to zero at the cusp: i.e. if x and y are the

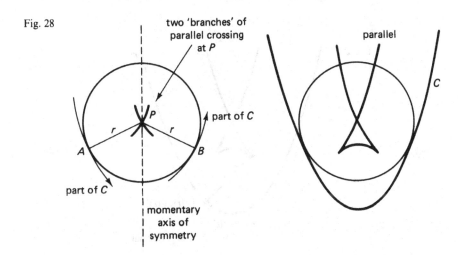

Fig. 28

functions of t giving the parametrisation, then $x' = y' = 0$ at the cusp. Now for the *parallel* to C we have instead of plain x and y the expressions from Section 5.1:

$$x - ry'/\sqrt{(x'^2 + y'^2)} \text{ and } y + rx'/\sqrt{(x'^2 + y'^2)},$$

where x and y come from the given curve C and r is the distance of the parallel from C. Differentiating these gives

$$x'(1 - r\kappa) \quad \text{and} \quad y'(1 - r\kappa), \tag{2}$$

where $\kappa = (x'y'' - x''y')/(x'^2 + y'^2)^{3/2}$.

Now assuming that the original curve C does *not* have any points where $x' = y' = 0$, the expressions in (2) can only both be zero when $r\kappa = 1$. (Also, when $r\kappa \neq 1$, they tell us, not surprisingly, that the tangent direction to the parallel C_r is the same as the tangent direction to C, namely the direction of the vector (x', y').) Thus:

> Whenever a cusp occurs on a parallel C_r at a particular parameter value t, then $\kappa(t)$ must be non-zero and $r = 1/\kappa(t)$.

See Fig. 29. The number $1/\kappa(t)$ is called the *radius of curvature* of C at the point with parameter value t, and $\kappa(t)$ is called the *curvature* of C. The parallel C_r is forced to slow down and stop at a parameter value t for which $r = 1/\kappa(t)$. It can be shown that, as in the figure, the parallel C_r executes a 180° turn provided that the derivative $\kappa'(t)$ is not also zero. We say that C has a *vertex* at the point with parameter value t if $\kappa'(t) = 0$.

For example, the parabola $(x, y) = (t, t^2)$ has a vertex at $(0, 0)$, given by $t = 0$. Here, $\kappa = 2$ so the parallel at distance $r = \frac{1}{2}$ will have a

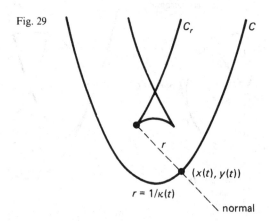

Fig. 29

C_r C

$(x(t), y(t))$

$r = 1/\kappa(t)$

normal

singular point when $t = 0$. However, this is just at the birth of the swallowtail (Fig. 25(b)) and there is no change of direction on the parallel $C_{1/2}$. This is because $\kappa'(0) = 0$.

5.11 *Exercise: The parabola revisited*

Verify the above statements about the parabola $y = x^2$. Also show that the derivative κ' of the curvature κ is never zero except at $t = 0$. In this case, $\kappa(t) = 2/(1 + 4t^2)^{3/2}$, which is certainly > 0 for all t, and also < 2 for all t (why?). Why does this show that, if $r < \frac{1}{2}$ (which includes all negative values of r), there are *no* cusps on the parallels? Compare Exercise 5.3.

5.12 *Exercise: The ellipse revisited*

For the ellipse, as in Exercise 5.5, show that $\kappa(t) = a/(a^2 \sin^2 t + \cos^2 t)^{3/2}$, using Formula (2) for κ in Section 5.10. Thus (taking $a > 0$), κ is always > 0; taking $a \geq 1$ show that in fact $1/a^2 \leq \kappa(t) \leq a$ for all t. (Hint: the denominator of $\kappa(t)$ is $((a^2 - 1)\sin^2 t + 1)^{3/2}$, and $0 \leq \sin^2 t \leq 1$ for all t.) Deduce that, for $a = \frac{3}{2}$, there are *no* cusps on the parallel C_r when $r > \frac{9}{4}$ or $r < \frac{2}{3}$. What if $a = 2$? Check by drawing parallels as in Exercise 5.5.

5.13 *Exercise: Other curves*

For the curve $y = x^3$ ($x = t$, $y = t^3$; compare Exercise 5.7) show that $\kappa(t) = 6t/(1 + 9t^4)^{3/2}$. Show that $\kappa' = 0$ when $t^4 = 1/45$, i.e. for $t = \pm 0.3861$ approximately. Deduce that κ has its maximum at the positive one of these and its minimum at the negative one. (Note $\kappa(t) \to 0$ as $t \to \infty$ and as $t \to -\infty$.) Deduce that

$$-1.7623 \leq \kappa(t) \leq 1.7623$$

approximately, for all t, and that there are *no* cusps on the parallel C_r if $-0.5674 < r < 0.5674$ approximately. Compare with your pictures in Exercise 5.7.

For $y = x^4$ ($x = t$, $y = t^4$) show that $\kappa(t) = 12t^2/(1 + 16t^6)^{3/2}$, $0 \leq \kappa(t) \leq 2.1515$ approximately, for all t, and there are *no* cusps on the parallel C_r when $r < 0.4648$ approximately. Confirm this by drawing the parallels.

§6
Evolutes   As r increases, the cusps on the parallel C_r to a given curve trace out a curve in the plane called the *evolute* of C. Thinking of the parallels as wavefronts spreading out from an initial disturbance along C, the evolute is a curve along which interference between wavefronts takes place. (Interference also takes place along the symmetry set; compare Section 5.9.)

To plot the evolute E when C is parametrised as usual (with x and y functions of t with $x' = y' = 0$ never happening) we just have to substitute $r = 1/\kappa$, using Formula (2) for κ in Section 5.10, in the parametrisation of the parallel C_r given in Equation (1) of Section 5.1. The result is:

$$E: \left(x - \frac{y'(x'^2 + y'^2)}{x'y'' - x''y'},\ y + \frac{x'(x'^2 + y'^2)}{x'y'' - x''y'} \right), \tag{1}$$

where we assume $\kappa \neq 0$, that is, $x'y'' - x''y' \neq 0$. If this fails, then the point (1) goes off to infinity, accompanied, of course, by an error message of the 'division by zero' kind. So long as we avoid actually trying to calculate (1) when $\kappa = 0$, there is no difficulty in plotting the evolute E by dots-only. When using join-the-dots some care is needed to avoid the drawing of 'asymptotes'. See Appendix A2. A point where $\kappa = 0$ on a curve is called an *inflexion*, so (compare Exercise 5.13) the curves $y = x^3$ and $y = x^4$ both have an inflexion at $(0,0)$, where $t = 0$. The former is called an *ordinary inflexion* because $\kappa'(0) \neq 0$.

6.1 *The evolute program*
We need to tell the computer the functions x, y, x', y', x'' and y'' of the parameter t in order to plot the evolute. It is instructive to add an evolute-plotting program to the end of the Parallels, Program 5.2. To plot the evolute *only*, simply omit lines 40–140.

Program: Evolute   Add the following to Parallels, Program 5.2

```
200 FOR I = 1 TO 100
210 LET T = TL + I*(TU − TL)/100
220 Calculate x and y for this t
230 Calculate x' and y'
240 Calculate x" and y"
```

We shall use X1, Y1, X2, Y2 for x', y', x'', y'' respectively.

```
250 LET DENOM = X1*Y2 − X2*Y1
260 IF DENOM = 0 THEN GOTO 320
270 LET W = (X1*X1 + Y1*Y1)/DENOM
280 LET X = X − Y1*W: LET Y = Y + X1*W
290 IF X < XL OR X > XU OR Y < YL OR Y > YU THEN
      GOTO 320
300 Convert to screen coordinates (u, v) as in Section 1.7
310 Put a dot at screen point (u, v)
320 NEXT I
```

It is particularly effective to draw *C* in one colour, some parallels *C_r* in a second colour and the evolute *E* in a third colour.

6.2 *Things to notice*

When you draw parallels and the evolute on the same picture, you should see the following:

The cusps on the parallels all lie on the evolute.

The cusps point at right angles to the evolute.

In fact (Fig. 30) the tangent line to the evolute *E* is along the *normal* line to the curve *C*. The tangent to the parallel, on the other hand, is parallel to the tangent line to *C* at the corresponding point of *C*. When the parallel has a cusp, then it is the limiting, or cuspidal tangent which is parallel to the tangent line to *C*. Also:

When *C* has a vertex ($\kappa' = 0$) the *evolute* has a cusp (or at any rate it has a singular point, where the derivatives with respect to *t* of both components of *E* in (1) above are zero).

To see that the tangent line to *E* is normal to *C* it is possible just to differentiate the coordinates of *E* as in (1) above and check that the result is a multiple of the vector $(-y', x')$ which is normal to *C*. Alternatively vector notation and use of standard formulae for the differential geometry of plane curves helps. (See Bruce and Giblin (1984), pp. 27, 33.) Writing $c(t) = (x(t), y(t))$, the *unit tangent* vector is $T = c'/\|c'\|$, where the double bars indicate length of a vector. The *unit normal* vector *N* is *T* turned anticlockwise through a right angle. Then the standard formulae (Serret–Frenet formulae for plane curves) are

$$T' = \kappa N\|c'\| \quad \text{and} \quad N' = -\kappa T\|c'\|.$$

Fig. 30

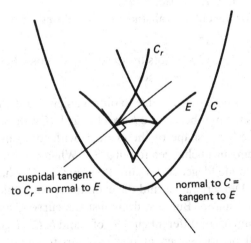

cuspidal tangent
to *C_r* = normal to *E*

normal to *C* =
tangent to *E*

The evolute is

$$e(t) = c(t) + N(t)/\kappa(t),$$

so that

$$\begin{aligned} e' &= c' + N'/\kappa - N\kappa'/\kappa^2 \\ &= T\|c'\| - T\|c'\| - N\kappa'/\kappa^2 \\ &= -N\kappa'/\kappa^2. \end{aligned}$$

So the tangent $e'(t)$ to the evolute e is parallel to $N(t)$ so long as $\kappa'(t) \neq 0$. The condition $\kappa'(t) = 0$ means that C has a *vertex* at this value of t; compare Section 5.10. If this happens then $e'(t) = 0$, i.e. both coordinates of the evolute have zero derivative and the evolute has a singular point. As a rule this manifests itself as a cusp on the evolute.

6.3 *Exercise: Parabola and ellipse*

Plot the evolute of the parabola $y = x^2$ ($x = t$, $y = t^2$) as well as parallels, and verify the assertions of Section 6.2. As in Exercise 5.11, $t = 0$ gives the unique vertex ($\kappa' = 0$) on the parabola. Verify that there is a corresponding cusp (on the vertical line of symmetry of the evolute) in your picture. (Compare Fig. 30.)

For the ellipse (see Exercises 5.5 and 5.12) with $a > 1$, verify that $\kappa' = 0$ precisely when $t = 0$, $\frac{1}{2}\pi$, π and $\frac{3}{2}\pi$ (no other values for $0 \leq t \leq 2\pi$). Draw the evolute for $a = 1.5$ and check that indeed it has four cusps. Which points on the ellipse have these four values of t? Which cusps on the evolute correspond to these values? (Look at the evolute as it is being drawn. What order do the cusps come in?) Try also $a = 2$. What happens to the cusps? Show that the coordinates of the cusps are, for any $a > 1$,

$$((a^2 - 1)/a, 0), \quad (0, 1 - a^2), \quad ((1 - a^2)/a, 0), \quad (0, a^2 - 1).$$

6.4 *Exercise: Cubic oval*

For the cubic oval studied in Exercises 4.5 and 5.6 check that

$$\begin{aligned} x'' &= -\tfrac{1}{2}\cos t, \\ y'' &= -\tfrac{1}{4}a(\sin t)(9\cos^2 t + 42\cos t + 37)/(6 + 2\cos t)^{3/2} \\ &\quad - \tfrac{1}{2}b\cos t. \end{aligned}$$

This time it is possible to observe significant changes on the *evolutes* as the numbers a and b are changed. (On the other hand for ellipses the basic shape of the evolute, with four cusps and no crossings, remains unchanged for all $a > 1$. When $a = 1$ in Exercise 6.3 then the evolute 'degenerates' into the centre of C, which is then a circle.)

Draw parallels and the evolute for *one* cubic oval, i.e. one choice of a and b. But also draw just the curve C and its evolute E for a number of different choices of a and b. (You could even retain them all on the screen at once, for up to three or so using different colours.) Try $a = 0.8$ and in succession $b = 0.17, 0.25, 0.32, 0.4$. For all of these, $x_\ell = -1$, $x_u = 2$, $y_c = 0$ (and, of course, $t_\ell = 0$, $t_u = 2\pi$) will do.

You should observe a swallowtail transition (Section 5.4) on the evolutes – just the same kind of transition that happens on the parallels of a single curve. (See Fig. 31.) It can be shown that in general this is the only kind of transition which occurs on evolutes of curves, as the curves themselves gradually change shape under the influence of one changing parameter (b in the above example).

6.5 *Exercise: Other cubics*

The evolute of the curve $y = x^3$ ($x = t$, $y = t^3$) goes off 'to infinity' at $t = 0$, since $\kappa(0) = 0$ (see Exercise 5.13). There are two cusps, corresponding to $t = \pm 0.3861$ approximately. Show that the co-ordinates of these cusps are (± 0.1544, ± 0.5756) approximately.

Try also the curve $y = x^3 + ax$ ($x = t$, $y = t^3 + at$) for various values of a. Are there any swallowtail transitions on the evolutes?

6.6 *Exercise: Cycloid*

Try drawing the evolute of the cycloid of Exercise 4.11 with $d = 1$. You should avoid $t = 0$ and $t = 2\pi$, so take perhaps $t_\ell = 0.01$, $t_u = 6.28$. Does the evolute look like another cycloid?

In fact it *is* another cycloid, indeed a congruent one. (This has

Fig. 31

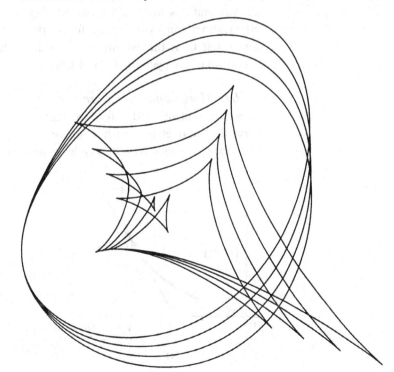

Fig. 32

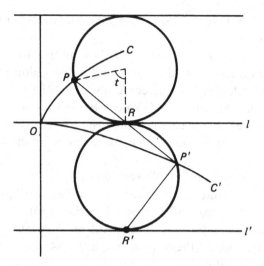

connexions with designing pendulums whose time of swing is *exactly* the same no matter what the angle of swing. See Yates (1974), p. 68.) Fig. 32 is intended as a hint to proving this result. Two circles of radius 1 rolling on lines l and l' determine cycloids C and C' but O is the bottom of the arch of C and the top of the arch of C'. The crucial fact is that RP is normal to C and $R'P'$ is normal to C'. Check this for say C directly from the parametrisation in Exercise 4.11. (We can also say that P is 'instantaneously rotating' about R, but that takes a little justification.) Why does it follow that RP' is *tangent* to C' and hence that C' is the evolute of C? Deduce also that the radius of curvature of the cycloid at P is $4\sin(\tfrac{1}{2}t)$.

6.6 *More about curvature*

As we have mentioned before (Sections 5.10 and 6.2) a point of a curve C, parametrised with x and y as functions of t, where the curvature satisfies $\kappa'(t) = 0$, is called a *vertex* of C. Thus vertices are

Fig. 33

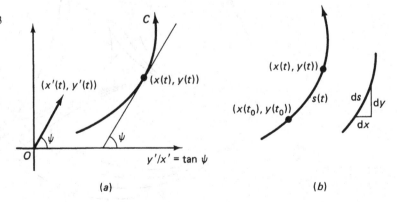

(a)   (b)

stationary points, usually maxima or minima, of the curvature. A geometrical interpretation of curvature is as follows. Let ψ be the angle from the positive x-axis to the tangent line to C (Fig. 33). Since the tangent direction is (x', y') we have $y' = x' \tan \psi$, provided $x' \neq 0$. Differentiating with respect to t, we get

$$y'' = x'' \tan \psi + x' \psi' \sec^2 \psi.$$

Substituting $\tan \psi = y'/x'$, $\sec^2 \psi = 1 + (y'/x')^2$, gives (compare (2) in Section 5.10):

$$\kappa = \frac{x' y'' - x'' y'}{(x'^2 + y'^2)^{3/2}} = \frac{\psi'}{(x'^2 + y'^2)^{1/2}}.$$

(If $x' = 0$ and $y' \neq 0$ then a similar argument gives the same result.) Now if $s(t)$ is the *arclength* along C from a given point (compare Exercise 4.11) to the point with parameter value t, then $(s')^2 = (x')^2 + (y')^2$. (In the language of differentials, $(\mathrm{d}s)^2 = (\mathrm{d}x)^2 + (\mathrm{d}y)^2$; see Fig. 33($b$).) Thus $\kappa = \psi'/s'$, which can also be written $\kappa = \mathrm{d}\psi/\mathrm{d}s$. Thus κ is the rate of increase of ψ with respect to arclength on C:

> *The curvature is the rate at which the tangent line to C turns, as you move along C at unit speed.*

When κ is very large the curve is *very curved* and when κ is small it is *straighter*. See Fig. 34. It is quite hard to spot precisely where, on C, the curvature reaches a maximum (at a vertex) and starts

Fig. 34

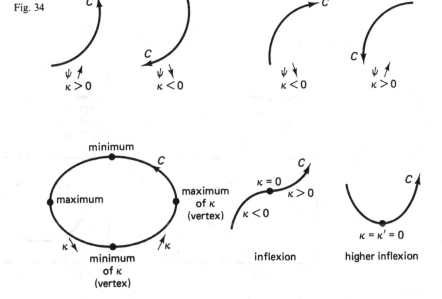

decreasing, with the curve flattening out. But the cusp on the evolute pinpoints this precisely.

6.7 *More on evolutes*

Draw again some of the evolutes described above, and verify by inspection that, for a cusp on the evolute, the direction of the cusp is directly away from points of minimum curvature and directly towards points of maximum curvature (Fig. 35), where C is oriented so that $\kappa > 0$.

Try the limaçons of Exercise 4.4 and study how their evolutes change as the parameter a changes. How many vertices do they have? Which limaçons have inflexions? (That is, how many cusps does the evolute have? Which evolutes go off to infinity?)

Why will two parallel curves always have the same evolute?

Appendix   *Join-the-dots*

We cover briefly the following matter in this appendix: how can we draw parametrised curves, and hence parallels, evolutes and so on, so that they look vaguely like *curves* on the screen rather than sequences of dots?

A.1 *The trouble-free case*

If a dots-only curve is known to lie entirely on the screen (i.e. entirely within the plotting rectangle in the (x, y)-plane, which is transferred to the screen by the coordinate changes of Section 1.7), then there is no problem. We simply join up the dots by straight segments. Thus it is only necessary to move the cursor to the first point calculated, and then to join each

Fig. 35

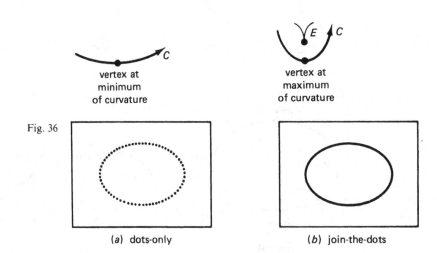

vertex at
minimum
of curvature

vertex at
maximum
of curvature

Fig. 36

(a) dots-only

(b) join-the-dots

subsequent point to the one before. Provided the dots are fairly close together this gives a good approximation to the required curve (Fig. 36).

In the program for drawing a parametrised curve (4.1) we need only replace line 9$\emptyset$ by two lines:

9$\emptyset$ If $i = 1$ then move the cursor to screen point (u, v)
95 Draw a straight segment from the cursor position to screen point (u, v)

After line 95 has been executed, the cursor is at the latest calculated screen point (u, v), which for $i > 1$ is the end of a segment; all is then prepared for drawing the next segment, starting at that point.

You can insert 'if $i > 1$' at the beginning of line 95, but leaving it out only makes the computer draw one extra 'segment' of length zero, from the $i = 1$ point to itself. Also the initial moving of the cursor (line 9$\emptyset$) can be placed outside the loop.

Try this method on, for example, Exercises 4.2, 4.4 and 4.5 above.

A.2 *Eliminating 'asymptotes'*

A snag arises with curves that go off to infinity (Fig. 37). The last point calculated along the upward arm is joined to the next point calculated, which is on the downward arm. The exact line which these two arms approach is called an *asymptote* to the curve; thus the spurious line in Fig. 37(*b*) is almost an asymptote, whence the title of this section.

There is absolutely no foolproof solution to this problem, but here is a simple solution which works in most cases. It applies to curves which go off the screen, even if your micro abruptly stops the program when given instructions to plot a point which is off the screen.

All we do is to join dots until the next point calculated is off the screen, then stop trying even to plot the dots, starting a new piece of joined dots curve when further points are calculated which lie within the screen. The

Fig. 37

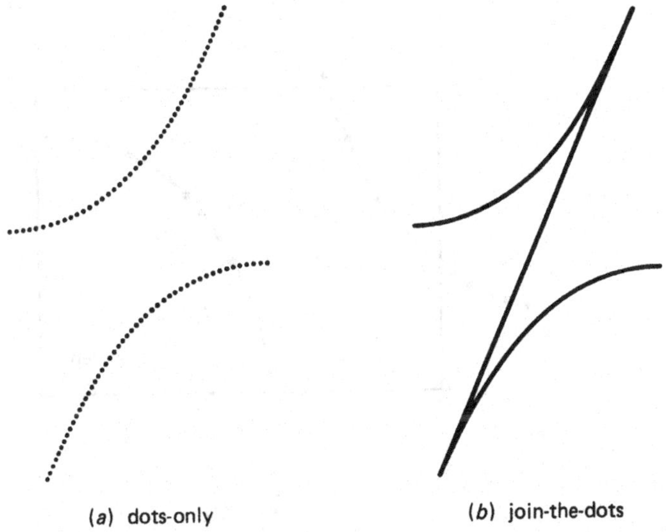

(*a*) dots-only   (*b*) join-the-dots

effect is to truncate pieces of curve which are going off the screen (Fig. 38) but acceptable pictures are produced so long as successively calculated points are not too far apart.

The idea is to use a separate number, k say, within the program, which takes values 0 and 1. For each calculated point within the screen $k = 1$, while points off the screen give $k = 0$. There are four cases:

(a) k changes from 0 to 1: move the cursor to the current point;

(b) k stays at 1: draw a segment;

(c) k changes from 1 to 0: suspend plotting;

(d) k stays at 0: keep plotting suspended.

Here is a program which puts this idea into effect. We suppose that a parametrised curve is being plotted, with x and y known functions of t; lines 1Ø–3Ø are as in Program 4.1.

```
35 LET K = Ø
4Ø FOR I = 1 TO N
5Ø LET T = TL + (I − 1)*(TU − TL)/(N − 1)
55 Calculate x for this t
6Ø Calculate y for this t
7Ø IF X < XL OR X > XU OR Y < YL OR
   Y > YU THEN LET K = Ø: GOTO 1ØØ
8Ø Calculate screen coordinates (u, v) as in Section 1.7
9Ø If k = Ø then move cursor to (u, v): LET K = 1
95 If k = 1 then join the current cursor position to (u, v) by a
   straight segment
1ØØ NEXT I
```

You should convince yourself that this really does do what is claimed, and try it out on examples such as Exercises 4.3 and 4.7 and those in §2 and §3.

Note that no attempt is made to plot points outside the plotting rectangle (line 7Ø), so the chaos mentioned in Section 1.6 is automatically avoided. You do nevertheless need to take care that any denominators occurring in

Fig. 38

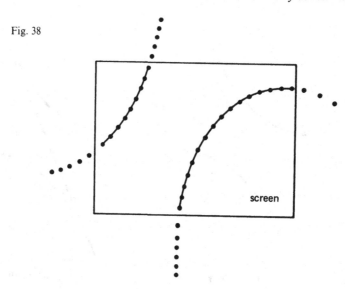

the functions x and y are never zero for the values of t actually used by the program. In practice, it is probably best to ignore this hazard and, if it arises, to add some small number such as 0.00001 to the starting value of t. That usually does the trick.

For micros that do not object to being given points off the screen (they refrain from plotting them, naturally, but carry on with the program), one can try slight variants of the above, replacing the forbidden region of line 7∅ by a somewhat larger one (Fig. 39). With any luck, the curve will then be drawn up to the edge of the screen. The numbers x_a, x_b, y_a, y_b can be extra inputs to the program, or can be chosen once for all. Line 7∅ becomes

7∅ IF X < XA OR X > XB OR Y < YA OR
    Y < YB THEN LET K = ∅: GOTO 1∅∅.

References

H. Abelson and A. diSessa *Turtle Geometry*, MIT Press, Cambridge, Mass., 1980

T. M. Apostol *Calculus*, Volume 1, Blaisdell Publishing Co., New York, 2nd Edn, 1967.

J. W. Bruce and P.J. Giblin *Curves and Singularities*, Cambridge University Press, Cambridge, 1984. (Second Edition, 1992.)

R. Courant *Differential and Integral Calculus*, Blackie and Son, London, 1937

R. Courant and H. Robbins *What is Mathematics?*, Oxford University Press, Oxford, 1947: (Paperback 1978).

H. S. M. Coxeter *Projective Geometry*, University of Toronto Press, Toronto, 2nd Edn, 1964.

Introduction to Geometry, Wiley, New York, 2nd Edn, 1969

H. M. Cundy and A. P. Rollett *Mathematical Models*, Oxford University Press, Oxford, 2nd Edn, 1961

P. J. Giblin and S. A. Brassett 'Local symmetry of plane curves', *Amer. Math. Monthly* **92** (1985) 689–707

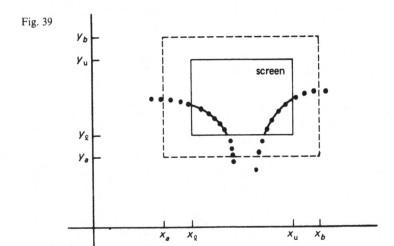

Fig. 39

E. H. Lockwood *A Book of Curves*, Cambridge University Press, Cambridge, 1967

A. Oldknow *Microcomputers in Geometry*, Ellis Horwood, Chichester, 1987

E. G. Rees *Notes on Geometry*, Springer-Verlag, Berlin, 1983

I. J. Schoenberg *Mathematical Time Exposures*, Math. Assoc. of America, Washington DC, 1982

I. R. Shafarevich *Basic Algebraic Geometry*, Springer-Verlag, Berlin, 1974

M. Spivak *Calculus*, Publish or Perish, Boston, Mass., 2nd Edn, 1980

R. C. Yates *Curves and their Properties*, National Council of Teachers of Math., Reston, Va, 1974

4

Numbers, Part 2

As we mentioned in the first chapter, general questions concerning whole numbers, rather than merely mechanical computations, can be extremely difficult to answer. Indeed this higher (as opposed to basic) arithmetic is one of the most difficult and fascinating branches of mathematics, and has been extensively studied by many of the greatest mathematicians. These mathematicians often spent an enormous amount of time and energy checking their conjectures with specific numbers and sifting through mountains of experimental data. (Mathematics is an experimental science after all. It differs from other experimental sciences, however, because often the amount of experimental evidence prior to the proof of a result might be very slim, and after the proof experimental evidence is strictly irrelevant, although psychologically reassuring.) Anyway, the computational feats of mathematicians of old are often extremely impressive, bearing in mind that they only had paper and pencil (or papyrus and stylus or whatever) to hand. What an advantage we have! Indeed what might Gauss have achieved with his own micro? Let us start our investigations. The emphasis throughout this chapter will be on the building blocks of arithmetic: the prime numbers.

§1
Prime numbers

Recall that a natural number x is prime if it is only divisible by 1 and itself (in other words cannot be written as a product of natural numbers a and b unless a or b is 1). It is fairly clear that any number can be factored as a product of prime numbers and the resulting factorization is unique up to the order of the factors. (It may be 'clear', but it is actually far from trivial to prove that this is so, the assertion concerning the uniqueness of the factorization being especially troublesome to prove. Indeed, it apparently took the genius of Gauss to appreciate that anything needed proving at all!) Prime numbers then are the multiplicative building blocks of arithmetic.

Our first task is to get ourselves a fairly long list of primes. There are a number of ways one can do this on a micro, and their efficiencies may vary somewhat from machine to machine. Here are some trivial, though useful observations to bear in mind, however, when designing your program.

(a) To check whether or not a number n is prime we need only consider possible divisors d between 2 and $\text{int}(\sqrt{n})$. The reason should be clear; if n has a divisor bigger than $\text{int}(\sqrt{n})$ it must have a divisor less than $\text{int}(\sqrt{n})$ as well. Moreover one need only check prime divisors (although as a means of proving that some given number is prime, rather than generating a list of primes, this is not recommended).

(b) One useful trick (already used in Chapter 1) for discovering if one natural number d divides another x (with no remainder of course) on your micro is to note that d divides x if and only if $\text{int}(x/d) = x/d$, i.e. the integer part of x/d is the whole of x/d. Most micros have INT available as a function which is very convenient. Of course, one has to be a little careful. Our computer only has a limited accuracy and this check may for instance show that $10^{10} + 1$ is divisible by 10^{10}. Generally such problems will not arise in this chapter, but the reader would do well to bear them in mind.

(c) Even numbers (other than 2) are not prime! This is hardly deep but bear it in mind when designing your programs and you may halve or quarter your computer's workload.

Here are a couple of methods for generating primes.

1.1 *Algorithms for generating primes*
Given n, introduce an array $a(i)$, $1 \leq i \leq n$, and set all of their initial values equal to 0. For all $2 \leq x \leq y \leq n$ consider the products xy and set $a(xy)$ equal to 1. After all of these products have been considered we run through the integers $2 \leq z \leq n$. It is easy to see that z is prime if and only if $a(z) = 0$.

Of course the algorithm above has taken neither of the observations (a) and (c) above into account, and so is rather inefficient. The following program has been written with the corresponding improvements in mind. (A further refinement concerns line 8∅ – can you explain it?)

1.2 *Program: Primes via products*
```
1∅ INPUT N
2∅ DIM A(N)
3∅ FOR K = 1 TO N
4∅ LET A(K) = ∅
5∅ NEXT K
```

```
 6Ø  LET M = INT(SQR(2*N + 1)) + 1
 7Ø  FOR I = 3 TO M STEP 2
 8Ø  FOR J = I TO INT((2*N + 1)/I) STEP 2
 9Ø  LET K = (I*J − 1)/2: LET A(K) = 1
1ØØ  NEXT J
11Ø  NEXT I
12Ø  FOR K = 1 TO N
13Ø  IF A(K) = Ø THEN PRINT; 2*K + 1; ",";
14Ø  NEXT K
```

One problem with this algorithm is that the array *a*(*i*) has a limited size determined by your micro's memory. On a 48K machine we have used it will list the primes between 3 and around 16 000. Since most of the numbers between 3 and 16 000 are *not* prime this is rather wasteful. How much more useful to list the first 16 000 primes (well actually 8000 since we are only storing the odd integers in our array). Another weakness is that we are asking our micro to carry out rather a lot of multiplications. In fact, it is more efficient to obtain the value of *k* in line 9Ø by repeated additions rather than products. (On one machine the running time for listing those primes < 16 000 was around five minutes for the program above. This was shortened by one or two minutes by incorporating this improvement.)

The algorithm described above is rather crude. A more refined version, with paper and pencil, is the *sieve of Eratosthenes*. One first writes down the sequence 2, 3, . . ., *n*. Next one crosses out successively 4, 6, 8, 10, . . .; i.e. 2^2 and every succeeding even number. Next delete 9, 15, 21, 27, i.e. 3^2 and then every multiple of 3 not yet deleted. The process continues by deleting 25, 35, 55, 65, . . ., i.e. 5^2 (the square of the next *remaining* number after 3) and then every multiple of 5 not yet crossed off. Continuing in this fashion we obtain a list of the prime numbers between 1 and *n*. The reader is urged to try the method out with paper and pencil before turning to his micro. Here is a program which implements Eratosthenes' method.

1.3 *Program: Sieve of Eratosthenes*
```
1Ø  INPUT N: DIM A(N)
2Ø  FOR I = 1 TO N
3Ø  LET A(I) = Ø
4Ø  NEXT I
5Ø  LET P = 1: LET Q = Ø
6Ø  FOR J = 1 TO N
7Ø  LET P = P + 2: LET Q = Q + 2*P − 2
```

```
8Ø  IF A(J) = Ø THEN PRINT; P; ","; ELSE GOTO 13Ø
9Ø  IF Q > N THEN GOTO 13Ø
1ØØ FOR K = Q TO N STEP P
11Ø LET A(K) = 1
12Ø NEXT K
13Ø NEXT J
```

You may find the program a little inscrutable: as usual to understand it better you are advised to run through its machinations with paper and pencil. You may prefer to write your own. In practice it actually does not appear to be much faster than our previous method. (It does have one psychological advantage: it starts producing the list of primes immediately, very slowly at first, but with increasing rapidity. We hope you see why.)

As we previously mentioned it would be nice to be able to obtain even longer lists of primes, so we need some method of circumventing the problem of array size. One obvious way to proceed is via the following algorithm for listing the first n primes.

First introduce an array $p(i)$, $1 \leq i \leq n$, and set $p(1) = 2$. Check 3 for divisibility by all of the current $p(i)$ (namely $p(1)$). If it is not divisible by any of them (it isn't, i.e. 2 does not divide 3) let the next term in the array $p(2) = 3$. Proceed in this way through the natural numbers. At the kth stage we have a number of primes $p(1), \ldots, p(r) < k$, and we check k for divisibility by these primes. If none of them divide k this becomes the next prime $p(r + 1)$. To save ourselves (or rather our micro) some time we can note that we need only check those $p(i)$s with $(p(i))^2 \leq k$, and, of course, the following program (as usual) does not consider even numbers as 'prime candidates'.

1.4 *Program: Primes via division*
```
1Ø  INPUT N
2Ø  DIM P(N)
3Ø  LET Z = 1: LET K = 3: LET P(1) = 3
4Ø  LET K = K + 2: LET J = Ø
5Ø  LET J = J + 1
6Ø  IF P(J)*P(J) > K THEN GOTO 9Ø
7Ø  IF K = INT(K/P(J))*P(J) THEN GOTO 4Ø
8Ø  IF J < Z THEN GOTO 5Ø
9Ø  PRINT K; ",";
1ØØ LET Z = Z + 1
11Ø LET P(Z) = K
12Ø IF Z < N THEN GOTO 4Ø
```

The main problem with this program is that it is *extraordinarily slow*! Of course it actually does a good deal more than produce a list of primes; it also computes the smallest prime factor of all the odd numbers considered. A more efficient method of producing longer lists of primes is to use modifications of one of the two programs we have already considered.

Perhaps the quickest method is to note that one can fairly easily modify Program 1.2 to print all primes lying in any *interval* of numbers of length 16 000 (or 2n). The following program prints out a list of all primes lying between r and $r + 2n + 1$ when r is *even*.

1.5 *Program: Primes via products 2*

```
1Ø INPUT R, N: DIM A(N + 1)
2Ø FOR K = 1 TO N + 1
3Ø LET A(K) = Ø
4Ø NEXT K
5Ø LET C = R + 2*N + 1: LET M = INT(SQR(C)) + 1
6Ø FOR I = 3 TO M STEP 2
7Ø LET S = 2*INT((INT(R/I) + 1)/2) + 1
8Ø IF S = 1 THEN LET S = 3
9Ø IF S > INT(C/I) THEN GOTO 13Ø
1ØØ FOR J = S TO INT(C/I) STEP 2
11Ø LET D = (I*J + 1 − R)/2: LET A(D) = 1
12Ø NEXT J
13Ø NEXT I
14Ø FOR K = 1 TO N + 1
15Ø IF A(K) = Ø THEN PRINT; R + 2*K − 1; ",";
16Ø NEXT K
```

Two remarks concerning the program are in order. The rather complicated expression in line 7Ø selects not merely the first integer s with $r + 1 \leq is$, but the first *odd* integer with this property. (Care is needed as usual when dealing with the function INT. On one machine this program crashed when we replaced division by 2 in line 7Ø with multiplication by 0.5.) The other remark is that if, by inserting a loop, you want to list all primes between 1 and $2n \times k$ for some $k \geq 2$ you can save yourself some time by leaving lines 2Ø–4Ø outside this loop, and resetting the $a(k)$ equal to zero in a new line 155.

This program is quite good at finding large primes; for example, it takes only 30 seconds on a slow machine to find the eight primes between $10^6 - 100$ and 10^6, only around 1 minute to find the nine primes between $10^7 - 100$ and 10^7, and about 3 minutes to list the five primes between $10^8 - 100$ and 10^8.

By now you should have a long list of prime numbers. Have a look at the list – what patterns do you observe? What lines of enquiry should we pursue?

1.6 *Mathematical excursion*

Before getting engrossed in detail one question may well have already occurred to you while considering the algorithms above. Are there infinitely many primes? If this question has not presented itself, it is probably because you thought it fairly obvious that there *are*. If so your intuition is correct! Can you prove this?

It was Euclid who first gave a proof of this theorem. *There are infinitely many prime numbers.*

The reasoning is so simple and beautiful we give it here. Suppose that there are only finitely many primes $p_1, \ldots, p_n$. Now consider

$$q = p_1 p_2 \ldots p_n + 1.$$

It is clearly not divisible by any of the primes $p_1, \ldots, p_n$ (because of the remainder 1 of course). Consequently the prime divisors of q provide new prime numbers, contradicting our assertion that $p_1, \ldots, p_n$ is a complete list.

Note that Euclid's proof, excellent though it is, would be so much more useful if it gave a formula for constructing a new prime from the $p_1, \ldots, p_n$. More of this later. It does predict the existence of a new prime $\leqslant p_1 p_2 \ldots p_n + 1$, but this is not a very useful estimate. Other better estimates are known. We mention only a result of Bertrand, usually referred to as Bertrand's postulate: namely for each $n \geqslant 1$ there is at least one prime satisfying $n < p \leqslant 2n$. In particular the $(r + 1)$st prime p_{r+1} is less than twice the rth prime $2p_r$.

A rather sharper result than Euclid's is the following theorem of Euler: *the sum of the reciprocals of the primes* $\Sigma 1/p = \frac{1}{2} + \frac{1}{3} + \frac{1}{5} + \frac{1}{7} + \frac{1}{11} + \ldots$ *is divergent; i.e. by taking sufficiently many terms this sum will exceed any fixed positive number.* See Hardy and Wright (1975) p. 17 for the proof (which is entirely elementary). In particular there are, of course, infinitely many terms in this series.

1.7 *Exercise*

You might like to design a program which uses Eratosthenes' method to obtain an extended list of primes, i.e. circumvents the problem of storage space discussed after Program 1.2. One possible method is to store the primes as they are produced in another array and use them to test intervals $1 \leqslant x \leqslant n$, $n + 1 \leqslant x \leqslant 2n$, $2n + 1 \leqslant x \leqslant 3n, \ldots$ for primes inductively. Of course you may have to do some juggling with array sizes, since the new array set aside for the primes naturally uses up storage space.

If, after scrutinizing your list of primes, you find that you cannot see any simple pattern emerging do not feel downhearted. Nobody else can either! The primes do appear to be rather an irregular bunch of characters. We shall start, however, by suggesting the following line of investigation. Consider the gaps between consecutive primes. How big can these gaps become? Generally the gaps do appear to get larger as we proceed further up the list. Nevertheless you may notice occasional *twin* primes, i.e. primes separated by a single non-prime. (Of course, the only possible *consecutive* primes are 2 and 3, after 3 there is always at least one non-prime separating consecutive primes.) Does this minimal gap eventually widen or are there infinitely many prime pairs?

2.1 *Gaps between consecutive primes*

The above questions concerning gaps in our list of primes could hardly be more different in their degree of difficulty. It is really rather easy to provide the following answer to our first question: the gaps between consecutive primes can be arbitrarily large. For suppose that $2, 3, 5, \ldots, p$ are the primes in ascending order to the prime p. Clearly each number up to and including p is divisible by one of these primes. Consequently if q is the product of $2, 3, 5, \ldots, p$ the $p - 1$ numbers $q + 2, q + 3, q + 4, \ldots, q + p$ are all composite, i.e. we have a gap of length at least $p - 1$.

The second problem is much deeper – indeed unsolved. You may, on the basis of an examination of your list, have conjectured that there are infinitely many twin primes ($10^6 - 39$ and $10^6 - 41$ are two such; check this!) If so congratulations; this conjecture is both famous and unsolved. At the moment there appear to be no techniques which can come near to proving this result. One *can* prove, however, that there are not too many prime pairs. Using an idea similar to the sieve of Eratosthenes (and much more besides) Brun in 1919 proved that the sum of reciprocals of twin primes

$$\frac{1}{3} + \frac{1}{5} + \frac{1}{7} + \frac{1}{11} + \frac{1}{13} + \frac{1}{17} + \frac{1}{19} + \frac{1}{29} + \frac{1}{31} + \ldots$$

is convergent. This is in contrast to Euler's result of Section 1.6 that the sum of the reciprocals of all primes is divergent. In a certain sense then Brun's result implies that twin primes are rather thin on the ground. Nevertheless, the question of whether or not the above sum has only finitely many terms remains unanswered. For a proof of Brun's result see Chapter 15 of Rademacher (1964).

2.2 *Exercises*

(a) Try writing a program which prints out all prime pairs $p, p + 2$ which lie between the integers $r, r + 2n + 1$. (Off hand we can only suggest making the obvious modification to Program 1.5. Any better ideas?)

(b) Do the same for prime quadruplets like

11, 13, 17, 19;   101, 103, 107, 109;   191, 193, 197, 199.

(Check that 9 933 611, 9 933 613, 9 933 617, 9 933 619 is such a quadruplet.) Before trying this convince yourself that we cannot have a prime quadruplet of the form n, $n + 2$, $n + 4$, $n + 6$ (and define what you mean by a prime quadruplet!).

§3
Primes and probability

Having admitted that there are no discernible patterns in our list of primes we try an alternative line of investigation. Consider the following rather simple experiment: a *fair* coin is tossed and the results of consecutive tosses noted down. The outcome of our experiment may begin HHTHTTHTTTHHTH . . . . Can we discern any pattern in this result? Generally not. Indeed hopefully not; one might almost make the lack of pattern a precondition on what we mean by a *fair* coin. So we have a random arrangement of heads and tails, no patterns; no useful observations to make? Well, one observation we can make concerns not the sequence itself but its *average long-term* behaviour. Namely the longer the experiment runs the nearer the ratio of heads to tails approaches 1.

Let us now return to our sequence of primes. What average or long-term behaviour is there to observe here? The most interesting property to consider is the growth of the number $\pi(n)$, which is defined to be the number of primes p with $1 \leqslant p \leqslant n$.

Your next task is to amend one of the previous programs to compute values of $\pi(n)$. This is fairly easily done, and you will save time of course if your new program does *not* print out a list of these primes.

3.1 *Exercise*

Having written this program you may care to examine the ratio $\pi(n)/n$ as n gets larger and larger. This ratio $\pi(n)/n$ is the chance of drawing a prime from a bucket containing the first n natural numbers. The limit of this ratio, as n gets larger and larger, represents the chance of drawing a prime from a very large bucket which contains all of the natural numbers.

3.2 *Answers and discussion*

If you run your program you should find the values of $\pi(n)$ shown in Table 1.

You will no doubt observe that the ratio $\pi(n)/n$ decreases as n gets larger and this is indeed the case. Much more is true, however: the ratio actually approaches 0. The chance of a random whole number being prime then is 0. That is a random number is *certain* not to be prime. (We will not pursue the philosophical implications of this statement; but see Knuth (1981) pp. 127–57.) It is far from clear from the numerical evidence that *the sequence*

Table 1.

n	$\pi(n)$	n	$\pi(n)$
1 001	168	60 001	6057
10 001	1229	70 001	6936
20 001	2262	80 001	7837
30 001	3245	90 001	8714
40 001	4203	100 001	9592
50 001	5133		

$\pi(n)/n$ *approaches zero as n increases*. We shall return to the lack of evidence later but first give a proof of this fact.

The proof hinges on the following result. If $p_1, p_2, p_3, \ldots$ is a list of all the primes then the infinite product $(1-1/p_1)(1-1/p_2)(1-1/p_3) \ldots$ which we denote by $\Pi(1-1/p)$ is zero.

This may seem fairly obvious, since each of the terms $(1-1/p_i)$ is less than 1 the partial products $(1-1/p_1) \ldots (1-1/p_r)$ decrease as r increases, that is as we multiply more factors together. But one should be careful, for the infinite product $(1-1/4)(1-1/9) \ldots (1-1/n^2) \ldots$ has the same property but is equal to $\frac{1}{2}$. (Prove this; it is quite easy.) We start with a non-rigorous proof that $\Pi(1-1/p) = 0$.

Let p be prime. The probability that a natural number n is not divisible by p is $(1-1/p)$. For every pth integer is divisible by p, so that the probability that a number *is* divisible by p is $1/p$, and the probability that it is *not* is $1-1/p$. If p_1 and p_2 are distinct primes the events 'n is not divisible by p_1' and 'n is not divisible by p_2' are independent. So the probability that n is divisible by neither is $(1-1/p_1)(1-1/p_2)$. Consequently the probability that any number chosen at random is divisible by none of the p_i is the infinite product $\Pi(1-1/p)$. On the other hand every number is divisible by *some* prime, so this probability is 0!

For a formal proof we consider the reciprocal $\Pi(1/(1-p^{-1}))$ and show that it gets arbitrarily large as we consider more products. This clearly implies the required result. However, the product $\Pi_{p \leqslant N}(1/(1-p^{-1}))$ is equal to $\Pi_{p \leqslant N}(1+1/p+1/p^2+\ldots)$, simply using the familiar formula for the sum of an infinite geometric progression. This second product on the other hand is the sum $\Sigma 1/n$ where the summation is over all those values of n whose prime factors are at most N. This follows from the prime factorisation result. Since all $n \leqslant N$ have prime factors $\leqslant N$ it follows that the product $\Pi(1/(1-p^{-1}))$ is at least $\Sigma_{n=1}^{N} 1/n$. As N increases the latter sum increases without bound, and the result is proved.

Now to our assertion about $\lim_{n \to \infty} \pi(n)/n$. For any natural numbers n and r we set $f(n, r)$ equal to the number of numbers x for which $1 \leqslant x \leqslant n$ and x is *not* divisible by the first r primes $p_1, \ldots, p_r$. A little thought shows that $\pi(n) \leqslant f(n, r) + r$. Now if we write $[x]$ for the largest integer $\leqslant x$ we claim that we can write $f(n, r)$ as

$$f(n, r) = n - \Sigma_i \left[\frac{n}{p_i}\right] + \Sigma_{i,j} \left[\frac{n}{p_i p_j}\right] - \ldots + (-1)^r \left[\frac{n}{p_1 p_2 \ldots p_r}\right] \qquad (1)$$

where the $i, j, \ldots$ are all distinct. This formula is obtained as follows. The term n/p_i is the number of numbers $1 \leqslant x \leqslant n$ divisible by p_i. So $[n] - \Sigma_i[n/p_i]$ is a first attempt at $f(n, r)$. Unfortunately numbers divisible by some p_i and a distinct p_j are counted twice in this sum. The third term of (1) accounts for this error, but counts twice those numbers divisible by three of the p_i's. The fourth term in (1) redresses this error and so on.

Now the number of square brackets in (1) is clearly

$$1 + \binom{r}{1} + \binom{r}{2} + \ldots + \binom{r}{r-1} + 1 = (1+1)^r = 2^r.$$

If we remove all of the square brackets in (1) above each bracket can lead to an error of at most 1, and we obtain

$$f(n, r) \leqslant n - \sum_i^n \frac{n}{p_i} + \sum_{i,j}^n \frac{n}{p_i p_j} - \ldots + (-1)^r \frac{n}{p_1 p_2 \ldots p_r} + 2^r$$

and so

$$\pi(r) \leqslant n - \sum_i^n \frac{n}{p_i} + \sum_{i,j}^n \frac{n}{p_i p_j} - \ldots + (-1)^r \frac{n}{p_1 p_2 \ldots p_r} + 2^r + r$$

$$= n \Pi_{i=1}^r (1 - p_i^{-1}) + 2^r + r.$$

Since the product $\Pi_{i=1}^r (1 - p_i^{-1})$ approaches 0 as $r \to \infty$ we see that by choosing r sufficiently large (and independent of n) we can make $\pi(n)/n \leqslant \Pi_{i=1}^r (1 - p_i^{-1}) + (2^r + r)/n$ smaller than any prescribed value. This yields the required result.

3.3 *Exercise*

Computing values of $\pi(n)$ for n much above 100 000 is likely to be too time-consuming for your micro. Gain more convincing evidence for the assertion that $\lim_{n \to \infty} (\pi(n)/n) = 0$ by finding the number of primes between 10^k and $10^k + 10^4$ say for $k = 4, 5, 6, 7$ (see below).

3.4 *Other powers*

The result $\lim_{n \to \infty} (\pi(n)/n) = 0$ is quite interesting but does not give us much information on how quickly or slowly $\pi(n)$ grows. Instead of considering the quotients $\pi(n)/n$ you may like to consider $\pi(n^2)/n$. Does this have a non-zero limit as n gets larger and larger? If for example $\lim_{n \to \infty} (\pi(n^2)/n) = 5$ this would tell us that there are, for large n, about $5n$ primes between 1 and n^2.

3.5 *Exercise*

Investigate the ratio $\pi(n^2)/n$ for large n (or easier $\pi(n)/\sqrt{n}$). Does this approach any limit as n gets large? Do the same for other powers, e.g. $\pi(n^{3/2})/n$, $\pi(n^{11/10})/n$.

3.6 *Answers and discussion*

In contrast to the behaviour of the ratio $\pi(n)/n$, the limit $\pi(n^2)/n$ as n gets large is non-zero, indeed this quotient tends to infinity. In

Table 2.

n	$\pi(n)$	$n/\ln n$	n	$\pi(n)$	$n/\ln n$
1 001	168	155	60 001	6057	5454
10 001	1229	1086	70 001	6936	6275
20 001	2262	2020	80 001	7837	7086
30 001	3245	2910	90 001	8714	7890
40 001	4203	3775	100 001	9592	8686
50 001	5133	4621			

other words for large n there are *many* more than n primes between 1 and n^2. In fact if you recall that $\Pi(1 - 1/n^2) = \frac{1}{2}$ and $\Pi(1 - 1/p) = 0$ a little thought should convince you that this is entirely reasonable. Indeed for any power $k > 1$ the quotient $\pi(n^k)/n$ tends to infinity as n increases – recall that we have already proved that for $k = 1$ the quotient has limit zero. Again you will find numerical evidence to support these assertions rather hard to come by.

There is a quite precise result, however, which describes the growth of $\pi(n)$, the number of primes $\leq n$ for n large, and is considered one of the most beautiful results of all mathematics.

3.7 *The Prime Number Theorem*
The limit as n increases of $\pi(n)/(n/\ln n)$ is 1. In other words for large n there are approximately $n/\ln n$ primes p with $p \leq n$. (The logarithm here note is the natural logarithm or logarithm to the base e.) In Table 2 we compare the values of $n/\ln n$ and $\pi(n)$, where the former has been rounded to the nearest integer. Again you will see that the numerical evidence for the Prime Number Theorem is hardly convincing, for $\pi(n)$ seems to be consistently larger than $n/\ln n$; indeed $n/10$ seems almost as good an approximation to $\pi(n)$ as $n/\ln n$ is! The reason for this is not very difficult to find. The function $\ln n$ grows *very* slowly; you can easily check the following on your micro:

$$\ln 10^3 = 6.90 \ldots, \quad \ln 10^4 = 9.21 \ldots, \quad \ln 10^5 = 11.51 \ldots$$
$$\ln 10^9 = 20.72 \ldots.$$

In particular, as n ranges from 10 000 to 100 000 the function $\ln n$ is more or less 10 which explains why $\pi(n)$ is about $n/10$ above. We would have to start counting primes out at 10^9 before we expected to see half as many as occur on average in the range 10^4–10^5. Computing $\pi(10^9)$, however, is not a practical proposition, even with a micro. To find more convincing evidence to support the Prime Number Theorem we suggest you do the following.

3.8 *Exercise*

Compute the number of primes lying in the intervals 10^4 to $10^4 + 10^4$, 10^5 to $10^5 + 10^4$, 10^6 to $10^6 + 10^4$, 10^7 to $10^7 + 10^4$. Do your results support the validity of the Prime Number Theorem? (Or have all the mathematicians got it wrong?)

(*Answer*   We found (about!) 931 primes in the first range, 861 in the second, 753 in the third and 614 in the last. Since ln n is more or less constant within each range the Prime Number Theorem predicts about $10^4/\ln 10^k$ primes in the range 10^k to $10^k + 10^4$, and these are, for $k = 4, 5, 6, 7$ respectively 1085, 869, 724, 620 when rounded. This is indeed more convincing evidence. Indeed misleadingly so! What are the predicted values if we do not assume ln n constant within each range?)

Given the discussion above it seems quite amazing that the Prime Number Theorem was first conjectured in 1792 by a 15-year-old schoolboy. The schoolboy in question was Carl Friedrich Gauss, one of the greatest mathematicians to have ever lived, but the conjecture proved too difficult for him (throughout his life – not just as a 15-year-old) and it was 1896 before it was finally established, independently by Hadamard and de la Vallée Poussin. We cannot resist setting an earlier weaker form due to Chebyshev as an exercise. Of course, it is a horribly hard exercise.

3.9 *Exercise*

Prove the following version of Chebyshev's result. For $n \geqslant 2$ we have

$$\tfrac{1}{2}(n/\ln n) \leqslant \pi(n) \leqslant 4(n/\ln n).$$

Without hints this is not merely hard – it is impossible. For hints see Cohn (1982), p. 38.

§4
Formulae for primes

Having spent some time and energy producing lengthy lists of primes it is natural to ask if we might not have been able to get our hands on them a little more easily. For example:

     (*a*) Is there a formula $f(n)$ involving the unknown n which on substitution of 1, 2, 3 ..., for n yields *all of the* prime numbers 2, 3, 5, 7, 11, . . . ?

Maybe this is too much to ask. What about:

     (*b*) Is there a formula $f(n)$ which yields *only* prime numbers for $n = 1, 2, 3, \ldots$?

or weaker still:

     (*c*) Is there a formula $f(n)$ which yields *infinitely many* prime numbers?

(Concerning question (*b*) the reader may care to consider the functions $f_1(n) = n^2 - n + 41$, $f_2(n) = n^2 - 79n + 1601$ ($= f_1(n - 39)$) introduced by Euler. Concerning (*c*), if you find yourself struggling to answer this you are missing the point.)

4.1 *Mathematical excursion*

You should have observed that $n^2 - n + 41$ yields primes for $0 \leqslant n \leqslant 40$, but not of course for $n = 41$. The second formula yields primes for $0 \leqslant n \leqslant 79$, but not for $n = 80$. (What are the factors?) It turns out that this is inevitable because of the following result.

4.2 *Theorem*

No polynomial $f(n)$ of degree $\geqslant 1$ with integral coefficients can be prime for all n, nor even for all sufficiently large n (i.e. eventually).

Proof   Let $f(n)$ be a polynomial. Changing the sign of f we may suppose that the coefficient of the leading power of n is positive. Since f is dominated by this term for large n, we find that $f(n)$ increases without bound as n gets larger. In particular, for suitably large n (say $n > N$) we have $f(n) > 1$. Now if $x > N$ and $f(x) = a_0 x^k + \ldots = y > 1$ then

$$f(x + ry) = a_0(x + ry)^k + \ldots = f(x) + y(\ldots)$$

is clearly divisible by y for every integer r. Moreover, $f(x + ry)$ increases without bound as r gets larger so there are infinitely many values of $f(n)$ which are divisible by y, and hence not prime.

What if we allow more complicated functions? For instance polynomials in two or more variables, like $f(n_1, n_2) = n_1^2 - 3n_1 n_2 + 5$. A slight modification of the above argument shows that no non-constant such polynomial will output prime numbers only.

If we move away from polynomials and allow ourselves the luxury of exponential functions there seems more hope of finding an example of the type sought in question (*b*). In fact there is a famous (and unfortunate) conjecture of Fermat in this direction. The basic idea is that it seems plausible that one will obtain prime (or at least prime-ish) numbers by adding or subtracting 1 from an integer which has many factors. Fermat (whom we have come across before) considered the numbers $2^n + 1$. For which values of n are these prime? (Check your list of primes.)

It is easy to see that if $2^n + 1$ is to be prime then n itself must be a power of 2. For if n contains an odd factor r, say $n = rs$, then $2^n + 1$ can be factored as a product $(2^{(r-1)s} - 2^{(r-2)s} + \ldots + 1)(2^s + 1)$.

Fermat conjectured that conversely if $n = 2^m$ for some m then $F_m = 2^n + 1$ is a prime. You can easily check that this is so for $m = 1$, 2, 3, 4. In 1732, however, Euler showed that the fifth Fermat number $F_5 = 2^{32} + 1$ was composite, indeed $F_5 = 641 \times 6\,700\,417$. Euler's achievement, of course, was not verifying that the two sides of this equality are equal, but finding the factors of F_5. This verification is nevertheless probably a non-trivial exercise on your micro. (Why?) Here is an indirect proof that 641 is a factor of F_5.

First note that $641 = 2^4 + 5^4 = 5 \times 2^7 + 1$. Consequently

$$2^{32} = 2^4 \times 2^{28} = (641 - 5^4) \times 2^{28} = 641a - (5 \times 2^7)^4$$
$$= 641a - (641 - 1)^4 = 641b - 1,$$

for some integers a and b. For a *direct* verification that F_6 is composite see §6. No prime F_m has been found beyond F_4, so Fermat's conjecture proved to be rather a disaster. A far more successful source of primes are the integers $2^n - 1$ considered by Mersenne. If n factors as a product rs it is not difficult to see that $2^r - 1$ is a factor of $2^n - 1$, so we need only consider the integers $M_p = 2^p - 1$ for p prime. You can check that M_p *is* prime for $p = 2, 3,$ 5, 7 but M_{11} is composite so it certainly is *not* true that M_p is prime for all prime p. Nevertheless the integers M_p are a source of very large primes. For example $2^{11213} - 1$ is a prime. You might well check that 11 213 is prime but we advise *against* a direct verification that $2^{11213} - 1$ is prime, for this number has 3375 digits. A little later, in §5, we shall discuss Mersenne primes in greater detail.

So far then our attempts to provide a formula which only produces prime numbers have failed. If we move on to question (*c*), above and only ask that our formula produces infinitely many primes then clearly $f(n) = n$ will do(!), as will $f(n) = 2n + 1$. It is a little more difficult to show that $f(n) = 4n + 1$ or $6n + 5$ will also produce infinitely many primes (see Davenport (1982), pp. 35, 36). It is true, but more difficult still to prove that $f(n) = 4n + 3$ or $6n + 1$ will also do the trick.

4.3 *Exercise*
Write a program which lists the first 1000 or so primes of the form $4n + 1$, $4n + 3$, $6n + 1$, $6n + 5$.

A wonderful theorem of Dirichlet asserts a far more general result than those mentioned above.

Dirichlet's Theorem
Let a and b be coprime natural numbers i.e. hcf(a, b) = 1. Then the formula $f(n) = a + nb$ yields infinitely many primes.
In other words the arithmetic progression a, $a + b$, $a + 2b$, $a + 3b$, . . . contains infinitely many primes.

Dirichlet's proof was a watershed in the theory of numbers, for it made use of powerful techniques from calculus, and marked the birth of *analytic* number theory. No other such general result is known, and the reader can make him or herself famous by proving or disproving the assertion: there are infinitely many primes in the sequence 1, 5, 10, 17, 26, 37, . . . (here $f(n) = n^2 + 1$). (A proof of Dirichlet's Theorem is really too difficult for a book of this sort. Nevertheless you might like to glance through that given in Rademacher (1964) pp. 121–36. If nothing else it might well give you a new respect for nineteenth-century man; they *may* have known less than we do, but their wits were every bit as sharp as ours.)

4.4 *Exercises*

(a)   As previously mentioned, Euler's formula $f_1(n) = n^2 - n + 41$ yields primes for $0 \leqslant n \leqslant 40$ but a composite number when $n = 41$. We now know that no polynomial function will yield only primes. Do some formulae yield more primes than others though? For what proportion of values of n is $f_1(n)$ prime? As far as we are aware it is unknown if the sequence $f_1(n)$ yields infinitely many primes. Nevertheless it *is* known that for the generator $g_1(n) = n^2 + n + 41$ exactly half of the first 2398 values are prime; indeed the proportion of primes in the first 10 000 000 values is 0.475 . . . . What proportion of the first 2397 values of f_1 are prime? (Don't rush to your computer!)

(b)   Using your micro try verifying the first assertion concerning the generator g_1.

(c)   The mathematician Stanislaw Ulam noticed a rather remarkable fact concerning prime numbers when doodling at a conference. Given a piece of squared paper we can number these squares in a spiral as shown in Fig. 1. Suppose we shade in those squares labelled by a prime number. Do we expect to see any pattern? Given that the primes appear to be a rather

Fig. 1
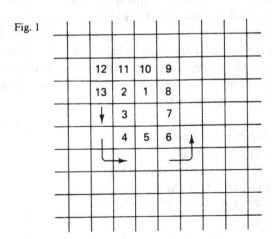

random collection of integers one might expect not. Amazingly there are, however, discernible patterns in the result: primes tend to cluster in straight lines! Write a program which places a dot at prime points of a 100×100 grid. As a help towards understanding this phenomenon you might also like to plot out *all* values of $f_1(n)$ (as in Exercise 4.4(*a*)) which lie inside this grid.

(*d*)   Actually there *do* exist formulae, of a sort, which yield all of the primes, and take no other values. One such, pointed out by Keith Devlin in the *Guardian*, is as follows.

First define a function k of two integer variables m, n (with $m \geqslant 1$, $n > 1$) by

$$k = (n - 1)! + 1 - mn$$

and then set

$$p = \tfrac{1}{2}(n - 2)\{|k^2 - 1| - (k^2 - 1)\} + 2.$$

One can show that p takes all prime values, as m and n vary, and no others. You might try running a program implementing this algorithm – if only to persuade yourself that it is not a very useful method of listing the primes. You might also like to prove the above assertion. (The key step is Wilson's Theorem mentioned in Chapter 1 (Section 8.13). Indeed one needs to use Wilson's Theorem and its converse: namely p is prime if and only if $(p - 1)! \equiv -1 \pmod{p}$.)

4.5 *Solution to Problem 4.4(c)*

The following program plots out the points in the plane corresponding to prime integers lying between 1 and n^2. The values of a, b specify, in screen coordinates, the starting point for the spiral. As written, consecutive points of this spiral have one screen coordinate in common and the other differs by 1. The resulting distance between consecutive points may be too small, so you may wish to alter the increments in u and v specified in lines 22Ø, 26Ø, 31Ø and 35Ø. One final point: our program first finds all primes between 1 and n^2 and then starts plotting these points out, so if nothing appears on the screen for a few minutes don't be dismayed.)

4.6 *Program: Prime grid*

```
1Ø  INPUT N, A, B
2Ø  LET M = N * N: DIM A(M)
3Ø  FOR K = 1 TO M
4Ø  LET A(K) = Ø
5Ø  NEXT K
```

```
 6∅  FOR I = 2 TO N
 7∅  FOR J = I TO INT(M/I)
 8∅  LET A(I * J) = 1
 9∅  NEXT J
1∅∅  NEXT I
2∅∅  LET K = 1: LET U = A: LET V = B: LET J = ∅
21∅  FOR I = 1 TO K
22∅  LET V = V − 1: LET J = J + 1: IF J > M THEN
       GOTO 4∅∅
23∅  IF A(J) = ∅ THEN put a dot at screen point (u, v)
24∅  NEXT I
25∅  FOR I = 1 TO K
26∅  LET U = U + 1: LET J = J + 1: IF J > M THEN
       GOTO 4∅∅
27∅  IF A(J) = ∅ THEN put a dot at screen point (u, v)
28∅  NEXT I
29∅  LET K = K + 1
3∅∅  FOR I = 1 TO K
31∅  LET V = V + 1: LET J = J + 1: IF J > M THEN
       GOTO 4∅∅
32∅  IF A(J) = ∅ THEN put a dot at screen point (u, v)
33∅  NEXT I
34∅  FOR I = 1 TO K
35∅  LET U = U − 1: LET J = J + 1: IF J > M THEN
       GOTO 4∅∅
36∅  IF A(J) = ∅ THEN put a dot at screen point (u, v)
37∅  NEXT I
38∅  LET K = K + 1
39∅  GOTO 21∅
4∅∅  END
```

The result of running Program 4.6 using a fairly large value of *n* is shown in Figure 2. Note the promised (especially diagonal) straight lines. Can you locate the number 1 on the diagram?

§5
Large prime numbers

We know that the list of primes is infinite, but it appears that there is no way of writing down this list in an explicit form. One consequence of these two facts has been the quest for large primes. Large numbers have a certain fascination all of their own, and an enormous amount of energy and money (= computer time) has been expended in the search for large primes.

To prove that an integer *p* is prime of course we need only check that it is not divisible by any natural number $n \le \sqrt{p}$, and, naturally,

Fig. 2

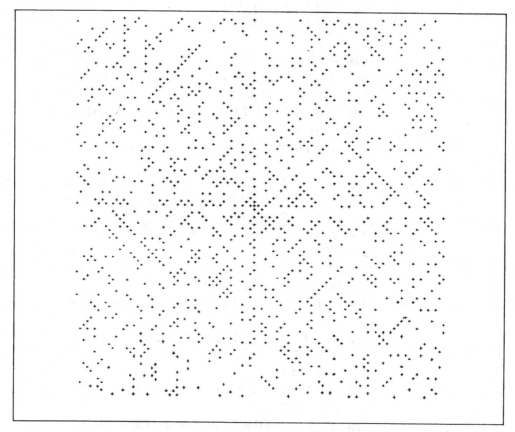

it is easy to construct computer programs which run such checks. So there seems to be no problem; we should be able to produce lots and lots of primes simply by running such programs. By now, however, you should know that there *is* a problem. Computers are fast (micros fastish) but they are far from instantaneous. We have seen (Program 1.4) that checking relatively small numbers for factors is a rather slow business. Even a computer which could do a million divisions a second (yours probably can't!) would take longer than the age of the universe to determine a prime with 50 digits. Yet we have already mentioned one prime with 3375 digits ($M_{11\,213} = 2^{11\,213} - 1$), and this is far from being a record. In 1971 Tuckerman showed that the Mersenne number $M_{19\,937} = 2^{19\,937} - 1$ was prime, a number with 6002 digits. In 1978 (here is some encouragement) two high school students, Nickel and Noll, showed that $M_{23\,209}$ is prime. In 1981 Slowinski proved that $M_{44\,497}$ is prime; this number has 13 395 digits .... The quest continues.

Given that even the mighty computer has its limits, how were these

Mersenne numbers shown to be prime? The answer is that there is a specific test that one can apply to the Mersenne numbers, the so-called Lucas–Lehmer primality test.

5.1 *Lucas–Lehmer primality test*
Define a sequence of integers S_k by $S_1 = 4$ and $S_k = S_{k-1}^2 - 2$ for $k > 1$. Then the Mersenne number $M_n = 2^n - 1$ is prime if and only if M_n divides S_{n-1}.

For a proof see Hardy and Wright (1975) pp. 223–5, or Knuth (1981) pp. 356–9. An elementary proof that M_n is prime if M_n divides S_{n-1} is given in Brace (1993). Since the test only concerns the divisibility of S_{n-1} by M_n clearly after computing each S_k we can reduce modulo M_n. That is, it is more convenient to define a sequence L_k of integers with $0 \leqslant L_k < M_n$ by

$$L_1 = 4, \quad L_k \equiv L_{k-1}^2 - 2 \pmod{M_n},$$

and check if $L_{n-1} = 0$. This is quite an improvement since the S_ks grow exceedingly rapidly. (You can check that $S_4 = 37\,634$; in fact it is clear from its definition that S_k is roughly 2^{2^k}.)

Let us now see how this test works in practice. We start by doing one computation by hand. Take $n = 7$ and the Mersenne number $2^7 - 1 = 127$ (recall from §4 that n must be prime if the Mersenne number M_n is to be prime). Here $L_1 = 4$, $L_1^2 - 2 = 4^2 - 2 = 14$ so $L_2 = 14$, $L_2^2 - 2 = 14^2 - 2 = 194 \equiv 67 \pmod{127}$, $L_3 = 67$; $L_3^2 - 2 = 4487 \equiv 42 \pmod{127}$, $L_4 = 42$; $L_4^2 - 2 = 1762 \equiv 111 \pmod{127}$, $L_5 = 111$; $L_5^2 - 2 = 12319 \equiv 0 \pmod{127}$, $L_6 = 0$ and $M_7 = 127$ passes the primality test.

Having done this trial computation you will notice that we have to consider numbers around the size of M_n^2 when determining the sequence L_k. If you write a short program you can quickly verify that the first 26 Mersenne numbers are

1, 3, 7, 15, 31, 63, 127, 255, 511, 1023, 2047, 4095, 8191, 16 383, 32 767, 65 535, 131 071, 262 143, 524 287, 1 048 575, 2 097 151, 4 194 303, 8 388 607, 16 777 215, 33 554 431, 67 108 863,

so that the above method runs into problems with any Mersenne number beyond M_{12}. The point is that one must then expect to have to deal with nine digit numbers and beyond, and your micro probably cannot store such integers exactly. It cannot even deal with the Mersenne numbers themselves beyond M_{26}. Clearly what we need is high precision arithmetic, i.e. some method of adding, subtracting, multiplying and dividing numbers with a large number of digits. This is the topic we turn to next.

5.2 *Exercise*
Write a program which uses the Lucas–Lehmer test to check M_2, M_3, M_5, M_7, and M_{11} for primality.

§6
Large numbers and multiple precision arithmetic

In this section we shall give some programs which enable us to carry out the standard arithmetic operations on (more or less) arbitrarily large numbers. Of course, as stated before, the main problem we have is that our micro can only deal with around eight figure arithmetic; integers with a larger number of digits are stored in principal part/exponent form and are essentially rounded. We shall overcome this problem by storing large integers as sequences or arrays; we need to define the usual arithmetic operations on these resulting arrays. The required programs are some of the most complicated which appear in this book, but we think that the effort is well worthwhile. There is a certain satisfaction to be gained from multiplying two 20 digit numbers in one second (!) or checking that $2^{101} - 1$ is not prime.

The basic idea is as follows: we can represent an n digit number $a = a_n a_{n-1} a_{n-2} \ldots a_2 a_1$ by the array $a(i) = a_i$, $1 \leqslant i \leqslant n$. Thus

$$a = a(1) + a(2) \times 10 + a(3) \times 10^2 + \ldots + a(n) \times 10^{n-1}.$$

Suppose we wish to add two such numbers a and b; we shall suppose that they both have n digits, but allow the possibility that the $a(i)$ or $b(i)$ are eventually zero. (Thus 7 can be thought of as a three digit number 007.) To add the two numbers

$$a = a(1) + a(2) \times 10 + \ldots + a(n) \times 10^{n-1}$$

and

$$b = b(1) + b(2) \times 10 + \ldots + b(n) \times 10^{n-1},$$

we simply use the standard method we all learned at primary school. So $a(1)$ and $b(1)$ are first added and then we write down the first digit of the resulting sum, which will be the first digit of $a + b$, and bring forward a carry figure x which is 1 or 0 depending on whether $a(1) + b(1)$ is > 9 or $\leqslant 9$. We now form the sum $a(2) + b(2) + x$; its first digit will be the second digit of $a + b$, and again we will have a carry figure x to bring forward. The process then repeats in the obvious way. One point to note: the sum of two n digit numbers generally has $n + 1$ digits so we must be careful to allow for this in our output. We have rather dodged this difficulty below by supposing we are adding two $n - 1$ digit numbers together. So when using this program take n to be one greater than the number of digits in a and b and take $a(n) = b(n) = 0$. (Of course this defect is easily corrected but we will need the version below later.)

We hope by now that the following program is clear.

6.1 *Program: Addition*

```
1Ø INPUT N
2Ø DIM A(N): DIM B(N): DIM C(N)
3Ø FOR I = 1 TO N
4Ø INPUT A(I)
5Ø NEXT I
6Ø FOR I = 1 TO N
7Ø INPUT B(I)
8Ø NEXT I

2Ø1Ø LET X = Ø
2Ø2Ø FOR I = 1 TO N
2Ø3Ø LET W = A(I) + B(I) + X
2Ø4Ø LET X = INT(W/1Ø)
2Ø5Ø LET C(I) = W − 1Ø*X
2Ø6Ø NEXT I

2Ø7Ø FOR I = 1 TO N
2Ø8Ø PRINT; C(N + 1 − I);
2Ø9Ø NEXT I
```

Note the integers a and b are read in from right to left; their sum c is printed out in standard form. If you prefer to read your numbers in from left to right replace A(I) in line 4Ø by A(N + 1 − I) and similarly for B(I) in line 7Ø.

Before proceeding to the other mathematical operations we make one observation that will greatly speed up the running of the above program. To carry out standard addition we essentially need to memorize the 'addition tables', i.e. the sums of all pairs of digits between 0 and 9. This is needed in line 2Ø3Ø above in our program, and we are, of course, using the fact that our micro can do such additions. But actually our micro has a much better memory than we have, it has access to the addition tables for sums of pairs of digits between 0 and $10^7 - 1$ (at least). Can we make use of this facility in the program above? The answer is yes of course! Let us suppose that exact eight figure arithmetic is possible on your micro. This means that we can certainly add *and* multiply four figure numbers exactly.

Consequently instead of storing our integers as arrays of single digits it will be more efficient to store them as arrays of four figure numbers. Thus if a is an integer with $a < 10^{4n}$ we can represent it as a sequence $a(1)$, $a(2)$, . . ., $a(n)$ of four figure numbers with

$$a = a(1) + a(2) \times 10^4 + a(3) \times 10^8 + \ldots + a(n) \times 10^{4(n-1)}.$$

(If your micro cannot do exact eight figure arithmetic work to the 'base' 1000.) The same method as before will now allow us to add two numbers expressed in this form together. In fact we simply replace lines 2040 and 2050 of our original program by

```
2040 LET X = INT(W/10000)
2050 LET C(I) = W − 10000*X
```

One point to note: it is possible that some of the four digit parts of the integers a, b and c will be less than 1000, i.e. have three or fewer digits. This is not important when inputting the summands a and b; the computer will recognise 0123 as 123. You may like to modify the output, however, by replacing lines 2070–2090 of our program with the following:

```
2070 FOR I = 1 TO N
2080 IF C(N + 1 − I) < 10 THEN PRINT; "000";: GOTO 2110
2090 IF C(N + 1 − I) < 100 THEN PRINT; "00";: GOTO 2110
2100 IF C(N + 1 − I) < 1000 THEN PRINT; "0";: GOTO 2110
2110 PRINT; C(N + 1 − I);
2120 NEXT I
```

Having dealt with addition it is not difficult to write a program for subtraction. The following program subtracts a number $e = e(n)e(n-1) \ldots e(1)$ from the number $d = d(n)d(n-1) \ldots d(1)$; the program assumes that $d \geq e$. We leave you to make the necessary improvements to make use of the four (or larger) digit subtraction available on your micro.

6.2 *Program: Subtraction*

```
10 INPUT N
20 DIM D(N): DIM E(N): DIM F(N)
30 FOR I = 1 TO N
40 INPUT D(I)
50 NEXT I
60 FOR I = 1 TO N
70 INPUT E(I)
80 NEXT I
```

```
3010 LET X = 0
3020 FOR I = 1 TO N
3030 LET W = D(I) − E(I) + X + 10
3040 LET Y = INT(W/10)
3050 LET F(I) = W − 10 * Y
3060 LET X = Y − 1
3070 NEXT I
3080 FOR I = 1 TO N
3090 PRINT; F(N + 1 − I);
3100 NEXT I
```

To help you to decipher this program we note that x keeps track of whether or not a carry figure has been used at the previous stage. Thus $x = 0$ if $y = 1$, which is so precisely when the difference $d(i) − e(i) + x \geq 0$ (no need for a carry) and $x = − 1$ if $y = 0$, which happens when $d(i) − e(i) + x < 0$, and a carry is required.

Next we consider multiplication; this is a little more difficult but the basic idea is simple enough: namely

$$(g(1) + g(2) \times 10 + \ldots + g(n) \times 10^{n-1})$$
$$\times (h(1) + h(2) \times 10 + \ldots + h(m) \times 10^{m-1})$$
$$= g(1)h(1) + (g(2)h(1) + g(1)h(2)) \times 10$$
$$+ (g(3)h(1) + g(2)h(2) + g(1)h(3)) \times 10^2 +$$
$$\ldots + g(n)h(m) \times 10^{m+n-2}$$

or more succinctly

$$\left(\sum_{i=1}^{n} g(i) \times 10^{i-1} \right) \left(\sum_{j=1}^{m} h(j) \times 10^{j-1} \right)$$

$$= \sum_{k=1}^{m+n-1} \left(\sum_{i+j=k+1} g(i)h(j) \right) \times 10^{k-1},$$

using summation notation. Writing x_k for the coefficient of the 10^{k-1} term in the above product (the sum $\Sigma_{i+j=k+1} g(i)h(j)$) the main problem we have is that this is no longer a single digit number. We rewrite x_k in the form $10r_k + s_k$ with $0 \leq s_k < 9$. Clearly the initial term of the product is s_1. We then write $s_2 + r_1$ in the form $10t_2 + u_2$. Clearly u_2 is the tens digit of the product and we next consider $s_3 + r_2 + t_2$, write this in the form $10t_3 + u_3$ and take u_3 for our hundreds digit. The process then continues.

Here is a program for multiplying the numbers $g(n)g(n − 1) \ldots g(1)$ and $h(m)h(m − 1) \ldots h(1)$. Note in lines 40 and 100 we have arranged for these numbers to be read in from left to right.

6.3 *Program: Multiplication*

```
 10 INPUT N, M
 20 DIM G(N + M): DIM H(N + M): DIM P(N + M)
 30 FOR I = 1 TO N
 40 INPUT G(N + 1 − I)
 50 NEXT I
 60 FOR I = N + 1 TO N + M
 70 LET G(I) = 0
 80 NEXT I
 90 FOR I = 1 TO M
100 INPUT H(M + 1 − I)
110 NEXT I
120 FOR I = M + 1 TO N + M
130 LET H(I) = 0
140 NEXT I
150 LET T = 0: LET R = 0
160 FOR K = 1 TO N + M
170 LET T1 = T: LET R1 = R
180 LET X = G(1)*H(K)
190 IF K = 1 THEN GOTO 230
200 FOR I = 2 TO K
210 LET X = X + G(I)*H(K + 1 − I)
220 NEXT I
230 LET R = INT(X/10)
240 LET S = X − 10*R
250 LET Y = S + R1 + T1
260 LET T = INT(Y/10)
270 LET U = Y − 10*T
280 LET P(K) = U
290 NEXT K
300 FOR I = 1 TO N + M
310 PRINT; P(M + N + 1 − I);
370 NEXT I
```

Again to make use of the computer's fast multiplication of four digit numbers only slight modifications are required. Namely in lines 230, 240, 260, 270 the number 10 is replaced by 10 000 and line 310 is replaced by

```
310 LET D = P(M + N + 1 − I)
320 IF D = 0 THEN PRINT; "0000";: GOTO 370
330 IF D < 10 THEN PRINT; "000"; D;: GOTO 370
340 IF D < 100 THEN PRINT; "00"; D;: GOTO 370
350 IF D < 1000 THEN PRINT; "0"; D;: GOTO 370
360 PRINT; D;
```

You can now use this program to check that the Mersenne number $M_{101} = 2^{101} - 1$ is *not* prime. In fact show that

$$M_{101} = 7\,432\,339\,208\,719 \times 341\,117\,531\,003\,194\,129.$$

The product is now easily obtainable: you should get $2\,535\,301\,200\,456\,458\,802\,993\,406\,410\,751$ as the answer. How does one prove that this number is indeed $2^{101} - 1$? The efficient way to proceed here is as follows. Consider the powers

$$2^1, \quad (2^1)^2 = 2^2, \quad (2^2)^2 = 2^4, \quad (2^4)^2 = 2^8, \quad (2^8)^2 = 2^{16}, \quad (2^{16})^2 = 2^{32},$$
$$(2^{32})^2 = 2^{64}.$$

Repeatedly squaring six times one obtains 2^{64}, i.e. one evaluates 2^{64} using only six multiplications. Since $101 = 64 + 32 + 4 + 1$ we can write $2^{101} = 2^{64} \times 2^{32} \times 2^4 \times 2$. The additional factors in this product have already been found and so the evaluation of 2^{101} requires a total of nine multiplications, and many of these do not require high precision arithmetic. One now finds

$$2^1 = 2, \quad 2^2 = 4, \quad 2^4 = 16, \quad 2^8 = 256, \quad 2^{16} = 65\,536,$$
$$2^{32} = 4\,294\,967\,296, \qquad 2^{64} = 18\,446\,744\,073\,709\,551\,616,$$
$$2^{32} \times 2^4 \times 2 = 137\,438\,953\,472$$

and

$$2^{101} = 2^{64} \times (2^{32} \times 2^4 \times 2)$$
$$= 2\,535\,301\,200\,456\,458\,802\,993\,406\,410\,752$$

as required. We shall return to this question of how to compute powers efficiently later.

6.4 *Exercise*
Check that $2^{2^6} + 1 = 274\,177 \times 67\,280\,421\,310\,721$.

At this stage a few remarks are in order. First you will have noticed that there was a jump in the numbering of lines in our programs for addition and subtraction. In Program 6.1 for example the jump occurs at line 8∅. The reason is that we shall need lines 2∅1∅–2∅6∅ as a subroutine in our later programs. It is in these lines that the real work of addition is carried out. Similarly in Program 6.2 lines 3∅1∅–3∅7∅ will be used as a subroutine. The problem with Program 6.3 is that for convenience we have read in the number of digits of g and h. Later it will be much *more* convenient to do our arithmetic with integers having a fixed number of digits. In other words our arrays will have a fixed dimension n. We shall use the following as a subroutine for multiplying two n digit numbers together (some of the leading digits being 0) to obtain an n digit output.

6.5 *Program: Multiplication subroutine*

```
4000 LET R = 0: LET T = 0
4010 FOR K = 1 TO N
4020 LET U = T: LET V = R: LET X = G(1)*H(K)
4030 IF K = 1 THEN GOTO 4070
4040 FOR I = 2 TO K
4050 LET X = X + G(I)*H(K + 1 - I)
4060 NEXT I
4070 LET R = INT(X/10): LET S = X - 10*R
4080 LET Y = S + U + V
4090 LET T = INT(Y/10): LET W = Y - 10*T
4100 LET P(K) = W
4110 NEXT K
```

Of course when used as a subroutine we need to add a final line (4120 RETURN). The same is true for the subroutines for addition and subtraction. We next consider the question of division. This is a considerably more difficult problem and we will devote a section to its solution.

§7
Division

Finally we come to the algorithm for division. If you ponder a while on the process of long division you will understand why this program will be the longest in this book. To implement the long division algorithm of our junior school days one needs to make estimates (= inspired guesses) and carry out the processes of multiplication and subtraction. Of course of these three ingredients the inspired guess is the most difficult.

The basic idea is quite simple. Suppose we wish to divide $q = q(b) q(b - 1) q(b - 2) \ldots q(1)$ by $r = r(a) r(a - 1) \ldots r(1)$, and suppose further that $b > a$. The key step in the whole process is to make a good guess at the leading digit s in this quotient. For example when dividing 237 114 by 622 this leading digit s is 3. Once a choice of s is made, 3 in this case, we take the first $(a + 1)$ digits of q, 2371 and subtract rs, i.e. 3×622. This difference $2371 - 3 \times 622 = 505$ is then taken as the leading part of the new number q to be divided. We hope that the following makes this clear

```
             3..
         _____
     622│237114
         1866
         ____
          505
         _____
         │50514│ ← new number q.
```

When doing long division by hand we always choose the exact value for s, but this is not a trivial problem, as you can discover for yourself by noting carefully the choices involved when doing a few concrete examples. One other observation: by repeating the above process we have essentially reduced the general problem to the cases $b = a + 1$ or a i.e. the problem of dividing a number with a or $a + 1$ digits by a second with only a digits. The division of 237 114 by 622 is an illustration of the second case; the division of 837 114 by 622 shows how the first case might arise. By choosing the leading digit to be zero in the first case we can reduce it to the second so it is this we now analyse. Thus we take $q = q(a + 1)q(a) \ldots q(1), r = r(a)r(a - 1) \ldots r(1)$ and suppose that $q(a + 1)q(a) \ldots q(2) < r$ so that division does produce a single digit answer.

The choice of leading digit s we shall use is that described by Knuth (1981) pp. 235–40; indeed our program is merely an implementation of the algorithm he gives. The most obvious method of choosing the leading digit s is to use the first couple of digits of q and r as the basis for one's guess. Knuth suggests taking

$$\hat{s} = \min\{\text{int}((10q(a + 1) + q(a))/r(a)), 9\}$$

as an estimate for s. Thus $\hat{s}$ is obtained by dividing the two leading digits of q by the leading digit of r. If the result is 9 or more we replace it by 9.

We now prove, following Knuth, that the estimate for $\hat{s}$ is never too small, i.e. $\hat{s} \geqslant s$, where s is the true value of the quotient. Since $s \leqslant 9$ this is clearly true when $\hat{s} = 9$, so we may suppose that $\hat{s} \leqslant 8$ and $\hat{s} = \text{int}((10q(a + 1) + q(a))/r(a))$. Clearly $\hat{s} r(a) \geqslant 10 q(a + 1) + q(a) - r(a) + 1$ and so

$$
\begin{aligned}
q - \hat{s}r &\leqslant q - \hat{s}r(a) \times 10^{a-1} \\
&\leqslant q(a + 1) \times 10^a + q(a) \times 10^{a-1} + \ldots + q(1) \\
&\quad - (q(a + 1) \times 10^a + q(a) \times 10^{a-1} - r(a) \times 10^{a-1} + 10^{a-1}) \\
&= q(a - 1) \times 10^{a-2} + \ldots + q(1) - 10^{a-1} + r(a) \times 10^{a-1} \\
&< r(a) \times 10^{a-1} \leqslant r.
\end{aligned}
$$

Since $q - \hat{s}r \leqslant r$, we have $\hat{s} \geqslant s$ as asserted. Having shown that $\hat{s}$ is never too small we now need to show that it is not too large either provided $r(a) \geqslant 5$. In fact we shall show that in this case $\hat{s} - 2 \leqslant s \leqslant \hat{s}$. For first we note that

$$\hat{s} \leqslant \frac{q(a + 1) \times 10 + q(a)}{r(a)} = \frac{q(a + 1) \times 10^a + q(a) \times 10^{a-1}}{r(a) \times 10^{a-1}}$$

$$\leqslant \frac{q}{r(a) \times 10^{a-1}} < \frac{q}{r - 10^{a-1}}$$

or $r = 10^{a-1}$ in which case clearly $\hat{s} = s$. Setting this latter case to one side we see that if $3 \leqslant \hat{s} - s$ then

$$3 \leqslant \hat{s} - s < \frac{q}{r - 10^{a-1}} - \frac{q}{r} + 1 = \frac{q}{r}\left(\frac{10^{a-1}}{r - 10^{a-1}}\right) + 1$$

so

$$\frac{q}{r} > 2\left(\frac{r - 10^{a-1}}{10^{a-1}}\right) \geqslant 2(r(a) - 1).$$

We now deduce, since $9 \geqslant \hat{s} \geqslant s + 3 = \mathrm{int}(q/r) + 3 \geqslant 2(r(a) - 1) + 3$, that $r(a) \leqslant 4$. Thus if $r(a) \geqslant 5$ we have $\hat{s} - 2 \leqslant s \leqslant \hat{s}$ as asserted. What is far more remarkable is that an analogue of this result remains true if instead of storing our integers as sequences of single digits we store them in blocks of four, working to base 10 000. The same argument with 10 replaced by 10^4 throughout shows that if $r(a) \geqslant 5000$ then $\hat{s}$, which is now a four figure number, satisfies $\hat{s} - 2 \leqslant s \leqslant \hat{s}$, i.e. is in error by at most 2.

How does one ensure that $r(a)$ is sufficiently large to be able to make use of this remarkable estimate? Clearly by multiplying both q and r by a suitable single digit number: $d = \mathrm{int}(10/(r(a) + 1))$ when working to base 10, $d = \mathrm{int}(10\,000/(r(a) + 1))$ when working to base 10 000 (this latter *is* a single digit number in this base). Having done this we can then use the estimates $\hat{s}$ for s. Ensuring that the correct value of s is eventually chosen is rather a subtle business. The reader is referred to Knuth for further details. Here is our program.

7.1 *Program: Division*

```
 10 INPUT N
 20 DIM A(N): DIM C(N + 1): DIM F(N + 1):
        DIM Q(N + 1): DIM R(N + 1): DIM S(N): DIM T(N)
 30 FOR I = 1 TO N
 40 INPUT Q(N + 1 − I)
 50 NEXT I
 60 FOR I = 1 TO N
 70 INPUT R(N + 1 − I)
 80 NEXT I

1000 FOR I = 1 TO N
1010 IF R(N + 1 − I) > 0 THEN GOTO 1030
1020 NEXT I
1030 LET  A = N + 1 − I:  LET  R = R(A):  IF  A = 1  THEN
        GOTO 1470
1040 LET D = INT(10/(R + 1))
1050 FOR I = 1 TO N
```

```
1060 IF Q(N + 1 - I) > 0 THEN GOTO 1080
1070 NEXT I
1080 LET B = N + 1 - I: IF B < A THEN GOTO 1520
1090 LET B1 = D: IF D = 1 THEN GOTO 1220
1100 FOR I = 1 TO N
1110 LET A(I) = R(I)
1120 NEXT I
1130 GOSUB 5000
1140 FOR I = 1 TO N
1150 LET R(I) = C(I): LET A(I) = Q(I)
1160 NEXT I
1170 GOSUB 5000
1180 FOR I = 1 TO N + 1
1190 LET Q(I) = C(I)
1200 NEXT I
1210 GOTO 1230
1220 LET Q(N + 1) = 0
1230 LET R = R(A): LET B = B + 1: LET J = 0
1240 LET Q = Q(B - J)
1250 IF Q = R THEN GOTO 1270
1260 LET E = INT((Q * 10 + Q(B - J - 1))/R): GOTO 1280
1270 LET E = 9
1280 IF R(A - 1) * E < = (Q * 10 + Q(B - J - 1) - R * E) * 10 +
     Q(B - J - 2) THEN GOTO 1300
1290 LET E = E - 1: GOTO 1280
1300 GOSUB 6000
1310 GOSUB 7000
1320 IF Z = 0 THEN GOTO 1350
1330 GOSUB 8000
1340 LET E = E - 1
1350 LET S(B - A - J) = E
1360 LET J = J + 1: IF J < B - A THEN GOTO 1240
1370 IF D > 1 THEN GOTO 1420
1380 FOR I = 1 TO N
1390 LET T(I) = Q(I)
1400 NEXT I
1410 GOTO 1430
1420 LET D1 = D: GOSUB 9000
1430 FOR I = B - A + 1 TO N
1440 LET S(I) = 0
1450 NEXT I
1460 GOTO 1550
1470 LET D1 = R: GOSUB 9000
```

```
1480  FOR I = 1 TO N
1490  LET S(I) = T(I): LET T(I) = Ø
1500  NEXT I
1510  LET T(1) = Z: GOTO 1550
1520  FOR I = 1 TO N
1530  LET S(I) = Ø: LET T(I) = Q(I)
1540  NEXT I
1550  PRINT "THE QUOTIENT IS";
1560  FOR I = 1 TO N
1570  PRINT; S(N + 1 − I); ",";
1580  NEXT I
1590  PRINT "THE REMAINDER IS";
1600  FOR I = 1 TO N
1610  PRINT; T(N + 1 − I); ",";
1620  NEXT I
1630  END
```

The subroutines are listed below.

```
5000  LET Z = Ø
5010  FOR I = 1 TO N
5020  LET X = A(I) * B1 + Z
5030  LET Z = INT(X/1Ø)
5040  LET C(I) = X − Z * 1Ø
5050  NEXT I
5060  LET C(N + 1) = Z
5070  RETURN

6000  LET Z = Ø
6010  FOR I = 1 TO A
6020  LET X = R(I) * E + Z
6030  LET Z = INT(Z/1Ø)
6040  LET F(I) = X − Z * 1Ø
6050  NEXT I
6060  LET F(A + 1) = Z
6070  RETURN

7000  LET Z = Ø
7010  FOR I = 1 TO A + 1
7020  LET T = B − A − J + I − 1: LET X = Q(T) − F(I) − Z
7030  IF X > = Ø THEN LET Q(T) = X − 1Ø * INT(X/1Ø)
7040  IF X < Ø THEN LET Q(T) = (X + 2Ø) − 1Ø * INT
          ((X/1Ø) + 2)
7050  LET Z = (Q(T) − X)/1Ø
```

```
7Ø6Ø NEXT I
7Ø7Ø RETURN

8ØØØ LET Z = Ø
8Ø1Ø FOR I = 1 TO A + 1
8Ø2Ø LET T = B − A − J + I − 1: LET X = R(I) + Q(T) + Z
8Ø3Ø LET Z = INT(X/1Ø)
8Ø4Ø LET Q(T) = X − Z * 1Ø
8Ø5Ø NEXT I
8Ø6Ø RETURN

9ØØØ LET Z = Ø
9Ø1Ø FOR I = 1 TO N
9Ø2Ø LET X = Z * 1Ø + Q(N + 1 − I)
9Ø3Ø LET T(N + 1 − I) = INT(X/D1)
9Ø4Ø LET Z = X − T(N + 1 − I) * D1
9Ø5Ø NEXT I
9Ø6Ø RETURN
```

Some remarks are in order concerning the above program (although we will not explain all of its subtleties here). First we note that we only ever have to multiply by single digit numbers and a program for doing this is given by the subroutine 5ØØØ. Also, because we wish to be able to divide any pair of numbers using this program, we need to consider separately the cases when $a = 1$ (r has only one digit) and $a > b$ (r has more digits than q). These are easily dealt with but account for lines 147Ø–154Ø. Finally we note that since we have multiplied q and r by a normalizing factor d we need to divide the remainder by d. Again long division by a single digit is easily done, in the subroutine 9ØØØ. Can you amend Program 7.1 to use three or four digit blocks?

§8

Mersenne numbers again

We now wish to produce some very large Mersenne primes using the Lucas–Lehmer test. Although we have solved the problem of high precision arithmetic, we have to surmount one remaining difficulty. How does one efficiently compute the powers of 2 involved in their definition? We shall need to compute large powers a little later too, when we come to general primality tests, so it is worth investing a little time on this problem.

Clearly if we want to compute 2^{121} for example it is most inefficient to multiply 2 by itself 121 times, and in an example above we have already indicated a sounder approach, based on the fact that the powers 2^1, 2^2, 2^4, 2^8, 2^{16}, 2^{32}, ... are easily found by repeated squaring. We then note that

$$121 = 1 \times 64 + 1 \times 32 + 1 \times 16 + 1 \times 8 + 0 \times 4 + 0 \times 2 + 1 \times 1$$

so that $2^{121} = 2^{64} \times 2^{32} \times 2^{16} \times 2^8 \times 2^1$. Clearly the key here is to find the *binary form* of the exponent 121, which is 1 111 001, i.e. $121 = 1 \times 2^6 + 1 \times 2^5 + 1 \times 2^4 + 1 \times 2^3 + 0 \times 2^2 + 0 \times 2^1 + 1 \times 2^0$. It is probably easier to get some idea of how this method works by trying a few examples than by reading a lengthy explanation. How would one compute 2^{39} or 2^{63} for example?

To implement the corresponding algorithm on a micro is not difficult. The program below computes 2^p by this method. It first determines the binary expansion of the number p, writing it as

$$p = 2^0 x(1) + 2^1 x(2) + \ldots + 2^{m-1} x(m),$$

with the $x(i) = 0$ or 1. This is the content of lines 6∅–9∅. We then set up a running product y, which is to be 2 if $x(1) = 1$ and 1 if $x(1) = 0$, and set $g = h = 2$. The rest of the program successively squares g (by multiplying g by h and then replacing g and h by their product) and multiplies the running product y by those squares which correspond to a binary digit $x(j)$ whose value is 1.

8.1 *Program: Powers*

```
 1∅ INPUT P
 2∅ LET M = INT(LN(P)/LN(2)) + 1:
    LET N = INT(P*∅.3∅1∅) + 1
 3∅ DIM X(M): DIM Y(N): DIM G(N): DIM H(N): DIM P(N)

 6∅ LET I = 1
 7∅ LET Y = P − 2*INT(P/2)
 8∅ LET X(I) = Y: LET P = (P − Y)/2: LET I = I + 1
 9∅ IF P < > ∅ THEN GOTO 7∅
1∅∅ LET M1 = I − 1
11∅ LET G(1) = 2: LET H(1) = 2: LET Y(1) = 1 + X(1)
12∅ FOR I = 2 TO N
13∅ LET G(I) = ∅: LET H(I) = ∅: LET Y(I) = ∅
14∅ NEXT I
15∅ FOR L = 2 TO M1
16∅ GOSUB 4∅∅∅
17∅ FOR I = 1 TO N
18∅ LET G(I) = P(I): LET H(I) = Y(I)
19∅ NEXT I
2∅∅ IF X(L) = ∅ THEN GOTO 25∅
21∅ GOSUB 4∅∅∅
22∅ FOR I = 1 TO N
```

```
23Ø  LET Y(I) = P(I)
24Ø  NEXT I
25Ø  FOR I = 1 TO N
26Ø  LET H(I) = G(I)
27Ø  NEXT I
28Ø  NEXT L
29Ø  END
```

4ØØØ Insert multiplication subroutine Program 6.5.

Even for relatively small powers this program is a vast improvement on the obvious method of repeated multiplication. For example it required $1\frac{1}{2}$ minutes on one machine to compute 2^{101}, while repeated multiplication took over 20 minutes. Note that if you actually want to *see* what the result of the computation is you will have to add a few lines to the above program.

A couple of points concerning the program design. Firstly, since we are using the multiplication subroutine, which multiplies g and h to obtain a product p, there is a certain amount of relabelling to be done in lines 17Ø–27Ø. Doubtless this could be done more efficiently; as usual we leave the high performance tuning to you. Secondly, m and n are estimates for the number of digits required to express p in binary and 2^p in decimal. Your computer may well only have natural logarithms $\ln$; 0.3010 is an approximation for $\log_{10} 2$. With this hint you should be able to work out where these estimates come from. Thirdly, it is actually more efficient to compute the binary expansion of p at the same time as one computes the powers. If you rewrite the program this way you won't need to introduce the array $x(m)$. Finally, the program only computes 2^p, whereas the pth Mersenne number is $2^p - 1$. By adding a new line

29Ø LET Y(1) = Y(1) − 1

you obtain the Mersenne number. (Why are there never any carry problems?)

8.2 *Lucas–Lehmer test again*

We now have all of the ingredients necessary to apply the Lucas–Lehmer test for the Mersenne primes, discussed in Section 5.1. The following program is a fairly straightforward implementation of this test. The required inputs are m, the number of digits of the Mersenne number $M_p = 2^p - 1$, p itself, and the Mersenne number read in from left to right. Naturally you can cobble this program to that which computes powers and save yourself this trouble.

8.3 *Program: Lucas–Lehmer*

```
 10 INPUT M, P: LET N = 2*M
 20 DIM A(N): DIM C(N + 1): DIM E(N): DIM F(N + 1):
    DIM P(N): DIM Q(N + 1): DIM R(N + 1): DIM S(N):
    DIM T(N): DIM X(N)
 30 FOR I = 1 TO M
 40 INPUT R(M + 1 − I): LET R(M + I) = 0:
    LET X(M + 1 − I) = R(M + 1 − I):
    LET X(M + I) = 0
 50 NEXT I
 60 FOR I = 2 TO N
 70 LET E(I) = 0: LET T(I) = 0
 80 NEXT I
 90 LET E(1) = 2: LET T(1) = 4
100 FOR L = 1 TO P − 2
110 GOSUB 4000
120 GOSUB 3000
130 FOR I = 1 TO N
140 LET R(I) = X(I)
150 NEXT I
160 GOSUB 1000
170 NEXT L
180 FOR I = 1 TO M
190 PRINT; X(M + 1 − I); ","
200 NEXT I
210 FOR I = 1 TO M
220 IF T(I) > 0 THEN GOTO 260
230 NEXT I
240 PRINT; "IS PRIME"
250 GOTO 270
260 PRINT; "IS NOT PRIME"
270 END

1000 Insert division subroutine

3000 LET Z = 0
3010 FOR I = 1 TO N
3020 LET X = P(I) − E(I) − Z
3030 IF X > = 0 THEN LET Q(I) = X − 10*INT(X/10)
3040 IF X < 0 THEN LET Q(I) = X + 20 −
     10*INT((X/10) + 2)
3050 LET Z = (Q(I) − X)/10
3060 NEXT I
```

```
3Ø7Ø RETURN

4ØØØ LET Z = Ø: LET T = Ø
4Ø1Ø FOR K = 1 TO N
4Ø2Ø LET U = T: LET V = Z: LET X = T(1)*T(K)
4Ø3Ø IF K = 1 THEN GOTO 4Ø7Ø
4Ø4Ø FOR I = 2 TO K
4Ø5Ø LET X = X + T(I)*T(K + 1 − I)
4Ø6Ø NEXT I
4Ø7Ø LET S = X − 1Ø*INT(X/1Ø): LET Z = INT(X/1Ø)
4Ø8Ø LET Y = S + U + V
4Ø9Ø LET W = Y − 1Ø*INT(Y/1Ø): LET T = INT(Y/1Ø)
41ØØ LET P(K) = W
411Ø NEXT K
412Ø RETURN
```

Some comments on the program are in order. First the division subroutine is obtained from Program 7.1 by deleting lines 1Ø–8Ø, 155Ø–163Ø and adding 155Ø RETURN. Second the reason for introducing the array $x(i)$ and lines 13Ø–15Ø is that we repeatedly divide by the Mersenne number M_p, which is stored as the array $r(i)$. However, if the leading digit of M_p is less than 5 the division subroutine will multiply up the divisor M_p and the dividend by some number (d in Program 7.1) before carrying out the division process. If lines 13Ø–15Ø are not included this multiple will be used as the divisor in all *subsequent* divisions while the corresponding dividends will *not* be multiplied by d. Of course, if the leading digit of M_p is greater than or equal to 5 lines 13Ø–15Ø may be omitted. Note also that subroutines 3ØØØ, 4ØØØ used above are not quite our standard subtraction and multiplication programs; a certain amount of relabelling has been done.

Since e in line 3ØØØ is a single digit number, namely 2, this subroutine could be written more efficiently.

You should be warned that although the Lucas–Lehmer test is *much* more efficient than any trial division method for testing the Mersenne numbers for primality, it is anything but instantaneous. On one of the slower machines it took about an hour to test $M_{127} = 2^{127} − 1$; it is in fact prime and is the 39 digit number

$$170\,141\,183\,460\,469\,231\,731\,687\,303\,715\,884\,105\,727.$$

The reason that the program takes rather a long time is that we need to perform around 120 operations of multiplication and division involving numbers of up to 78 digits in length. Of course when running the program it is more efficient to work to base 1000 or 10 000 if possible. Because of the time involved you might like to add a line 1Ø5 PRINT; L; ","; to keep you in touch with how the computation is proceeding.

You may be interested to know that M_{127} was, until 1951, the largest known prime, and was proved to be prime *without* the aid of a computer by Lucas in 1875.

8.4 *Exercise*

Check that $2^p - 1$ is prime for $p = 2, 3, 5, 7, 13, 17, 19, 31, 61, 89, 107, 127$. These are, in fact, the first 12 Mersenne primes. We know, of course, that $2^n - 1$ is *not* prime unless n is a prime p. Check that $2^p - 1$ is not prime for some primes p not in the above list (e.g. take $p = 11, 23, 37, 67$).

The Mersenne primes were first discussed by Marin Mersenne, who, in 1644, asserted that $2^p - 1$ is prime for $p = 2, 3, 5, 7, 13, 17, 19, 31, 67, 127, 257$ and for no other p less than 257. Mersenne gave no proof of his assertions (of course he did not have the Lucas–Lehmer primality test or a micro available) and for over 200 years nobody knew if his list was correct or not. In 1772 Euler showed that $2^{31} - 1$ was indeed prime, and this was the largest known prime until Lucas's *tour de force* in 1875. Lucas also showed that $2^{67} - 1$ was not prime and other errors have since been found in Mersenne's assertions. (There are two further errors not obtainable by comparing the two lists above: $2^{257} - 1$ is *not* prime but $2^{251} - 1$ is.)

A recent (1992) Mersenne prime $2^{756839} - 1$ was found at the Atomic Energy Authority, Harwell. It is natural to ask if there are infinitely many Mersenne primes. This has not been established, but there are various plausible arguments suggesting that there are indeed arbitrarily large Mersenne primes. Even more striking is the fact that these primes appear to be fairly regularly distributed. Of course the numerical evidence for believing these arguments is necessarily limited; at the time of writing there are only about thirty Mersenne primes known. Given this constraint, the evidence for regularity of distribution, and hence the evidence that there *are* infinitely many Mersenne primes, is amazing. See the book by Schroeder (1986) pp. 30–4.

8.5 *Mathematical excursion: Perfect numbers*

A number n is said to be *perfect* if it is equal to the sum of its divisors, including 1 but not the number itself. The smallest such number is 6 ($6 = 1 + 2 + 3$) and the next is 28 ($= 1 + 2 + 4 + 7 + 14$). One can fairly easily check that if $2^p - 1$ is prime then $n = 2^{p-1}(2^p - 1)$ is a perfect number. This assertion is due to Euclid. The divisors of n are 2^r, $0 \leqslant r \leqslant p - 1$ and $2^r(2^p - 1)$, $0 \leqslant r \leqslant p - 1$, and so the sum of the divisors other than n itself is

$$(2^0 + 2^1 + 2^2 + \ldots + 2^{p-2})(2^p - 1 + 1) + 2^{p-1}$$
$$= (2^{p-1} - 1) \times 2^p + 2^{p-1} = 2^{p-1}(2^p - 1)$$

as required. So corresponding to each Mersenne number there is a perfect number, and the first eight perfect numbers obtained in this way are consequently obtained by taking $p = 2, 3, 5, 7, 13, 17, 19$ and 31; the perfect number corresponding to $p = 31$ is 2 305 843 008 139 952 128. Euler showed that any *even* perfect numbers must be of this form, so there is a one to one correspondence between even perfect numbers and Mersenne primes. For an elementary proof of this fact see Hardy and Wright (1975) pp. 239, 240. In particular it is not known whether or not there are an infinite number of even perfect numbers. Even more annoyingly it is still not known if there is an odd perfect number. This is a good example of how difficult an easily stated problem can be.

The following are some properties of even perfect numbers which you can easily deduce from their Euclidean form.

(a) Show that every even perfect number is of the form $1 + 2 + 3 + \ldots + m$ for some m i.e. is triangular.

(b) Show that every even perfect number ends in a 6 or an 8.

(c) Show that the sum of the reciprocals of the divisors of a perfect even number, including the number itself, is 2.

(d) Prove that if $n = 2^{p-1}q$ is a perfect number, with $p \geqslant 1$ and q prime then $q = 2^p - 1$.

(e) Show that the digital root of any even perfect number other than 6 is 1. (To obtain the digital root of a number repeatedly add its digits until only a single digit remains. This digital root is the remainder obtained after division by the number 9, so work modulo 9.)

(f) Use your program for high precision multiplication to verify that $2^{30}(2^{31} - 1)$ is indeed 2 305 843 008 139 952 128.

§9
General primality tests

So far we have rather concentrated on producing long lists of primes. Given any number n, how does one go about proving, or disproving, that n is prime? Naturally if n is a Mersenne number one simply applies the Lucas–Lehmer primality test, but this test only applies to these very special numbers.

The most obvious way of checking whether or not a number n (like 3 215 031 751) is prime is by trial division, but if n has no small prime factors this method is really very inefficient. For example on a computer that can do one million trial divisions per second it would take about one million years to verify a prime with 40 digits. Of course one might try the sieve of Eratosthenes. As a method for producing lists of primes this is very efficient; the time spent on any one prime is rather small. Unfortunately, checking that n is prime involved producing all primes between 1 and n, or at least between 1 and $\sqrt{n}$, and again even on the biggest computers this takes far too long if n is rather large.

A far more useful test, which strictly speaking is not a test at all, concerns Fermat's Theorem discussed in Chapter 1, Section 8.5. Recall this theorem states that if n is prime and x is not a multiple of n then

$$x^{n-1} \equiv 1 (\text{mod } n). \tag{1}$$

For $x = 2$ this was known to the fifth century BC Chinese, who also asserted the converse, namely if $2^{n-1} \equiv 1 (\text{mod } n)$ then n is prime. If this were so we would have a very useful primality test; for we already have a very efficient way of computing large powers of 2 by repeated squaring; see Program 8.1. Sadly this converse is false (although the Chinese mathematicians in question are in good company: Leibniz also believed this converse result was true). For example if $n = 341 = 11 \times 31$ then $2^{340} \equiv 1 (\text{mod } 341)$. (Don't use your micro, simply note that $2^5 \equiv 1 (\text{mod } 31)$ and $2^{10} \equiv 1 (\text{mod } 11)$, by Fermat's Theorem, so that $2^{340} \equiv 1 (\text{mod } 31)$ and $2^{340} \equiv 1 (\text{mod } 11)$. A little thought now shows that the required conclusion follows.)

So one possible primality test bites the dust. However, we should not discard this idea out of hand. Although the Chinese converse is false, in practice it is not far from being true! In other words numbers n which pass the test

$$2^{n-1} \equiv 1 (\text{mod } n) \tag{2}$$

are usually prime. For example of those numbers $n < 10^{10}$ for which (2) is true, 455 052 512 are prime and only 14 884 are not. Thus the probability that a number $n < 10^{10}$ passes this test and is *not* prime is around 0.000 03. Such numbers are called *pseudoprimes to the base* 2. More generally any non-prime n satisfying $\text{hcf}(n, b) = 1$ and

$$b^{n-1} \equiv 1 (\text{mod } n) \tag{3}$$

is called a *pseudoprime to the base b*. There is overwhelming numerical evidence that pseudoprimes to any base b are rare by comparison with true primes, and such a result was established by Erdös in 1950. We now wish to write a program which implements test (2). This is not very difficult now; we have all the relevant pieces already available, we need only assemble the pieces in the correct order. We shall assume that the number to be tested for primality has eight digits or less, it is input as p, and also as an array $u(1), \ldots, u(8)$, reading p as an eight digit number from right to left. Larger numbers could be considered, of course, and you can modify the program listed below to deal with them.

As written the program carries out the primality test to the base 2 i.e. checks (2). One can easily change the base by rewriting lines 11$\emptyset$–14$\emptyset$ of the program. We have replaced *n* by *p*, since this was the label used in Section 8.5. (If your computer cannot do *exact* eight digit arithmetic you may run into problems if *p* is an eight digit number.)

9.1 *Program: Pseudoprimality test*

```
 1Ø  INPUT P: LET P = P − 1:
     LET M = INT(LN(P)/LN(2)) + 1: LET N = 16
 2Ø  DIM X(M): DIM Y(N): DIM G(N): DIM H(N):
     DIM P(N): DIM A(N): DIM C(N + 1): DIM F(N + 1):
     DIM Q(N + 1): DIM R(N + 1): DIM S(N): DIM T(N):
     DIM U(N)
 3Ø  FOR I = 1 TO 8
 4Ø  INPUT U(I): LET U(8 + I) = Ø
 5Ø  NEXT I
6Ø-16Ø As in Program 8.1
17Ø  FOR I = 1 TO N
18Ø  LET Q(I) = P(I): LET R(I) = U(I)
19Ø  NEXT I
2ØØ  GOSUB 1ØØØ
21Ø  FOR I = 1 TO N
22Ø  LET G(I) = T(I): LET H(I) = Y(I)
23Ø  NEXT I
24Ø  IF X(L) = Ø THEN GOTO 33Ø
25Ø  GOSUB 4ØØØ
26Ø  FOR I = 1 TO N
27Ø  LET Q(I) = P(I): LET R(I) = U(I)
28Ø  NEXT I
29Ø  GOSUB 1ØØØ
3ØØ  FOR I = 1 TO N
31Ø  LET Y(I) = T(I)
32Ø  NEXT I
33Ø  FOR I = 1 TO N
34Ø  LET H(I) = G(I)
35Ø  NEXT I
36Ø  NEXT L
37Ø  LET Y(1) = Y(1) − 1
38Ø  FOR I = 1 TO N
39Ø  IF Y(I) < > Ø THEN GOTO 43Ø
4ØØ  NEXT I
41Ø  PRINT "IS A PSEUDOPRIME"
42Ø  GOTO 44Ø
```

430 PRINT "IS NOT A PSEUDOPRIME"
440 END

1000 Insert division subroutine

4000 Insert multiplication subroutine

The program above works quite rapidly; on one of the slower micros it took around two minutes to check an eight digit number. (98 765 431 is a pseudoprime to the base 2. Is it prime?)

One possible refinement of the primality test just discussed is to apply it with various different values of b. Since pseudoprimes to any base are rare, one reasons that numbers which are simultaneously pseudoprimes to a number of bases must be *extremely* rare. This appears to be correct, but unfortunately there *are* non-primes n which are pseudoprimes to every base b with hcf$(b, n) = 1$. An example of such a *Carmichael number* is $561 = 3 \times 11 \times 17$. (To see that this does indeed pass the pseudoprimality test to every base b with hcf$(b, 561) = 1$, one notes that, by Fermat's Theorem, $a^2 \equiv 1 \pmod 3$, $a^{10} \equiv 1 \pmod{11}$, $a^{16} \equiv 1 \pmod{17}$ for any a with hcf$(a, 561) = 1$, and taking a respectively equal to b^{280}, b^{56}, b^{35} one finds that $b^{560} \equiv 1$ modulo 3, 11 and 17 as required.)

Nevertheless the idea of applying several tests is a good one. Before investigating it further we shall strengthen our pseudoprimality test. Suppose that n is a prime with $n > 2$. The equation $x^2 \equiv 1 \pmod n$ has just two solutions ($x = 1$ and $x = n - 1$) satisfying $0 \leqslant x \leqslant n - 1$, as you can easily check. If an odd number n satisfied (3) i.e. $b^{n-1} \equiv 1 \pmod n$ then clearly $x = b^{(n-1)/2}$ is a solution of $x^2 \equiv 1 \pmod n$. So if n is prime we must have $b^{(n-1)/2} \equiv 1$ or $n - 1 \pmod n$. This *is* a stronger test than before since taking $b = 5$ we find that the Carmichael number $n = 561$ fails our new test. (Check on your micro that $5^{280} \equiv 67 \pmod{561}$.)

In fact we can further strengthen our pseudoprimality test as follows. Given a positive odd integer n to be tested, first write $n - 1 = 2^r m$, where m is odd.

$$\text{If } either \quad b^m \equiv 1 \pmod n \quad or \quad b^{2^i m} \equiv n - 1 \pmod n$$
$$\text{for some } 0 \leqslant i \leqslant r - 1, \tag{4}$$

we shall say that n is a *strong pseudoprime to the base b* (we include the primes here). As with our pseudoprime test any integer n which fails this test is definitely composite. Unfortunately for every base b there are infinitely many strong pseudoprimes which are not primes, but since strong pseudoprimes are pseudoprimes these strong pseudoprimes are again very rare.

Before we move on to the problem of implementing the strong pseudoprime test on a micro we prove that a prime is indeed a strong pseudoprime. For if n is prime $b^{2^r m} \equiv 1 \pmod{n}$ and taking square roots $b^{2^{r-1} m} \equiv 1$ or $n - 1 \pmod{n}$. In the latter case n passed the strong pseudoprimality test, so let us suppose $b^{2^{r-1} m} \equiv 1 \pmod{n}$. Taking square roots again we find $b^{2^{r-2} m} \equiv 1$ or $n - 1 \pmod{n}$. Again in the latter case n passes the test. We continue to extract roots, and stop only when $b^{2^i m} \equiv n - 1 \pmod{n}$ for some $0 \leqslant i \leqslant r - 1$. But if this fails for each i then, taking $i = 0$, $b^m \equiv 1 \pmod{n}$ and again n passes the test.

We now turn to the question of how best to use this test on a micro. Our first (trivial) observation is that since we are assuming that n is odd clearly $n - 1$ is obtained by decreasing the last digit of n by 1. This is useful if n has been fed in as an array. We next need to extract all of the powers of 2 from $n - 1$. Of course whether $n - 1$ is divisible by 2 or not is decided simply by considering its final digit. Since our long division subroutine contains an algorithm for division by a single digit number the numbers r and m are easily determined. (Of course if n has eight digits or less there is no need to use this subroutine.)

We now compute $b^m \pmod{n}$ as before and test to see if this is congruent to 1 or $n - 1 \pmod{n}$. If it is then n passes the test. Otherwise we square, to obtain b^{2m}, and reduce modulo n. If the result is $n - 1$ again n passes the test. If not we square again, and successively squaring and reducing modulo n we check the congruence $b^{2^i m} \equiv n - 1 \pmod{n}$ for $0 \leqslant i \leqslant r - 1$. If this *fails* for each i we know that n is composite.

9.2 *Exercise*
Write a basic program implementing the algorithm just described.

9.3 *Exercise*
In Hardy and Wright (1975) p. 78 the following theorem is proved.

> *Let p be an odd prime, k a positive integer less than p and let $n = kp + 1$ or $kp^2 + 1$. If $2^k \not\equiv 1 \pmod{n}$ and $2^{n-1} \equiv 1 \pmod{n}$ then n is prime.*

The proof is elementary, and we encourage you to look it up. This result essentially gives a source of numbers for which the pseudoprimality test is actually a primality test. It was used by Miller and Wheeler in 1951 to find a prime number larger than $2^{127} - 1$ (the record holder at that time). In fact they showed that $180(2^{127} - 1)^2 + 1$ is prime. Find some large primes using the above result.

As stated previously, although it is true that strong pseudoprimes (to some base b) which are not primes are very rare, they do exist. Consequently if n passes the strong pseudoprimality test this does not establish the primality of the number n, although any number failing the test is, we know, composite. However, there are *very* few integers that are simultaneously strong pseudoprimes to several bases. For example Pomerance, Selfridge and Wagstaff announced in 1980 that there is only one integer $n < 25 \times 10^9$ which is simultaneously a strong pseudoprime to the bases 2, 3, 5, 7, and this integer is

$$3\,215\,031\,751 = 151 \times 751 \times 28\,351.$$

Thus by applying the strong pseudoprime test four times one can determine the primality or otherwise of any integer $< 25 \times 10^9$ (other than $3\,215\,031\,751$). By comparison with the sieve of Eratosthenes the resulting test is rather rapid.

9.4 *Exercise*
Select some large (odd) primes and non-primes from the lists you have already compiled and apply the strong pseudoprimality test to the bases 2, 3, 5 and 7.

The advantages of the tests just described are only really felt when dealing with numbers considerably larger than 10^8. We shall see in the next section that trial division is quite an efficient way of determining whether or not an eight digit number is prime. Moreover, it has the advantage of yielding a prime factorization if the number considered is *not* prime. As the numbers tested increase, however, the number of computations involved in the trial division method increases very rapidly. In fact, the most obvious method of determining whether or not n is prime by trial division involves around $\sqrt{n}$ divisions. Actually one can reduce this to $\frac{1}{3}\sqrt{n}$ quite easily (see the next section) but it is the factor $\sqrt{n}$ which is important. By comparison, consider the pseudoprimality test (1). The main part of the computation involved raising 2 to the power $n-1$ and successively reducing modulo n. The key observation is that the method employed entails considerably fewer than n multiplications and divisions. In fact an inspection of Program 9.1 shows that the pseudoprimality test for an integer n (labelled p in Program 9.1) involves round $3 \ln(n)/\ln(2)$ multiplications and divisions, or fewer.

Table 3 shows various values for n, $\sqrt{n}$ and $\ln(n)/\ln(2)$ (rounded to the nearest digit). Clearly the pseudoprimality test will involve *far* fewer computations than trial division for even moderately large n. For smaller values of n the fact that Program 9.1 involves $3 \ln(n)/\ln(2)$ operations and trial division $\frac{1}{3}\sqrt{n}$ operations narrows

Table 3.

n	$\sqrt{n}$	$\ln(n)/\ln(2)$
10^4	10^2	13
10^6	10^3	20
10^8	10^4	27
10^{12}	10^6	40
10^{20}	10^{10}	67

the gap between the running time of these tests. In addition the pseudoprimality test does entail dealing with numbers around the size of n^2. However, the effect of these factors when n is large is negligible by comparison with the relative growths of $\sqrt{n}$ and $\ln(n)/\ln (2)$; this is especially true if n is greater than 10^8, for then *both* tests involve high precision arithmetic.

For further information on primality tests see Pomerance (1980) and Dixon (1984).

§10
Factorizing large numbers

We know that every positive integer can be expressed in a unique way as a product of primes. How does one find this prime factorization? For large numbers this is a difficult problem. The most obvious method of factoring some number n is by successively dividing n by the primes $p = 2, 3, 5, \ldots$ satisfying $p \le \sqrt{n}$. If p_1 is the first such prime to divide n we note the factor p_1 and are reduced to factoring the smaller number n/p_1. When factoring this new smaller number we should note that the primes $p < p_1$ have already been considered, and since they do *not* divide n they will not divide n/p_1. Assuming that you have an array $p(i)$ of the primes in ascending order, $1 \le i \le r$, and the integer n to be tested satisfies $n \le p(r)^2$ the following algorithm will factor n.

10.1 *Program: Factorisation by division*

```
10 INPUT N: LET K = 1: PRINT N; " = ";
20 IF N = 1 THEN GOTO 80
30 LET Q = INT(N/P(K)): LET R = N − P(K)*Q
40 IF R > Ø THEN GOTO 70
50 PRINT; P(K); "*";
60 LET N = Q: GOTO 20
70 IF Q > P(K) THEN LET K = K + 1: GOTO 30
80 PRINT; N;
```

Before running this program you will need to input a list of primes $p(i)$. The number of these required depends on the size of the integer n to be factored. For example if $n < 10^6$ we need only input the 168 primes less than 10^3, and this algorithm will factor n quite quickly. For genuinely large n (say n around 10^{12}) this type of algorithm is far too slow to be of any practical use. One observation, which saves us the labour of first producing an array of primes, is that our algorithm will factor the integer n as a product of primes provided the increasing sequence $p(k)$ contains all of the primes. For if one of the ps is composite clearly the current value of n will fail to be divisible by p since it is not divisible by *any* of the factors of p. This suggests that we replace the sequence of primes 2, 3, 5, 7, 11, 13, 17, . . . by the sequence 2, 3, 5, 7, 11, 13, 17, 19, 23, 25, . . . obtained by alternately adding 2 and 4 after the first three terms. (Check that this sequence does include all of the primes.) Here is a program for finding all members of this latter sequence less than *about m*.

10.2 *Program: Factor sequence*
```
1Ø  INPUT M: LET R = INT(M/3) + 1
2Ø  DIM P(R)
3Ø  LET P(1) = 2: LET P(2) = 3: LET P(3) = 5: LET K = 3
4Ø  LET P(K + 1) = P(K) + 2: LET P(K + 2) = P(K + 1) + 4
5Ø  LET K = K + 2: IF K < = R − 2 THEN GOTO 4Ø
```

(As an aid to understanding this program note that $p(i) = 3i − 4$ if i is odd. This explains the choice of r in line 1Ø. Can you see why we are not definite about the largest value of this sequence?)

10.3 *Exercises*

(*a*) Take $m = 1000$ and combining Programs 10.1 and 10.2 try factoring some numbers $n < 10^6$.

(*b*) In Knuth (1981) pp. 341–2 a modification of factorisation by division due to Alway is described. Use Knuth's algorithm B as the basis for a BASIC program. Is the result more efficient than that described above?

(*c*) It is a rather amazing fact that a number n has, on average, about ln ln n prime factors. Of course some numbers (like $n = 2^{100}$) have many more factors while others (like $n = 2^{127} − 1$) have fewer; the number ln ln n is simply an average. What makes this result surprising is that the function ln ln n grows *extremely* slowly. For example ln ln 10^7 is about 3 while ln ln 10^{80} is little more than 5. Thus a number around 10^7 will usually have about three prime factors and a number near 10^{80} around five.

By selecting random seven digit numbers and factoring using Programs 10.1 and 10.2 see if your observations are in agreement with the results above.

10.4 *Project*

This section has done little beyond introducing the problem of factorization. A large number of interesting and ingenious methods have been developed for factoring large numbers. Read the fascinating account given by Knuth (1981) and devise an efficient series of factoring algorithms.

10.5 *Cryptography and large primes*

The quest for large primes, which we have discussed in this chapter, has, over the past ten years or so, become a matter of some interest to major financial institutions and government agencies. Cryptography, the ancient art of encoding and decoding secret messages, is of great importance in this age of instant communication. How, for example, can a bank ensure that the electronic information it receives from other banks is authentic? A new class of codes, called *public key cryptosystems*, has revolutionised this question of authentication, and the more general problem of the secure transfer of data. A public key cryptosystem is one in which all users of the system can publish their encryption key, that is the method by which others can encode information for the user, while keeping the decryption or decoding key known only to themselves. More precisely in such a system it must be a straightforward task to find encryption and decryption keys, but require a prohibitively large amount of time to determine, from the encryption key *only*, the decryption key. Such systems involve so called trap-door functions, and one of the best known (the RSA system) relies on the fact that it is much easier to find large primes than factor large numbers. So any breakthrough in algorithms for finding large primes or factoring large numbers may have consequences for national security! For details of these developments see Schroeder (1986) Part IV.

References   J. W. Bruce 'A really trivial proof of the Lucas–Lehmer primality test', to appear in *Amer. Math. Monthly* (1993).

F. J. Budden *The Fascination of Groups*, Cambridge University Press, Cambridge, 1972

P. M. Cohn *Algebra*, Volume 1, Wiley, London, 1974

H. Davenport *The Higher Arithmetic*, Cambridge University Press, Cambridge, 5th Edn, 1982

J. D. Dixon *American Math. Monthly*, **91**, 6 (1984) 333–52

G. H. Hardy and E. M. Wright *An Introduction to the Theory of Numbers*, Oxford University Press, Oxford, 4th Edn 1975

D. E. Knuth *The Art of Computer Programming*, Volume 2, *Seminumerical Algorithms*. Addison-Wesley. Reading, Mass., 1981

C. Pomerance *The Mathematical Intelligencer*, **3**, 3 (1980) 97–105

H. Rademacher *Lectures on Elementary Number Theory*, Blaisdell Publishing Company, New York, 1964

M. R. Schroeder *Number Theory in Science and Communication*, Springer–Verlag, Berlin, 1986.

I. Stewart *Concepts of Modern Mathematics*, Penguin Books, Harmondsworth, 1975

B. A. Venkov *Elementary Number Theory*, Wolters-Noordhoff, Groningen, 1970

5

Curves, Part 2

In this second chapter on curves, we shall attempt some slightly more ambitious things, and launch into two investigations where mathematical reasoning and computer examples go hand in hand. First we consider families of lines in the plane and their envelopes. Among other things, this gives us a new perspective on the evolutes of Chapter 3, §5. Next we consider the generally very hard problem of drawing with the computer the set of points in the plane satisfying an equation of the form $f(x, y) = 0$, i.e. the problem of drawing *level sets*, or *contours* of a function. After that we come to our two investigations, one on the topic of Cartesian ovals, an interesting family of plane curves related to refraction of light, and the other on simple plane linkages.

§1   We begin with an example.

Envelopes of lines

1.1 *Embroidery with chords of a circle*

Let m be a fixed number, usually a whole number such as 2, 3 or 4. We shall draw a circle, radius 1 and centre $(0, 0)$ in the plotting rectangle, and then draw a succession of chords of this circle, joining points at angles t and mt (Fig. 1) for say 60 values of t between 0 and 2π. Here is a program for this.

Fig. 1

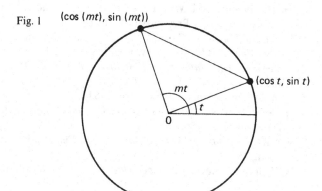

(cos (mt), sin (mt))

(cos t, sin t)

mt

t

0

Program: Chords 1

```
1Ø  INPUT M
2Ø  LET XL = − 1.7: LET XU = 1.7: LET YC = Ø
3Ø  Calculate yₗ, yᵤ (see Section 1.7 of Chapter 3)
4Ø  Calculate scaling factors xₛ, yₛ
5Ø  FOR I = 1 TO 2ØØ
6Ø  LET T = Ø.Ø314159∗I
7Ø  LET X = COS(T): LET Y = SIN(T)
8Ø  Convert (x,y) to screen coordinates (u, v) as in Section 1.7
     of Chapter 3
9Ø  Put a dot at screen point (u, v)
1ØØ NEXT I
```

So far, this plots the circle; now for the chords.

```
2ØØ FOR J = 1 TO 6Ø
21Ø LET T = 3.14159∗J/3Ø
22Ø LET X = COS(T): LET Y = SIN(T)
23Ø Convert to screen coordinates (u, v)
24Ø Move the cursor to screen point (u, v)
25Ø LET X = COS(M∗T): LET Y = SIN(M∗T)
26Ø Convert (x,y) to screen coordinates (u, v)
27Ø Draw the straight line from cursor position to screen
     point (u, v)
28Ø NEXT J
```

If 60 chords produce just a mess then try fewer, amending lines 2ØØ and 21Ø accordingly (for n chords, $t = 2\pi j/n$). This suggests, however, that your graphics resolution is not adequate for the effective drawing of envelopes. Try in succession $m = 2$, $m = 3$ and $m = 4$, and note that in each case a new curve appears to form, to which the chords are all *tangents*. The new curve is called the *envelope* of the chords. It has $m − 1$ cusps; see Fig. 2 for the case $m = 3$.

1.2 *Formulae for envelopes*

The theory of envelopes is something we cannot cover in the space available here. Instead we shall adopt a purely experimental approach in this section, hoping that you will try your own experiments in this rich and beautiful field. For a more theoretical and explanatory approach, see for example Bruce and Giblin (1984), Chapter 5. Our one theoretical comment here is as follows. Suppose that

$$p(t)x + q(t)y + r(t) = 0 \tag{1}$$

is the equation of a line in the plane whose coefficients are functions of a parameter t. For example in the chords example above it is the equation of the chord, namely

$$(\sin(mt) - \sin t)x + (\cos t - \cos(mt))y - \sin t = 0.$$

Then *the points of the envelope satisfy both* Equations (1) *and*

$$p'(t)x + q'(t)y + r'(t) = 0 \tag{2}$$

where p' is the derivative of p with respect to t, etc. Thus, solving Equations (1) and (2) for x and y gives

$$x = (r'q - rq')/(pq' - p'q), \quad y = (rp' - r'p)/(pq' - p'q), \tag{3}$$

which can be regarded as a parametrisation of the envelope by t since it expresses (x, y) on the envelope in terms of t.

For the chords example, this reduces (after some trigonometrical trickery) to

$$x = (m \cos t + \cos(mt))/(m + 1), \quad y = (m \sin t + \sin(mt))/(m + 1).$$

Fig. 2

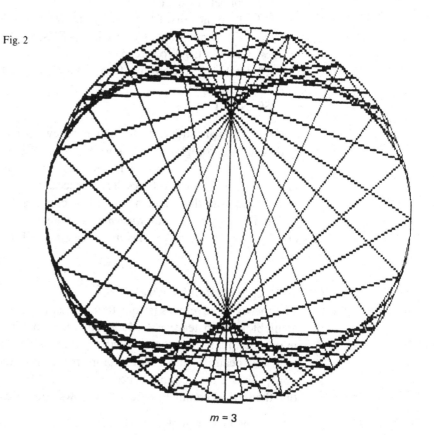

$m = 3$

It is of course possible to plot this as a parametrised curve, and indeed it is instructive to do so and to compare the result with the chords picture. Note the similarity between this parametrisation and the spirograph curve (Section 4.12 in Chapter 3), but note the essential difference of sign. *Is* the above curve a spirograph?

In the chords example, the straight lines stay entirely within the plotting rectangle, since they are inside the circle and *that* is entirely within the plotting rectangle. So nothing goes outside the screen area during plotting. However, in many examples it is much more convenient to draw the lines right across the screen. This presents problems if your micro objects to being given points outside the screen, for you must then calculate exactly where the line hits the boundary of the plotting rectangle. See the appendix for more details of this; here, we shall assume that, given *any* two points, the micro will draw that part of the line joining the points which lies within the plotting rectangle.

Here is a brief indication of why Equations (1) and (2) give the envelope. It is plausible (Fig. 3) that the points of the envelope can be approximated by intersection points of nearby lines in the family – here, the lines 1, 2, 3 and 4 give three intersection points of 1 and 2, 2 and 3, 3 and 4. If δt is a small change in t, then Equation (1) and

$$p(t + \delta t)x + q(t + \delta t)y + r(t + \delta t) = 0 \tag{4}$$

are two 'nearby lines'. Now if δt is small, then $(p(t + \delta t) - p(t))/\delta t \approx p'(t)$, so subtracting Equation (1) from Equation (4) gives approximately Equation (2), with the approximation becoming better as $\delta t \to 0$. Thus we can use Equations (1) and (2) instead of Equations (1) and (4) to obtain points of the envelope.

1.3 *Drawing lines across the screen*

Suppose we are given two distinct points (a_1, a_2) and (b_1, b_2) in the (x, y)-plane, at least one of which lies within the plotting rectangle. The point which is a distance d from (a_1, a_2) along the line joining the two points is

Fig. 3

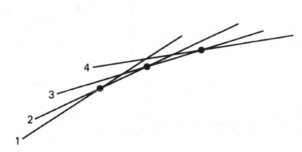

$$(a_1, a_2) + \frac{d(b_1 - a_1, b_2 - a_2)}{\sqrt{((b_1 - a_1)^2 + (b_2 - a_2)^2)}}. \qquad (5)$$

(Thus $d = 0$ gives (a_1, a_2), $d = $ (distance from (a_1, a_2) to (b_1, b_1)) gives (b_1, b_2), $d < 0$ gives points in the direction *away from* (b_1, b_2), and so on.) To extend the line right across the screen it is enough (even a little extravagant!) to join two points, given by $d = +r$ and $d = -r$, where r is the *diagonal* of the plotting rectangle in the (x, y)-plane (Fig. 4). There is no doubt that both the latter points are *beyond* the edge of the plotting rectangle, so long as (a_1, a_2) itself is within the rectangle. Of course,

$$r = \sqrt{((x_u - x_\ell)^2 + (y_u - y_\ell)^2)}. \qquad (6)$$

1.4 *More chords of a circle*

Consider the chord of the unit circle joining the point at angle t with the point at angle $\pi - mt$ (thus replacing mt with $\pi - mt$ in Program 1.1). If you try this just changing line 250 of Program 1.1 you will obtain a tangle of lines inside the circle but no envelope curve. The reason for this is simple: the envelope is now *outside* the circle, and the chords have to be extended at both ends to make the envelope visible. See Fig. 5.

Applying the technique of 1.3, the following program will serve.

> *Program: Chords 2*
> 10 INPUT XL, XU, YC, M
> 20 Calculate y_ℓ, y_u as in Section 1.7 of Chapter 3
> 30 Calculate scaling factors x_s, y_s
> 40 LET R = SQR((XU − XL)↑2 + (YU − YL)↑2)
> 50–100 As in Program 1.1

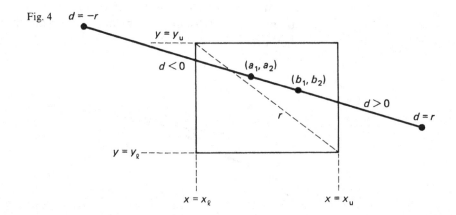

Fig. 4

```
2ØØ  FOR J = 1 TO 6Ø
21Ø  LET T = 3.14159*J/3Ø
22Ø  LET A1 = COS(T): LET A2 = SIN(T)
23Ø  LET B1 = COS(3.14159 − M*T):
     LET B2 = SIN(3.14159 − M*T)
```

You could, to be sure, use $b_1 = -\cos(mt)$, $b_2 = \sin(mt)$ here.

```
24Ø  LET L = SQR((B1 − A1)*(B1 − A1) +
     (B2 − A2)*(B2 − A2))
25Ø  IF L = Ø THEN GOTO 32Ø
```

Note: what is more likely than $l = 0$ is that for certain j (e.g. $j = 10$, 30, 50 when $m = 2$), l will be calculated as a *very small* number and that will make the calculations which follow very inaccurate. You could say 'IF ABS(L) < Ø.ØØ1 THEN GOTO 32Ø' in line 25Ø to avoid this (or explicitly omit those j for which (a_1, a_2) and (b_1, b_2) turn out to be the same point, because t and $\pi - mt$ differ by a multiple of 2π).

```
26Ø  LET X = A1 + R*(B1 − A1)/L:
     LET Y = A2 + R*(B2 − A2)/L
27Ø  Convert to screen coordinates (u, v) as in Section 1.7 of
     Chapter 3
28Ø  Move the cursor to screen point (u, v)
29Ø  LET X = A1 − R*(B1 − A1)/L:
     LET Y = A2 − R*(B2 − A2)/L
3ØØ  Convert to screen coordinates (u, v)
```

Fig. 5(i)

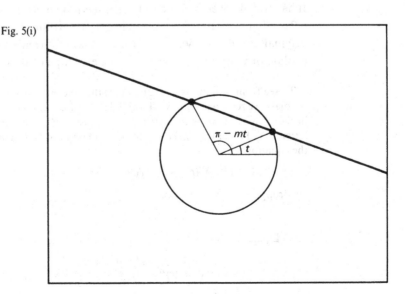

Fig. 5(*ii*)

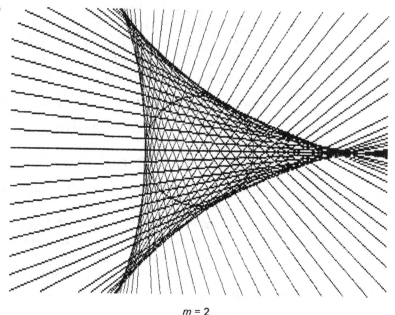

$m = 2$

310 Draw a line from cursor position to screen point (u, v)
320 NEXT J

Try $x_\ell = -3.5$, $x_u = 3.5$, $y_c = 0$, $m = 2$; and $x_\ell = -3$, $x_u = 3$, $y_c = 0$, $m = 4$. You should find that the envelope now has $m + 1$ cusps.

1.5 *Envelopes of normals to a curve*

It has already been pointed out in the section on evolutes (see Section 6.2 in Chapter 3) that the tangent line to the evolute E is normal to the original curve C. If we draw a good many normals to C then the evolute of C springs to the eye as the envelope of these normals.

To see from Equations (1), (2) and (3) that the evolute *is* the envelope of normals, we reason as follows. To avoid confusion between coordinates x, y in the plane and the parametrising functions for C, temporarily write the latter as X, Y: thus $((X(t), Y(t))$ is the general point of C. The normal line has the equation

$$(x - X(t)) X'(t) + (y - Y(t)) Y'(t) = 0$$

i.e. dropping t from the notation,

$$X'x - Y'y - (XX' + YY') = 0.$$

Thus Equation (3) gives

$$\begin{aligned}
x &= ((-X'^2 - Y'^2 - XX'' - YY'') Y' \\
&\quad + (XX' + YY') Y'')/(X'Y'' - X''Y') \\
&= X - Y'/\kappa,
\end{aligned}$$

where $\kappa = (X'\,Y'' - X''\,Y')/(X'^2 + Y'^2)^{3/2}$ is the curvature of C (compare Section 5.10 in Chapter 3). Similarly

$$y = Y + X'/\kappa,$$

so that the point (x, y) on the envelope is precisely the point of the evolute for the value of t in question. (See Equation (1) in §6 of Chapter 3.)

The argument is shorter in vector notation and using unit speed parametrisations; see Bruce and Giblin (1984), p. 89.

The point which is a distance r down the normal to a curve C (parametrising functions x and y) at the point of C with parameter t has already been used in the work on parallels. As in Equation (1) of Section 5.1, Chapter 3, the point is

$$(x - ry'/\sqrt{(x'^2 + y'^2)},\ y + rx'/\sqrt{(x'^2 + y'^2)}).$$

To draw the envelope of normals we draw the line joining (x, y) on C to this point, with $r =$ diagonal of the plotting rectangle as in Section 1.3 above. As before, 60 is about the right number of normals to draw to avoid a mess of lines on the screen.

A good physical interpretation of the evolute comes out of this envelope. For we can imagine rays (of heat, light, electromagnetic radiation) emanating from C as source and propagating down the normals to C. They *focus* along the evolute (Fig. 6). This fits in well with the evolute as the locus of cusps on the parallels to C (Section 5.10 in Chapter 3), for the parallels are the evolving wavefronts of the radiation and they focus at cusp points.

1.6 *Program: Normals*
This program draws 60 normals to a curve for which x, y, x' and y' are known functions of t, for $t_1 \le t \le t_u$.

```
10  INPUT TL, TU, XL, XU, YC
20  Calculate yℓ, yu as in Section 1.7 of Chapter 3
30  Calculate scaling factors xs, ys
40  LET R = SQR((XU − XL)↑2 + (YU − YL)↑2)
50  FOR J = 1 TO 60
60  LET T = TL + J∗(TU − TL)/60
70  Calculate x and y for this t
80  Convert (x,y) to screen coordinates (u, v)
90  Move the cursor to screen point (u, v)
100 Calculate x′ ( = X1) and y′ ( = Y1)
110 LET W = SQR(X1∗X1 + Y1∗Y1)
120 LET X = X − R∗Y1/W: LET Y = Y + R∗X1/W
130 Convert (x,y) to screen coordinates (u, v)
```

Fig. 6

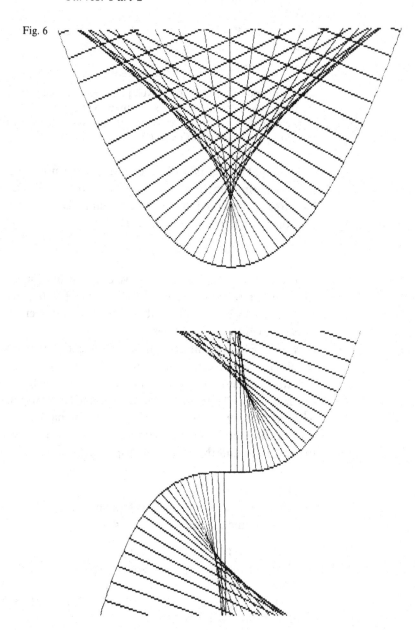

140 Draw a line from cursor position to screen point (u, v)
150 NEXT J

If you want to put the curve C in as well, then either do this as join-the-dots, or as dots-only for many more values of t than 60 (maybe 250 values). If you do a dots-only plot of C for 60 values of t

then of course you will simply replot the end-points of the 60 normals, and nothing new will appear.

1.7 *Exercise: Parabola and ellipse*

For the parabola, $x = t$, $y = t^2$, take $t_\ell = -1$, $t_u = 1$, $x_\ell = -1$, $x_u = 1$, $y_c = 0.7$. Compare with Fig. 6.

For the ellipse $x = a \cos t$, $y = \sin t$, take $t_\ell = 0$, $t_u = 2\pi$, $y_c = 0$ and

$$
\begin{aligned}
x_\ell &= -1.5, \quad x_u = 1.5, \quad a = 1.2; \\
x_\ell &= -2, \quad\;\; x_u = 2, \quad\;\; a = 1.5; \\
x_\ell &= -4, \quad\;\; x_u = 4, \quad\;\; a = 2.
\end{aligned}
$$

1.8 *Exercise: Cubic curves*

Let $x = t$, $y = t^3$, taking $t_\ell = -1$, $t_u = 1$, $x_\ell = -2$, $x_u = 2$, $y_c = 0$. In this case the normals as drawn only focus on the evolute for $t > 0$; for $t < 0$ the curvature is < 0 and the normals need to be drawn the *other* way in order to focus. Can you amend the program so that this is done? See Section 1.10 below and Fig. 6.

For the cubic oval, as in Exercise 5.6 of Chapter 3, try $t_\ell = 0$, $t_u = 2\pi$, $x_\ell = -0.2$, $x_u = 1.2$, $y_c = 0.1$, $a = 0.8$, $b = 0.17$ (compare Exercise 6.4 of Chapter 3). Try other values of a and b, adjusting the other numbers accordingly.

1.9 *Exercise: Quartic curve*

Let $x = t$, $y = t^4$, taking $t_\ell = -1$, $t_u = 1$, $x_\ell = -1$, $x_u = 1$, $y_c = 0.6$. This time the curvature is positive for all t and the normals focus in the picture, except that normals near $t = 0$ try to focus very far away, since $\kappa = 0$ at $t = 0$ so the evolute goes off to infinity. (Compare Exercise 5.13 of Chapter 3.)

1.10 *Focusing all the normals*

It is possible to make all the normals focus by calculating κ for each t, using the formula $\kappa = (x' y'' - x'' y')/(x'^2 + y'^2)^{3/2}$ (so you need x'' and y''), and then, for values of t which make $\kappa < 0$, changing r to $-r$ in line 12Ø of Program 1.6. So you need to insert

> 112 Calculate x'' and y'' (written X2, Y2)
> 114 LET H = (X1 * Y2 − X2 * Y1)
> 116 IF H < Ø THEN LET R = − R

while leaving line 12Ø as it is.

A good example to try this on (besides Exercise 1.8) is a limaçon (see Exercise 4.4 in Chapter 3), which, for $2 < a < 4$, has inflexions where κ changes sign.

1.11 *Envelopes of reflected rays*

As a final example of an envelope of lines we consider the following situation. Take a curve *C* and a point *S* and regard *S* as a *source* and *C* as a *mirror*. Rays of light emerge from *S* and are *reflected* from *C* (Fig. 7). These reflected rays focus along a curve in a very similar way to the focusing of the normals along the evolute. The curve of focusing is a bright curve – also a hot curve when the rays are sunlight; hence the name *caustic* curve. An example from nature is the bright curve you see on the surface of the coffee in a cup in sunlight: light from the distant sun *S* is reflected from the rounded inner surface of the cup and the coffee surface acts as a screen to make the reflected light visible to us along the bright focusing curve (Fig. 8).

How can we plot the reflected rays? Extend the reflected ray backwards, as in Fig. 7. The three marked angles are all equal, because of the straight line just drawn and because the ray from *S* to *P* makes the same angle with the tangent as the reflected ray does. (This is the *law of reflexion*.) Making *PQ = PS* it now follows by congruent triangles that *QS* is perpendicular to the tangent line at *P* to *C*: in fact, *Q is the reflexion of S in the tangent line to C at P*.

Thus, given *C* and *S*, we can find the reflected ray for each position of *P* on *C* by first calculating the reflexion *Q* of *S* in the tangent line and then drawing the line from *P* in the direction of *QP* extended.

Now *SQ* has direction *normal* to *C* at *P* = (*x, y*) (where *x* and *y* are, as usual, functions of *t*), so any point on *SQ* has coordinates of the form

$$(s_1 - hy', \ s_2 + hx') \quad \text{for some number } h, \tag{7}$$

Fig. 7

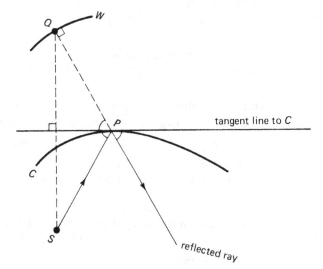

where $S = (s_1, s_2)$. (Recall that (x', y') has the direction of the tangent to C and $(-y', x')$ has the direction of the normal to C.) We want to choose h so that the distance, namely $h(x'^2 + y'^2)^{1/2}$, from S to this point equals *twice* the distance from S to the tangent line. Using the equation of the tangent line we find

$$h = \frac{2(s_1 - x)y' + 2(y - s_2)x'}{x'^2 + y'^2}. \tag{8}$$

Thus, Q is given by substituting Equation (8) into Formula (7).

We now want to draw C, mark S in some way, and draw the reflected rays from about 40 points of C (not the incident rays as these will only confuse the picture). In fact it can be instructive in some examples to draw the reflected rays starting at Q rather than at P. The reason for this will be explained later.

There is one additional refinement worth considering, which arises because some of the reflected rays may not in fact come to a focus on the same side of C as S. They may be *diverging* after reflexion. These rays do not then contribute to the actual caustic; nevertheless something can be gained by drawing them backwards (from P towards Q) for they will then come to a focus, albeit on the 'wrong' side of C. This is completely analogous to the problem discussed in Section 1.10, where normals sometimes focus on the 'wrong' side of a curve. See Project 1.20 below.

Fig. 8

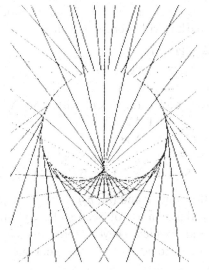

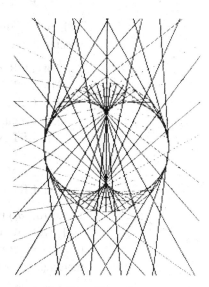

reflected rays only are drawn

rays reflected from the top are extended backwards to focus

1.12 *Program: Caustic*

We assume that the curve C is given by parametrisation with x and y known functions of t, where $t_\ell \leq t \leq t_u$. The derivatives x' and y' will as usual be denoted by X1 and Y1. The source S has coordinates (s_1, s_2), denoted (S1, S2).

```
1Ø  INPUT TL, TU, XL, XU, YC, S1, S2
2Ø  Calculate yₑ, yᵤ as in Section 1.7 of Chapter 3
3Ø  Calculate scaling factors xₛ, yₛ
4Ø  LET R = SQR((XU − XL)↑2 + (YU − YL)↑2)
5Ø  FOR I = 1 TO 2ØØ
6Ø  LET T = TL + I*(TU − TL)/2ØØ
7Ø  Calculate x and y for this t
8Ø  IF X < XL OR X > XU OR Y < YL OR Y > YU
    THEN GOTO 11Ø
9Ø  Convert (x,y) to screen coordinates (u, v) as in Section 1.7
    of Chapter 3
1ØØ Put a dot at screen point (u, v)
11Ø NEXT I
```

Thus lines 5Ø–11Ø plot the curve C.

```
2ØØ LET X = S1: LET Y = S2
21Ø IF X < XL OR X > XU OR Y < YL OR Y > YU
    THEN GOTO 3ØØ
22Ø Convert (x,y) to screen coordinates (u, v)
23Ø Put a dot at screen point (u, v)
```

This marks the source S with a dot. Of course you can be more spectacular and mark it with a cross or a star.

```
3ØØ FOR J = 1 TO 4Ø
31Ø LET T = TL + J*(TU − TL)/4Ø
32Ø Calculate x and y for this t
33Ø Calculate x' and y' for this t (written X1, Y1)
34Ø LET A1 = X: LET A2 = Y
35Ø LET H = (2*(S1 − X)*Y1 +
    2*(Y − S2)*X1)/(X1*X1 + Y1*Y1)
36Ø LET B1 = S1 − H*Y1: LET B2 = S2 + H*X1
```

So far (a_1, a_2) is the point P and (b_1, b_2) is the point Q as in Section 1.11; we now use the formula of Section 1.3 to calculate a point (c_1, c_2) on QP extended which is beyond the boundary of the plotting rectangle (at any rate provided P is in the rectangle).

```
37Ø LET L = SQR((B1 − A1)*(B1 − A1) +
    (B2 − A2)*(B2 − A2))
```

380 IF L = Ø THEN GOTO 44Ø

390 LET C1 = A1 − R*(B1 − A1)/L: LET C2 = A2 − R*
(B2 − A2)/L

Note that *l* can only be zero if $P = Q$, and this can only happen if the source S is at the point P on the mirror curve C. In practice we avoid this case, but line 38Ø is put in just as a precaution.

4ØØ Convert (x, y) to screen coordinates (u, v)

Since $(x, y) = (a_1, a_2)$ this refers to the point $P = (a_1, a_2)$; if you want to draw the reflected rays from the point Q then precede line 4ØØ with the following line 395:

395 LET X = B1: LET Y = B2
4Ø5 Move the cursor to screen point (u, v)
41Ø LET X = C1: LET Y = C2
42Ø Convert (x,y) to screen coordinates (u, v)
43Ø Draw a line from cursor position to screen point (u, v)
44Ø NEXT J

1.13 *Exercise: C a circle*

Thus $x = \cos t$, $y = \sin t$. Take $t_\ell = 0$, $t_u = 2\pi$. For the case where the reflected rays are drawn from the point P (thus without line 395 above) you can take $x_\ell = -2$, $x_u = 2$, $y_c = 0$ so that just the source coordinates are varying from one experiment to another (and indeed all the other inputs could be fixed by defining them in an additional line 5, say).

Try $(s_1, s_2) = (0, 0)$ (you should find all reflected rays pass through $(0, 0)$ again; why is this?).

Try in succession $(s_1, s_2) = 0, (0.25), (0, 0.4), (0, 0.5), (0, 0.75), (0, 0.9), (0, 1.001)$ (to avoid having S on C), $(0, 2), (0, 10), (0, 100)$.

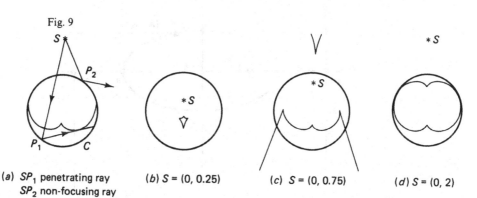

Fig. 9

(a) SP_1 penetrating ray
SP_2 non-focusing ray

(b) $S = (0, 0.25)$

(c) $S = (0, 0.75)$

(d) $S = (0, 2)$

When $s_2 > 0.5$ you should find that not all the reflected rays are coming to a focus: only certain parts of the circle are contributing to the envelope of reflected rays which is the caustic. When $s_2 > 1$ then of course S is *outside* the circle, and we are allowing rays to penetrate once before being reflected from the far side (Fig. 9(a)). (With sunlight on a cup of coffee the rays slant in over the edge of the cup!) Fig. 9 also shows the shapes of three 'complete' caustic curves, where the non-focusing rays are extended backwards to focus on the 'wrong side' of C.

1.14 *Exercise: C an ellipse*
Here $x = a \cos t$, $y = \sin t$. Again take $t_\ell = 0$, $t_u = 2\pi$. Try say $a = 1.5$ and various positions for S moving up the y-axis as in Exercise 1.13, comparing with the circle case. Try also $a = 1.5$ and S far away in various directions, e.g. $S = (100 - k, \ 100 + k)$ for $k = 0, 10, 20, \ldots,$ 100. Why does the symmetry of the ellipse show that essentially all shapes of caustic are obtained by considering S in just one quadrant? Try $S = (0, 1000)$ and various values for a, such as 1.5, 1.8, 2.

For $a = 1.5$, try $S = (-1.118, 0)$. You should find that all the reflected rays pass through a point (actually $(+1.118, 0)$). These two points are the foci of the ellipse (see below, Exercise 4.2 of Chapter 3 and Exercise 2.10 of Chapter 2). Each point is called a *focus*; the reason for the name is clear!

1.15 *More about ellipses*
Let $P = (a \cos t, \sin t)$ be any point on the ellipse and let e be the

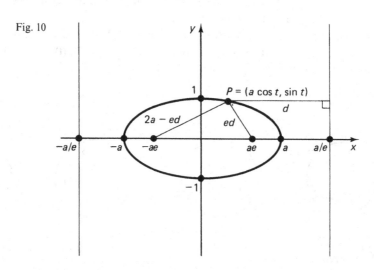

Fig. 10

eccentricity of the ellipse, defined by $e = (a^2 - 1)^{1/2}/a$ when $a \geq 1$ (compare Exercise 2.10 of Chapter 2). It is easy to check (try it!) that: distance of P from $(ae, 0) = e \times$ (distance of P from line $x = a/e$), provided $e > 0$, i.e. the ellipse is *not* a circle. This amounts to checking that

$$(a \cos t - ae)^2 + \sin^2 t = e^2(a/e - a \cos t)^2.$$

Equally well, replacing e by $-e$, we have:
distance of P from $(-ae, 0) = e \times$ (distance of P from line $x = -a/e$). See Fig. 10.

Hence *the sum of the distances of P from* $(-ae, 0)$ *and* $(ae, 0)$ *is* $e(a/e + a/e) = 2a$, *which is constant for all positions of P*. (Compare Section 3.1 below on Cartesian ovals.)

The lines $x = \pm a/e$ are called the *directrices* of the ellipse, and the property, 'distance to focus $= e$ times distance to corresponding directrix', can be used as a definition of an ellipse, though it fails for a circle, where $e = 0$.

Let $S = (-ae, 0)$, $S' = (ae, 0)$, $P = (a \cos t, \sin t)$. Draw SF and $S'F'$, perpendiculars onto the tangent line at P, as in Fig. 11. The tangent line has the equation $a(\sin t)y + (\cos t)x - a = 0$, so the ratio of the lengths $SF/S'F'$ is

$$\frac{a + ae \cos t}{a - ae \cos t} = \frac{1 + e \cos t}{1 - e \cos t}.$$

(Note: $-1 < e \cos t < 1$ since $0 < e < 1$ and $-1 \leq \cos t \leq 1$.) This is the same as the ratio PS/PS' since, by the above, the latter equals

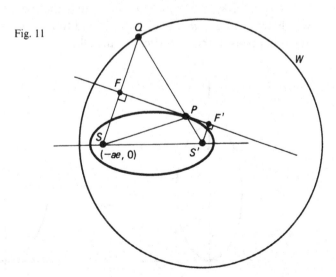

Fig. 11

the ratio of the distances from the two directrices, namely $(a \cos t + a/e)/(a/e - a \cos t)$. Hence the triangles PFS and $PF'S'$ are similar, so the angles at P are equal: SP and PS' make equal angles with the tangent. Thus, as in the last example of Exercise 1.14, incident rays SP are reflected through S'.

As a mathematical exercise, deduce that QPS' is a straight line, where Q is as usual the reflexion of S in the tangent line. Why does it follow that, as P moves round the ellipse, Q moves round a circle? Check this result also by calculating Q as in Section 1.11, Formula (7) and Equation (8), and the distance QS'. Given the two axes of the ellipse, how can you find the points S and S' (the foci) just with a pair of compasses? (Use the 'sum of distances = $2a$' property.)

1.16 *Exercise: Parabola*

Here $x = t$, $y = t^2$ (this is just as interesting as the more general $x = at$, $y = at^2$ with equation $ay = x^2$). Try $S = (0, \frac{1}{4})$. You should find all the reflected rays parallel to the y-axis. Equally, with incident rays parallel to the y-axis, i.e. S very far away in the y-axis direction, all reflected rays pass through $(0, \frac{1}{4})$. Try $S = (0, 1000)$. Needless to say, $(0, \frac{1}{4})$ is called the *focus* of the parabola.

Prove that the distance of any point P on the parabola from the focus equals the distance of P from a certain fixed line parallel to the x-axis. (This line is called the *directrix* of the parabola.)

Consider the ellipse of Fig. 12, which has equation $2x^2/a + (y - a)^2/a^2 = 1$, i.e. $x^2 - y = y^2/2a$. If $a \to \infty$ then the equation becomes $y = x^2$: the parabola is a limiting case of an ellipse. The eccentricity e of this ellipse satisfies $a/2 = a^2(1 - e^2)$, so $e^2 = 1 - 1/2a$; as $a \to \infty$, $e \to 1$. Show that the foci of the ellipse, which are at $(0, a \pm ae)$, tend to $(0, \frac{1}{4})$ and to infinity on the y-axis. What happens to the directrices of the ellipse?

Fig. 12

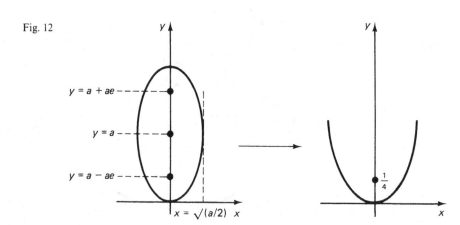

Use the program to draw the caustic for the parabola with S far away in various directions. This gives a rather beautiful curve (in fact a nodal cubic; compare Exercise 4.7 in Chapter 3), except when S is far away in the y-direction, when the caustic collapses completely to the focus $(0, \frac{1}{4})$.

We now consider some examples where the reflected rays are drawn from the point Q rather than from P; this is done by inserting line 395 into Program 1.12.

1.17 *Exercise: Ellipse*
Take C as in Exercise 1.14, with $a = 1.5$, $S = (-1.118, 0)$, $t_\ell = 0$, $t_u = 2\pi$, $x_\ell = -3$, $x_u = 5$, $y_c = 0$. Compare Section 1.15: S is at a focus, and Q lies on a circle, W say, centred at the other focus and of radius $2a = 3$. All the reflected rays are *radii* of this circle. Note that, therefore, the reflected rays are all along the normal lines to the circle W (Fig. 11).

1.18 *Exercise: Circle*
For C a circle ($a = 1$ in Exercise 1.14, so $x = \cos t$, $y = \sin t$), take $t_\ell = 0$, $t_u = 2\pi$, $x_\ell = -3$, $x_u = 3$, and (a) $y_c = 0$, $S = (0, 0.3)$; (b) $y_c = -0.2$, $S = (0, 0.5)$; (c) $y_c = -0.6$, $S = (0, 0.75)$; (d) $y_c = -0.8$, $S = (0, 0.9)$; (e) $y_c = -0.8$, $S = (0, 1)$.

Although the locus W of the point Q (where the reflected rays are extended back to) is not explicitly drawn, you should be able to make out its shape fairly clearly from the picture. (Alternatively, draw it in after C is drawn!) It should then be fairly clear that *the reflected rays are all normal lines to W.* (You may guess that W is actually a limaçon in these examples, and indeed that is true; can you prove it?)

1.19 *Orthotomics*
Note that if, for any mirror C, we replace the incident ray SP (Fig. 7) by a ray QP then (assuming a finite speed of light) the new ray will reach P at the same instant as the old ray would have done, since SP, QP are equal in length. In fact the source S can be completely replaced by the locus W of Q, and the reflected rays become simply normals to W: the caustic becomes the envelope of normal lines to W.

To see why QP really is always normal to W we may indulge in a little vector notation, writing $c(t)$ for P, $w(t)$ for Q and s for S. Let $T(t)$ and $N(t)$ be the unit tangent and normal vectors to C at P, so that $N' = -\kappa T \|c'\|$ (compare Section 6.2 in Chapter 3). Then $w = s + 2((c - s).N)N$, where we drop t from the notation and use $\cdot$ to denote the usual scalar product of vectors (so $(c - s) . N$ is, up to sign, the distance from S to the tangent line at P). Differentiation gives

$$w' = -2\kappa \|c'\| (((c - s) . T)N + ((c - s) . N)T),$$

so that the *tangent* to W is along the direction given by the right-hand side of this equation. The *normal* is then at right-angles to this direction, so has direction:

$$2\kappa \|c'\| (((c - s) . T)T - ((c - s) . N)N),$$

using $T . N = 0$. On the other hand, QP has direction:

$$c - w = c - s - 2((c - s) . N)N.$$

However,

$$c - s = ((c - s) . N)N + ((c - s) . T)T,$$

since T and N are perpendicular unit vectors; thus, so long as κ and c' are non-zero, *QP has the same direction as the normal to W*. The curve W is called the *orthotomic* of C with respect to S. (See also Yates (1974), pp. 15, 160, Lockwood (1967), p. 153, and Bruce and Giblin (1984), p. 92.)

Since the reflected rays are normals to W, it follows that *the caustic is the evolute of W* (compare Section 1.5). If we know the curvature of W then we can draw the caustic directly as the evolute of W, as in §6 of Chapter 3. By separating the cases where the curvature κ_W of W is positive or negative we can also draw the reflected rays in the correct direction from P for focusing. With the curvature of C assumed positive, this direction is:

$$\text{away from} \quad Q \quad \text{if} \quad \kappa_W > 0;$$
$$\text{towards} \quad Q \quad \text{if} \quad \kappa_W < 0.$$

(In the Program 1.12, the reflected rays are always drawn away from Q.) We shall leave it as a project to incorporate this refinement into Program 1.12, given the following formula for κ_W. (Compare Bruce and Giblin (1984), p. 147.)

Write g for the distance SP and p for the perpendicular $\frac{1}{2}SQ$ in Fig. 7. (In the above reference, g appears as r.) Then

$$g = \sqrt{((x - s_1)^2 + (y - s_2)^2)},$$

where $P = (x, y)$ and x, y are as usual functions of t, and

$$p = ((x - s_1)y' - (y - s_2)x')/\sqrt{(x'^2 + y'^2)}.$$

The formula for κ_W is then

$$\kappa_W = (2g^2 \kappa - p)/2g^3 \kappa.$$

You need to beware of $\kappa_W = 0$: the point on the caustic is then at infinity, and such points are ignored for plotting purposes!

1.20 *Project*

Use the formula above for κ_W to amend Program 1.12 so that reflected rays are drawn (from P or from Q as you like) in the direction in which they focus.

Try the examples of Exercise 1.18 with the reflected rays drawn in the correct direction for focusing. This makes a difference for $S = (0, s_2)$ with $s_2 > 0.5$ (why is this?).

Try an ellipse with various values for a (including $a = 1$, a circle), with S far away. For a circle, note that the full caustic, revealing what nature hides, is a symmetrical curve showing two cusps of the kind which occur on the coffee-cup caustic (Fig. 8).

1.21 *Project: Plotting caustics*

Instead of drawing the reflected rays and noting their envelope we can, as noted in Section 1.19, draw the caustic curve itself by plotting the evolute of W. Now that we have given the curvature of W and the direction of the normal (from Q to P) put together a program for plotting the caustic directly in this way. You have then before you a rich field for experiment and observation. You can of course try again all the above examples where C is an ellipse or parabola. Here is one further suggestion.

Arrange the program so that, for each parameter value t, first a point of C and then a point of the caustic is plotted (rather than first all of C and then all of the caustic). For a circle C, which points of C are plotted as the *cusps* on the caustic are being formed? You should find, for S inside C, four points, marked × in Fig. 13(a). For S outside C there are two points, as in Fig. 13(b). In the latter case note also that the points of contact of the tangents to S from C are also points of the caustic, which is *tangent* to C at these points. (Compare Bruce and Giblin (1984), pp. 145, 143.)

Fig. 13

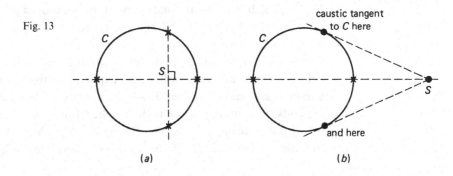

(a)   (b)

1.22 *Project: More envelopes*

A rich source of envelopes of lines is the following simple construction. For each angle t in a certain range, $t_\ell \leqslant t \leqslant t_u$, consider the line through $(0, 0)$ at angle t. Let h be a function of t and consider the line l_t through $(h(t)\cos t, h(t)\sin t)$ perpendicular to the line at angle t. Then draw the envelope of lines l_t. Thus a general point on the line l_t has coordinates $(h(t)\cos t - s\sin t, h(t)\sin t + s\cos t)$ for arbitrary s. If you want to allow t to be any angle then it's better to have h periodic with period 2π; then $t = 0$ and $t = 2\pi$ give the same l_t. Try $h(t) = \sin(nt)$ for $n = 2, 3, 4$ say. Do the curves look familiar? (Compare Section 4.12 of Chapter 3; can you establish a connexion?)

§2

Contours (level sets)

2.1 *Contours and implicit functions*

The subject of contours is a big one, and we have space here only to scratch the surface (or perhaps cut the surface?). The idea is to sketch the points (x, y) in the plane which satisfy a given equation

$$f(x, y) = c,$$

where c is constant. For example, the equation $x^2 + y^2 = c$ gives a circle for $c > 0$, a single point $(0, 0)$ for $c = 0$ and nothing at all for $c < 0$. The reasons for the names 'contour' and 'level set' are as follows: writing $z = f(x, y)$, the graph of f in three-dimensional space with coordinates (x, y, z) is the set of points $(x, y, f(x, y))$, and those points of this surface at 'level' c (i.e. where the plane $z = c$ cuts the surface) form a curve which is called the *contour* of the surface at level c. See Fig. 14, where $z = x^2 + y^2$ is drawn in (*b*). The curve $f(x, y) = c$, $z = c$ in the plane $z = c$ then projects down to the curve $f(x, y) = c$, $z = 0$ in the plane $z = 0$, and regarding this as the (x, y)-plane, the contour of the surface projects to the curve $f(x, y) = c$ in the (x, y)-plane. As c changes, so the contour will change: lowering c for $f(x, y) = x^2 + y^2$ causes the circle in Fig. 14 to shrink and finally vanish as c becomes negative.

On geographical maps of hills the contours are, of course, projected down to the (x, y)-plane of the map in the manner of Fig. 14, and by the spacing and shape of the contours a practised eye can judge the shape of the hill (i.e. the graph $z = f(x, y)$) which gave rise to the contours.

From a mathematical point of view, the equation $f(x, y) = c$ defines a curve implicitly rather than explicitly in the manner of the parametrisations of Chapter 3, §4. The connexion between the two methods of defining a curve is the Implicit Function Theorem (see for example Bruce and Giblin (1984), p. 57). This says that, in suitable circumstances, if $f(x_0, y_0) = c$, then the solutions to

Fig. 14

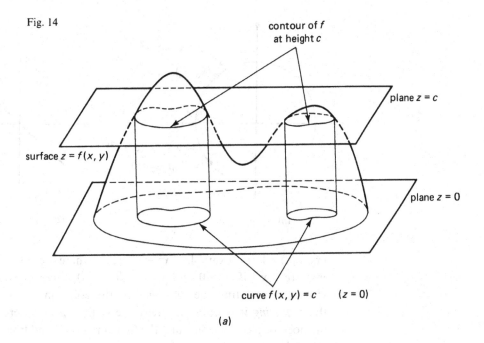

contour of *f*
at height *c*

plane *z* = *c*

surface *z* = *f*(*x*, *y*)

plane *z* = 0

curve *f*(*x*, *y*) = *c*   (*z* = 0)

(*a*)

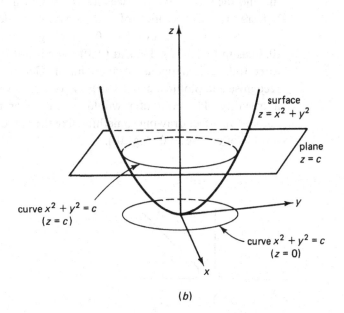

surface
$z = x^2 + y^2$

plane
z = *c*

curve $x^2 + y^2 = c$
(*z* = *c*)

curve $x^2 + y^2 = c$
(*z* = 0)

(*b*)

$f(x, y) = c$ where x is close to x_0 and y is close to y_0, can be written in the form $y = g(x)$ for a function g. That is $f(x, y) = c$ can be *solved* for y in terms of x near to a known solution point. (The suitable circumstances are that the partial derivative $\partial f/\partial y$ is non-zero at

Fig. 15

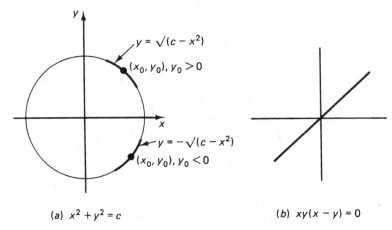

(a) $x^2 + y^2 = c$ (b) $xy(x - y) = 0$

(x_0, y_0).) For example $x^2 + y^2 = c$, where $c > 0$, becomes $y = \sqrt{(c - x^2)}$ if $y_0 > 0$ and $y = -\sqrt{(c - x^2)}$ if $y_0 < 0$ (Fig. 15(a)). However, asserting the *existence* of the solution $y = g(x)$ is one thing; *finding* it is quite another. We shall consider here just two methods of plotting contours, the first very crude and time-consuming and the second with a measure of sophistication.

Here is one source of difficulty. Consider the equation $x^2 y - x y^2 = 0$, i.e. $xy(x - y) = 0$, which give three lines through $(0, 0)$ as in Fig. 15(b). Thus at $(0, 0)$ there is not just one curve, but three (all, as it happens, straight lines). Getting the computer to recognise and plot in a neighbourhood of such a *singular point* is not a triviality. The computer would much prefer to round off the corners, in effect drawing something like the curve $xy(x - y) = c$ for a value of c close to 0 (Fig. 16).

Fig. 16

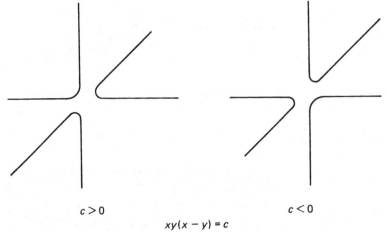

$c > 0$ $c < 0$

$xy(x - y) = c$

Singular points can be identified in advance as those points of the contour where both partial derivatives, $\partial f/\partial x$ and $\partial f/\partial y$, are zero. Other points of the contour are *regular* points, and near a regular point we can either solve for y in terms of x (if $\partial f/\partial y \neq 0$) or for x in terms of y (if $\partial f/\partial x \neq 0$) and obtain just *one* piece of smooth curve as the contour. (Indeed we usually have the choice of expressing y in terms of x or x in terms of y.) (Compare Bruce and Giblin (1984), p. 60.) We shall not, however, enter here into the tricky problem of identifying the singular points in advance, but just plunge ahead and see what can be achieved by relatively simple methods.

2.2 *The method of sign changes (scanning the screen)*
In this subsection we consider level sets $f(x, y) = 0$. This is no loss of generality, since the constant c can be absorbed into the function f, provided the value of c is given.

Suppose the point (x, y) moves along a line in the plane given by $y = y_0$, a constant. What happens as this line *crosses* the contour $f(x, y) = 0$? As a rule, f changes sign ($+$ to $-$ or $-$ to $+$), as in Fig. 17(*a*). If we are unlucky (Fig. 17(*b*)), the line might *touch* the contour and f might then fail to change sign. However, even in that case we expect nearby lines to be better behaved (Fig. 17(*c*)), so we don't miss much of the contour by looking for sign changes in f.

The idea, then, is to scan across the screen many times, putting a dot whenever there is a change of sign in f between one point and the previous one. If there are n horizontal lines $y = y_0$ and n points on each at which f is evaluated, that makes n^2 evaluations – a very expensive operation in computer time if n is at all large. However, you can always go away and have a cup of tea (or an overnight sleep,

Fig. 17

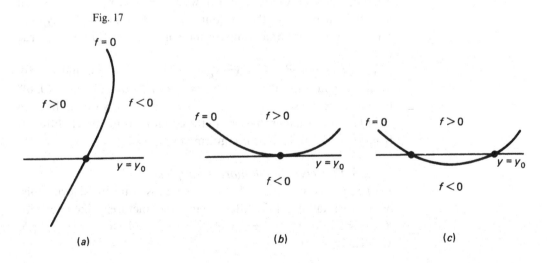

$f = 0$

$f > 0$ $f < 0$

$y = y_0$

(*a*)

$f = 0$ $f > 0$

$y = y_0$

$f < 0$

(*b*)

$f = 0$ $f > 0$

$y = y_0$

$f < 0$

(*c*)

or a fortnight's holiday, depending on n), while the picture is forming!

2.3 *Program: Scan*
```
1Ø INPUT XL, XU, YC, N
2Ø Calculate yₗ, yᵤ as in Section 1.7 of Chapter 3
3Ø Calculate scaling factors xₛ, yₛ
4Ø FOR I = 1 TO N
5Ø LET Y = YL + I*(YU – YL)/N
6Ø FOR J = 1 TO N
7Ø LET X = XL + J*(XU – XL)/N
8Ø Calculate f(x, y), calling the result F
9Ø IF J = 1 THEN GOTO 13Ø
1ØØ IF F*G > Ø THEN GOTO 13Ø
```

Here G stands for the previous value of F; see line 13Ø

```
11Ø Convert (x, y) to screen coordinates (u, v)
12Ø Put a dot at screen point (u, v)
13Ø LET G = F
14Ø NEXT J
15Ø NEXT I
```

At line 1ØØ, the current and previous values of $f(x, y)$ are compared for sign, except that at the start of a new j-loop there *is* no previous value. Perhaps you can use your knowledge of your own micro to speed up the program.

In Exercises 2.4 and 2.5, use Scan to plot the contour $f(x, y) = 0$.

2.4 *Exercise: Cubic curves*
Take $f(x, y) = xy(x - y)$ (Fig. 15), with $x_\ell = -2$, $x_u = 2$, $y_c = 0$ and $n = 50$. Which part of the contour $f(x, y) = 0$ is missing? Why? Try $f(x, y) = x(x^2 - y^2)$ and compare the computer picture with a true one.

Take $f(x, y) = y^2 + x^3 - x^2$, $x_\ell = -1$, $x_u = 2$, $y_c = 0$ and $n = 50$. What do you think the contour $f = 0$ *really* looks like near $(0, 0)$? (Compare Exercise 4.7 in Chapter 3.) When x is very small, the term x^3 in f is much smaller than x^2, so the equation is not much different from $y^2 - x^2 = 0$. Does this confirm your guess?

2.5 *Exercise: Some more examples*
Let $f(x, y) = x^2y - xy^2 + y^4 - x^2y^2$. Perhaps you can factorize this, before or, failing that, after seeing the picture! Likewise with $f(x, y) = x^2 - x^2y^2 - y^3 + x^2y^3 + y^5 - x^4$. (Take $x_\ell = -1.5$, $x_u = 1.5$, $y_c = 0$.)

Take $f(x, y) = y^2 - 2x^2 y + x^4$. What goes wrong here?

Take $f(x, y) = x^3 - xy^2 + y^2 - 4$, taking $x_\ell = -4$, $x_u = 4$, $y_c = 0$.

Take $f(x, y) = x^3 - 6y^2 + y^3$, with $x_\ell = -7$, $x_u = 7$, $y_c = 3$. In this example, you can find the singular points, given by $\partial f / \partial x = \partial f / \partial y = 0$. What does $f = 0$ look like near $(0, 0)$? Compare the remarks in Exercise 2.4 above.

Take $f(x, y) = x^4 - x^2 y + y^3$. Here, $f = 0$ gives a curve with three branches crossing at $(0, 0)$. (Close to $x = y = 0$, the x^4 term is relatively insignificant.)

There are more examples in Exercises 4.8 and 4.9 of Chapter 3.

2.6 *An incremental method*

After trying a few of the above exercises you will be in a good position to appreciate how bad the scanning method is. Here is a first attempt at producing a method of following the contour instead of stumbling over it. The method assumes that:

(*a*) there are no singular points on the piece of contour being followed (i.e. on $f(x, y) = c$, the equations $\partial f / \partial x = \partial f / \partial y = 0$ have no solution);

(*b*) we know fairly accurately *one* point (x_0, y_0) on the required contour $f(x, y) = c$.

In fact any point (x_0, y_0) at which f is defined must lie on *some* contour of f, namely the contour $f(x, y) = f(x_0, y_0)$. What we try to do is to tiptoe along *that* contour in tiny steps. There is no need to know in advance whether (*a*) holds: if a singular point is encountered the method simply comes to a halt, though in practice the singular point will probably not be encountered precisely.

Here's how the method works. Starting at (x_0, y_0) we want ideally to move a short distance along a chord of the contour $f(x, y) = c$

Fig. 18

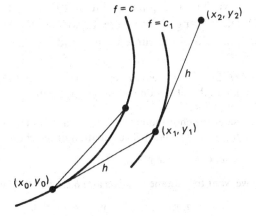

(where $c = f(x_0, y_0)$) to a nearby point. Failing that, what we do is to move a short distance h, one way or the other, along the *tangent* to the contour at (x_0, y_0); see Fig. 18, where the distance h has been somewhat exaggerated. Admittedly the new point (x_1, y_1) will probably not lie exactly on the original contour of f, but if h is small then we may expect it to lie on a very close contour $f(x, y) = c_1$ for c_1 close to c. We now move along the tangent to *this* contour a distance h, and so on. We obtain a sequence of points (x_0, y_0), (x_1, y_1), (x_2, y_2), . . . which form a surprisingly good approximation to the original contour, as you will see.

We need to find the point (x_1, y_1) and to do this we need to know the tangent line to the contour $f(x, y) = c$ at (x_0, y_0). It is not difficult to show that this tangent line has the equation

$$(x - x_0)(\partial f / \partial x)_0 + (y - y_0)(\partial f / \partial y)_0 = 0, \tag{1}$$

where $(\partial f / \partial x)_0$ and $(\partial f / \partial y)_0$ are the partial derivatives of f with respect to x and y respectively evaluated at (x_0, y_0). (Thus to find $\partial f / \partial x$, pretend y is a constant, and differentiate f with respect to x.) One of the two points of this tangent line at a distance h from (x_0, y_0) is then the point (x_1, y_1) given by

$$\left.\begin{array}{l} x_1 = x_0 - \dfrac{h(\partial f / \partial y)_0}{\sqrt{((\partial f / \partial x)_0^2 + (\partial f / \partial y)_0^2)}}, \\[3mm] y_1 = y_0 + \dfrac{h(\partial f / \partial x)_0}{\sqrt{((\partial f / \partial x)_0^2 + (\partial f / \partial y)_0^2)}}. \end{array}\right\} \tag{2}$$

Here, $\partial f / \partial x$ and $\partial f / \partial y$ are evaluated at (x_0, y_0).

Note that it is crucial that $\partial f / \partial x$ or $\partial f / \partial y$ is non-zero at (x_0, y_0); otherwise (2) makes no sense. Compare Fig. 13 of Chapter 3, where the curve has a singular point at $(0, 0)$, and indeed there *is* no well-defined tangent line there. Landed at $(0, 0)$ we should not know which branch of the curve to take and the method breaks down.

Proof of (2)   It is easy to check that the point (2) is a distance h from (x_0, y_0), and that it lies on the line (1). We indicate here why (1) represents the tangent line.

Consider the chord joining (x_0, y_0) to a point $(x_0 + a, y_0 + b)$ also on the contour $f = c$ (Fig. 19(a)). The equation of the chord is

$$b(x - x_0) = a(y - y_0), \tag{3}$$

and we want to examine this as a and b tend to 0. Now

$$f(x_0 + a, y_0 + b) - f(x_0, y_0) = c - c = 0,$$

and we can write this straightforward fact in the following totally baffling way:

$$0 = a \left(\frac{f(x_0 + a) - f(x_0, y_0)}{a} \right) + b \left(\frac{f(x_0 + a, y_0 + b) - f(x_0 + a, y_0)}{b} \right)$$

$$= ap + bq,$$

say. Now p is precisely the slope of the chord (Fig. 19(b)) of the graph of $f(x, y_0)$ joining the points with $x = x_0$ and $x = x_0 + a$. As $a \to 0$ this tends to the slope of the tangent to the graph, i.e. to

$$\frac{\mathrm{d}}{\mathrm{d}x} f(x, y_0) = \frac{\partial f}{\partial x}$$

at $x = x_0$, $y = y_0$. (Note that the graph of $f(x, y_0)$ can also be regarded as a slice, or section, of the graph in three dimensions of the function $z = f(x, y)$, by the plane $y = y_0$.) Similarly, $q \to \partial f / \partial y$ at (x_0, y_0) as a and b both $\to 0$. Rewriting Equation (3) as $p(x - x_0) + q(y - y_0) = 0$ (using $ap + bq = 0$), and letting a and b tend to 0 now gives (1) as the tangent line.

2.7 *Program: Contour*
10 INPUT XL, XU, YC, XØ, YØ, H, N

The number n here is the number of times which the procedure of Section 2.6 is repeated to obtain successive points approximately on the contour through (x_0, y_0).

20 Calculate y_ℓ, y_u as in Section 1.7 of Chapter 3
30 Calculate scaling factors x_s, y_s
40 LET X = XØ: LET Y = YØ
50 FOR I = 1 TO N
60 Calculate $\partial f / \partial x$ (= FX), $\partial f / \partial y$ (= FY) in terms of x
   and y

Fig. 19

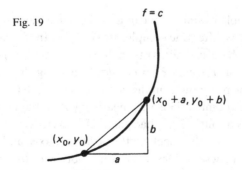

(a)

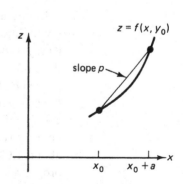

(b)

70 LET W = SQR(FX * FX + FY * FY)
80 IF W = Ø THEN PRINT "SINGULAR! ": END

This takes care of the unlikely event that you hit exactly on a singular point, where $\partial f/\partial x = \partial f/\partial y = 0$. Line 8Ø just throws in the sponge; alternatively you could use some standard 'remedy' such as adding 0.001 to x and hoping that this lands you at a point where $w \neq 0$.

90 IF X < XL OR X > XU OR Y < YL OR Y > YU THEN GOTO 12Ø
1ØØ Convert (x,y) to screen coordinates (u,v)
11Ø Put a dot at screen point (u, v)
12Ø LET X = X − H * FY/W: LET Y = Y + H * FX/W
13Ø NEXT I

A possible amendment to the program is to allow several contours of f to be drawn one after another, for different starting points (x_0, y_0). You really need in that case to choose a large standard value of n and have a device for stopping the plot of one contour and going on to the next when one is 'complete', or you are tired of watching it. Another useful addition is the ability to return to line 4Ø but with h replaced by $-h$. This plots the *same* contour (approximately) going the other way, and is especially useful when the contours are not closed.

2.8 *Exercise: Circles*

Let $f(x, y) = x^2 + y^2$. Taking any (x_0, y_0) the computer should plot approximately the circle through (x_0, y_0), centre $(0, 0)$. Take for example $(x_0, y_0) = (1, 0)$, $x_\ell = -2$, $x_u = 2$, $y_c = 0$, $h = 0.1$, $n = 100$; you will find that the curve does not join up, after going right round, at all convincingly. However, $h = 0.01$, $n = 700$ gives a much better circle.

In this simple example we can actually calculate how far out the point plotted is, after one complete revolution. In fact, as in Fig. 20, if (x, y) is on the circle radius r then the next point $(\bar{x}, \bar{y})$ plotted is on the circle radius $\bar{r}$ where $\bar{r}^2 = r^2 + h^2$. Repeating this, the ith point plotted by the program is on the circle radius $\sqrt{(1 + (i - 1)h^2)}$. With $h = 0.1$, point number 73 is very nearly back on the positive x-axis, giving radius about 1.31, a bad miss. However, with $h = 0.01$, it is point 640 or so which is back on the positive x-axis, and gives radius about 1.03. (These values of i were obtained by stopping the program and reading off i by a PRINT I command; can you *calculate* the value of i which most nearly brings the point back to the positive x-axis?)

Fig. 20

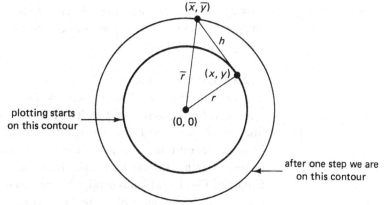

2.9 *Exercise: Circles?*

Suppose that, in line 120 of Program 2.7, you replace FY and FX by their expressions in terms of the variables X and Y; what happens? Try this program with $f(x, y) = x^2 + y^2$, as in Exercise 2.8, with $h = 0.1$. The curve closes up rather well, but is it circular? (Remember that the program will calculate the expressions for $\partial f / \partial x$ and $\partial f / \partial y$ at whatever are the *current* values of x and y.)

2.10 *Exercise: Two cubic curves*

Let $f(x, y) = y^2 - x + x^3$, $(x_0, y_0) = (1, 0)$. Thus we are trying to plot the curve $f(x, y) = 0$. Take $x_\ell = -0.5$, $x_u = 1.5$, $y_c = 0$, choosing h and n appropriately. This curve does in fact have an oval between $x = 0$ and $x = 1$; compare Exercise 4.5 of Chapter 3. Try also $(x_0, y_0) = (-1, 0)$ and appropriate x_ℓ, x_u, etc.

Take $f(x, y) = (y - bx)^2 - a^2(x - x^3)$ for various values of the constants a and b, and $(x_0, y_0) = (0, 0)$. Compare Exercise 4.5 of Chapter 3 again.

2.11 *Exercise*

Take $f(x, y) = \sin(xy) + \frac{1}{2}x^2 + \frac{1}{2}y^2$. Starting at any point (x_0, y_0), do you expect the contour of f to be a closed curve, or to go off to infinity? Try $(x_0, y_0) = (0.3, 0.3)$ with $x_\ell = -3$, $x_u = 3$, $y_c = 0$, $h = 0.01$ and $n = 700$. Also try $(x_0, y_0) = (1, 1)$ with $x_\ell = -4$, $x_u = 4$, $y_c = 0$, $h = 0.01$ and $n = 1400$. (Fig. 21, (*a*).) Try to form an impression of the contours through points (x_0, y_0) as $x_0 \to 0$. What do you think the contour through the (singular) point $(0, 0)$ looks like?

2.12 *Exercise*

Take $f(x, y) = x^4 + y^4 + xy$. Try drawing contours of f starting at various points $(x_0, 0)$, $x_0 = 1, 0.5, 0.3, 0.1, 0.01, 0.001$ (take $x_\ell = -2$,

$x_u = 2$, $y_c = 0$). See Fig. 21 (*b*). Form an idea of how the contours change as $x_0 \to 0$. What does the contour through the (singular) point (0, 0) look like?

2.13 *Exercise: A monkey puzzle*

Let $f(x, y) = x^3 - xy^2$. The surface $z = f(x, y)$ in three-dimensional space is called a *monkey saddle*. The contour $f = 0$ consists of three lines, $x = 0$, $x = y$ and $x = -y$, dividing the plane into six regions. Draw some contours in each of these six regions, and sketch them on paper, marking against each one the value of f on that contour. Compare Fig. 16, which is similar but not identical. Build up in this way an idea of the shape of the surface $z = f(x, y)$. Why do you think it is called a monkey saddle? (Hint: think of the tail.) See Hilbert and Cohn-Vossen (1952), p. 191. Compare Chapter 1, Exercise 2.2.

If you try plotting the contour $f = 0$ using the program, starting at (0, 1) or $(-1, -1)$ or $(1, -1)$, the straight line $x = 0$ or $x = y$ or $x = -y$ is drawn correctly, despite the singular point at (0, 0). Why is this? (Remember to change h to $-h$ if you want the contour plotted in the opposite direction.)

2.14 *Exercise*

Take $f(x, y) = y(y - x^2)$, which has a singular point at (0, 0), the contour through (0, 0) consisting of the line $y = 0$ and the parabola $y = x^2$. Using the program to plot the contour through $(-1, 0)$ gives the line $y = 0$ (why is this?) but starting at (1, 1) the contour avoids the origin and tries to bend along the x-axis. This is because, by the

Fig. 21

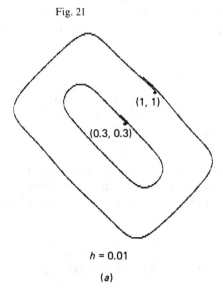

$h = 0.01$

(*a*)

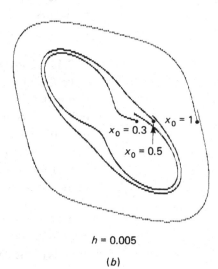

$h = 0.005$

(*b*)

time the plotting is near $(0, 0)$, it is not the contour $f = 0$ which is being plotted but the contour $f = c$ for a small c. (Why is the line $y = 0$ different in this respect?)

2.15 *Exercise: Two transitional families*

In Section 4.15 of Chapter 3, two families of curves are given in a (more or less) parametrised form. Show that the first family can be written as $(x^2 - a)^3 - y^2 = 0$. Try plotting this by the approximate method here, for $a = -0.5$, $a = 0$, $a = 0.5$ in succession (don't forget to find a point on each curve first, at which to start). Also try the second family of Section 4.15, Chapter 3, given by $(a - x^2)^3 - y^2 = 0$.

2.16 *Exercise: Does f exist?*

Note that Program 2.7 does not require f to be known, merely its derivatives $\partial f / \partial x$ and $\partial f / \partial y$, as functions of x and y. Suppose you use xy for '$\partial f / \partial x$' (i.e. FX = X∗Y in line 6∅) and $x^2 + y^2$ for '$\partial f / \partial y$' (i.e. FY = X∗X + Y∗Y in line 6∅). Are you then plotting the contours of any function f? If not, what *are* you plotting? (Compare Euler lines, Chapter 7.) How can you tell whether two given functions are in fact $\partial f / \partial x$ and $\partial f / \partial y$ for some function f? (Hint: $\partial^2 f / \partial x \, \partial y$. See books on advanced calculus, under 'line integrals', for example Taylor and Mann (1983), pp. 470–1.)

2.17 *Project*

Here is a rather ambitious suggestion for improving Program 2.7. From (x_0, y_0) go a distance h along the tangent line, but *then* move in very small steps (possibly of order about h^2) at right-angles to the tangent line until there is a sign change in $f(x, y) - f(x_0, y_0)$, indicating that the contour has been crossed. Choose the point just before the sign change as your next point approximately on the contour, replacing (x_1, y_1) as in (2) of Section 2.6 above. In which direction should you go at right-angles to the tangent line? Clearly you need to know which way the curve bends (Fig. 22). This depends on the *second* derivative of f; the condition can be obtained, for example, by supposing $\partial f / \partial y \neq 0$ at (x_0, y_0) so that y can be expressed as a function $y = g(x)$ on the curve $f(x, y) = c$ near to (x_0, y_0) (compare Section 2.1). This requires simply that the tangent line to the curve is not parallel to the y-axis. When $\partial f / \partial y > 0$ the vector $(\partial f / \partial x, \partial f / \partial y)$, evaluated at (x_0, y_0), points upwards and is normal to the curve $f = c$. The condition for this curve to bend upwards is $g''(x_0) > 0$, and this can be calculated by differentiating $f(x, g(x)) = c$ twice with respect to x.

When all this is worked out we find that the movement perpendicular to the tangent is given by adding $(k(\partial f/\partial x), k(\partial f/\partial y))$, $k > 0$, when

$$\frac{\partial^2 f}{\partial x^2}\left(\frac{\partial f}{\partial y}\right)^2 - 2\frac{\partial^2 f}{\partial x \partial y}\frac{\partial f}{\partial x}\frac{\partial f}{\partial y} + \frac{\partial^2 f}{\partial y^2}\left(\frac{\partial f}{\partial x}\right)^2 < 0,$$

where everything is evaluated at (x_0, y_0). Likewise we should take $k < 0$ when this expression is > 0. (When the expression is equal to 0 there is an inflexion (Fig. 22(c)), and we have a problem!) The point (x_1, y_1) then has the form

$$\left(x_0 - h\frac{\partial f}{\partial y} + k\frac{\partial f}{\partial x},\ y_0 + h\frac{\partial f}{\partial x} + k\frac{\partial f}{\partial y}\right),$$

where k should be taken > 0 or < 0 as determined above.

Having found (x_1, y_1) you now move h along the tangent line at (x_1, y_1) and then at right-angles to the tangent line in small steps, in a direction determined as above where now everything is evaluated at (x_1, y_1). And so on!

§3
Cartesian ovals This section is in effect an extended exercise in mathematics and computer graphics combined.

3.1 *Definition of the ovals*

In the section above on envelopes of reflected rays we pointed out a striking fact about ellipses (see Section 1.15). Within an ellipse there are two points called the foci: incident rays from one focus all pass, after reflexion from the ellipse, through the other focus. Furthermore the sum of the distances of a point P from the two foci is the same for all points P on the ellipse.

There is a generalization of this idea which is very interesting both geometrically and physically. Take two fixed 'foci' O and I in the

Fig. 22

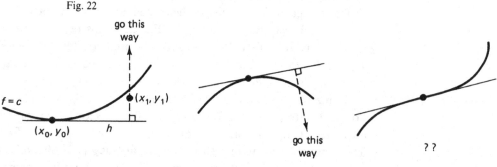

(a) contour above tangent   (b) contour below tangent   (c) inflexion
line so move up   line so move down

Fig. 23

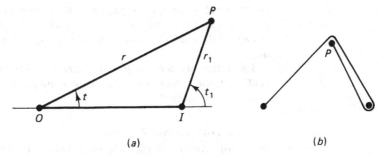

(a)　　　　　　　　　　(b)

plane and consider a point P which moves so that the distances $OP = r$ and $IP = r_1$ satisfy

$$r + mr_1 = a, \tag{1}$$

for constants m and a (see Figure 23(a)). (Thus $m = 1$ gives an ellipse, and then a is the *whole* length of the major axis.) Note that $r \geq 0$ and $r_1 \geq 0$. We can assume that $|m| \geq 1$, i.e. $m \geq 1$ or $m \leq -1$, for otherwise we simply interchange the points O and I. The locus of P is called a *Cartesian oval*. (If the *product* rr_1 is constant then the resulting curve is called a *Cassinian* curve. See for example Yates (1974), p. 8.)

When m is a whole number or a simple fraction, e.g. $m = 2$ or $\frac{3}{2}$, there is an ingenious construction for the oval, using two pins, a pencil and a piece of string, which the great physicist James Clerk Maxwell published when still a schoolboy (see Goldman (1983)). For $m = 2$ this method is illustrated in Fig. 23(b). We hope you get the idea.

The physical interpretation of Cartesian ovals come from *refraction* of light, and applies to negative values of m, say $m = -e$ where $e \geq 1$. *If light from O is refracted at the oval* (refractive index e; see below for the law of refraction), *then the refracted rays, extended backwards, all pass through I.* See Fig. 24.

To prove this we assume that the oval is given a parametrisation c by arclength, denoted s (compare Bruce and Giblin (1984), p. 25). Then the angle α between $c(s) = \overrightarrow{OP}$ and the tangent vector $T(s)$ satisfies $\cos \alpha = -r'(s)$, where $r = $ length OP and the prime stands for d/ds. This is because

$$c(s) \cdot T(s) = -r(s)\cos \alpha$$

from Fig. 24, and

$$c(s) \cdot c(s) = (r(s))^2.$$

Now, differentiating the second equation,

$$c(s) \cdot T(s) = r(s)r'(s),$$

and the result follows, so long as $r(s) \neq 0$, and that is needed even to define α and β. Similarly $\cos \beta = -r_1'(s)$, where $r_1 = $ length IP. Hence $\cos \alpha / \cos \beta = r'(s)/r_1'(s)$, and from $r(s) - er_1(s) = a$ this ratio is equal to e for all s.

The statement $\cos \alpha / \cos \beta = e$ is the *Law of Refraction* (Snell's Law), and is often stated as $\sin \bar{\alpha} / \sin \bar{\beta} = e$ where $\bar{\alpha}$ and $\bar{\beta}$ are angles with the normal instead of the tangent.

3.2 *How to plot the ovals*

We shall now try to plot the oval, taking $O = (0, 0)$, $I = (1, 0)$ and angle $IOP = t$. We need to turn Equation (1) into a formula for just r in terms of t. To do this apply the cosine formula from trigonometry to the triangle IOP:

$$r_1 = \sqrt{(r^2 - 2r \cos t + 1)}.$$

Then the required polar equation for the oval (compare Section 4.13 in Chapter 3) is

$$r + m\sqrt{(r^2 - 2r \cos t + 1)} = a. \tag{2}$$

Rearranging and squaring gives

$$r^2(1 - m^2) - 2r(a - m^2 \cos t) + a^2 - m^2 = 0. \tag{3}$$

Since we have squared Equation (2) to obtain Equation (3), Equation (3) also includes the curve with constants $-m$ and a along with the original curve given by m, a. Remember that $r \geq 0$ and that, in Equation (2), it is the positive square root. (In fact, all the solutions to Equation (2) which have $r < 0$ can be obtained by replacing m, a by $-m$, $-a$ and then having $r \geq 0$ as we are assuming.) We shall see later that only one of the two pairs (m, a) and $(-m, a)$ can give an

Fig. 24

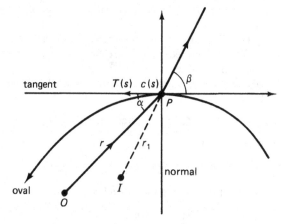

oval with real points on it and for which r and r_1 are both positive. So in fact Equation (3) will produce whichever one is the *real* oval.

So here is how the plotting goes, assuming a and m are given and $m^2 \neq 1$ (see Exercise 3.6 below). From Equation (3),

$$r = \frac{m^2 \cos t - a \pm m\sqrt{(1 - 2a \cos t + a^2 - m^2 \sin^2 t)}}{m^2 - 1}. \quad (4)$$

For each t, we work out the expression under the square root sign in Equation (4), rejecting this value of t if the expression is < 0. When the expression is ≥ 0, both values of r are calculated, but only values $r \geq 0$ are used. Finally, for each $r \geq 0$ we work out $(x, y) = (r \cos t, r \sin t)$ and plot this by a dot on the screen. (In this example, a join-the-dots program is not recommended: it is considerably more ambitious than a dots-only program.)

In the following program, the range $0 \leq t \leq 2\pi$ is divided into 500 equal intervals, i.e. t is increased by $\pi/250$ at each step. Also dots will be placed at $O = (0, 0)$ and $I = (1, 0)$.

3.3 *Program: Oval*

```
10 INPUT XL, XU, M, A
20 LET YC = 0
30 Calculate yₑ as in Section 1.7 of Chapter 3
40 Calculate scaling factors xₛ, yₛ
50 LET X = 0: LET Y = 0
60 Convert to screen coordinates (u, v) as in Section 1.7
   of Chapter 3
70 Put a dot at screen point (u, v)
80 LET X = 0: LET Y = 1
90 Convert (x,y) to screen coordinates (u, v)
100 Put a dot at screen point (u, v)
```

Thus far we have dots marking the points O and I.

```
110 FOR I = 1 TO 500
120 LET T = 3.14159 * I/250
130 LET W = 1 − 2 * A * COS(T) +
          A * A − M * M * SIN(T) * SIN(T)
140 IF W < 0 THEN GOTO 290
150 LET W1 = M * M * COS(T) − A + M * SQR(W)
160 IF W1 < 0 THEN GOTO 220
```

Note that with $m^2 > 1$ we have $w_1 \geq 0$ if and only if $r \geq 0$, from Equation (4) above.

17Ø LET R = W1/(M*M − 1)
18Ø LET X = R*COS(T): LET Y = R*SIN(T)
19Ø IF X < XL OR X > XU OR Y < YL OR Y > YU
     THEN GOTO 22Ø
2ØØ Convert to screen coordinates (u, v)
21Ø Put a dot at screen point (u, v)

This deals with one of the two signs in Equation (4); now for the other one.

22Ø LET W2 = M*M*COS(T) − A − M*SQR(W)
23Ø IF W2 < Ø THEN GOTO 29Ø
24Ø LET R = W2/(M*M − 1)
25Ø LET X = R*COS(T): LET Y = R*SIN(T)
26Ø IF X < XL OR X > XU OR Y < YL OR Y > YU THEN
     GOTO 29Ø
27Ø Convert (x,y) to screen coordinates (u, v)
28Ø Put a dot at screen point (u, v)
29Ø NEXT I

(We hope that those who find this program unnecessarily long will set to and shorten it!)

3.4 *Exercise*

Take $x_\ell = -1$, $x_u = 2$, $m = 2$ and in succession $a = 1.5$, $a = 2$ and $a = 3$. Note that for $a = 1.5$ some values of t give *two* values of r (two points plotted) and some give *no* values of r (nothing happens on the screen). What happens for $a = 2$ and $a = 3$? How is this related to the position of $(0, 0)$ relative to the oval? Try other values of $m > 1$ and make a conjecture on the relationships between a and m which determine which of O and I lies inside the oval.

3.5 *Exercise: Bounded ovals*

Given that, as above, $m^2 \neq 1$, why must the curve necessarily be *bounded* – i.e. why can r in Equation (4) never go to infinity?

3.6 *Exercise:* $m = \pm 1$

Consider the case $m^2 = 1$, so that Equation (3) becomes a *linear* equation for r. If $a > 1$ or $a < -1$ show that every value of t gives exactly one value of r, and also that m must be $+1$ so the oval is an ellipse. (That is $|a| > 1$ and $m = -1$ gives no real solutions with r and r_1 both ≥ 0. Hint: in the triangle POI, the sum of two sides must be at least equal to the third side.) For $-1 < a < 1$ and $m = 1$ the curve is in fact a *hyperbola*. Note that $\cos t = a$ gives no value of r (or gives $r = \infty$ if you prefer; compare Section 4.6 of Chapter 3): the curve *does* go to infinity. Try plotting this curve (say for $a = 0.5$); of course, you will need to amend Program 3.3 so that it calculates the one solution r of Equation (3).

3.7 *Exercise:* $m = -2$

Put $m = -2$ and try the following: (*a*) $x_\ell = -1$, $x_u = 2$, $a = 0$; (*b*) $x_\ell = -1$, $x_u = 3$, $a = -1$; (*c*) $x_\ell = -1$, $x_u = 4$, $a = -1.5$; (*d*) $x_\ell = -1$, $x_u = 5$, $a = -2$; (*e*) $x_\ell = -2$, $x_u = 6$, $a = -2.2$; (*f*) $x_\ell = -2$, $x_u = 7$, $a = -3$; (*g*) $x_\ell = -3$, $x_u = 8$, $a = -4$. Make a note of the changes in shape, and the number of points plotted for each t; also whether O and I lie inside or outside the oval. Which ovals have inflexions – points where they cross their tangent lines? (Compare Fig. 34 of Chapter 3.) Make a conjecture on the relationship between a and m which holds when inflexions are present. (All this is investigated theoretically below; see Fig. 27.)

The word 'oval' is often restricted in its use to curves without inflexions, but 'Cartesian oval' is the traditional name for the curves we are studying, even when they have inflexions. A fully consistent terminology seems always beyond reach!

3.8 *Exercise: Two ovals at once*

Try removing lines 16Ø and 23Ø from Program 3.3 (the tests for positive r). Check that the effect is to plot the ovals given by (m, a) and $(-m, -a)$ at the same time.

3.9 *Some theory of the ovals*

A good deal of light is thrown on the experimental results we hope you have obtained above, by means of a very simple diagram. The condition for a point P to exist at distances r from $O = (0, 0)$ and r_1 from $I = (1, 0)$ (Fig. 23) is

$$|r - r_1| \leq 1 \leq r + r_1.$$

(Think of circles, centre O radius r and centre I radius r_1. We need those circles to *meet*.) Now take axes in the plane labelled r_1 and r and consider the region defined by

$$r_1 \geq 0, \ r \geq 0, \ |r - r_1| \leq 1 \leq r + r_1. \tag{5}$$

This region is the shaded strip in Fig. 25.

Note that $r_1 - r = 1$ automatically gives $t = t_1 = \pi$ (see Fig. 23, remembering the length of OI is 1), so that P is on the x-axis to the *left* of O.

Likewise $r - r_1 = 1$ gives $t = t_1 = 0$, so that P is on the x-axis to the *right of I*.

Finally $r_1 + r = 1$ makes $t = 0$, $t_1 = \pi$ and P is on the x-axis *between O and I*.

Thus the whole boundary of the shaded region in Fig. 25 makes P lie on the x-axis.

Now consider Equation (1) above, defining the Cartesian oval, and which in Fig. 25 represents a straight line of slope $-m$ through $(0, a)$ on the r-axis (remember that $m > 1$ or $m < -1$). Possible positions for P correspond precisely to intersections, if any, between this line and the shaded region; further, by the way the line enters and leaves this region we can tell where the oval crosses the x-axis in relation to the points O and I.

Note that, given (r_1, r) inside the shaded region of Fig. 25, there will be *two* points, P_1 and P_2 say, on the oval and symmetrical about the x-axis. They have angles of the form t and $-t$ as in Fig. 26(a). (Angle $-t$ means t clockwise or $2\pi - t$ anticlockwise.) So, going right round the oval corresponds to going along the segment where the line $r + mr_1 = a$ meets the shaded region, and back again, as in Fig. 26(b).

We shall now apply the insight gained from the above discussion to the elucidation of the shape of Cartesian ovals.

3.10 *Exercise*

Let $m > 1$. Explain why the line (1) in the (r_1, r)-plane meets the shaded strip (Fig. 25; (5)) precisely when $a \geq 1$, and why it meets the end of the strip ($r_1 + r = 1$) precisely when $1 \leq a \leq m$. Deduce that, for:

Fig. 25

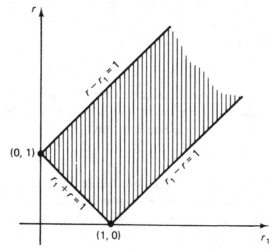

$$a < 1 \quad \text{there is no curve;}$$
$$a = 1 \quad \text{there is just one point, } I;$$
$$1 < a < m \quad O \text{ is outside the oval and } I \text{ inside;}$$
$$a = m \quad O \text{ is on the oval and } I \text{ inside;}$$
$$m < a \quad O \text{ and } I \text{ are inside the oval.}$$

Now compare with any experimental results you obtained in Exercise 3.4, and try other values of a and m to test the above.

3.11 *Exercise*
Now take $m < -1$. Explain why $a \leqslant 1$ is required for the line (1) to meet the strip (5). Deduce that for

$$a = 1 \quad \text{there is just one point, } I;$$
$$m < a < 1 \quad O \text{ is outside the oval and } I \text{ inside;}$$
$$a = m \quad O \text{ is on the oval and } I \text{ inside;}$$
$$a < m \quad O \text{ and } I \text{ are inside the oval.}$$

Compare with Exercise 3.7 above.

3.12 *Exercise*
Using Program 3.3 with say $m = -2$, $a = 1.5$, *does* give a real oval, despite the fact that the condition $a \leqslant 1$ of Exercise 3.10 is violated. Why is this? (Compare the remarks following Equation (3) above.)

3.13 *Detecting inflexions*
Let us try to refine the list of Exercise 3.10 or 3.11 by discovering which Cartesian ovals have inflexions. A direct attack by calculating the condition for inflexions is rather complicated so let us take an

Fig. 26

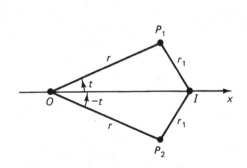

(a)

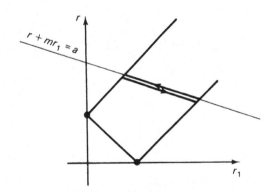

(b)

oblique approach, using the symmetry of any Cartesian oval about the *x*-axis (Fig. 27).

The equation (1) of the oval, turned into Cartesian coordinates (which are much less convenient for *most* aspects of the study of Cartesian ovals!), is $f(x, y) = 0$ where

$$f(x, y) = \sqrt{(x^2 + y^2)} + m\sqrt{((x - 1)^2 + y^2)} - a.$$

Let us calculate the condition for $\partial f/\partial y = 0$ and $\partial f/\partial x \neq 0$ at a point of the oval: this is the condition for the tangent line at that point to be vertical; compare Equation (1) in Section 2.6 above, where the point is called (x_0, y_0). Assuming $r = \sqrt{(x^2 + y^2)}$ and $r_1 = \sqrt{((x - 1)^2 + y^2)}$ are both non-zero, it is easy to check that $\partial f/\partial y = 0$ precisely when

$$y/r + my/r_1 = 0,$$

which gives $y = 0$ (the *x*-axis), or $r_1 + mr = 0$.

Consider $y = 0$, so that $r = |x|$, $r_1 = |x - 1|$. If *also* $\partial f/\partial x = 0$, we find

Fig. 27

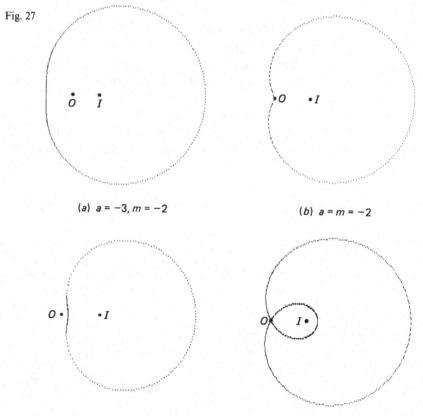

(a) $a = -3, m = -2$

(b) $a = m = -2$

(c) $a = -1.5, m = -2$

(d) $a = m = -2$, the complete limaçon

$$x/r + m(x - 1)/r_1 = 0,$$

which implies that $|m| = 1$, and we are excluding that case. So $\partial f/\partial x \neq 0$ and it follows that, *at any point where the oval crosses the x-axis, other than O $(r = 0)$ or I $(r_1 = 0)$, it does so smoothly with a vertical tangent line.* There is no singular point such as a crossing (Fig. 27(*d*)), where $\partial f/\partial x$ and $\partial f/\partial y$ would *both* be zero (compare Section 2.1 above).

Furthermore, $r = 0$ is only possible when $a^2 = m^2$, by Equation (3), and that gives $a = m$ by Exercises 3.10 and 3.11. Also $r_1 = 0$ is possible only when $r = a$, by Equation (1), and of course $r = 1$ for the point I where $r_1 = 0$, so in fact $a = 1$. Let us exclude $a = m$ and $a = 1$ for the moment.

We can now use the other equation above, $r_1 + mr = 0$, to find the condition for the oval to have points *off* the x-axis, where the tangent line is vertical, and assuming $a \neq m$ and $a \neq 1$ this is equivalent, as in Fig. 27(*c*), to the existence of inflexions.

From $r_1 + mr = 0$ and $r + mr_1 = a$ we have $r_1 = ma/(m^2 - 1)$ and $r = -a/(m^2 - 1)$. The question then is: when does this point (r_1, r) lie within the region given by (5)? We invite you to check that this happens precisely when $m - 1 \leq a \leq m + 1$, where $m < -1$. (Note that $r_1 + mr = 0$ certainly implies $m < 0$, and we are assuming $|m| > 1$.) This enables us to refine the list in Exercise 3.11 as follows:

$m + 1 < a < 1$	O outside, I inside, no inflexions;
$a = m + 1$	two inflexions about to be born (the curve looks very flat there);
$m < a < m + 1$	O outside, I inside, two inflexions;
$a = m$	O on curve, I inside; see Section 3.14 below;
$m - 1 < a < m$	O and I inside, two inflexions;
$a = m - 1$	O and I inside, two inflexions have coincided at a very flat place;
$a < m - 1$	O and I inside, no inflexions.

Confirm this experimentally with the examples of Exercise 3.7 above and with others of your own devising.

3.14 *The case a = m*

In this case, apart from the solution $r = 0$, Equation (3) has the solution

$$r = \frac{2a}{1 - a^2} (1 - a \cos t).$$

When $a = m < -1$ this is a fixed positive multiple of $1 - a \cos t$, and the curve is identified as a limaçon (compare Exercise 4.4 and Section 4.13 of Chapter 3). Since $a < -1$ the complete limaçon has a crossing at $r = 0$, as in Fig. 27(d). But how much of this curve actually satisfies $r > 0$, $r_1 > 0$? Try plotting say $a = m = -2$. Explain the difference between Fig. 27, (b) and (d).

What about the case $a = 1$? Does that also give a limaçon? (How are $a = m$ and $a = 1$ related in Fig. 25?)

3.15 *Approximate ovals*

Use the equation $f(x, y) = 0$ in 3.13 and the approximate method of Section 2.6 to plot some Cartesian ovals approximately. Compare with the true pictures.

§4
Simple linkages

Consider three rigid bars and four pivots O, P, Q and R as shown in Fig. 28(a) where O and R are fixed points in the plane and the bars can turn freely, in the plane, about the four pivots. This is about the simplest example of a *linkage* (it is often called a *four bar linkage*, counting OR as the fourth bar, both of whose ends are fixed). We shall develop a program for *plotting the curve on which the mid-point S of the bar PQ moves* as the rods turn about the pivots. The study of linkages, and in particular of the curves they can describe, is part of *robotics*. Naturally the important problems arising from more complex linkages which are part of mechanisms are harder to solve than the one considered here, but we hope to convey something of the flavour of this very interesting topic.

Fig. 28

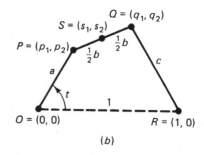

(a)   (b)

Fig. 29

4.1 *The range of movement of P*

Clearly, *P* has to move on a circle, centre *O*, and *Q* has to move on a circle, centre *R*. It is quite possible for *PQR* to become straight as *P* rotates about *O* (Fig. 29), in which case *P* is obliged to change direction to prevent the linkage from disintegrating. Thus *P* may possibly travel back and forth over an *arc*, rather than going all the way round the circle centre *O*. Even so, the mid-point *S* of *PQ* can travel smoothly along its path, without any sudden reversals.

Suppose the position of *P* is given (as well as those of *O* and *R*). Then *Q* lies on two circles, the one centre *P* of radius *PQ* = *b* and the other centre *R* of radius *RQ* = *c*. We also write *a* for *OP* and scale the figure so that *OR* = 1, taking in fact *O* = (0, 0) and *R* = (1, 0), as in Fig. 28(*b*). Let us write, temporarily, *e* for the distance *PR*: thus *e* is the distance apart of the centres of the circles. The condition for the circles to meet (and so give a real position for *Q*) is

$$|b - c| \leqslant e \leqslant b + c. \tag{1}$$

(The same condition came up in Section 3.9 above.) See Fig. 30. The condition for the circles to be *tangent*, making two of the rods lie in a straight line and giving *one* position for *Q*, is that one $\leqslant$ in (1) should be = . The circles meet in *two* points when both $\leqslant$ are < . There is one exceptional case, namely *e* = *b* − *c* = 0 (which requires also *a* = 1) for which the circles *coincide* and *Q* can be any point which is a distance *c* from *R*. We shall avoid this case in what follows, except as a 'transition' between more general cases. (As an extreme example, consider *a* = *b* = *c* = 1. Use commonsense to describe the motion of the linkage in that case.)

Let *t* be the anticlockwise angle from *OR* to *OP* (Fig. 28) so that $P = (p_1, p_2) = (a \cos t, a \sin t)$. Then, by the cosine formula, $e^2 = a^2 + 1 - 2a \cos t$, and squaring (1) we obtain

Fig. 30

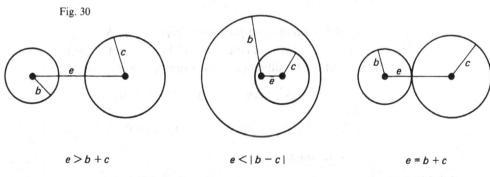

$e > b + c$

circles which don't meet

$e < |b - c|$

$e = b + c$

tangential circles

$$\frac{a^2 + 1 - (b + c)^2}{2a} \leqslant \cos t \leqslant \frac{a^2 + 1 - (b - c)^2}{2a}. \tag{2}$$

This tells us the range of values which t can take as the bar OP rotates about O and the linkage stays connected. Again, an equality sign in (2) indicates that two of the three rods are in a straight line.

4.2 *Exercise*
From the fact that (2) confines $\cos t$ between two fixed limits what can you say about the set of values of t which satisfy (2)?

4.3 *Exercise: Full circle*
If the lower limit in (2) is $\leqslant -1$ and the upper limit is $\geqslant 1$, then (2) imposes *no* restrictions on t, so that the bar OP can rotate full circle. Show that this is equivalent to

$$|b - c| \leqslant |a - 1| \leqslant a + 1 \leqslant b + c.$$

4.4 *Exercise: No solutions*
Show that the condition for (2) to have no solutions at all is

$$a + 1 < |b - c| \quad \text{or} \quad b + c < |a - 1|.$$

When $b > c$ the first of these states that, even with the rods PO, OR, RQ stretched out in a straight line they still aren't long enough for the rod PQ to be fitted in: $a + 1 + c < b$. Interpret the condition when $b \leqslant c$ and also the second condition when $a < 1$ and when $a \geqslant 1$.

4.5 *Exercise: State of collapse*
Show that an equality sign occurs in (2) for $t = 0$ or $t = \pi$ if and only if $|a - 1|$ or $a + 1$ equals $|b - c|$ or $b + c$ (four cases). This indicates that the whole linkage has collapsed to a straight line (why?). We shall usually avoid these cases below.

4.6 *Calculating positions of P, Q and S*
With P as above the equations of the two circles (centre P, radius b, and centre R, radius c) whose intersection is Q are

$$x^2 + y^2 - 2p_1 x - 2p_2 y + a^2 - b^2 = 0$$

and

$$x^2 + y^2 \quad - 2x \quad\quad + 1 - c^2 = 0. \tag{3}$$

Subtraction gives

$$2x(1 - p_1) - 2yp_2 + a^2 - b^2 + c^2 - 1 = 0, \tag{4}$$

and we can use Equations (3) and (4) to find $Q = (x, y)$. Let us write (q_1, q_2) for Q.

Provided $p_2 \neq 0$ (i.e. $t \neq 0$ and $t \neq \pi$) we can substitute for y from Equation (4) into Equation (3) and solve the resulting quadratic for x. In fact let us quietly ignore $p_2 = 0$ and tell the computer to skip on to the next point when this happens. It is possible to include these points by a separate argument, or to use a technique such as that in Exercise 1.4 of Chapter 2, but for present purposes it is scarcely worth the trouble. Indeed we could deliberately choose the values of t used in the program so that $t = 0$ and $t = \pi$ are avoided.

Write Equation (4) in the form

$$y = kx + l,$$

where

$$k = (1 - p_1)/p_2 \quad \text{and} \quad l = (a^2 - b^2 + c^2 - 1)/2p_2. \tag{5}$$

Then the solutions for Q turn out to be

$$\left.\begin{array}{l} q_1 = \dfrac{1 - kl \pm \sqrt{w}}{1 + k^2}, \quad w = c^2(1 + k^2) - (k + l)^2 \\[2mm] q_2 = kq_1 + l. \end{array}\right\} \tag{6}$$

Having found Q then of course the mid-point S of PQ is

$$S = (s_1, s_2) = (\tfrac{1}{2}(p_1 + q_1), \tfrac{1}{2}(p_2 + q_2)).$$

Note that $w \geq 0$ must be equivalent to (1), when $p_2 \neq 0$, since both represent the condition for a real solution for (q_1, q_2).

Let us replace the $\pm$ sign in (6) by a new variable $m = \pm 1$, so that

$$q_1 = \frac{1 - kl + m\sqrt{w}}{1 + k^2}. \tag{7}$$

For a start, let us choose m, plot all points for which $w \geq 0$, then reverse the sign of m and plot again. The program below plots the position of P, Q and S; it is a great advantage if three different colours can be used. As with Cartesian ovals, we consider only dots-only plotting.

4.7 *Program: Linkage*

```
1Ø INPUT XL, XU, A, B, C
2Ø LET YC = Ø
3Ø Calculate yℓ, yu as in Section 1.7 of Chapter 3
4Ø Calculate scaling factors xs, ys
5Ø LET M = 1: LET DT = 3.14159/15Ø
```

```
6Ø FOR J = 1 TO 2
7Ø LET T = Ø
8Ø FOR I = 1 TO 299
9Ø LET T = T + DT
```

This method of incrementing *t* is used to help in later modifications (below).

```
1ØØ LET P1 = A * COS(T): LET P2 = A * SIN(T)
11Ø IF P2 = Ø THEN GOTO 32Ø
```

Alternatively, put *t* = 0.001 say in line 7Ø; then line 11Ø is not needed.

```
12Ø LET K = (1 − P1)/P2
13Ø LET L = (A * A − B * B + C * C − 1)/(2 * P2)
14Ø LET W = C * C * (1 + K * K) − (K + L) * (K + L)
15Ø IF W < Ø THEN GOTO 32Ø
16Ø LET Q1 = (1 − K * L + M * SQR(W))/(1 + K * K)
17Ø LET Q2 = K * Q1 + L
18Ø LET S1 = Ø.5 * (P1 + Q1)
19Ø LET S2 = Ø.5 * (P2 + Q2)
2ØØ LET X = P1: LET Y = P2
21Ø IF X < XL OR X > XU OR Y < YL OR Y > YU
     THEN GOTO 24Ø
22Ø Convert (x,y) to screen coordinates (u, v) as in Section 1.7
     of Chapter 3
23Ø Put a white dot at screen point (u, v)
```

This marks the position of *P* by a white dot.

```
24Ø LET X = Q1: LET Y = Q2
25Ø IF X < XL OR X > XU OR Y < YL OR Y > YU
     THEN GOTO 28Ø
26Ø Convert (x,y) to screen coordinates (u, v)
27Ø Put a red dot at screen point (u, v)
```

This marks the position of *Q* by a red dot.

```
28Ø LET X = S1: LET Y = S2
29Ø IF X < XL OR X > XU OR Y < YL OR Y > YU
     THEN GOTO 32Ø
3ØØ Convert (x,y) to screen coordinates (u, v)
31Ø Put a yellow dot at screen point (u, v)
```

This marks the position of the mid-point *S* of *PQ* with a yellow dot.

32∅ NEXT I
33∅ LET M = − 1
34∅ NEXT J

4.8 *Exercise*

Take $x_\ell = -2$, $x_u = 3$, and $a = 1.8$, $b = 2$, $c = 1.3$. Note that these values satisfy the condition of Exercise 4.3 so the whole circle is traversed by P. You may be puzzled by sudden jumps in the positions of Q and S. Where is P when these occur? Read on! The S-curve is in *two pieces which cross over one another*. (Fig. 31 (*a*).)

4.9 *Exercise*

Take $x_\ell = -2$, $x_u = 3$, $a = 1.3$, $b = 2$, $c = 1.2$. This time there is no solution at first, and the positions for P (the white dots in the

Fig. 31

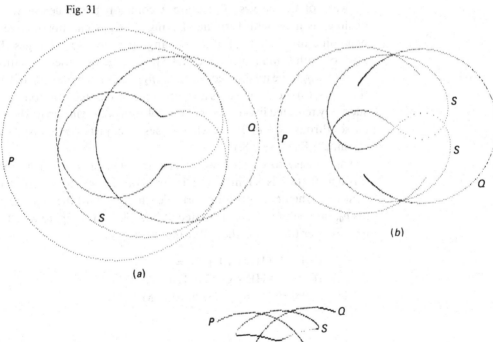

(a)

(b)

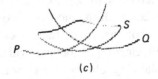

(c)

program) make up a wide arc. (How wide? See (2) above.) You should find that the *S*-curve, once completed, is *all in one piece*, though you may need to have a little faith if the *S*-points (yellow points) are somewhat sparse in places! (Fig. 31(*b*).) (Why are they sparse?) You can make them less so by say DT = 3.14159/300 in line 5∅ and I = 1 TO 599 in line 8∅.

4.10 *Exercise*

Try $x_\ell = -2$, $x_u = 3$, $a = 1$, $b = 0.7$, $c = 1$. This time the *two pieces* of the *S*-curve, for $m = 1$ and for $m = -1$, *are entirely separate* (do not cross). (Fig. 31(*c*).) There is no continuous movement of the linkage taking *S* from a point on one piece to a point on the other. Actually, this applies to the *S*-curve in Exercise 4.8 as well.

4.11 *Eliminating some of the jumps*

Maybe it is time to do something about some of those jumps in the drawing of the curves. These are a common phenomenon when dealing, as here, with formulae having ± signs and possibly zero denominators. From (5) above, changing p_2 to $-p_2$ changes the signs of both *k* and *l*, and if we make no change in *m* then Equation (7) shows q_1 to be unaffected. Thus, as p_2 passes from one side of 0 to the other, (6) shows that q_2 is abruptly reversed in sign: the point *Q* is suddenly reflected in the *x*-axis. In the plotting this will occur when *P* passes through $(-a, 0)$, i.e. when *t* goes from just $< \pi$ to just $> \pi$. (Compare Exercise 4.8.)

This is easy to correct: we reverse the sign of *m* when p_2 goes through 0 (this is slightly better for a further modification than detecting when *t* goes through π). We simply record the value of p_2 (as p_0, say) before it is recalculated at line 1∅∅ and compare with the new p_2 after this. Thus the following will suffice:

```
 75  IF I > 1 THEN LET P∅ = P2
115  IF I = 1 THEN GOTO 12∅
117  IF P∅*P2 < = ∅ THEN LET M = − M
```

4.12 *Exercises*

Use the modified program to redo Exercises 4.8–4.10 above. In Exercise 4.10, for example, where the *S*-curve is in two separate pieces, with the modified program half of one piece is drawn, then half of the other, then back to the first. Why is this? A further refinement (see below) will draw all of one piece first. Try the following, observing and noting changes in the *S*-curve.

(a) $a = 1, b = 2, c = 0.5$;

(b) $a = 1, b = 1.6, c = 0.5$;

(c) $a = 1, b = 1.4, c = 0.5$.

Has something happened between (b) and (c)? At what value of b (keeping $a = 1, c = 0.5$) is there a 'transition'? Compare Exercise 4.5.

(d) $a = 1, b = 0.8, c = 0.5$;

(e) $a = 1.1, b = 0.7, c = 0.5$;

(f) $a = 1.5, b = 0.65, c = 0.5$.

This is another transitional case. Which of the four in Exercise 4.5 is it?

(g) $a = 1.2, b = 0.5, c = 0.5$.

What has happened to the S-curve between (e) and (g)?

(h) $a = 1.5, b = 0.3, c = 0.5$;

(i) $a = 1.7, b = 0.1, c = 0.5$.

This is rather a dull case; see Exercise 4.4.

4.13 *Further work on the jumps*

There are still jumps of a kind in the plotting, as in the reworking of Exercise 4.10, where each piece of the S-curve is drawn in two stages. It would be nice to mimic the real linkage more closely by making P *reverse* direction every time P, Q and R become collinear. At the same moment we want to switch to the other solution for Q (i.e. change the sign of m). To do this we change dt to $-$ dt and m to $-m$ every time w has just become negative (see Equations (6) in Section 4.6). Thus we change line 15Ø to

15Ø IF W < Ø THEN LET DT = $-$ DT: LET M = $-$ M: GOTO 32Ø

There is a snag: P is no longer stepping sedately round a circle, oblivious of whether Q exists or not, but may return over a broad arc, as in Fig. 32. Thus it may possibly need more than 300 steps to return to its starting point. Perhaps it is best at this stage to forget about drawing all the solutions, i.e.

delete lines 6Ø, 33Ø, 34Ø,

and replace 299 by 599 or so in line 8Ø for complete safety. This

Fig. 32

covers the case when P goes almost to $t = \pi$ before reversing direction. Also introduce m as a further input in line 1Ø, and delete 'LET M = 1:' from line 5Ø. Start with $m = 1$ and then run the program again with $m = -1$.

There is one further snag! If it so happens that the starting value of t does not give a real solution for Q (i.e. gives $w < 0$) then the program will not know what to do in order to reach a position for P where Q is real. One way round this is to introduce a new input t_0 in line 1Ø, representing the starting value of t, and to replace line 7Ø by

7Ø   LET T = TØ∗3.14159/18Ø

Thus the starting angle is input in *degrees* at line 1Ø and is automatically converted to radians at line 7Ø. In each example, a little experiment will find a suitable t_0 which *does* give a real solution for Q.

Here are suitable values for the first few exercises above. Exercise 4.8: any value, e.g. $t_0 = 0$, will do, since every value of t gives a real solution for Q; Exercise 4.9: $t_0 = 180$; Exercise 4.10: $t_0 = 90$ (here the upper closed half of the S-curve is completed quickly, by about the value $i = 170$, since P moves over a relatively short arc in the upper half of the circle centre O); Exercise 4.12(*a*): $t_0 = 180$; (*b*): $t_0 = 180$ (in the last two the whole S-curve is drawn since the arc on which P moves is all in one piece on the circle).

4.14 *Some mathematical observations*
Here are some mathematical observations which draw together the various examples given so far and which suggest many more examples to try for yourself.

For a given linkage of the kind considered here there is a certain part of the circle, centre O and radius a, which consists of actual positions for P – namely the part given by (2) in Section 4.1 above. It

Fig. 33

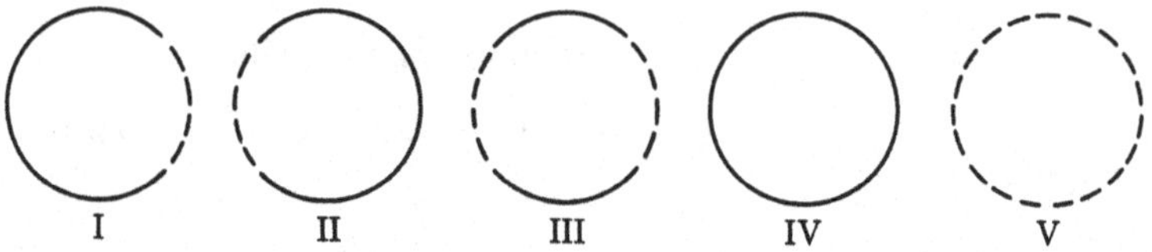

I   II   III   IV   V

I: $|a - 1| < |b - c| < a + 1 < b + c$
II: $|b - c| < |a - 1| < b + c < a + 1$
III: $|a - 1| < |b - c| < b + c < a + 1$
IV: $|b - c| < |a - 1| < a + 1 < b + c$
V': $a + 1 < |b - c|$
V": $b + c < |a - 1|$

turns out that there are just five different forms which this part of the circle can take, according to the relative sizes of the four numbers $|b - c|, b + c, |a - 1|, a + 1$. See Fig. 33, where the solid part of the circle is the part in question. Cases IV and V have already been noted in Exercises 4.3 and 4.4 above.

As an exercise, take all the examples given above and classify each according to which of the five cases it fits. How can you tell, from a knowledge of the case, I, II, III or IV, how many pieces there are in the *S*-curve? Remember that, as in Exercise 4.8, two pieces can sometimes cross over, but they are nevertheless 'separate' in that no motion of the linkage can take *S* from one piece to the other.

Note that case IV will always give two pieces in this sense, for a complete circuit for *P* involves *two* signs changes for *m* as in the discussion of Section 4.11, and therefore *m* returns to its original value after a circuit for *P*. The point *S* corresponding to the *other* choice for *m* at $t = 0$ is not accessible. In fact a real linkage needs to be taken apart and put together again to obtain the other piece of the *S*-curve.

If *a*, *b* and *c* are allowed to change then an inequality $<$ defining one of the cases I–V above can become $=$ and then reverse into $>$. When just *one* $<$ reverses in this way the following transitions take place:

Fig. 34

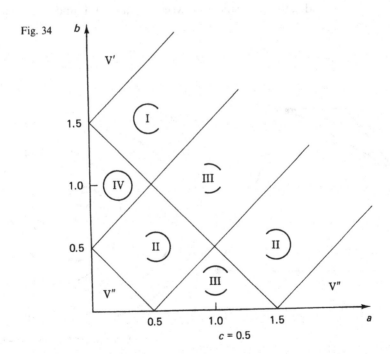

$c = 0.5$

$$V'-I \; < \; \genfrac{}{}{0pt}{}{IV}{III} \; > \; II-V''.$$

All of these except V'—I are illustrated in the examples above. To see the transition I → V' start with (a) of Exercise 4.12 and increase b in steps until it is > 2.5.

You should check that all the transitions in the diagram *are* illustrated by the examples above, and find other examples of your own which show these transitions happening.

A good method for finding your way around the various cases is as follows. Let us fix c, say $c = 0.5$. Then all the inequalities in Fig. 33 involve a and b only, and we can draw a diagram of the plane with coordinates (a, b) where different regions of the plane correspond to the different cases. Of course, only $a > 0$ and $b > 0$ are of interest. This is done in Fig. 34. We leave it as an exercise to verify that the figure is correct!

Notice that around the point $(a, b) = (0.5, 1)$ all four 'non-trivial' cases, I, II, III and IV, occur. So you can do a 'tour' of these cases by making (a, b) travel in a circle round this point.

4.15 *Exercise*
Examine the inequalities in (2) of Section 4.1 to establish the various cases I, II, III, IV, V', V'' above. (For example, $\cos t = (a^2 + 1 - (b + c)^2)/2a$ has two solutions with $0 < t < 2\pi$ provided the right side is between -1 and $+1$, and this is equivalent to

Fig. 35

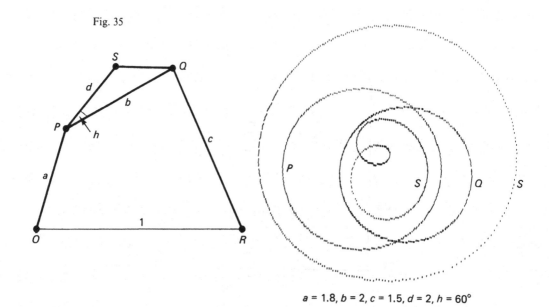

$a = 1.8, b = 2, c = 1.5, d = 2, h = 60°$

$|a - 1| < b + c < a + 1$. Similarly, $\cos t = (a^2 + 1 - (b - c)^2)/2a$ has two solutions provided $|a - 1| < |b - c| < a + 1$. When they *both* have two solutions we are in case III. Look carefully at $t = 0$, $t = \pi$ to separate I and II.)

4.16 *Missing cases*
Obviously the set of positions for P giving real Q is symmetric about the x-axis (the line OR). But why can it never be like the two *dotted* pieces in the case III diagram (Fig. 33)?

4.18 *Amended program*
Write a program which takes into account all the amendments above, and which allows you to stop plotting one piece of the S-curve (if it *is* in two pieces) once it is complete, change m and return to the start to plot the other piece. Both pieces should be on the screen at the end.

4.19 *Plotting the paths of other points*
Instead of plotting the path of the mid-point of PQ we can attach a point S rigidly to the bar PQ, by bars PS, QS as in Fig. 35 and plot the path of *this* point S. With length $PS = d$ and angle $QPS = h$ the formulae for s_1 and s_2 become:

$$s_1 = p_1 + df_1/b, \quad s_2 = p_2 + df_2/b,$$

where

$$f_1 = (q_1 - p_1)\cos h - (q_2 - p_2)\sin h,$$
$$f_2 = (q_1 - p_1)\sin h + (q_2 - p_2)\cos h.$$

Amend the program so that d and h can be accepted as additional inputs and the locus of this point S plotted. (The old S is given by $d = \frac{1}{2}b$, $h = 0$.)

Some pretty curves can be obtained in this way, for example by taking PSQ equilateral (i.e. $d = b$ and $h = \pi/3$) and using the examples of Exercise 4.12 above.

4.20 *Flashing mechanisms*
Write a program which displays the actual rods OP, PQ, QR momentarily for each value of t, flashing them on the screen and then very quickly rubbing them out by plotting over them in the background colour. You can get an impression of the actual linkage in motion this way. You definitely should incorporate the 'turnaround' facility which reverses P's direction of travel and passes to the other solution for Q when P, Q and R become collinear (see Section 4.13).

Fig. 36

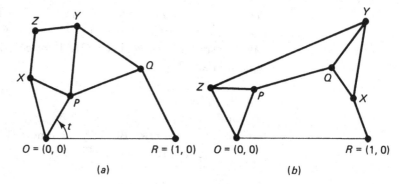

(a)   (b)

After all this *is* what happens: the linkage doesn't vanish when solutions for Q cease to be real!

4.21 *Project: Other linkages*

Naturally there are endless extensions of the above discussion to more complicated linkages. Fig. 36(*a*) shows one simple extension: one can plot the path of Z, or the mid-point of ZY, or .... Again, angle $t = ROP$ determines everything up to some choices of sign (how many?). Write a program to draw the path of Z for this linkage.

Fig. 36(*b*) is a different kettle of fish, however. Here, angle ROP does not, in any obvious way, determine the positions of Q, X, Y, Z even with choices of sign. In fact *how* can we possibly determine the positions of this linkage, given the lengths of all the rods?

Appendix:
Drawing lines
across the screen

A.1 *Where does a line cut the edge of the screen?*
If your micro does not allow points which lie off the screen to be even mentioned, then there is a problem drawing, say, a segment from a given point outwards in a given direction. This is often required in the drawing of envelopes, as in §1. Compare Section 1.3.

Suppose we are given a point $a = (a_1, a_2)$ *inside* the plotting rectangle, i.e. satisfying $x_\ell < a_1 < x_u$, $y_\ell < a_2 < y_u$, and that $b = (b_1, b_2)$ is any other point in the plane. The *half-ray* from (a_1, a_2) towards (b_1, b_2), is the segment *from* (a_1, a_2) *towards* (b_1, b_2), (Fig. 37). Which side of the rectangle will it cross?
Let

$$\left. \begin{array}{l} e_\ell = (x_\ell - a_1)(b_2 - a_2), \\ e_u = (x_u - a_1)(b_2 - a_2), \\ f_\ell = (y_\ell - a_2)(b_1 - a_1), \\ f_u = (y_u - a_2)(b_1 - a_1). \end{array} \right\} \tag{1}$$

Then the conditions for the half-ray to cross the various sides are those given in Fig. 37. To prove this note that, if (b_1, b_2) is replaced by any other point of the half-ray, say by

$$(a_1, a_2) + \lambda(b_1 - a_1, b_2 - a_2), \quad \lambda > 0,$$

then the effect is to multiply all of e_ℓ, e_u, f_ℓ, f_u by λ. Thus the conditions in the figure are unchanged. Hence it is enough to verify these conditions when (b_1, b_2) lies *on* a side of the rectangle. For the top side, for example, this means that $b_2 = y_u$ and $x_\ell \leqslant b_1 \leqslant x_u$. It then follows that $e_\ell \leqslant f_u \leqslant e_u$, for

$$x_\ell - a_1 \leqslant b_1 - a_1 \leqslant x_u - a_1, \quad \text{and} \quad y_u - a_2 = b_2 - a_2 \geqslant 0,$$

so that

$$(x_\ell - a_1)(b_2 - a_2) \leqslant (b_1 - a_1)(y_u - a_2) \leqslant (x_u - a_1)(b_2 - a_2),$$

which is the required result.

It is now an easy matter to calculate the point at which the half-ray meets the edge of the plotting rectangle. In fact, if this point is (x, y) on the line $x = x_\ell$ or $x = x_u$ then, for some λ,

$$a_1 + \lambda(b_1 - a_1) = x,$$

which gives

$$\lambda = (x - a_1)/(b_1 - a_1). \tag{2}$$

Note that $b_1 - a_1$ cannot be 0 since a_1 equals neither x_ℓ nor x_u. The corresponding value of y is then given by

$$a_2 + \lambda(b_2 - a_2) = y,$$

i.e. from Equation (2),

$$
\begin{aligned}
y &= \frac{a_2(b_1 - a_1) + (x - a_1)(b_2 - a_2)}{b_1 - a_1} \\
&= \frac{a_2 b_1 - a_1 b_2 + x(b_2 - a_2)}{b_1 - a_1}.
\end{aligned}
\tag{3}
$$

If, on the other hand, the half-ray meets the edge of the plotting rectangle at (x, y) where $y = y_\ell$ or $y = y_u$, then

$$x = \frac{a_1 b_2 - a_2 b_1 + y(b_1 - a_1)}{b_2 - a_2}. \tag{4}$$

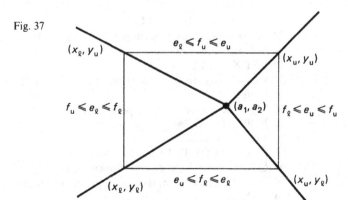

Fig. 37

half-ray from (a_1, a_2) towards (b_1, b_2)

Thus the procedure suggested for discovering *where the half-ray from* (a_1, a_2) *in the direction of* (b_1, b_2) *meets the boundary of the plotting rectangle* is as follows:

(a) calculate e_ℓ, e_u, f_ℓ, f_u as in Equations (1);
(b) if $e_u \leqslant f_\ell \leqslant e_\ell$ then $y = y_\ell$ and x comes from Equation (4);
(c) if $e_\ell \leqslant f_u \leqslant e_u$ then $y = y_u$ and x comes from Equation (4);
(d) if $f_u \leqslant e_\ell \leqslant f_\ell$ then $x = x_\ell$ and y comes from Equation (3);
(e) if $f_\ell \leqslant e_u \leqslant f_u$ then $x = x_u$ and y comes from Equation (3).

Remember that these assume (a_1, a_2) is within the plotting rectangle.

Naturally there are other ways to find the point (x, y): perhaps the reader can find a better way! At least with the method given here there is no danger of running into zero denominators or having to calculate very large numbers, as there might be if you try to find where the half-ray meets *each* of the four lines $x = x_\ell$, $x = x_u$, $y = y_\ell$, $y = y_u$ and then choose the one of these four intersections which is on an edge of the plotting rectangle. Of course, the half-ray might pass through a *corner* of the plotting rectangle; in that case two of (b)–(e) above will apply, and will give the same answer.

Sometimes it is necessary to calculate the point of the half-ray from (a_1, a_2) *away from* (b_1, b_2) which lies on the boundary of the plotting rectangle. To do this, simply replace b by $2a - b$ (Fig. 38). This has the effect of reversing the signs of e_ℓ, e_u, f_ℓ, f_u in Equations (1), so that the conditions for the half-ray to meet the four sides are those in Fig. 39. For example, $e_\ell \leqslant f_u \leqslant e_u$ in Fig. 37 becomes $-e_\ell \leqslant -f_u \leqslant -e_u$, i.e. $e_u \leqslant f_u \leqslant e_\ell$.

A.2 *Applications to envelope drawing*

The examples of envelopes of lines where the above is relevant are : Section 1.4 (chords of a circle drawn right across the screen); Section 1.5 (envelopes of normals); and Section 1.11 *et seq.* (envelopes of reflected rays).

For the chords of a circle, both points (a_1, a_2) and (b_1, b_2) are within the plotting rectangle and we want to extend the segment *both ways*. The following program will then draw the envelope of chords; compare Section 1.4.

```
10 INPUT XL, XU, YC, M
20 Calculate yₗ, yᵤ as in Section 1.7 of Chapter 3
30 Calculate scaling factors xₛ, yₛ
40 LET X = 1: LET Y = 0
50 Convert (x,y) to screen coordinates (u, v) as in Section 1.7 of
   Chapter 3
60 Move the cursor to screen point (u, v)
70 FOR I = 1 TO 200
80 LET T = 0.0314159*I
90 LET X = COS(T): LET Y = SIN(T)
100 Convert (x,y) to screen coordinates (u, v)
110 Draw a segment from the cursor position to (u, v)
120 NEXT I
```

Thus far the program draws the unit circle by join-the-dots.

```
200  FOR J = 1 TO 60
210  LET T = 3.14159*J/30
220  LET A1 = COS(T): LET A2 = SIN(T)
230  LET B1 = COS(3.14159 − M*T):
     LET B2 = SIN(3.14159 − M*T)
240  LET EL = (XL − A1)*(B2 − A2): LET EU = (XU − A1)*
     (B2 − A2): LET FL = (YL − A2)*(B1 − A1):
     LET FU = (YU − A2)*(B1 − A1)
250  IF EU < = FL AND FL < = EL THEN LET Y = YL:
     GOTO 290
260  IF EL < = FU AND FU < = EU THEN LET Y = YU:
     GOTO 290
270  IF FU < = EL AND EL < = FL THEN LET X = XL:
     GOTO 300
280  IF FL < = EU AND EU < = FU THEN LET X = XU:
     GOTO 300
290  LET X = (A1*B2 − A2*B1 + Y*(B1 − A1))/(B2 − A2):
     GOTO 310
300  LET Y = (A2*B1 − A1*B2 + X*(B2 − A2))/(B1 − A1)
```

Thus (x, y) is the point where the half-ray *from a towards b* meets the boundary of the plotting rectangle.

```
310  Convert to screen coordinates (u, v)
320  Move the cursor to screen point (u, v)
330  IF EL < = FL AND FL < = EU THEN LET Y = YL:
     GOTO 370
```

Fig. 38

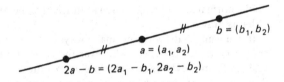

Fig. 39

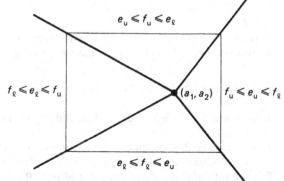

half-ray *from* (a_1, a_2) *away from* (b_1, b_2)

340 IF EU < = FU AND FU < = EL THEN LET Y = YU:
GOTO 370
350 IF FL < = EL AND EL < = FU THEN LET X = XL:
GOTO 380
360 IF FU < = EU AND EU < = FL THEN LET X = XU:
GOTO 380
370 LET X = (A1∗B2 − A2∗B1 + Y∗(B1 − A1))/(B2 − A2):
GOTO 390
380 LET Y = (A2∗B1 − A1∗B2 + X∗(B2 − A2))/(B1 − A1)

This point (x, y) is then the point where the half-ray from a *away from* b meets the boundary of the plotting rectangle.

390 Convert to screen coordinates (u, v)
400 Draw a segment from the cursor position to (u, v)
410 NEXT J

Doubtless this program is more complicated than necessary: it is based on a very literal interpretation of the conditions of Figs. 37 and 39. Perhaps the reader can speed things up!

A.3 *Exercise: Applications to envelopes of normals*
Apply the above ideas to the envelope of normals to a curve which lies entirely within the plotting rectangle. This is easier than Section A.2 above, for we need only calculate the intersection of the normal, drawn in one direction from a point on the curve, with the bounds of the plotting rectangle. Thus, comparing with Section 1.5, (a_1, a_2) is the point (x, y) of the curve, and (b_1, b_2) is the point

$$(x - ry'/\sqrt(x'^2 + y'^2), \ y + rx'/\sqrt(x'^2 + y'^2))$$

on the normal line, r being chosen as in 1.5. It is the half-ray from a towards b that is drawn.

If you want to draw the normal always in the focussing direction, then r should be replaced by $-r$ whenever the curvature is < 0, and again the half-ray from a towards this revised point b is the one to draw. (Alternatively draw the half-ray from a away from the original point b.)

Of course, the same ideas apply to the drawing of envelopes of reflected rays.

A.4 *Exercise*
Why do only some inequalities between the numbers e_ℓ, e_u, f_ℓ, f_u occur in the conditions of Figs. 37 and 39? For example, why does $e_\ell \leqslant e_u \leqslant f_\ell$ not occur?

References   H. Abelson and A. diSessa *Turtle Geometry*, MIT Press, Cambridge, Mass., 1980

T. M. Apostol *Calculus*, Volume 1, Blaisdell Publishing Co., New York, 2nd Edn, 1967

J. W. Bruce and P. J. Giblin *Curves and Singularities*, Cambridge University Press, Cambridge, 1984. (Second Edition, 1992.)

R. Courant *Differential and Integral Calculus*, Blackie and Son, London, 1937

R. Courant and H. Robbins *What is Mathematics?*, Oxford University Press, Oxford, 1947: (Paperback 1978).

H. S. M. Coxeter *Projective Geometry*, University of Toronto Press, Toronto, 2nd Edn, 1964

H. S. M. Coxeter *Introduction to Geometry*, Wiley, New York, 2nd Edn, 1969

H. M. Cundy and A. P. Rollett *Mathematical Models*, Oxford University Press, Oxford, 2nd Edn, 1961

P. J. Giblin and S. A. Brassett Local symmetry of plane curves, *Amer. Math. Monthly*, **92** (1985) 689–707

M. Goldman *The Demon in the Aether*, Paul Harris Publishing, Edinburgh, 1983

D. Hilbert and S. Cohn-Vossen *Geometry and the Imagination*, Chelsea Publishing, New York, 1952

E. H. Lockwood *A Book of Curves*, Cambridge University Press, Cambridge, 1967

A. Oldknow *Microcomputers in Geometry*, Ellis Horwood, Chichester, 1987

E. G. Rees *Notes on Geometry*, Springer-Verlag, Berlin, 1983

I. J. Schoenberg *Mathematical Time Exposures*, Math. Assoc. of America, Washington DC, 1982

I. R. Shafarevich *Basic Algebraic Geometry*, Springer-Verlag, Berlin, 1974

M. Spivak *Calculus*, Publish or Perish, Boston, Mass., 2nd Edn, 1980

A. E. Taylor and W. R. Mann *Advanced Calculus*, John Wiley, New York, 3rd Edn, 1983

R. C. Yates *Curves and their Properties*, National Council of Teachers of Math., Reston, VA, 1974

6

Special Numbers

This chapter will be all about special numbers such as $\sqrt{2} = 1.414213\ldots$, the square root of 2, $\pi = 3.141592\ldots$, which arises in measuring the perimeters and areas of circles, and $e = 2.718281\ldots$, the base of natural logarithms. We shall see that attempts to calculate such numbers more and more accurately have fascinated mathematicians since ancient times, and we shall describe some of the most recent of these attempts. All of the methods we describe can be easily tried out on a micro.

§1
Decimals

First we talk briefly about the decimal system for representing numbers, and how it is implemented on a micro. A symbol such as 3.806, which is called a finite or terminating decimal, is shorthand for the fraction (or rational number)

$$3 + \frac{8}{10} + \frac{0}{100} + \frac{6}{1000} = \frac{3806}{1000}.$$

Suppose we have a fraction whose denominator contains no prime factors other than 2 and 5. (So the denominator has the form $2^a 5^b$ for integers $a \geq 0, b \geq 0$.) Then multiplying numerator and denominator by a suitable number will bring the fraction to the form $n/10^c$, and this is a finite decimal. For example,

$$\tfrac{1}{2} = 0.5, \ \tfrac{6}{5} = 1.2, \ \tfrac{3}{20} = 0.15, \ \tfrac{7}{50} = 0.14,$$

as we find by the familiar process of division. The micro also displays numbers such as 3/20 in this way. Try

PRINT 3/2Ø   and   PRINT 6/125.

However the micro will only display a finite decimal like this if it has fewer than, say, nine digits. To see how your micro deals with longer decimals and larger numbers try

PRINT 1ØØØ.ØØØØØØØ1,   PRINT 3/1ØØØØØØØØØØ
and   PRINT 1234567890.

When we try to use the division process to express rationals like $\tfrac{1}{3}$, whose denominator has factors other than 2 and 5, the process never ends. We get a recurring decimal. This is indicated by a dot over the recurring digit, or dots over the first and last of a recurring block of digits:

$$\frac{1}{3} = 0.3333\ldots \qquad = 0.\dot{3}$$
$$\frac{1}{7} = 0.14285714\ldots \qquad = 0.\dot{1}4285\dot{7}$$
$$\frac{19}{15} = 1.26666\ldots \qquad = 1.2\dot{6}$$

The micro can store only a certain number of the decimal digits of such numbers. In fact it usually stores more digits than it displays, as you can see by running the following.

1.1 *Program*
10 LET X = 1/3: LET Y = 3∗X
20 PRINT X, Y

Having run this, add

30 LET X = the number displayed by 20: LET Y = 3∗X
40 PRINT X, Y

Notice the difference? Clearly the X used in line 10 to calculate Y is not the X which is displayed in line 20.

The moral of this very brief introduction is that the micro cannot do all its arithmetic exactly, but it rounds off at about the tenth decimal place. For a small number of calculations this causes no problems, but after a large number the cumulative effect can become very significant. Deciding how such errors affect computer calculations is part of 'error analysis' – an increasingly important area of mathematics.

1.2 *Remark*
We shall be describing, in what follows, methods which can approximate various numbers to arbitrarily many decimal places, with varying efficiency. Naturally, if you want $\sqrt{2}$ or π to 100 decimal places, you need more than an efficient algorithm for approximating the number: you need some way of handling strings of 100 decimal places when the computer only has eight or ten significant figures on the screen. That is a fascinating challenge, but we shall not go into it here. If you wish to attempt such calculations yourself, then you might try using the routines for high precision arithmetic described in Chapter 4.

§2   Another arithmetic operation which the micro only carries out
Square roots   approximately is the calculation of square roots. Try running, for
              example, this program.

2.1 *Program*
     1Ø LET X = SQR(2): LET Y = X*X
     2Ø PRINT X, Y

followed by the same program, but giving X the value displayed for
X first time round. Notice the difference? Again it is clear that the X
displayed in line 2Ø is not the X used to calculate Y in line 1Ø.

In fact $\sqrt{2}$, like $\frac{1}{3}$, does not have a finite decimal expansion but an
infinite one. Unlike $\frac{1}{3}$, however, the decimal expansion of $\sqrt{2}$ is not a
recurring one, due to the fact that $\sqrt{2}$ is not rational. (You can read
an explanation of this phenomenon, 'recurring implies rational', in
Courant and Robbins (1947) p. 66.)

2.2 *Mathematical exercises*
(a)   Prove that $\sqrt{2}$ is not rational. (Almost any book on Analysis
      will cover this point, or see Courant and Robbins (1947),
      p. 59.) The idea is that if we assume $\sqrt{2} = p/q$ then $2q^2 = p^2$
      and it is not very hard to deduce p, and then q, must be *even*.
      But then every fraction can be reduced to lowest terms with
      numerator and denominator not *both* even, and this is a
      contradiction.

(b)   An alternative proof can be based on Fig. 1. You should use
      elementary geometry to check that the diagram really does fit
      together. Let s_1, s_2 be the sides of the big and little squares,
      respectively, and let d_1, d_2 be their diagonals. Then

$$d_1 = s_1 + s_2$$
$$s_1 = s_2 + d_2.$$

Fig. 1

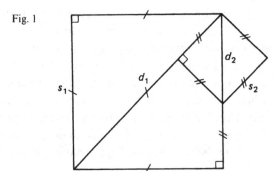

The construction can be continued to give squares of sides $s_3, s_4, \ldots$ and diagonals $d_3, d_4, \ldots$ which get shorter and shorter. Write down expressions for d_2 and s_2 analogous to the above expressions for d_1 and s_1.

Assuming $\sqrt{2} = d_1/s_1$ is rational, why does it follow that, for some (small) length l, s_1 and d_1 are both *whole number* multiples of l? Why do the above equations show s_2 and d_2 are whole number multiples of the *same* l? Why, continuing with s_3 and d_3, s_4 and $d_4, \ldots$ must this ultimately be impossible?

The fact that $\sqrt{2}$ is irrational makes no difference of course to the micro, since it only works with finite decimals. The interesting question is, how does the micro calculate its value for SQR(2), SQR(3), . . . ? There are several ways to do this but a particularly effective one can be obtained from the Newton–Raphson method of Chapter 2, though it was already known and used by the Ancient Babylonians. It is an example of an iteration method, otherwise known as the method of 'refining guesses'. (There is a lot more on iteration in Chapter 8.)

2.3 *Square roots by iteration*

To find $\sqrt{c}$ where $c > 0$ we make an initial guess $a > 0$. Whichever side of $\sqrt{c}$ this first guess lies, the number c/a must lie on the other (for example if $a > \sqrt{c}$ then $1/a < 1/\sqrt{c}$ so $c/a < \sqrt{c}$). So it is likely that

$$b = \tfrac{1}{2}(a + c/a)$$

will be a better approximation to $\sqrt{c}$. Applying this formula again with b instead of a should give an even better approximation to $\sqrt{c}$, and we can repeat the process as often as we wish. In fact we are constructing the sequence $a_0, a_1, a_2, \ldots$, given by

$$a_0 = a, \quad a_{n+1} = \tfrac{1}{2}(a_n + c/a_n), \quad n = 0, 1, 2, \ldots \tag{1}$$

where a is the initial guess at $\sqrt{c}$. To see this in action try the following.

2.4 *Program: Square root*
```
10 INPUT C
20 LET A = C
30 PRINT A
40 LET A = 0.5*(A + C/A): GOTO 30
```

The initial guess is made in line 20 and the iteration step (or refined guess) occurs in line 40.

Use several values of c and compare the results with SQR(C) as given by the micro. The initial guess $a = c$ is not especially good in most cases, but it does work for all $c > 0$.

In fact no matter which values of c and a we start with, the sequence a_n given by (1) converges to $\sqrt{c}$. The mathematical shorthand for this is

$$\lim_{n \to \infty} a_n = \sqrt{c},$$

or

$$a_n \to \sqrt{c} \quad \text{as } n \to \infty,$$

and we say that the sequence a_n, $n = 0, 1, 2, \ldots$, has *limit* $\sqrt{c}$. This means that the numbers $\epsilon_n = a_n - \sqrt{c}$, $n = 0, 1, 2, \ldots$, which represent the errors in the successive approximations to $\sqrt{c}$, can be made as small as may be required by taking n large enough. Put another way, by making n large enough we can ensure that the numbers a_n agree with $\sqrt{c}$ to as many decimal places as may be required. Roughly speaking two numbers agree to n decimal places if they differ by less than $1/10^n$. (They certainly agree to n decimal places if they differ by less than $1/(2 \times 10^n)$.)

2.5 *Convergence of the method*

The convergence of a_n to $\sqrt{c}$ can be illustrated by sketching the graphs $y = x$ and $y = \frac{1}{2}(x + c/x)$. These are given in Fig. 2 for the case $c = 100$.

Using the graph $y = x$ allows us to bring the value

$$a_1 = \frac{1}{2}(a_0 + c/a_0)$$

back down to the x-axis (follow the arrows!) ready to be fed into the iteration formula again:

Fig. 2

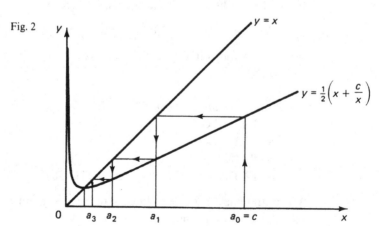

$$a_2 = \tfrac{1}{2}(a_1 + c/a_1).$$

The following facts are easily checked; (b) and (c) are best done by calculus.

(a) $y = \tfrac{1}{2}(x + c/x)$ meets $y = x$ at $(\sqrt{c}, \sqrt{c})$

(b) For $x > \sqrt{c}$ the graph $y = \tfrac{1}{2}(x + c/x)$ is increasing (as x increases) and lies below $y = x$.

(c) For $0 < x < \sqrt{c}$ the graph $y = \tfrac{1}{2}(x + c/x)$ is decreasing (as x increases) and lies above $y = x$.

If $c > 1$ then, by (a) and (b), we have $c = a_0 > a_1 > a_2 > \ldots$ and $a_n \to \sqrt{c}$ as $n \to \infty$. If $0 < c < 1$ then the initial guess $a_0 = c$ is less than $\sqrt{c}$ but the next guess a_1 is greater than $\sqrt{c}$ and once again $a_1 > a_2 > a_3 > \ldots$, with $\lim_{n \to \infty} a_n = \sqrt{c}$.

Remark   We shall make extensive use of this graphical approach to iteration in Chapter 8.

2.6 *Speed of convergence*

This method of calculating square roots converges extraordinarily quickly. Indeed, for $n = 0, 1, 2, \ldots$,

$$a_{n+1} - \sqrt{c} = \tfrac{1}{2}(a_n + c/a_n) - \sqrt{c}$$

$$= \frac{a_n^2 + c - 2a_n\sqrt{c}}{2a_n}$$

$$= (a_n - \sqrt{c})^2/2a_n.$$

Thus if $a_n \geqslant \tfrac{1}{2}$ for all n, which is certainly true if $c > 1$, then

$$\epsilon_{n+1} \leqslant \epsilon_n^2, \quad n = 0, 1, 2, \ldots,$$

where $\epsilon_n = a_n - \sqrt{c}$ is the error term at the nth iteration.

This inequality tells us that the convergence of the terms a_n to $\sqrt{c}$ is 'error-squaring' or 'quadratic'. This means, roughly speaking, that the iteration step from a_n to a_{n+1} doubles the number of correct decimal digits. For example, with $c = \tfrac{1}{2}$ the sequence a_n begins

$a_1 = 0.75$	1 correct
$a_2 = 0.70833333$	2 correct
$a_3 = 0.70710784$	5 correct
$a_4 = 0.70710678$	8 correct (at least)
$a_5 = 0.70710678$	

It is this quadratic rate of convergence which is the standard by which all calculations of special numbers have to be judged. We shall see that many other methods of calculating special numbers such as

π and e, which look at first sight very promising, are in fact hopelessly slow by comparison.

2.7 *Square roots by exponentiation*

You may be wondering why we have not mentioned the other way of calculating square roots on the micro; namely, by using the ↑ instruction. This can be used much more generally to calculate numbers like $2 \uparrow 0.51 = 2^{0.51}$, $0.3 \uparrow 0.4 = 0.3^{0.4}$ etc, and we would not expect therefore that the Newton–Raphson method would be used here. In fact this instruction is related to the exponential function via the formula

$$a^b = \exp(b \ln a).$$

Some micros actually evaluate SQR by using the same routines as $\uparrow 0.5$, whilst others use the Newton–Raphson method, which is much faster.

2.8 *Exercise*

Write a simple loop to determine whether your machine evaluates SQR(2) faster than $2 \uparrow 0.5$.

2.9 *Exercise*

(a)   Write a program to print the sequence

$$a_0 = a, \quad a_{n+1} = \tfrac{1}{3}(2a_n + c/a_n^2), \quad n = 0, 1, 2, \ldots$$

for any given $c > 0$ and initial value a. Try $c = 8$, $c = 27$. You will probably believe at once that a_n converges to $\sqrt[3]{c}$, the cube root of c.

(b)   *Assuming $a_n \to l$ for some number $l \neq 0$ show from the above iteration formula that $l = \sqrt[3]{c}$. (Use $a_{n+1} \to l$, $1/a_n^2 \to 1/l^2$, etc.)*

(c)   (Harder.) Show that a_n does converge to some number l.

(d)   Make an informed guess at an iteration formula which will give the fourth, fifth or more generally the kth root of c. Try it out in a program.

§3
The number π by regular polygons

We now turn to the number π, which has fascinated mathematicians since ancient times. The familiar formula $2\pi r$ gives the perimeter of a circle of radius r, whilst the formula πr^2 gives its area. Thus we can think of π as the semi-perimeter of a circle of radius 1.

But how are we to calculate π? How do we know, for example, that $\pi \approx \frac{22}{7}$? This could perhaps be established by actual measurements of a large carefully drawn circle, but it would hardly give us the very accurate estimate

$$3\tfrac{10}{71} < \pi < 3\tfrac{1}{7},$$

which was already known to Archimedes of Syracuse in the third century BC!

On the micro the value of PI (or sometimes of $\pi/2$) is stored correct to about ten decimal places ready to be used when required. At the time of writing π is known accurate to many millions of decimal places, and there is no possibility of recurrence since π, like $\sqrt{2}$, is irrational (a fact not proved till 1770 by Lambert). This means that any method of calculating π must involve some infinite process, and it is amazing how frequently the number π turns up in such infinite processes, as we shall see.

3.1 *Archimedes's method for π*

First we describe the ingenious method used by Archimedes to obtain the estimates above. We shall see that it is essentially an iteration process and so well suited to computer demonstration. The idea is to calculate the perimeters of regular polygons which lie inside and outside a circle of radius 1, and to use these lengths as lower and upper estimates for 2π. For example, using squares we have (see Fig. 3)

$$4\sqrt{2} < 2\pi < 8$$

so that

$$2\sqrt{2} < \pi < 4,$$

since the inner square, the circle and the outer square have successively bigger perimeters.

On the other hand using hexagons we have (see Fig. 4)

$$6 < 2\pi < 6(2/\sqrt{3})$$

Fig. 3

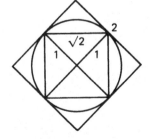

Fig. 4

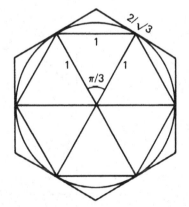

so that

$$3 < \pi < 2\sqrt{3}.$$

Obviously we are going to get better and better estimates by increasing the number of sides, and it is a good graphics exercise to write a program which plots such inner and outer polygons. Some typical results of such a program are illustrated in Fig. 5.

Fig. 5

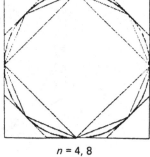

$n = 6$

$n = 6, 12$

$n = 4, 8$

Archimedes's achievement was to find an effective way of calculating with great accuracy the lengths of the perimeters of polygons with many sides. To see how his method works consider a small part of a regular n-gon as shown in Fig. 6.

Since the polygon has n sides, $\theta = \pi/n$, and so

$$n(2 \sin(\pi/n)) < 2\pi < n(2 \tan(\pi/n)),$$

which gives the relationship between semi-perimeters:

$$n \sin(\pi/n) < \pi < n \tan(\pi/n). \tag{1}$$

This is a special case of the inequality

$$\sin \theta < \theta < \tan \theta, \quad (0 < \theta < \pi/2)$$

with $\theta = \pi/n$. (See any textbook on Analysis, or Courant and Robbins (1947), p. 308.)

The formula (1) is not much use unless we can calculate $\sin(\pi/n)$ and $\tan(\pi/n)$, when n is very large. Archimedes's idea was to start with $n = 6$ (hexagons) and *repeatedly double* the number of sides. For $n = 6$ we have $\sin(\pi/6) = 1/2$ and $\tan(\pi/6) = 1/\sqrt{3}$ and for $n = 12$, 24, 48, ... the values of $\sin(\pi/n)$ and $\tan(\pi/n)$ can be found by repeated use of the half-angle formulae:

$$\sin \theta = 2 \sin(\tfrac{1}{2}\theta)\cos(\tfrac{1}{2}\theta), \quad \cos \theta = 2 \cos^2(\tfrac{1}{2}\theta) - 1.$$

Using these we find that

$$\tan(\tfrac{1}{2}\theta) = \frac{\sin \theta \tan \theta}{\sin \theta + \tan \theta}, \quad \sin(\tfrac{1}{2}\theta) = \sqrt{(\tfrac{1}{2} \tan(\tfrac{1}{2}\theta)\sin \theta)}, \tag{2}$$

a pair of formulae ideally suited to calculating $\sin(\tfrac{1}{2}\theta)$ and $\tan(\tfrac{1}{2}\theta)$ if $\sin \theta$ and $\tan \theta$ are known.

Starting with $n = 6$ and repeatedly doubling gives polygons of 6×2^k sides for $k = 0, 1, 2, \ldots$. Let us write a_k and b_k for the semi-perimeters of these inner and outer polygons. Also write θ_k for the angle $\pi/(6 \times 2^k)$, $s_k = \sin \theta_k$, $t_k = \tan \theta_k$. We have

$$a_k = 6 \times 2^k s_k, \quad b_k = 6 \times 2^k t_k.$$

Fig. 6

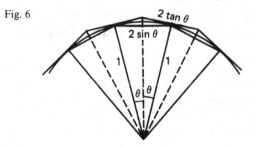

Thus

$$3 = a_0 < a_1 < a_2 < \ldots < \pi < \ldots < b_2 < b_1 < b_0 = 2\sqrt{3}.$$

Using $\theta_{k+1} = \frac{1}{2}\theta_k$, and Equation (2), we get

$$b_{k+1} = 6 \times 2^{k+1} t_{k+1} = 6 \times 2^{k+1} \frac{s_k t_k}{s_k + t_k} = \frac{2a_k b_k}{a_k + b_k},$$

and

$$a_{k+1} = 6 \times 2^{k+1} s_{k+1} = 6 \times 2^{k+1} \sqrt{(\tfrac{1}{2}t_{k+1}s_k)} = \sqrt{(b_{k+1}a_k)}.$$

Thus we can calculate the semi-perimeters a_k, b_k by using the iteration process:

$$a_0 = 3, b_0 = 2\sqrt{3}, b_{k+1} = \frac{2a_k b_k}{a_k + b_k}, a_{k+1} = \sqrt{(b_{k+1}a_k)}. \tag{3}$$

3.2 *Exercise*

We do not have to start with a six-sided polygon; we could start with any number, and then keep doubling as before. This does not affect the iteration formulae but it does affect a_0 and b_0. What would they be if we started with a square? With a regular m-sided polygon?

The following program shows the above *Archimedean algorithm* in action.

3.3 *Program: Archimedes*

```
1∅ LET A = 3: LET B = 2*SQR (3)
2∅ PRINT A, B
3∅ B = 2*A*B/(A + B): A = SQR(B*A)
4∅ GOTO 2∅
```

Archimedes himself carried out the iteration as far as $k = 4$, which corresponds to polygons with 96 sides. He had to calculate the square roots involved by hand of course and used results such as $265/153 < \sqrt{3} < 1351/780$. It is still not known for sure how he established these very accurate square root estimates. However, there are plausible conjectures: for two quite different ones see Kline (1972) p. 134 and Fowler (1987) Part 1, Chapter II.

3.4 *Exercise*

Let $c_k = \cos \theta_k = s_k/t_k = a_k/b_k$. Then $c_{k+1} = \sqrt{[\frac{1}{2}(1 + c_k)]}$ by a well-known half-angle formula. Use (3) to show that

$$a_{k+1} = a_k/c_{k+1},$$

by noting that

$$b_{k+1} = a_{k+1}/c_{k+1}.$$

Write a program to use this algorithm for calculating the sequences $a_k, b_k, k = 0, 1, 2, \ldots$.

3.5 *Exercise*

There is a variant of Archimedes's method due to N. Cusanus (1450). He took regular polygons with 2^k sides ($k = 2, 3, 4, \ldots$) and *fixed perimeter*, put equal to 2 for convenience. Let r_k, R_k be the radii of the corresponding inscribed and circumscribed circles. Show that

$$r_2 = \tfrac{1}{4}, \quad R_2 = \tfrac{1}{4}\sqrt{2},$$
$$r_{k+1} = \tfrac{1}{2}(r_k + R_k)$$

and

$$R_{k+1}^2 = R_k r_{k+1}.$$

Since

$$1/R_k < \pi < 1/r_k$$

this gives an algorithm for π. Write a program to implement it.

The sequences a_k, b_k do appear to converge reasonably quickly (to π), but not so quickly as the iteration sequence for finding square roots considered earlier. In fact the rate of convergence here is only linear, satisfying the inequality (see Exercise 3.6)

$$b_{k+1} - a_{k+1} \le \tfrac{1}{4}(b_k - a_k), \quad k = 0, 1, 2, \ldots. \tag{4}$$

This implies that

$$b_{k+2} - a_{k+2} \le \tfrac{1}{16}(b_k - a_k), \quad k = 0, 1, 2, \ldots,$$

so that by doing two more iterations at any stage the error is divided by at least 16. This produces at least one extra decimal place of accuracy for two more iterations. Later on (see §6) we shall give an iteration sequence which converges quadratically to π (compare Section 2.6 above). The extra speed of convergence will be quite apparent.

3.6 *Exercise*

(*a*) With a_k, b_k as above (see (3)), show that

$$b_{k+1}^2 - a_{k+1}^2 = \frac{2a_k^2 b_k}{(a_k + b_k)^2}(b_k - a_k), \quad k = 0, 1, 2, 3, \ldots$$

Now use $2a_k \leqslant a_{k+1} + b_{k+1}$, $4a_k b_k \leqslant (a_k + b_k)^2$ to establish (4).

(b)   Experiment with the algorithm for a_k, b_k to see whether $(b_{k+1} - a_{k+1})/(b_k - a_k)$ is *much* less than $\frac{1}{4}$. Do you think $\frac{1}{4}$ in (4) could be replaced by a smaller constant (independent of k)? (Harder: can you prove it?)

3.7 *Exercise*

(a)   Modify line 1∅ of Program 3.3 so that other starting values a_0, b_0 with $0 < a_0 < b_0$ can be used. Experiment to see whether the sequences a_k, b_k are still convergent. (Compare Exercise 3.2.)

(b)   Now just assume the last two formulae of (3), taking any starting values as in (a) above. Write $c_k = a_k/b_k$ and let $\theta_k = \cos^{-1} c_k$, θ_k being acute. (Compare Exercise 3.4.) Show that $2c_{k+1}^2 = 1 + c_k$, and deduce from a well-known half-angle formula that $\theta_{k+1} = \frac{1}{2}\theta_k$ $(k = 0, 1, 2, \ldots)$. Now use $\sin \theta_k = 2 \sin \theta_{k+1} \cos \theta_{k+1}$ to deduce that

$$a_{k+1}/\sin \theta_{k+1} = 2a_k/\sin \theta_k, \quad k = 0, 1, 2, \ldots .$$

Writing $n_k = a_k/\sin \theta_k$, repeated use of the above formulae now shows $\theta_k = \theta_0/2^k$ and $n_k = 2^k n_0$, so that $\theta_k n_k$ is actually constant, equal to $\theta_0 n_0$.

Now $\theta_k n_k = a_k(\theta_k/\sin \theta_k)$, and since the angle $\theta_k \to 0$ as $k \to \infty$ (it is repeatedly halved), we can use the known fact that $\theta/\sin \theta \to 1$ as $\theta \to 0$. (This is proved in any calculus text or in Courant and Robbins (1947) p. 307.) We find $a_k \to \theta_0 n_0$. By evaluating $\theta_0 n_0$ show that

$$a_k \to \frac{a_0 b_0}{\sqrt{(b_0^2 - a_0^2)}} \cos^{-1}\left(\frac{a_0}{b_0}\right)$$

as $k \to \infty$. Since $b_k = a_k/c_k$ and $c_k \to 1$, b_k has the same limit as a_k.

(c)   The modification of Program 3.3 in (a) can now be regarded, using (b), as an algorithm for calculating $\cos^{-1} x$ for any given x with $0 < x < 1$. Write a program which accepts x as input and calculates appropriate sequences a_k, b_k with limit $\cos^{-1} x$. Check your program with $x = \sqrt{3}/2 = 0.866\,025\,4 \ldots$ ($\cos^{-1} x = \pi/6 = 0.523\,598\,7 \ldots$) or $x = \frac{1}{2}$ (here $\cos^{-1} x = \pi/3 = 1.047\,197\,5 \ldots$).

3.8 *Exercise*

(a)   Again with a_k, b_k satisfying the last two formulae of (3), but with a_0, b_0 arbitrary, $0 < a_0 < b_0$, let $c_k = a_k/b_k$ as in Exercise 3.7(b).

Show that $a_{k+1}c_{k+1} = a_k$ (this just uses the last formula of (3)). By repeated use of this show that

$$c_0 c_1 c_2 \ldots c_k = a_0 c_0 / a_k = a_0^2 / a_k b_0.$$

(b) Write a program which, for given a_0, b_0, calculates the successive products

$$c_0, \quad c_0 c_1, \quad c_0 c_1 c_2, \quad c_0 c_1 c_2 c_3, \ldots$$

By (a) these products have limit a_0^2 / b_0 times the limit of $1/a_k$, which you can look up in Exercise 3.7(b). Deduce the products have limit

$$c_0 \sqrt{(1 - c_0^2)} / \cos^{-1} c_0.$$

Check your program with some special values of a_0, b_0.

(c) With $a_0 = 2\sqrt{2}$, $b_0 = 4$, the limit in (b) is $2/\pi$. So if you work out $2/c_0$, $2/c_0 c_1$, $2/c_0 c_1 c_2$, ... the limit will be π. Write a program to implement this. How 'fast' is it compared with the straightforward Archimedean algorithm in Program 3.3?

3.9 Remark

The values $a_0 = 2\sqrt{2}$, $b_0 = 4$ in Exercise 3.8(c) correspond to taking inner and outer polygons with 4, 8, 16, 32, ... sides instead of 6, 12, 24, 48, ... sides as in Section 3.1. The sixteenth century French mathematician François Viète used this to produce the remarkable formula

$$2/\pi = \sqrt{\tfrac{1}{2}} \times \sqrt{(\tfrac{1}{2} + \tfrac{1}{2}\sqrt{\tfrac{1}{2}})} \times \sqrt{(\tfrac{1}{2} + \tfrac{1}{2}\sqrt{(\tfrac{1}{2} + \tfrac{1}{2}\sqrt{\tfrac{1}{2}})})} \times \ldots.$$

In fact this is the first explicit analytic expression for π ever discovered.

§4

π: other methods of approximation

The fundamental theorem of calculus, which relates integrals (areas under curves) to derivatives (slopes of curves), made its appearance in the seventeenth century, and mathematics was thereby transformed forever. The number π soon began to crop up all over the place, but one example which just predates the fundamental theorem is Wallis's product, published in 1655.

4.1 Wallis's product

Let

$$a_1 = \frac{1 \times 3}{2 \times 2} = \frac{3}{4}, \quad a_n = \frac{(2n-1)(2n+1)}{(2n)^2} a_{n-1}, \quad n = 2, 3, 4, \ldots$$

Thus

$$a_2 = \frac{1 \times 3 \times 3 \times 5}{2 \times 2 \times 4 \times 4} = \frac{45}{64}, \quad a_3 = \frac{1575}{2304}, \text{ etc.}$$

Wallis's formula is $\lim_{n \to \infty} a_n = 2/\pi$, which can be written in the more spectacular way

$$\frac{1 \times 3 \times 3 \times 5 \times 5 \times 7 \times \ldots}{2 \times 2 \times 4 \times 4 \times 6 \times 6 \times \ldots} = \frac{2}{\pi}. \tag{1}$$

Notice that

$$\frac{a_n}{a_{n-1}} = \frac{4n^2 - 1}{4n^2} = 1 - \frac{1}{4n^2},$$

so that

$$a_n = \left(1 - \frac{1}{4 \times 1^2}\right)\left(1 - \frac{1}{4 \times 2^2}\right) \cdots \left(1 - \frac{1}{4n^2}\right), \quad n = 1, 2, 3, \ldots$$

In particular, the sequence a_n is decreasing.

4.2 *Program: Wallis*
```
1Ø LET A = 3/4: LET N = 1
2Ø PRINT A: LET N = N + 1: LET A = A * (1 − 1/(4 * N * N))
3Ø GOTO 2Ø
```

You should be impressed at how slowly this sequence appears to be converging. As a practical method of calculating π the sequence is a non-starter, but it is of theoretical importance and we shall briefly describe the proof.

The idea is to consider the integrals

$$I_n = \int_0^{\pi/2} \sin^n x \, dx, \quad n = 0, 1, 2, \ldots.$$

The graphs $y = \sin^n x$, $n = 0, 1, 2, \ldots$, are illustrated in Fig. 7, and it is clear that the areas go down as n increases:

$$I_0 > I_1 > I_2 > \ldots. \tag{2}$$

By using the 'reduction formula' $I_{n+2} = ((n - 1)/n) I_n$, which follows from integration by parts, it can be shown that:

$$I_{2n} = c_n \pi/2, \quad I_{2n-1} = 1/2nc_n, \quad n = 1, 2, 3, \ldots,$$

where

$$c_n = \frac{1 \times 3 \times 5 \times \ldots \times (2n - 1)}{2 \times 4 \times 6 \times \ldots \times 2n}.$$

Note that $a_n = (2n + 1)c_n^2$. From (2) we get

$$1 > \frac{I_{2n}}{I_{2n-1}} > \frac{I_{2n+1}}{I_{2n-1}}$$

and the right-hand side equals $2n/(2n + 1)$ which has limit 1 as $n \to \infty$. Thus I_{2n}/I_{2n-1} is forced to have limit 1 ('sandwich rule': it is sandwiched between 1 and something else which tends to 1). But

$$I_{2n}/I_{2n-1} = \pi n c_n^2 = \pi(n/(2n + 1))a_n \to \tfrac{1}{2}\pi a_n.$$

This proves $\tfrac{1}{2}\pi a_n \to 1$, as required.

4.3 *Rate of convergence*

Starting from $\pi n c_n^2 < 1$ (see above) we obtain

$$a_n - 2/\pi < 1/n\pi, \quad n = 1, 2, 3, \ldots.$$

Note that the left-hand side is also > 0 since a_n *decreases* to its limit $2/\pi$. The only guarantee of accuracy this gives is that if, say, we want a_n to agree with $2/\pi$ up to six decimal places, it is enough to have $n > 10^6/\pi$, about 300 000 terms! By that time the cumulative effect of rounding errors in the later places could well be affecting accuracy at the fifth decimal place!

4.4 *The Leibniz–Gregory series*

Another early appearance of π is in the Leibniz-Gregory formula

$$\pi/4 = 1 - \tfrac{1}{3} + \tfrac{1}{5} - \tfrac{1}{7} + \ldots. \tag{3}$$

More precisely if

Fig. 7

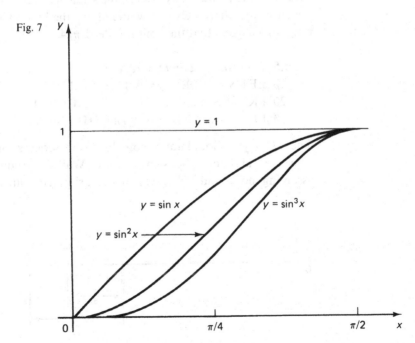

$$s_n = 1 - \tfrac{1}{3} + \ldots + (-1)^n/(2n+1), \quad n = 0, 1, 2, \ldots,$$

then the sequence s_n converges to $\pi/4$. It is often convenient to write an infinite sum such as $1 - \tfrac{1}{3} + \tfrac{1}{5} - \ldots$ in the form

$$\sum_{n=0}^{\infty} (-1)^n/(2n+1).$$

Such an infinite sum (or series, as it is known) is said to be *convergent* with sum s if the sequence s_n of partial sums

$$s_n = \sum_{k=0}^{n} \frac{(-1)^k}{2k+1} = 1 - \tfrac{1}{3} + \tfrac{1}{5} - \ldots + \frac{(-1)^n}{2n+1}$$

form a convergent sequence with limit s: $s_n \to s$ as $n \to \infty$. Thus a convergent infinite series corresponds to a convergent sequence of partial sums.

Because of the alternating signs, and the fact that

$$1 > \tfrac{1}{3} > \tfrac{1}{5} > \tfrac{1}{7} > \ldots,$$

it is evident that

$$\tfrac{2}{3} = s_1 < s_3 < \ldots < s_4 < s_2 < s_0 = 1,$$

as illustrated in Fig. 8.

Now $s_{2n} - s_{2n-1} = 1/(4n+1)$ and $1/(4n+1) \to 0$ as $n \to \infty$, so the odd terms creep up and the even terms down, ultimately getting as close together as we please. Hence the sequence s_n is *convergent* and the terms are alternately below and above the limit. The following program suggests that the limit is indeed $\pi/4$.

4.5 *Program: Leibniz–Gregory*
```
10 LET S = 1: LET N = Ø: LET T = 1
20 PRINT S: LET N = N + 1: LET T = - T
30 LET S = S + T/(2*N + 1): GOTO 20
```

Once again you should notice how slowly this series is converging. It converges at about the same rate as Wallis's product and so, assuming no round-off errors in the arithmetic, an assumption

Fig. 8

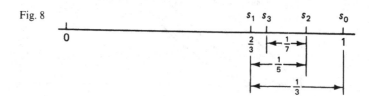

which we cannot make in practice, it takes about 10^k terms to get k decimal places correct.

We now give the proof that this series has sum $\pi/4$ and we shall then see how the series can be modified to give much faster convergence.

The proof relies on the fact that

$$\frac{d}{dx} \tan^{-1} x = \frac{1}{1 + x^2},$$

so that the shaded area in Fig. 9 is given by

$$\int_0^1 \frac{dx}{1 + x^2} = \left[\tan^{-1} x \right]_0^1 = \frac{\pi}{4}.$$

We shall use the fact that $1/(1 + x^2)$ is the sum to infinity of the geometric series

$$1 - x^2 + x^4 - x^6 + \dots,$$

which has common ratio $-x^2$. This series is only convergent when $|x| < 1$ so we must take care when using it near $x = 1$. In any case we have

$$f_n(x) = 1 - x^2 + \dots + (-1)^n x^{2n} = \frac{1 + (-1)^n x^{2n+2}}{1 + x^2}$$

$$= \frac{1}{1 + x^2} + \frac{(-1)^n x^{2n+2}}{1 + x^2},$$

and so the graphs $y = f_n(x)$, $n = 0, 1, 2, \dots$, lie alternately above and

Fig. 9

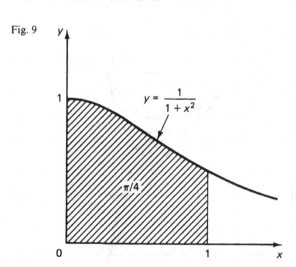

below $y = 1/(1 + x^2)$. The first few of these graphs are illustrated in Fig. 10.

The area under the graph of f_n is

$$\int_0^1 f_n(x)\,dx = \left[x - \frac{x^3}{3} + \ldots + (-1)^n \frac{x^{2n+1}}{2n+1} \right]_0^1$$

$$= 1 - \tfrac{1}{3} + \ldots + (-1)^n \frac{1}{2n+1}$$

$$= s_n.$$

It follows that these areas are alternately greater than and less than the area

$$\int_0^1 \frac{dx}{1 + x^2} = \frac{\pi}{4}.$$

Fig. 10

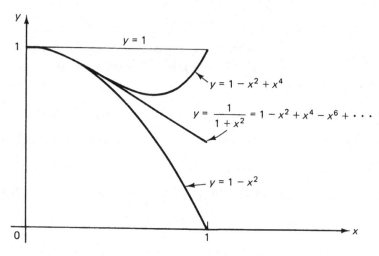

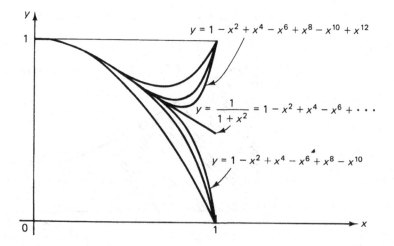

That is $s_{2n-1} < \pi/4 < s_{2n}$ for $n = 1, 2, 3, \ldots$. But we *know* $s_n \to l$ for some l. Hence $l \leqslant \pi/4 \leqslant l$, which proves $l = \pi/4$.

4.6 *Exercise*
Write a program to print the partial sums of the series $\sum_{k=1}^{\infty} (-1)^{k+1}/k$, i.e. to print $s_1, s_2, s_3, \ldots$ where

$$s_n = 1 - \frac{1}{2} + \frac{1}{3} - \frac{1}{4} + \ldots + \frac{(-1)^{n+1}}{2n}.$$

Does this series appear to converge? If so, slowly or quickly? As a mathematical exercise, use the integral

$$\int_0^1 \frac{dx}{1+x}$$

(whose value is ln 2) to show that $s_n \to \ln 2$ as $n \to \infty$.

4.7 *A faster algorithm for π*
Making only a slight change in the previous proof we obtain Gregory's series

$$\tan^{-1} x = \int_0^x \frac{dt}{1+t^2} = x - \frac{x^3}{3} + \frac{x^5}{5} - \frac{x^7}{7} + \ldots, \qquad (4)$$

if $0 < x < 1$. The infinite series $x - x^3/3 + \ldots$ is an example of a *power series*, i.e. a series of powers of x. It gives us a different infinite series for each value of x. For example, since $\tan \pi/6 = 1/\sqrt{3}$ the value $x = 1/\sqrt{3}$ gives

$$\frac{\pi}{6} = \frac{1}{\sqrt{3}} - \frac{1}{3}\left(\frac{1}{\sqrt{3}}\right)^3 + \frac{1}{5}\left(\frac{1}{\sqrt{3}}\right)^5 - \frac{1}{7}\left(\frac{1}{\sqrt{3}}\right)^7 + \ldots$$

$$= \frac{1}{\sqrt{3}}\left[1 - \frac{1}{3} \times \frac{1}{3} + \frac{1}{5} \times \frac{1}{3^2} - \frac{1}{7} \times \frac{1}{3^3} + \ldots\right]$$

so

$$\pi = 2\sqrt{3}\left[1 - \frac{1}{3} \times \frac{1}{3} + \frac{1}{5} \times \frac{1}{3^2} - \frac{1}{7} \times \frac{1}{3^3} + \ldots\right].$$

This series converges much more quickly as you can see by printing the partial sums with the following program.

4.8 *Program: Gregory*

```
1Ø LET S = 1: LET N = Ø: LET T = 1: LET X = 1/3: LET
   A = 1
2Ø PRINT 2 * SQR(3) * S: LET N = N + 1: LET T = - T
```

30 LET A = A∗X: LET S = S + T∗A/(2∗N + 1)
40 GOTO 20

In fact, the smaller the value for x which we use in Equation (4), the faster the series converges. As long ago as 1706, Machin noticed that

$$\frac{\pi}{4} = 4 \tan^{-1}\frac{1}{5} - \tan^{-1}\frac{1}{239}, \tag{5}$$

so the infinite series, with $x = 1/5$ and $y = 1/239$, gives

$$\pi = 16\left[\frac{1}{5} - \frac{1}{3} \times \frac{1}{5^3} + \frac{1}{5} \times \frac{1}{5^5} - \frac{1}{7} \times \frac{1}{5^7} + \cdots\right]$$
$$- 4\left[\frac{1}{239} - \frac{1}{3} \times \frac{1}{239^3} + \frac{1}{5} \times \frac{1}{239^5} - \frac{1}{7} \times \frac{1}{239^7} + \cdots\right],$$

which again converges quickly, as the following shows.

4.9 *Program: Machin*

10 LET S = 0: LET N = 0: LET T = − 1
20 LET X = 1/5: LET Y = 1/239: LET A = 1/5: LET B = 1/239
30 LET N = N + 1: LET T = − T
40 LET S = S + 4∗T∗(4∗A − B)/(2∗N − 1)
50 PRINT S: LET A = A∗X∗X: LET B = B∗Y∗Y: GOTO 30

4.10 *Exercise*

Prove Equation (5) by showing that if $\theta = \tan^{-1}(1/5)$ and $\varphi = \tan^{-1}(1/239)$ then $\tan(4\theta - \varphi) = 1$.

This formula of Machin was used for many years in high precision calculations of π. However, in 1961, Shanks and Wrench used the slightly more complicated formulae

$$\left.\begin{array}{l}\pi = 24 \tan^{-1}(1/8) + 8 \tan^{-1}(1/57) + 4 \tan^{-1}(1/239)\\ \text{and}\\ \pi = 48 \tan^{-1}(1/18) + 32 \tan^{-1}(1/57) - 20 \tan^{-1}(1/239),\end{array}\right\} \tag{6}$$

to calculate π correct to 100 000 decimal places. These series converge somewhat faster than Machin's formula, and both formulae were used to provide a double check. A few years later, the fictitious Dr Matrix was reported by Martin Gardner (1966) p. 100, to have predicted that the one millionth digit of $\pi = 3.141\ 59\ldots$ was 5, and this was confirmed in 1974 when the Equations (6) were used to calculate π to over one million decimal places. Two years later in 1976 an entirely new method of calculating π was announced which has now superseded methods based on the $\tan^{-1} x$ series. We turn to this new method in §6 below.

§5

The harmonic series and Euler's series for π^2

We shall consider briefly the following two series, which serve to illustrate the possibilities, and the limitations of the micro.

The harmonic series is

$$1 + \tfrac{1}{2} + \tfrac{1}{3} + \tfrac{1}{4} + \tfrac{1}{5} + \ldots$$

and Euler's series for π^2 (actually $\pi^2/6$) is

$$1 + \frac{1}{2^2} + \frac{1}{3^2} + \frac{1}{4^2} + \frac{1}{5^2} + \ldots$$

It is easy, of course, to print out the partial sums of these series:

5.1 *Program: Harmonic/Euler*

```
10 LET S = 1: LET T = 1: LET N = 1
20 PRINT S, T: LET N = N + 1
30 LET S = S + 1/N: LET T = T + 1/(N*N)
40 GOTO 20
```

Watching the terms

$$s_n = 1 + \frac{1}{2} + \ldots + \frac{1}{n}, \quad t_n = 1 + \frac{1}{2^2} + \ldots + \frac{1}{n^2}, \quad (n = 1, 2, \ldots)$$

being printed it is clear that the terms s_n are increasing much faster than the terms t_n. However, even after millions have gone by the terms s_n have still not passed 20 and the terms t_n have not passed 2. Their accuracy at this point is dubious. Eventually of course the micro will set first $1/n^2$, and then later (much later) $1/n$, equal to 0. From then on s_n and t_n will both be constant. As far as convergence is concerned, all we can infer is that t_n is more likely to be convergent than s_n.

In fact the sequence t_n is convergent and the sequence s_n increases without bound: the value of s_n can be made as large as we please by taking n big enough. But n has to be *huge* even for modest values of s_n. By considering the curve $y = 1/x$ between $x = 1$ and $x = n$ it can be shown that

$$\ln n + 1/n < s_n < \ln n + 1.$$

5.2 *Exercise*

Prove the above inequality. The area under the curve is ln*n*. Break the interval $1 \leqslant x \leqslant n$ into *n* intervals of length 1.

Thus if $s_n \geqslant 20$ the right-hand inequality shows that $\ln n > 19$, i.e. $n > e^{19}$, which is about 180 million: after this many terms the sum s_n will still not exceed 20. The left-hand inequality also shows $s_n \to \infty$ as $n \to \infty$. For other proofs that s_n is divergent, we refer the reader to any book on Analysis (see 'harmonic series'); the fact appears to have been known early in the fourteenth century.

On the other hand

$$t_n = 1 + \frac{1}{2^2} + \frac{1}{3^2} + \ldots + \frac{1}{n^2}$$

$$< 1 + \frac{1}{1 \times 2} + \frac{1}{2 \times 3} + \ldots + \frac{1}{(n-1)n}$$

$$= 1 + \left(1 - \frac{1}{2}\right) + \left(\frac{1}{2} - \frac{1}{3}\right) + \ldots + \left(\frac{1}{n-1} - \frac{1}{n}\right)$$

$$= 2 - 1/n < 2, \quad \text{for all } n.$$

This approach, which is due to Leibniz, shows that t_n is convergent to a limit $t < 2$ and also that

$$t - t_n = \frac{1}{(n+1)^2} + \frac{1}{(n+2)^2} + \ldots$$

$$< \frac{1}{n(n+1)} + \frac{1}{(n+1)(n+2)} + \ldots$$

$$= \left(\frac{1}{n} - \frac{1}{n+1}\right) + \left(\frac{1}{n+1} - \frac{1}{n+2}\right) + \ldots,$$

so

$$0 < t - t_n < 1/n.$$

This means for example that the value t_{1000} will give us t correct to three decimal places.

5.3 *Exercise*

Use Program 5.1 to find t correct to three decimal places.

5.4 *Euler's brilliant idea*

The question of what exactly the sum t is, completely defeated Leibniz and Bernoulli, who referred the problem to the great Swiss mathematician Leonard Euler. He began by calculating partial sums of the series. In 1731 he had the sum correct to six places, in 1733 he had it correct to 20 places and in

1734 he finally got it correct to infinitely many, by showing that the sum was $\pi^2/6 = 1.6449 \ldots$. His method is one of the most celebrated examples of how valuable a single inspired but unrigorous idea can be.

Euler started from the familiar fact that if the polynomial

$$p(x) = 1 + a_1 x + \ldots + a_n x^n$$

has n roots $\alpha_1, \ldots, \alpha_n$ then

$$p(x) = (1 - x/\alpha_1)(1 - x/\alpha_2) \ldots (1 - x/\alpha_n),$$

so

$$a_1 = -(1/\alpha_1 + 1/\alpha_2 + \ldots + 1/\alpha_n).$$

He then used the series expansion of $\sin x$ to obtain

$$\frac{\sin x}{x} = 1 - \frac{x^2}{3!} + \frac{x^4}{5!} - \ldots$$

Putting $x = \sqrt{u}$ gives

$$f(u) = \frac{\sin \sqrt{u}}{\sqrt{u}} = 1 - \frac{u}{3!} + \frac{u^2}{5!} - \ldots$$

He then applied the result about the roots of polynomials to f! The roots of f are precisely the numbers $u = \pi^2, (2\pi)^2, (3\pi)^2, \ldots$ (as $u \to 0$, $f(u) \to 1$ so 0 is *not* a root of f) and so he concluded that:

$$a_1 = -\frac{1}{3!} = -\left(\frac{1}{\pi^2} + \frac{1}{(2\pi)^2} + \frac{1}{(3\pi)^2} + \ldots\right)$$

or

$$\frac{\pi^2}{6} = 1 + \frac{1}{2^2} + \frac{1}{3^2} + \ldots$$

The method is breathtakingly direct and can in fact be made rigorous, though only at the expense of introducing unpleasant details. Other methods of demonstrating that the sum is $\pi^2/6$ have since been discovered, many of which are based on Fourier series. For an ingenious elementary method see Apostol (1974), Exercise 8.46.

5.5 *Exercise*

(*a*) Use the fact that

$$\frac{\pi^2}{6} = 1 + \frac{1}{2^2} + \frac{1}{3^2} + \frac{1}{4^2} + \ldots$$

to show that

$$\frac{\pi^2}{8} = 1 + \frac{1}{3^2} + \frac{1}{5^2} + \frac{1}{7^2} + \ldots,$$

and

$$\frac{\pi^2}{12} = 1 - \frac{1}{2^2} + \frac{1}{3^2} - \frac{1}{4^2} + \ldots$$

(Hint: It is permissible to add and subtract terms of series such as these. Working with $\pi^2/(2^2 \times 6)$ helps. Compare Chapter 1, Exercises 3.3) (*b*) Write programs to evaluate partial sums of the second and third series. Do they seem to be any better than the first one for speed?

Euler used his technique to show that $\Sigma_{n=1}^{\infty} 1/n^4 = \pi^4/90, \ldots$, and these sums of even power of $1/n$ have been extensively studied. Much less is known about the sums $\Sigma_{n=1}^{\infty} 1/n^3, \Sigma_{n=1}^{\infty} 1/n^5, \ldots$. For example it was only shown as recently as 1979 that $\Sigma_{n=1}^{\infty} 1/n^3 = 1.202 \ldots$ is an irrational number, but it is still not known whether this number is a rational multiple of π^3.

§6
The fastest algorithm for π?

In 1976 an entirely new method of calculating π was announced by E. Salamin and R. P. Brent (independently), which has the advantage of exceptionally fast (quadratic) convergence. For example, in 1986 the method was used by Japanese mathematicians to calculate π correct to 33 million decimal places!

6.1 *Arithmetic–geometric means*

At the heart of this new method is a procedure of which Gauss as a boy was very fond. Starting with two positive numbers a_0 and b_0 $(0 < b_0 < a_0)$, let us repeatedly calculate arithmetic and geometric means in the following way, which is reminiscent of the Archimedean algorithm:

$$a_{n+1} = \tfrac{1}{2}(a_n + b_n), \quad b_{n+1} = \sqrt{(a_n b_n)}, \quad n = 0, 1, 2, \ldots . \quad (1)$$

Evidently

$$b_0 < b_1 < b_2 < \ldots < a_2 < a_1 < a_0,$$

and

$$\frac{a_{n+1}}{b_{n+1}} = \frac{a_n + b_n}{2\sqrt{(a_n b_n)}}$$

$$= \tfrac{1}{2}\left(\sqrt{\frac{a_n}{b_n}} + \sqrt{\frac{b_n}{a_n}}\right) \quad (n = 0, 1, 2, \ldots).$$

Putting $r_n = a_n/b_n$ we have $r_0 > 1$ and

$$r_{n+1} = \tfrac{1}{2}(\sqrt{r_n} + 1/\sqrt{r_n}),$$

which is reminiscent of Newton's Method for finding square roots. From the graph of $y = \tfrac{1}{2}(\sqrt{x} + 1/\sqrt{x})$ (Fig. 11) it is clear that the sequence r_n tends to 1 as $n \to \infty$, so that a_n and b_n both converge to a common limit, which is denoted $L(a_0, b_0)$ and called the *arithmetic–geometric mean* of a_0 and b_0. As the graph suggests, this convergence is extremely rapid. Indeed

$$r_{n+1} - 1 = \tfrac{1}{2}(\sqrt{r_n} + 1/\sqrt{r_n}) - 1 = (\sqrt{r_n} - 1)^2/2\sqrt{r_n}$$

$$= \frac{(r_n - 1)^2}{2\sqrt{r_n}(\sqrt{r_n} + 1)^2},$$

so

$$r_{n+1} - 1 \leqslant \tfrac{1}{8}(r_n - 1)^2.$$

Thus the convergence of r_n to 1 is *quadratic* (compare Section 2.6 above). To see how quickly the sequences a_n, b_n converge to their common limit try the following.

6.2 *Program: A–G mean*

```
10 INPUT A, B
20 PRINT A, B
30 LET C = (A + B)/2: LET D = SQR(A*B)
40 LET A = C: LET B = D
50 GOTO 20
```

Try some inputs A, B (corresponding to a_0 and b_0) to find their arithmetic–geometric mean.

The question which exercised the young Gauss was: given a_0, b_0, what is the value of $L(a_0, b_0)$? The answer which he (and Lagrange some years before him) gave was quite unexpected. In fact

$$L(a_0, b_0) = \pi/2I(a_0, b_0), \tag{2}$$

where

$$I(a, b) = \int_0^{\pi/2} \frac{d\theta}{\sqrt{(a^2\cos^2\theta + b^2\sin^2\theta)}}.$$

Fig. 11

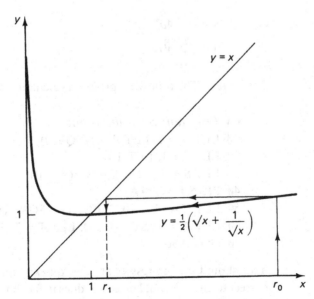

Now $I(a, b)$ is a so called elliptic integral. It cannot be evaluated by the usual process of finding an indefinite integral among the standard functions. So Equation (2) does not provide a good method of finding $L(a_0, b_0)$. However, as we have seen, $L(a_0, b_0)$ can be calculated very quickly by the iteration itself, and so Equation (2) came to be known as Gauss's method for evaluating elliptic integrals. Moreover, Gauss was able to use the iteration process associated with the arithmetic–geometric mean to give a quick method of calculating another elliptic integral:

$$J(a, b) = \int_0^{\pi/2} \sqrt{(a^2 \cos^2 \theta + b^2 \sin^2 \theta)}\,d\theta,$$

which is the length of that part of the ellipse $x^2/a^2 + y^2/b^2 = 1$ lying in the first quadrant. In this case the formula is

$$J(a_0, b_0) = \left(a_0^2 - \tfrac{1}{2} \sum_{n=0}^{\infty} 2^n(a_n^2 - b_n^2) \right) I(a_0, b_0). \tag{3}$$

But what has all this to do with the calculation of π? The remarkable achievement of Salamin and Brent was to use further results about elliptic integrals, which are too complicated for us to describe here, in order to eliminate all the elliptic integrals from Equations (2) and (3), leaving behind a relationship between π and the sequences a_n, b_n. If we put $a_0 = 1$, $b_0 = 1/\sqrt{2}$ and $L_0 = L(1, 1/\sqrt{2})$, then the Salamin–Brent Formula is:

$$\pi = \frac{4L_0^2}{1 - \displaystyle\sum_{n=0}^{\infty} 2^n(a_n - b_n)^2}.$$

Thus the sequence of numbers

$$\frac{4a_n^2}{1 - \displaystyle\sum_{k=0}^{n} 2^k(a_k - b_k)^2}, \quad n = 0, 1, 2, \ldots,$$

has limit π. The following program calculates this sequence.

6.3 *Program: Salamin–Brent*

```
10 LET A = 1: LET B = 1/SQR(2)
20 LET S = 1: LET T = 1
30 LET S = S − T*(A − B)*(A − B)
40 PRINT 4*A*A/S
50 LET C = (A + B)/2: LET D = SQR(A*B)
60 LET A = C: LET B = D: LET T = 2*T
70 GOTO 30
```

You should be impressed at how quickly this program gives π correct to eight decimal places. It does in fact converge quadratically to π; i.e. each iteration of the algorithm roughly doubles the number of correct digits after the decimal point. However, there is one catch. In order to calculate π correct to a given number of digits with this method, you need first to calculate rather more digits of $b_0 = 1/\sqrt{2}$. This can be done using, for example, the method of §2.

So much work has now been done on the arithmetic–geometric mean and its applications to high precision calculations of π and other special numbers, that a whole book has been devoted to the subject. See Borwein and Borwein (1987). A number of mathematicians and computer scientists have implemented the algorithm (and others related to it) to calculate π to many millions of decimal places and will no doubt continue to do so. Indeed, this apparently useless exercise has had one practical spin-off. The computations involved demand 100% accuracy over billions of calculations, and so they are increasingly being used as a 'test' of the computer itself!

§7
The number e and logarithms

The number e is not of such great antiquity as the number π, but it has fascinated mathematicians in a similar way since its introduction in the early seventeenth century, in connection with the new idea of logarithms. Logarithms were developed by the Scottish mathematician J. Napier and, independently, by the Swiss mathematician J. Bürgi as a method of speeding up the process of multiplying real numbers. A simplified explanation of how the number e arises in this process can be given as follows.

First take a large positive integer n (e.g. $n = 10^7$) and consider two numbers a and b, which are to be multiplied. Suppose that it is possible to find numbers x and y such that

$$a = (1 + x/n)^n \quad \text{and} \quad b = (1 + y/n)^n. \tag{1}$$

Then

$$ab = (1 + x/n)^n (1 + y/n)^n = (1 + (x + y)/n + xy/n^2)^n. \tag{2}$$

Since n is large, the term xy/n^2 is very much smaller than $(x + y)/n$, and so

$$ab \approx (1 + (x + y)/n)^n.$$

Thus the product ab is given, approximately, by an expression which has the same form as those appearing in Equations (1).

Now suppose that we have a look-up table available for finding the value of x in Equations (1) which corresponds to a given a, and vice versa. Then the tedious process of multiplying a and b can be replaced by the easier process of looking up x and y, adding them and finding the entry which corresponds to $x + y$, in the reverse direction. Compiling such a table will of course take a long time, but once it is available the speed of multiplication is greatly enhanced.

Of course, the above process does not always give the product *ab* exactly, but then nor does your micro! What is important is the degree of accuracy of the product, and this can be controlled in the above process by choosing *n* large enough. Thus we are led, in a natural way, to consider what happens to the expression $(1 + x/n)^n$ as *n* tends to infinity. This matter can be investigated on a micro by plotting the sequence of graphs:

$$y = (1 + x/1)^1, \quad y = (1 + x/2)^2, \ y = (1 + x/3)^3, \ldots.$$

The result appears in Fig. 12. It can be seen that these graphs appear to converge to the familiar graph of the function e^x, which is also plotted for comparison purposes. Indeed, one way to *define* e^x is by means of the formula:

$$e^x = \lim_{n \to \infty} (1 + x/n)^n. \tag{3}$$

Actually, there is quite a lot of work involved in making this definition watertight. First, the existence of the limit must be established for each real number *x*, and then we must check that the limit satisfies the usual power law:

$$e^x e^y = e^{x+y},$$

which is needed for natural logarithms, i.e. logarithms to the base e.

Fig. 12

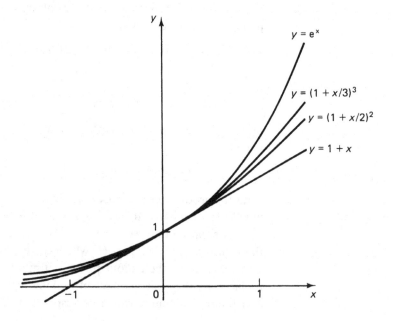

Since the details involved in this justification are unpleasant, we concentrate here on the actual value of the number 3, which is obtained by putting $x = 1$ in Equation (3):

$$e = \lim_{n \to \infty} (1 + 1/n)^n. \tag{4}$$

The following program calculates and prints the terms $(1 + 1/n)^n$, for $n = 1, 2, \ldots$. Note that only the four basic arithmetic operations are used; the $\uparrow$ operation is avoided because its evaluation requires the number e!

7.1 *Program: Definition of* e
```
1Ø LET N = Ø
2Ø LET N = N + 1
3Ø LET A = 1 + 1/N: LET P = A
4Ø FOR I = 1 TO N − 1
5Ø LET P = A * P
6Ø NEXT I
7Ø PRINT N, P
8Ø GOTO 2Ø
```

On running this program you will soon realise that the sequence $(1 + 1/n)^n$ is very slowly convergent. Many terms are required before $(1 + 1/n)^n$ is remotely close to the value 2.718281828, which your computer or calculator supplies. It looks as if Equation (4) may be a good definition of e, but is useless for calculating e.

However, with a little ingenuity, we can make much more efficient use of Equation (4). Some of the terms $(1 + 1/n)^n$ can be evaluated with fewer than the $n - 1$ multiplications used in Progam 7.1. For example, the term $(1 + 1/8)^8$ can be written in the form

$$(1 + 1/8)^8 = (((1 + 1/8)^2)^2)^2,$$

and so its evaluation requires only three multiplications (one for each of the 'squares') rather than seven. This saving occurs whenever n is of the form 2^k, because

$$(1 + 1/2^k)^{2^k} = (\ldots ((1 + 1/2^k)^2)^2 \ldots)^2,$$

where k squares are performed. The following program calculates these particular terms, which form a subsequence of $(1 + 1/n)^n$.

7.2 *Program: Subsequence*
```
1Ø LET K = Ø: LET T = 1
2Ø LET K = K + 1: LET T = Ø.5 * T
3Ø LET P = 1 + T
```

```
4Ø FOR I = 1 TO K
5Ø LET P = P*P
6Ø NEXT I
7Ø PRINT K, P
8Ø GOTO 2Ø
```

This program is much more satisfactory and, within about 16 terms, e is given correct to five decimal places. However, rounding errors in the arithmetic operations of the micro means that further accuracy cannot be obtained this way.

7.3 *Exercise*

(a)   Use a modification of Program 7.1 to investigate the sequence $(1 + 1/n)^{n+1}$, $n = 1, 2, \ldots$. More generally, investigate the sequence $(1 + 1/n)^{n+\alpha}$, $n = 1, 2, \ldots$, for values of α between 0 and 1.

(b)   Use a modification of Program 7.2 to calculate the sequence

$$\left(1 + \frac{1}{2^k - 1}\right)^{2^k}, \quad k = 1, 2, \ldots,$$

which is a subsequence of $(1 + 1/n)^{n+1}$.

(c)   Prove that the subsequences

$$\left(1 + \frac{1}{2^k}\right)^{2^k}, \quad k = 1, 2, \ldots,$$

$$\left(1 + \frac{1}{2^k - 1}\right)^{2^k}, \quad k = 1, 2, \ldots,$$

are increasing and decreasing, respectively. It is rather harder to prove the corresponding results for the sequences $(1 + 1/n)^n$ and $(1 + 1/n)^{n+1}$.

§8
The power series
for e^x

In this section we calculate e using the power series representation:

$$e^x = 1 + x + \frac{x^2}{2!} + \frac{x^3}{3!} + \ldots . \tag{1}$$

This formula can be obtained from the definition of e^x in §7 by several different means. For example, we could expand $(1 + x/n)^n$, using the Binomial Theorem, and then let n tend to infinity, taking great care with the limiting process. Alternatively, we could use the definition to prove that

$$\frac{d}{dx} e^x = e^x,$$

and then apply Taylor's Theorem to the function $f(x) = e^x$ to obtain the Taylor series of $f(x) = e^x$, which is just Equation (1) (see any calculus text for the details). Another possibility is to take Equation (1) as the definition of e^x. Whichever method is used, it is a messy business to prove that Equation (1) is equivalent to the definition of e^x given in §7, and so we shall concentrate again on the calculation of e from Equation (1). The following program uses Equation (1), with $x = 1$, to calculate the partial sums:

$$1, \ 1 + 1, \ 1 + 1 + \frac{1}{2!}, \ 1 + 1 + \frac{1}{2!} + \frac{1}{3!}, \dots,$$

of the series

$$e = 1 + 1 + \frac{1}{2!} + \frac{1}{3!} + \dots \tag{2}$$

8.1 *Program: Series for* e
```
1Ø LET N = Ø: LET S = 1: LET P = 1
2Ø LET N = N + 1: LET P = P/N
3Ø LET S = S + P
4Ø PRINT N, S
5Ø GOTO 2Ø
```

Here the variable s denotes the successive partial sums of e and p denotes the terms of the sequence $1/n!$ The program is remarkably efficient, giving e correct to about eight decimal places by about the eleventh term. Before discussing the speed of convergence of the series (2), we suggest that you try the following exercise.

8.2 *Exercise*
(a) Modify Program 8.1 to calculate partial sums of the series (1) for other values of x. How does the speed of convergence depend on the size of x?
(b) Write a program to plot graphs of the partial sum functions

$$y = 1, \ y = 1 + x, \ y = 1 + x + x^2/2!, \dots,$$

of the series (1). In what manner do these graphs approach the graph $y = e^x$?

We now return to the matter of the speed of convergence of the series (2). To explain this speed we need to examine the difference between e and the nth partial sum of the series (2) for e:

$$s_n = 1 + 1 + \frac{1}{2!} + \frac{1}{3!} + \dots + \frac{1}{n!}.$$

Special numbers

In fact it can be proved that

$$0 < e - s_n < \frac{1}{n!n}, \quad \text{for } n = 1, 2, \ldots, \tag{3}$$

so that, in particular,

$$0 < e - s_{11} < \frac{1}{11!11} \approx 2 \times 10^{-9}.$$

This explains why s_{11} gives e correct to eight decimal places.

In the following exercise we ask you to deduce the inequality (3) from the series (2).

8.3 *Exercise*
(a)   Use the fact that

$$e - s_n = \frac{1}{(n+1)!} + \frac{1}{(n+2)!} + \frac{1}{(n+3)!} + \ldots,$$

to deduce that

$$0 < e - s_n < 1/n!n, \quad n = 1, 2, \ldots.$$

(Hint: notice that $(n+k)! \geq (n+1)^k n!$, for $k = 1, 2, \ldots$.)

(b)   Obtain the more general inequality

$$0 < e - s_n(x) < x^{n+1}/n!(n+1-x), \quad n = 1, 2, \ldots, x > 0,$$

where

$$s_n(x) = 1 + x + \frac{x^2}{2!} + \ldots + \frac{x^n}{n!}.$$

The inequality given in Exercise 8.3 (b) shows that the series (1) for e^x converges extremely rapidly for small values of x. We shall see an application of this property in Section 8.5.

8.4 e *is irrational*
Many calculators give the value e = 2.718281828, which might lead you to suspect that the decimal expansion of e is recurring! However, the estimate (3), proved in Exercise 8.3, can be used to give a neat proof that the number e is irrational, so that its decimal expansion is not recurring. Since the proof is short, we include the details.

Let us suppose that e is rational, i.e. e = m/n, where m, n are positive integers. Then, by the inequality (3),

$$0 < e - s_n < 1/n!n,$$

and so

$$0 < n!(e - s_n) < 1/n.$$

Since $e = m/n$ and $s_n = 1 + 1 + 1/2! + \ldots + 1/n!$, we have

$$0 < n!(m/n - (1 + 1 + 1/2! + \ldots + 1/n!)) < 1/n. \tag{4}$$

The expression in the middle of (4) is, however, an integer, which must lie strictly between 0 and 1. This is a contradiction, and so e cannot be rational.

In fact e is a *transcendental* number (as is π), one which is the root of no polynomial equation with integer coefficients. This is much harder to prove.

8.5 *Calculating* e *more accurately*

It is natural to ask whether there exist methods of calculating e which are as fast as the Salamin–Brent method described in §6. In fact there are methods based on the arithmetic–geometric mean for calculating the function e^x, but they are much too involved to describe here (see Borwein and Borwein (1987), Chapter 7).

We do, however, include one final method for calculating e which is faster than the methods described earlier. With the help of the high precision arithmetic routines from Chapter 4, this method could be used on a micro to obtain a large number of decimal digits of e.

The method is based on the fact that if we know, say, $e^{1/8}$ very accurately, then we can calculate e accurately by repeated squaring:

$$e = (((e^{1/8})^2)^2)^2.$$

Now we can calculate $e^{1/8}$ from the power series expansion (1):

$$e^{1/8} = 1 + \frac{1}{8} + \frac{1}{2!} \times \left(\frac{1}{8}\right)^2 + \frac{1}{3!} \times \left(\frac{1}{8}\right)^3 + \ldots. \tag{5}$$

Your reaction to this may well be that we could also calculate e itself with this series, so what is the advantage? But remember Exercise 8.2, where you saw how much more quickly the series for e^x converges if x is small. This means that fewer terms of the power series (5) need to be calculated to obtain $e^{1/8}$ to a given accuracy.

This method can of course be used with any number of the form 2^k, instead of 8. If high precision arithmetic is available, then care is required in choosing the number of terms of the series for $e^{1/2^k}$ and also in estimating the error introduced by the k 'squarings', which are needed. The following program implements the method using the micro's arithmetic, so that you can see it in action.

8.6 *Program*
```
1Ø INPUT K
2Ø LET X = Ø.5
3Ø FOR I = 1 TO K − 1
4Ø LET X = Ø.5*X
5Ø NEXT I
6Ø LET N = Ø: LET S = 1: LET P = 1
7Ø LET N = N + 1: LET P = X*P/N
8Ø LET SN = S + P
9Ø IF P > Ø THEN LET S = SN: GOTO 7Ø
1ØØ FOR I = 1 TO K
11Ø LET S = S*S
12Ø NEXT I
13Ø PRINT S
```

The program calculates $1/2^k$ in lines 2Ø–5Ø, and $e^{1/2^k}$ in lines 6Ø–9Ø (as accurately as the micro is able). Finally lines 1ØØ–13Ø calculate and print e.

You should find that the program works best for $k = 3$. The explanation for this is that, although the value of $e^{1/2^k}$ is calculated accurately for larger values of k, the rounding errors from the repeated squarings in line 11Ø destroy the accuracy of the value given for e. Thus the method does require the use of high precision arithmetic in order to show its true colours!

References   T. M. Apostol *Mathematical Analysis*, Addison-Wesley, Reading, Mass., 2nd Edn, 1974

J. M. Borwein and P. B. Borwein *Pi and the AGM*, Wiley-Interscience, Chichester, 1987

R. Courant and H. Robbins *What is Mathematics?* Oxford University Press, Oxford, 4th Edition 1947: (Paperback 1978)

D. Fowler *The Mathematics of Plato's Academy*, Oxford University Press, Oxford, 1987

M. Gardner *New Mathematical Diversions from Scientific American*, Simon and Schuster, New York, 1966 (New edition, Univ. of Chicago Press, 1984)

M. Kline *Mathematical Thought from Ancient to Modern Times*, Oxford University Press, Oxford, 1972

7

Differential equations

Sir Isaac Newton is certainly one of the greatest scientists to have ever lived. He is generally reckoned to have been one of the three most outstanding mathematicians of all time, along with Archimedes and Gauss, and his discoveries in physics are unrivalled in their width and influence. What was Newton's secret? How did he achieve as much as he did? Obviously there is no simple answer, but Newton had one secret, which he guarded jealously, and which he believed to be vital. It was '*Data aequatione quotainque fluentes quantitoe involuente fluxions invenire et vice versa*' or in English 'solve differential equations'.

Nowadays this 'secret' is entirely unremarkable; we are all aware that many processes and phenomena in the world are governed by differential equations. The very fact that Newton's secret is now common knowledge clearly indicates its worth and power. Of course his secret was rather hard won; he did have to invent differential equations before pronouncing his dictum concerning solving them!

In this chapter we shall see what the microcomputer can do for those intending to follow Newton's advice. Our eventual viewpoint will be considerably more modern than Newton's. It turns out that in certain circumstances *solving* differential equations is not as useful as *watching* them.

§1
Differential equations and tangent segments

Much of science is devoted to the problems of predicting the future behaviour of some physical system or other. Often the underlying physical law will describe the *rate* at which the system evolves; what we require is a description of *how* it evolves.

1.1 *Example*

A body falls in a vacuum due to the action of gravity. If the body starts at rest at time $t = 0$ experiment shows that the velocity of the body is proportional to the time elapsed. If s measures the distance of the body from its initial position find s in terms of t.

Here we have $ds/dt = kt$ for some constant k so integration yields $s = \frac{1}{2}kt^2 + c$, where c is a constant; in fact $c = 0$ since $s = 0$ when

281

$t = 0$. The constant k, which can be determined experimentally, you will recognise as the acceleration due to gravity g ($= 9.8 \text{ m/s}^2$ approximately).

Here is another example of a differential equation which can be solved by a little trick.

1.2 *Example*

The bacteria in a culture increase at a rate proportional to the number present. If the original number of bacteria increases by 50% in one half-hour, how long does it take to quintuple this original number?

The key to solving this problem is to express the first sentence in mathematics. Let x represent the number of bacteria, and t the time after some fixed instant. The rate of increase with respect to time is nothing other than dx/dt, and so we find that $dx/dt \propto x$ or $dx/dt = kx$ for some constant $k > 0$. If we turn this on its head we find that $dt/dx = k^{-1}x^{-1}$, and integrating this yields $t = k^{-1}\ln x + c$. Taking exponentials $e^{kt} = e^{\ln x}e^{ck}$ and so $x = ae^{kt}$ for some constants $k, a > 0$ (the constant a is e^{-ck}). As ever it is easy to check that this function *is* a solution of the differential equation, the problem was *finding* it!

We now return to the original question. It is clear from the expression for x that the constant a is the amount of bacteria present at time $t = 0$. We are told that when $t = \frac{1}{2}$ the value of x has increased by 50%, in other words $x = \frac{3}{2}a$. Thus $ae^{\frac{1}{2}k} = \frac{3}{2}a$ and so $\frac{1}{2}k = \ln(\frac{3}{2})$; we have determined the constant k, and we can now answer the question. For the amount of bacteria has increased five fold when $ae^{kt} = 5a$, i.e. $e^{kt} = 5$. Taking logarithms we find that $kt = 2\ln(\frac{3}{2})t = \ln 5$ so $t = \ln 5/2 \ln (3/2)$ hours (about 0.992 hours or 59.5 minutes).

The trick used in solving the differential equation in Example 1.2 is the first of many which can be used to solve various classes of differential equations. These tricks which deal, for example, with separable variable equations, homogeneous equations, integrating factor equations, tend to dominate the introductory accounts of the theory. In fact to some extent the whole theory is dominated by special techniques, and the older texts, especially, lack any unifying theme. We are going to use our micro to move away from this obsession with explicit solutions to view the whole subject *geometrically*.

Our two examples of differential equations (Examples 1.1 and 1.2) both eventually reduced to the form

$$dx/dt = f(t) \tag{1}$$

for some given function f of the variable t. *Solving* such equations involves finding a function x of t satisfying this equation, and is clearly equivalent to integrating the function f. We know, however, that some functions can be extremely difficult to integrate. Instead of getting enmeshed in the tricks and troubles of integration let us consider Equation (1) from a geometric viewpoint.

The expression dx/dt represents the slope of the graph of the solution $x(t)$ of our differential equation (this is sometimes abbreviated to DE). These solution curves are, near each of their points, approximated by small portions of their tangent lines with the known slope $f(t)$ (see Fig. 1). Consequently we may gain some idea of the *shape* of these *integral curves* by drawing in sufficiently many small segments of tangent lines. This is a job for a computer of course.

Here is the basic idea. First to simplify matters we shall only consider the region $-1 \leqslant x, t \leqslant 1$ in the (t, x)-plane. The program you will write will be easily modified to draw tangent segments in a more general region. (Alternatively by suitably scaling the t, x-coordinates one can change the differential equation and reduce the region of interest to this 2×2 square centred at the origin.) For a suitable value of n one now cuts the t-axis and x-axis up into $2n$ segments obtaining a grid of $(2n + 1)^2$ points in the (t, x) plane. In the diagram (Fig. 2) we have taken $n = 4$; some of the points of the grid are marked with a dot.

We know the slope of the tangent line to the solution curve at (t, x) is $f(t)$ so we now draw a segment of some fixed length l through each point $(t(i), x(i))$ of the grid with slope $f(t(i))$. The resulting picture should give us some idea of the shape of the solution curves of the differential equation.

Before considering the program in detail we mention some possible sources of problems. First since the program requires the use of computer graphics you should bear in mind what was said in

Fig. 1

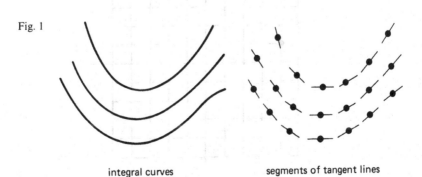

integral curves   segments of tangent lines

the introductory section of Chapter 3. In particular with some micros one must be careful that none of the line segments end up off the screen. Since the segments *l* are of a fixed length this is not too difficult to arrange. Also since line segments are needed here (plotting points is not enough) even the information required to draw these segments is going to be machine dependent. Aside from these general considerations, however, one needs to choose the value *l* for the length of the line segment quite carefully. If *l* is chosen too large one has problems with the segments running off the screen, but more seriously one loses the shape of the solution curves. On the other hand if the length of *l* is too small then the range of possible slopes is limited. For example if the length of *l* is the distance between two adjacent pixels on the screen there are only four possible directions for the segment *l*. A good choice of length *l* can be found by experimenting with differential equations whose solutions are known.

One final point. Clearly this method for obtaining the shape of integral curves works equally well with DEs of the more general form

$$dx/dt = f(t, x) \tag{2}$$

so we shall write our program so that it considers functions *f* of *both* variables *t* and *x* (that is considers the more general Equation (2)).

1.3 *Program: Tangent segments to integral curves*
```
10 INPUT N, L
20 FOR I = 1 TO 2*N + 1
30 LET T = (I − 1)/N − 1
```

Fig. 2

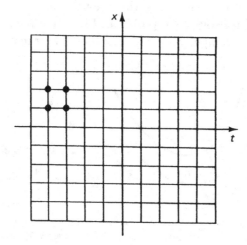

```
4Ø FOR J = 1 TO 2*N + 1
5Ø LET X = (J − 1)/N − 1
6Ø Calculate z = f(t, x) from the formula for f
7Ø LET R = L/SQR(Z*Z + 1)
8Ø LET S = R*Z
9Ø Calculate screen point (u, v) corresponding to (t, x)
1ØØ Put a dot at screen point (u, v)
11Ø Calculate   screen   point   (u', v')   corresponding   to
      (t + r, x + s)
12Ø Draw line segment joining (u, v) to (u', v')
13Ø NEXT J
14Ø NEXT I
```

Some comments are now in order. First the value of t stays the same inside the j-loop; do *not* replace t by $t + r$. The value n determines the mesh size of the grid covering the square $-1 \le t$, $x \le 1$. A fixed value of n cuts this square into $2n \times 2n$ blocks. At the vertices of this grid a segment of length l and slope f is drawn. (The values $n = 15$, $l = 0.05$ are quite convenient.) In line $9Ø$ by ensuring that the screen point (u, v) does not come within distance l of the edge of the screen one can avoid having to check that the segment stays within the screen. Finally some micros do not specify segments by their end-points but rather by their initial points and the *changes* in the value of the (u, v)-coordinates between end and initial point. In this case in line $11Ø$ one needs to compute the changes in the screen values corresponding to r and s.

Using this program we shall now investigate a number of DEs.

1.4 *Exercises*
Using Program 1.3 above investigate the shape of the solution curves of the following differential equations. (Compare Fig. 3.)

(*a*) $dx/dt = 2t$, $dx/dt = 3t^2$

(*b*) $dx/dt = \sin(\pi t)$, $dx/dt = \sin(2\pi t)$

(*c*) $\dfrac{dx}{dt} = \dfrac{1}{1 + t^2}$, $\dfrac{dx}{dt} = \dfrac{1}{\sqrt{(4 - t^2)}}$

(*d*) $dx/dt = e^t - x$, $dx/dt = 4(x^2 - t^2)$, $dx/dt = 4(x^2 + t^2)$

(*e*) $dx/dt = -2tx - tx^4$, $dx/dt = -t/x$.

We presume that you ran into trouble with the last example above, $dx/dt = -t/x$, for the obvious reason that the right-hand side of this equation is not well defined when $x = 0$. This problem is easily overcome by ensuring that the value $x = 0$ is never used in Program 1.3. For example we might consider tangent segments at points of a grid centred at $(0, 0.01)$ rather than $(0, 0)$ by changing line 5Ø to

    5Ø LET X = (J − 1)/N − Ø.99.

Provided $n < 100$, which it certainly will be in practice, the values of x considered will be non-zero.

For DEs such as $dx/dt = 1/t(x − t^3)$, where the denominator of the function on the right-hand side is more complicated, it is more difficult to ensure that the values of x and t considered will not result in division by zero. However these problems are, to some extent,

Fig. 3

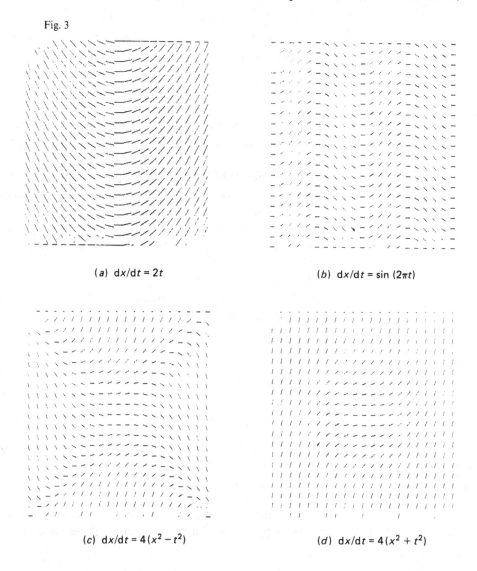

(a) $dx/dt = 2t$

(b) $dx/dt = \sin(2\pi t)$

(c) $dx/dt = 4(x^2 − t^2)$

(d) $dx/dt = 4(x^2 + t^2)$

rather artificial. For a zero of the denominator $t(x - t^3)$ corresponds to a point where the tangent to the integral curve is vertical. After all the DE $dx/dt = f(t, x)/g(t, x)$ is essentially the same as $dt/dx = g(t, x)/f(t, x)$ and so zeros of the denominator should cause no more problems than those of the numerator. A slight redesign of Program 1.3 reflects this fact; one simply observes that the coordinates of the end-point of the tangent line segment at (t, x) of length a are easily found without having to divide by the function g (see Fig. 4). For if this end-point is at $(t + r, x + s)$ then $r = cg(t, x)$,　　$s = cf(t, x)$,　　for　some　$c > 0$.　Moreover, $r^2 + s^2 = c^2(g^2 + f^2) = a^2$ so $c = a/\sqrt{(g^2 + f^2)}$. We now replace lines 6∅, 7∅, 8∅ in Program 1.3 by

```
55 DEF FNF(T, X) = f(t, x): DEF FNG(T, X) = g(t, x)
6∅ LET W = FNF(T, X): LET Z = FNG(T, X)
7∅ LET C = A/SQR(W*W + Z*Z)
8∅ LET R = C*Z: LET S = C*W
```

Note: the lower case f and g correspond to the functions appearing in the DE and need to be explicitly typed in. The resulting program will now quite happily deal with DEs like $dx/dt = -1/x$, $dx/dt = 1/t(x - t^3)$. We only have problems with the general DE $dx/dt = f(t, x)/g(t, x)$ if f and g *both* vanish at one of the points on the grid we are considering. Generally speaking, however, solutions of the pair of equations $f(t, x) = g(t, x) = 0$ are isolated points and we can arrange for our grid of points not to contain such solutions.

1.5 *Exercises*
Using the modification of Program 1.3 investigate the solution curves of the following differential equations (see Fig. 5):

(*a*)　$dx/dt = -t/x$,　$dx/dt = x/t$

(*b*)　$dx/dt = (2t + x)/(t - 2x)$

(*c*)　$dx/dt = x(x^3 - 2t^3)/t(2x^3 - t^3)$.

Fig. 4

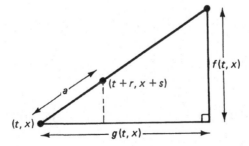

§2
Euler lines
Having drawn the tangent segments for the various differential equations of Exercises 1.4 and 1.5 above one natural idea presents itself. Why not join up these tangent segments to obtain an approximation to an integral curve? This idea actually occurred to Euler some time ago. (Euler lived from 1707 to 1783.)

In Fig. 6 we have drawn a solution curve of the DE $dx/dt = f(t, x)$ and the tangent at the point (t, x). Points near (t, x) which lie on the tangent 'very nearly' lie on the integral curve. Thus for small δt the point $(t + \delta t, x + \delta x)$ marked in the diagram is a good approximation to a subsequent point on the integral curve. Of course since $\delta x/\delta t$ is the slope of the tangent at (t, x) we have $\delta x/\delta t = dx/dt$ at (t, x) which in turn is $f(t, x)$. So for our next point on the integral curve we select $(t + \delta t, x + f(t, x) \delta t)$.

The smaller δt is, the closer this point is to lying on the integral curve.

Iterating this procedure, starting with some initial point (t_0, x_0) one produces polygonal lines with vertices

$$(t_0, x_0), (t_1, x_1) = (t_0 + \delta t, x_0 + f(t_0, x_0) \delta t),$$
$$(t_2, x_2) = (t_1 + \delta t, x_1 + f(t_1, x_1) \delta t), \ldots$$

These polygonal lines are referred to as *Euler lines*, in honour of the great man himself, and are approximations to the integral curves of our DE. As the reader might appreciate, the cumulative errors generated by this method can be quite substantial, and shortly we will discuss some possible improvements. First we present a program which sketches an Euler line of the differential equation $dx/dt = f(t, x)$ through some point $(t_0\ x_0)$.

Fig. 5

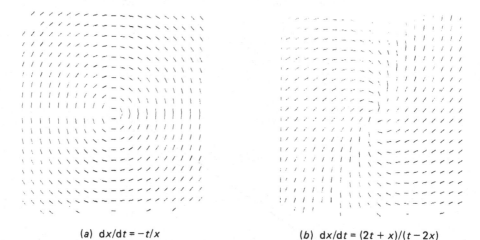

(a) $dx/dt = -t/x$ (b) $dx/dt = (2t + x)/(t - 2x)$

2.1 *Program: Euler lines*
```
1Ø INPUT TL, TU, XL, XU, D
2Ø INPUT T, X, N
3Ø IF N = Ø THEN GOTO 11Ø
4Ø FOR I = 1 TO N
5Ø Calculate screen point (u, v) corresponding to (t, x)
6Ø Check (u, v) lies on the screen: if not go to 2Ø
7Ø Put a dot at screen point (u, v)
8Ø LET X = X + f(t, x)*D: LET T = T + D
9Ø NEXT I
1ØØ GO TO 2Ø
11Ø END
```

As usual $f(t, x)$ is the function appearing in our DE and needs to be keyed in and the four numbers t_l, t_u, x_l, x_u specify the window in the (t, x)-plane inside which we are working. The number d is the length δt, and needs to be fairly small. Line 3Ø allows you to terminate the program by inserting any values for t, x and setting $n = 0$.

After you have supplied this information the program asks for an initial point (t, x) and a number n, which determines the number of times the Euler construction is repeated. The program then plots out the result as a sequence of n points which should give a good idea of the shape of the integral curve through (t, x). By varying our choices of initial point (t, x) we can build up a picture of how the integral curves of our DE $dx/dt = f(t, x)$ fit together. This picture may be enhanced by joining consecutive points by line segments. We leave you to incorporate this improvement. (On some machines returning to line 2Ø will make the screen contents move up by one line. To avoid this you will need to define a graphics or writing window.)

One word of warning concerning this program. It seems reasonable to suppose that the smaller the value of d, the time increment selected, the more accurate the corresponding pictures will be (compare Fig. 10). However, smaller values of d necessitate larger

Fig. 6

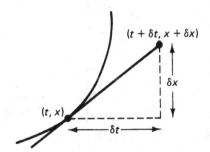

choices of n and the rounding errors resulting from the larger number of computations involved may well result in *less* accurate pictures.

2.2 *Exercises*
Plot out the integral curves for the DEs listed in Exercises 1.4.

2.3 *Exercises*
(a) Modify Program 2.1 so that it plots out points on the integral curves of the DE $dx/dt = f(t, x)/g(t, x)$. The changes involved are little different to those previously discussed for Program 1.3; the value l of 1.3 now appears as d, the time increment.

(b) Run your modified program with the examples of Exercise 1.5.

(c) Inserting values of t, x and n in Program 2.1 can be rather tedious. Add a few extra lines to Program 2.1 to *automatically* select initial points for the Euler line process. You can do this by choosing points along the edge of the window, but be sure to use two values $+ d$ and $- d$, for the small increment δt. The reason should be clear from Fig. 7.

§3
*Mathematical
excursion*

Our discussion of Euler lines, and the evidence of our experiments using Program 2.1 strongly suggest the following result.

3.1 *Existence and Uniqueness Theorem*
If $f(t, x)$ is a differentiable function of t and x then through every point (t_0, x_0) there is a unique integral curve of the differential equation $dx/dt = f(t, x)$.

This theorem is not phrased entirely accurately, and one can weaken the hypothesis of differentiability, but it covers most of the cases one is likely to meet. Its proof is not particularly easy. The Euler line approach can be used to construct a proof; see for example Petrovski (1966) pp. 29–31. The more usual proof uses the clever idea of replacing the DE $dx/dt = f(t, x)$ by the equivalent integral equation $x(t) = x(0) + \int_0^t f(s, x(s))ds$; see Petrovski

Fig. 7

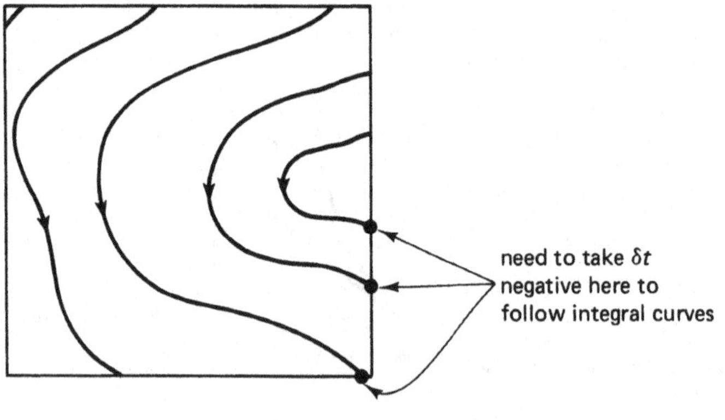

need to take δt negative here to follow integral curves

(1966) pp. 38–41. This may not seem such a brilliant move, of course, but it is in fact an extremely useful reformulation of the problem. The proof proceeds by producing a sequence of ever better approximations to the solution sought. One starts with an initial, possibly poor, approximation to a solution of our differential equation say $x = x_1(t)$ and produces a better approximation via the formula

$$x = x_2(t) = x_1(0) + \int_0^t f(s, x_1(s)) \, ds.$$

This in turn is then improved by setting

$$x_3(t) = x_2(0) + \int_0^t f(s, x_2(s)) \, ds.$$

As we iterate this procedure the functions $x_1(t)$, $x_2(t)$, $x_3(t)$, ... become better and better approximations to the required solutions. Thus although Theorem 3.1 is an existence theorem only, both proofs lead to algorithms for constructing approximate solutions.

3.2 *Exercise*

Consider the DE $dx/dt = x$. We know, of course, that the general solution of this equation is $x = ce^t$ for any constant c. It is instructive to see how the methods of proof described above apply in this case.

(a)   Starting with the initial function $x(t) = c$, any constant, as a (very poor) approximation to the solution, show how the method of successive approximations leads to the power series expansion $c(1 + t + t^2/2! + t^3/3! + \ldots + t^n/n! + \ldots)$ for ce^t.

(b)   We now use the Euler line method. We shall suppose that $x(0) = c$. The value of the solution x at a nearby point δt is then $x(0) + x(0)\delta t = x(0)(1 + \delta t)$. Using the Euler line method show that the approximate value of x at $n\delta t$ is $x((n-1)\delta t) + x((n-1)\delta t)\delta t = x(0)(1 + \delta t)^n$. Writing $n\delta t = t$ we deduce that an approximate value of $x(t)$ is $c(1 + t/n)^n$. What do you know about this expression as n becomes large? (If you didn't know this before you should now!) Compare Chapter 6, §7.

§4
*Improving the
Euler line method*

Useful as the Euler line method is for obtaining solutions of ordinary DEs it is not very accurate unless the increment δt is very small and then one can run into problems with rounding errors. There are more efficient methods for sketching solution curves, and although this is *not* primarily a book on Numerical Analysis we want to briefly mention these alternatives.

4.1 *Improvement I*

Here is a good example of how a rather silly idea can lead to a useful algorithm. Recall that the basic equation we use to solve the DE $dx/dt = f(t, x)$ is

$$\delta x = f(t, x)\, \delta t \tag{1}$$

where δt is the fixed increment in t, δx the corresponding increment in x. One possible objection to our basic equation is that it has an evident bias to the (t, x) end of the segment constructed. A more equable formula for the increment is

$$\delta x = \tfrac{1}{2}(f(t, x) + f(t + \delta t, x + \delta x))\, \delta t \tag{2}$$

which has no such bias. The problem with this approach, however, is that δx appears on both sides of equation (2). One rescues the idea by the simple device of replacing $x + \delta x$ on the right-hand side of (2) by the value given by the simple Euler method. This yields the new equation

$$\delta x = \tfrac{1}{2}(f(t, x) + f(t + \delta t, x + f((t, x)\, \delta t))\, \delta t.$$

We now show how to modify the basic Euler program to incorporate this improvement.

One can do this by relacing line 8∅ of Program 2.1 by

75 LET Z = X + $f(t, x)$ * D
8∅ LET X = X + ($f(t, x)$ + $f(t + d, z)$) * D/2
85 LET T = T + D

This method *is* more efficient than the Euler line method (this isn't entirely clear!). Note that since f is used three times in this program it is a good idea to make it a user defined function, defined on a new line 12∅, with corresponding changes in lines 75 and 8∅. When considering a new DE one then only needs to alter a single expression rather than three such.

4.2 *Improvement II*
An even more accurate, indeed very powerful, method of solving ordinary differential equations numerically, is the so called Runge–Kutta method. In common with improvement I it aims at giving a more accurate value for the increment δx. Rather than attempt to justify the method we simply state the procedure for obtaining the required increment δx. It is, in fact, obtained in four stages as follows

$$\left.\begin{aligned}
\delta x_1 &= f(t, x)\, \delta t \\
\delta x_2 &= f(t + \tfrac{1}{2}\delta t, x + \tfrac{1}{2}\delta x_1)\, \delta t \\
\delta x_3 &= f(t + \tfrac{1}{2}\delta t, x + \tfrac{1}{2}\delta x_2)\, \delta t \\
\delta x_4 &= f(t + \delta t, x + \delta x_3)\, \delta t
\end{aligned}\right\}$$

$$x = x + (\delta x_1 + 2\delta x_2 + 2\delta x_3 + \delta x_4)/6$$

To implement the Runge–Kutta method we replace line 8Ø of Program 2.1 with

75 LET C1 = FNF(T, X)∗D: LET C2 = FNF(T + D/2, X + C1/2)∗D
8Ø LET C3 = FNF(T + D/2, X + C2/2)∗D: LET C4 = FNF(T + D, X + C3)∗D
85 LET T = T + D: LET X = X + (C1 + 2∗C2 + 2∗C3 + C4)/6.

(If the function $f(t, x)$ appearing in the DE $dx/dt = f(t, x)$ does not depend on x then finding a solution reduces to integrating the function $f(t)$. The Euler line method corresponds to evaluating the integral by means of inscribed rectangles. Our first improvement then corresponds to the trapezoidal method, while the Runge–Kutta method is the analogue of Simpson's Rule.)

To illustrate the need for more accurate methods of solving differential equations we have drawn (Fig. 8(*a*) and (*b*)) solution curves for the DE $dx/dt = 4(x^2 - t^2)$ using the Euler line method and Runge–Kutta. In both cases the increment d is 0.05. Clearly there are quite substantial differences in the pictures – indeed in single integral curves as Fig. 8(*c*) shows. (See also Figure 10(*c*), (*d*) and (*e*).)

Naturally the Euler line method yields a more accurate picture if the increment d is decreased, say to 0.01. But as remarked above some care is needed, since very small values of d may give rise to rounding errors. To be sure you really do have the right overall picture of the integral curves of some DE, a little experimentation is required. (If a decrease in d yields much the same picture you can be fairly happy.) Generally Runge–Kutta should be the preferred method.

Fig. 8

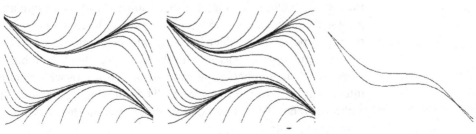

(*a*) integral curves via Euler line method (d = 0.05)

(*b*) integral curves via Runge–Kutta (d = 0.05) (see Exercise 5.7 (*c*))

(*c*) integral curves through (−1, 0.75). Euler's method yields upper curve, Runge–Kutta the lower curve (d = 0.05 in both cases)

Many interesting models used in physics, biology, and economics involve two DEs rather than one. Typically one has two quantities x and y varying with time t and related by the differential equations

$$dx/dt = g(t, x, y), \quad dy/dt = h(t, x, y). \tag{1}$$

One seeks solution curves in the three-dimensional space with coordinates (t, x, y), the curve being specified in the form $(t, x(t), y(t))$ where $x(t)$ and $y(t)$ satisfy Equations (1). Physically one can think of Equations (1) as specifying the velocity $(dx/dt, dy/dt)$ of a particle in the (x, y)-plane as a function of its position (x, y) and the time t. Ignoring the first component of the solution curves, the plane curves $(x(t), y(t))$ are trajectories of the corresponding motions of particles in the (x, y)-plane. Now in many applications the velocity of the particle $(dx/dt, dy/dt)$ is independent of the time t, and depends only on the position (x, y) of the particle (often reflecting the fundamental fact that physical laws are time independent). Thus we have the simpler equations

$$dx/dt = g(x, y), \quad dy/dt = h(x, y). \tag{2}$$

Such a pair of DEs is called an *autonomous system* (that is a time-independent system) and it is equations of this type that we shall spend most of the rest of this chapter considering. For obvious reasons we shall refer to the plane curves $(x(t), y(t))$, with x and y satisfying Equations (2) as *trajectories* of this autonomous system. The complete collection of trajectories of the system is referred to as the *phase portrait*.

Without further ado let us consider an example.

5.1 *Prey–Predator systems (Volterra's equations)*

On an island there live foxes and rabbits. The foxes eat rabbits and the rabbits eat clover of which there is an abundant supply. When the rabbit population is high the foxes flourish and their population grows. This increase, however, will eventually lead to a decrease in the rabbit population, which in turn produces a famine for the foxes, whose population decreases. With the foxes depleted the rabbits are safer and their numbers grow, and so on. How can we model the interdependence of the two species? The following analysis of Vito Volterra (1860–1940) shows that we can represent this system as an autonomous DE.

First, Volterra reasons, in the absence of foxes the rabbit population x will be described by the standard DE

$$dx/dt = ax, \quad a > 0. \tag{3}$$

This simply states that the rate of increase of the rabbit population, dx/dt, is proportional to the number of rabbits present; compare Example 1.2. This leads to exponential population growth, i.e. Equation (3) has solutions $x = ke^t$, for any constant k. Since there are foxes present however, y in number, a certain number of encounters between fox and rabbit are inevitable in unit time. It is reasonable to suppose that this number is proportional to the product xy. Moreover, of these encounters a certain proportion will result in an eaten rabbit, and one is led to modify Equation (3) to obtain

$$dx/dt = ax - bxy, \quad a, b > 0 \tag{3'}$$

Similarly one obtains the DE

$$dy/dt = -cy + dxy, \quad c, d > 0 \tag{4}$$

governing the change in the population of foxes. For in the absence of rabbits the foxes die out, and their increase depends on the number of their encounters with rabbits. The constants a, b, c and d are, of course, determined by a number of factors; for example the reticence of the rabbit, the speed of the fox, the terrain of the island.

We now wish to study the evolution of the rabbit and fox populations with time. One way of approaching the problem is to eliminate t by writing

$$dy/dx = (dy/dt)/(dx/dt) = (-cy + dxy)/(ax - bxy) \tag{5}$$

and use previous programs.

Alternatively one can use the basic equations

$$\left. \begin{array}{l} \delta x = (ax - bxy)\,\delta t \\ \delta y = (-cy + dxy)\,\delta t \end{array} \right\} \tag{6}$$

and the obvious variant of the Euler line method to obtain solution curves. As usual one cannot plot typical integral curves for the *whole* (x, y)-plane so one has to restrict one's attention to especially relevant regions. Of special interest, as we shall see, are points where the two derivatives dx/dt, dy/dt vanish. These are so called stationary points or equilibrium positions of our autonomous system. For at such points the populations of rabbits and foxes do not alter with time. Here we have equilibrium positions when $ax - bxy = 0$ *and* $-cy + dxy = 0$, in other words at the two points $(0, 0)$, $(c/d, a/b)$. Of course, we are largely interested in the solution curves which lie in the quadrant $x \geqslant 0$, $y \geqslant 0$, and physically the equilibrium point $x = y = 0$ is of little interest!

Before investigating the solutions of our autonomous system,

Equations (3′), (4), we need a program for drawing the trajectories of general autonomous systems. The following program is the obvious modification of Program 2.1 which drew Euler lines.

5.2 *Program: Autonomous systems*
```
10 INPUT XL, XU, YL, YU, D
20 INPUT X, Y, N
30 IF N = Ø THEN GOTO 11Ø
40 FOR I = 1 TO N
50 Calculate screen point (u, v) corresponding to (x, y)
60 Check (u, v) lies on screen; if not go to 2Ø
70 Plot point at (u, v)
80 LET X = X + g(x, y)*D: LET Y = Y + h(x, y)*D
90 NEXT I
100 GOTO 2Ø
110 END
```

We hope that the structure of this program is clear. The functions g and h are those appearing in Equations (2). On inputting x, y and n the trajectory through the point (x, y) is plotted as a series of n points. These points represent the approximate positions of the particle, initially at (x, y), after time $t = 0, d, 2d, \ldots, (n-1)d$. When all such points have been plotted, or one such lies outside the window $x_\ell \leq x \leq x_\mathrm{u}$, $y_\ell \leq y \leq y_\mathrm{u}$, the program returns to line 2Ø where a new initial point is requested, together with a value of n. The program is terminated by inserting any values for x and y and the value 0 for n.

Naturally to obtain fairly good approximations to the true trajectories one needs d to be small, but not *too* small or else rounding errors will occur.

Fig. 9 shows a typical print out of trajectories for the autonomous equations (3′) and (4) obtained by using Program 5.2 (the values of a, b, c, d are 4.0, 2.5, 2.0 and 1.0 respectively).

5.3 *Exercises*
Try running your program on the following autonomous systems. Unless otherwise specified consider the (x, y) range is to be $-1 \leq x$, $y \leq 1$. Three of these are illustrated in Fig. 10.
(Note:(a)–(j) each have a single stationary point at the origin.)

(a) $\mathrm{d}x/\mathrm{d}t = -x$, $\mathrm{d}y/\mathrm{d}t = -y$
(b) $\mathrm{d}x/\mathrm{d}t = x$, $\mathrm{d}y/\mathrm{d}t = -2y$
(c) $\mathrm{d}x/\mathrm{d}t = x$, $\mathrm{d}y/\mathrm{d}t = -y$
(d) $\mathrm{d}x/\mathrm{d}t = y$, $\mathrm{d}y/\mathrm{d}t = -x$

(e) $dx/dt = -x$, $dy/dt = -x + y$
(f) $dx/dt = 3x + 4y$, $dy/dt = -3x - 3y$
(g) $dx/dt = x$, $dy/dt = y^2$
(h) $dx/dt = y^2$, $dy/dt = x$
(i) $dx/dt = x^2$, $dy/dt = y(2x - y)$
(j) $dx/dt = -xy$, $dy/dt = x^2 + y^2$

Fig. 9

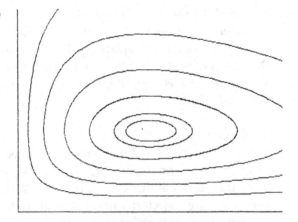

Integral curves for Volterra's equations

Fig. 10

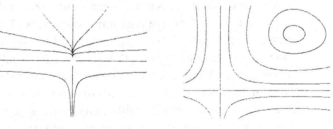

$dx/dt = x$, $dy/dt = y^2$ $dx/dt = x(1-y)$, $dy/dt = -y(1-x)$

Euler line method
$d = 0.05$

Euler line method
$d = 0.01$

Runge–Kutta, $d = 0.05$
(this is the right picture)

$dx/dt = 3x + 4y$, $dy/dt = -3x - 3y$,
integral curve through (0.2, 0 2)

Differential equations

(k) $dx/dt = x(1 - y)$, $dy/dt = -y(1 - x)$, $-\frac{1}{2} \leqslant x, y \leqslant \frac{3}{2}$
(stationary points at $(0, 0)$, $(1, 1)$).

(l) $dx/dt = -x(1 - 3y^{2/3}(1 - x)/(1 + x))$,
$dy/dt = y - 3xy^{2/3}/(1 + x)$, $-\frac{1}{2} \leqslant x, y \leqslant \frac{3}{2}$.
(Some care is needed here with the fractional power of y:
Y↑0.6667 will run into problems when $y \leqslant 0$.)

5.4 *Exercise*

Consider a general DE of the type discussed in §1,
$dx/dt = f(t, x)/g(t, x)$; replacing t by x and x by y this becomes
$dy/dx = f(x, y)/g(x, y)$. Show that trajectories of the autonomous
system $dx/dt = g(x, y)$, $dy/dt = f(x, y)$ correspond to solution
curves of this DE.

5.5 *Exercise*

A function f of two variables x and y is said to be a *first integral* of the
autonomous system $dx/dt = g(x, y)$, $dy/dt = h(x, y)$ if f is constant
along trajectories of this system. If f is a first integral then the level
curves of f are trajectories or a union of trajectories, so the phase
portrait of a system with a first integral can be obtained using the
methods of Chapter 5, §2. (Actually this is not much easier than the
Euler line method: indeed the method for sketching level curves discussed in Chapter 5, Section 2.6 really amounts to the same thing.)

Show that the Volterra equations, Equations (3′) and (4), have a
first integral $x^c \exp(-dx)y^a \exp(-by)$. ('Most' autonomous systems
do not possess first integrals; those that do are usually referred to as
conservative. Conservative systems play an important role in
mechanics, where the first integral corresponds to the total energy of
the system. In many physical situations we may suppose that this total
energy remains constant, i.e. is *conserved* as the system evolves, so that
trajectories correspond to subsets of the level curves of the energy
function. Of course if, in mechanics, we are to take frictional forces
into account the corresponding system will cease to be conservative.)

Before going on to discuss more theoretical aspects of autonomous systems we want to consider another 'real life' example.

5.6 *Example: The pendulum*

You may be familiar with the DE for simple harmonic motion

$$d^2 x/dt^2 + \lambda x = 0. \tag{7}$$

Amongst other things this equation governs the motion of a

pendulum, provided the displacement of the bob from the vertical is small. The DE which actually governs the pendulum is, you may recall,

$$\mathrm{d}^2 x/\mathrm{d}t^2 + (g/a) \sin x = 0 \qquad (8)$$

where x measures the displacement, in radians, of the pendulum from the vertical, g is the acceleration due to gravity and a the length of the pendulum. (In what follows we shall assume that we are dealing with a rigid pendulum hinged at one end with mass concentrated at the other, which we shall refer to as the bob.) One now argues that for small x the functions $\sin x$ and x very nearly agree. Replacing $\sin x$ by x and g/a by λ then reduces Equation (8) to Equation (7) which we can solve exactly, the solution being a linear combination of the trigonometric functions sine and cosine.

What we wish to do here is study the DE Equation (8) directly, using our Program 5.2. Of course in its present form Equation (8) is a second order DE, i.e. one involving a second derivative, and not an autonomous system. The following trick, however, converts Equation (8) to an autonomous system which we can then study.

Suppose we write $y = \mathrm{d}x/\mathrm{d}t$, i.e. we take y to be the angular velocity of the bob. Equation (8) can be rewritten as $\mathrm{d}y/\mathrm{d}t = -(g/a) \sin x$. In other words the single second order DE Equation (8) can be replaced by the autonomous system

$$\mathrm{d}x/\mathrm{d}t = y, \quad \mathrm{d}y/\mathrm{d}t = -(g/a) \sin x. \qquad (9)$$

Before rushing to our keyboards to churn out lots of pictures of the resulting trajectories let us first consider what such pictures actually represent. Clearly the x-coordinate is, as before, the angular displacement of the pendulum and, as stated, the y-coordinate represents the angular velocity of the pendulum. So for example position a in Fig. 11 represents an equilibrium position, with $x = 0$ (the

Fig. 11

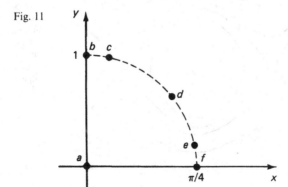

pendulum vertical) and $y = \mathrm{d}x/\mathrm{d}t = 0$ (the pendulum motionless). Position *b* on the other hand represents a vertical pendulum having unit velocity in the positive direction. As we move through positions *c–f* the pendulum moves away from the vertical, and its velocity drops, until at position *f* it is inclined at an angle of $\pi/4$ to the vertical and is motionless.

5.7 *Exercises*

(*a*)   Use Program 5.2 (and some commonsense) to investigate the motion of a pendulum.

(*Comments*   Since *x* is an angle we need only consider *x* in the range $-\pi \leqslant x \leqslant \pi$. On the other hand *y* is the angular velocity of the bob and so can assume any value. The stationary points are found by solving the equations $y = \sin x = 0$ and consequently occur at the points $(-\pi, 0)$, $(0, 0)$, $(\pi, 0)$. The first and last of these corresponds to the pendulum being motionless and vertically above the hinge or pivot; this is an *unstable* equilibrium point. On the other hand the stationary point $(0, 0)$, which corresponds to the pendulum hanging motionless below the hinge is a *stable* equilibrium or stationary point. Compare Fig. 12.)

(*b*)   When considering the pendulum above we have ignored any effect of friction at the pivot or in the form of air resistance on the bob. Consequently the resulting autonomous system is conservative. Show that $2g(1 - \cos x) + ay^2$ is a first integral for this system. (Compare Exercise 5.5.)

(*c*)   Rewrite Program 5.2 to incorporate analogues of the improvements to the Euler line method discussed in §4.

For example the analogue of the Runge–Kutta method discussed in Section 4.2 determines approximate solutions of the autonomous system $\mathrm{d}x/\mathrm{d}t = g(x, y)$, $\mathrm{d}y/\mathrm{d}t = h(x, y)$ as

Fig. 12

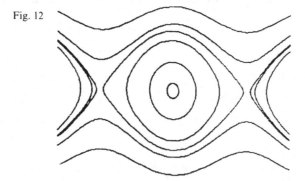

Integral curves for the autonomous system arising from the penulum. (We have taken $g/a = 1$, used Euler's method, and considered (x,y) in the range $-5 \leqslant x \leqslant 5$, $-3 \leqslant y \leqslant 3$.)

follows. Given an arbitrary point (x, y) we seek the point $(x + \delta x, y + \delta y)$ corresponding to an increment δt in t. The values of δx, δy are obtained from the following ten equations

$$\delta x_1 = g(x, y)\,\delta t \qquad\qquad\qquad \delta y_1 = h(x, y)\,\delta t$$
$$\delta x_2 = g(x + \tfrac{1}{2}\delta x_1, y + \tfrac{1}{2}\delta y_1)\,\delta t \qquad \delta x_2 = h(x + \tfrac{1}{2}\delta x_1, y + \tfrac{1}{2}\delta y_1)\,\delta t$$
$$\delta x_3 = g(x + \tfrac{1}{2}\delta x_2, y + \tfrac{1}{2}\delta y_2)\,\delta t \qquad \delta x_3 = h(x + \tfrac{1}{2}\delta x_2, y + \tfrac{1}{2}\delta y_2)\,\delta t$$
$$\delta x_4 = g(x + \delta x_3, y + \delta y_3)\,\delta t \qquad\quad \delta x_4 = h(x + \delta x_3, y + \delta y_3)\,\delta t$$
$$\delta x = \tfrac{1}{6}(\delta x_1 + 2\delta x_2 + 2\delta x_3 + \delta x_4) \quad \delta y = \tfrac{1}{6}(\delta y_1 + 2\delta y_2 + 2\delta y_3 + \delta y_4)$$

(See Fig. 10.)

§6
Stationary points and stability

After you have plotted trajectories for a large number of autonomous systems, using the Euler line method, you should have observed the following points.

(*a*) Suppose that the point (x_0, y_0) is a non-equilibrium point, so one of dx/dt, dy/dt is non-zero at (x_0, y_0). You will have observed that near such a point the integral curves of the autonomous system are smooth and fit together nicely. Indeed the integral curves give the plane the appearance of raked sand, or combed hair, near (x_0, y_0). This is hardly surprising for if we consider the autonomous equations as specifying the velocity of particles in the plane then this velocity at (x_0, y_0) is non-zero, and consequently one expects the trajectories through points near (x_0, y_0) to be approximately linear with slope $(dy/dt)/(dx/dt)$. In other words away from stationary points the integral curves behave very well, and predictably, at least locally.

(*b*) The behaviour of integral curves near stationary or equilibrium points can be considerably more complicated. The first thing one notes when plotting these curves is how slowly the tracing point moves near stationary positions. This results in unsightly holes in our version of the phase portrait of the system. This phenomenon is easily understood, for the distance between consecutive points produced by the Euler line method $\sqrt{((\delta x)^2 + (\delta y)^2)}$ is approximately $\sqrt{((dx/dt)^2 + (dy/dt)^2)}\,\delta t$ where δt is the fixed increment in t (labelled d in Program 5.2). Near a stationary point dx/dt and dy/dt are small and so consecutive points are close together. As an example consider the autonomous system $dx/dt = -x$, $dy/dt = -y$, with a stationary point at the origin. Here, by integrating just as in Example 1.2, one obtains the solutions $x(t) = ae^{-t}$, $y(t) = be^{-t}$, where a and b are arbitrary constants, and the integral curves are as indicated in Fig. 13(*a*).

The arrows on the trajectories give the direction in which these curves are transversed as t increases. What the diagram does not

Fig. 13

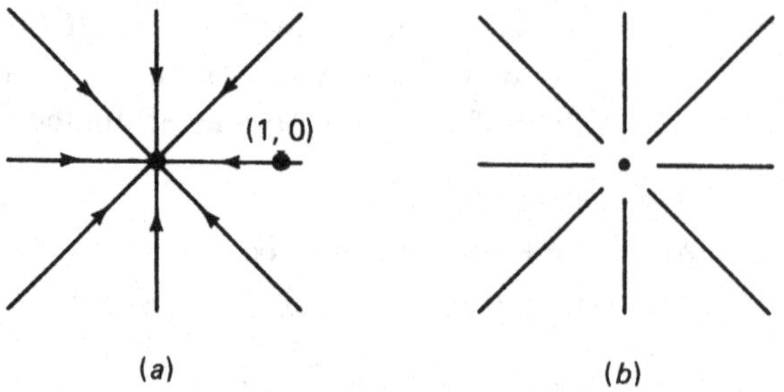

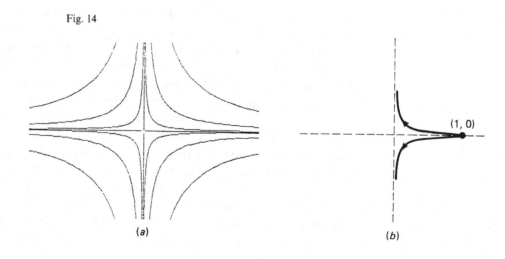

(a)   (b)

show is that the integral curves never actually reach the origin (0, 0). For example the integral curve through the point (1, 0) is parametrised as $(e^{-t}, 0)$ and although e^{-t} approaches 0 as t gets larger, e^{-t} is strictly positive for all values of t. Consequently, when plotting trajectories for this autonomous system (or ones like it), there is always some small neighbourhood or region near (0, 0) inside which the trajectories do not go, and the computer produces a picture as in Fig. 13(b).

(c) Different types of stationary point produce different problems. As another example consider the autonomous system $dx/dt = -x$, $dy/dt = y$. Again this system has a stationary point at the origin and a general trajectory is given by $x(t) = ae^{-t}$, $y(t) = be^t$ where a and b are constants. In particular these trajectories are level curves of the function xy (xy is a first integral of this system since $x(t)y(t) = ab$ is constant). One easily checks then that the integral curves are as in Fig. 14(a).

Fig. 14

(a)   (b)

Consider this time the trajectory through the point $(1, 0)$ which is parametrised as $(e^{-t}, 0)$. The form of the parametrisation leads one to believe that when plotting this trajectory consecutive points will cluster together as we approach the origin and the sequence of points produced by the Euler line method will never reach this equilibrium point. In practice something different happens, namely a trajectory started at $(1, 0)$ tends to veer off to one side or other of the equilibrium point, and move away rapidly producing a picture as in Fig. 14(b). The reason again is easy to understand. The Euler line method is an *approximate* method for plotting out integral curves; indeed our micro is a machine that produces *approximate* answers to precise problems (such as: find the decimal expansion of $\sqrt{2}$). Starting our trajectory at $(1, 0)$ we note that if any subsequent point on the approximate trajectory does not lie *on* the x-axis it will be swept away from this axis by the flow of the differential equation, never to return.

(d) As a final example let us consider the autonomous system $\mathrm{d}x/\mathrm{d}t = y$, $\mathrm{d}y/\mathrm{d}t = -x$. Here one can check that $(a \sin t, a \cos t)$ are solutions of these equations where a is any constant. (Indeed $\mathrm{d}y/\mathrm{d}t = \mathrm{d}^2 x/\mathrm{d}t^2$ and since $\mathrm{d}y/\mathrm{d}t = -x$ the function $x(t)$ is a solution of $\mathrm{d}^2 x/\mathrm{d}t^2 = -x$.) Consequently the integral curves of this system are as in Fig. 15(a). However, when plotting these curves by the Euler line method any slight error will mean that the trajectory will not close up exactly after one revolution about the origin. Typical experimental trajectories are illustrated in Fig. 15(b).

These problems are rather annoying, but they do have their positive aspects. As we mentioned above, deviations from true trajectories produced by the Euler line method are necessary consequences of the fact that this method only yields *approximate* solutions (a secondary factor is the rounding errors produced by the computer). Suppose now that we have an autonomous system which models some physical process, like a swinging pendulum or a

Fig. 15

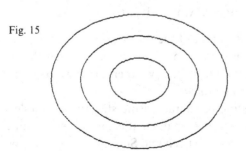 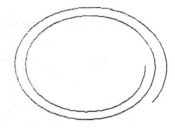

(a) Runge–Kutta   (b) Euler line method ($d = 0.05$, starting at $(0.5, 0)$)

prey–predator system. Nobody would ever assert that such a model was *perfect*, a simple pair of DEs can hardly be expected to capture all of the subtleties of fox–rabbit combat, and even if our equations for the pendulum are modified to take into account air resistance countless other phenomena (such as the effect of temperature changes on the length of the pendulum, air resistance on its temperature, eddies on its air resistance . . .) will *not* be accounted for. What one hopes is that the trajectories of the autonomous system which is used to model the process in question describe its behaviour *approximately*. Given this we can see that some of the problems our micro has plotting integral curves mentioned above have a deeper significance. For example if the system described in (*c*) modelled some physical process then the trajectory passing through (− 1, 0) could not arise as a series of observations of that process, no matter what initial conditions were selected. For if at any stage the point describing the evolution of the physical system moves slightly away from the *x*-axis it will continue to move away. In some sense the *x*-axis represents the set of initial conditions which yield *unpredictable* behaviour. In practice subsequently the trajectory will *certainly* move away from the *x*-axis never to return, but we have no way of knowing in which direction.

The situation with regard to the example in (*d*) is even worse. Here every set of initial conditions yields unpredictable behaviour, in other words the corresponding autonomous system cannot arise as a useful model of any physical process. In fact, only autonomous systems which are *structurally stable* have any place in describing real life situations. Roughly speaking a pair of DEs

$$\mathrm{d}x/\mathrm{d}t = h(x, y), \quad \mathrm{d}y/\mathrm{d}t = g(x, y) \tag{1}$$

is *structurally stable* if for any pair of functions $H(x, y)$, $G(x, y)$ close to $h(x, y)$, $g(x, y)$ respectively, the phase portrait of the perturbed autonomous system.

$$\mathrm{d}x/\mathrm{d}t = H(x, y), \quad \mathrm{d}y/\mathrm{d}t = G(x, y) \tag{2}$$

is equivalent to that of the original. To be more precise, we want a two-way continuous correspondence between the portraits taking trajectories to trajectories; we then say that the systems (1), (2) are *qualitatively equivalent*.

The question of characterising structurally stable systems is one which has exercised mathematicians for some time. See Arnold (1973), Chapter 3, Hirsch and Smale (1974) p. 312. We only remark that in some sense we cannot expect our micro to draw an accurate phase portrait of an unstable system, since any slight rounding error, or errors resulting from the particular algorithm used, may produce a quite different phase portrait.

6.1 *Exercise*

The prey–predator system discussed in Section 5.1 is a highly unstable autonomous system. As we remarked the trajectories near the stationary point $(c/d, a/b)$ are all closed curves winding once around this point. The discussion of the preceding section leads one to believe that the Volterra equations may not be a very good model for the fox–rabbit conflict. A better model is that due to Holling–Tanner discussed in Arrowsmith and Place (1982) pp. 147–51. Here the prey population $x(t)$ and the predator population $y(t)$, at time t, are related by the autonomous system

$$dx/dt = r(1 - xK^{-1})x - wxy(D + x)^{-1}$$
$$dy/dt = s(1 - Jyx^{-1})y$$

with $r, s, K, D, J > 0$. The reference above contains a derivation of these equations and some discussion of the form of the corresponding phase portrait. Sketch the phase portraits corresponding to various values of r, s, K, D, J (e.g. $r = 1$, $s = 0.2$, $K = 7.0$, $J = 1$, $D = 1.0$). Take w (the limiting predation rate) to be 1.

6.2 *Exercise*

(a) Similarly our equation for simple harmonic motion, Equation (8) of §5, and the resulting autonomous system Equations (9) of §5, is not a good model for the motion of a simple pendulum; in practice we cannot ignore frictional forces. These forces oppose the motion of the bob and are proportional to its velocity. Initially we consider the analogue of equation (7) of §5 above

$$d^2x/dt^2 + (g/a)x + k\,dx/dt = 0$$

(where k is some positive constant). This yields the autonomous system

$$dx/dt = y \quad dy/dt = -(g/a)x - ky. \tag{3}$$

Consider the phase portraits of this system (i) for $k = 0$, (ii) for $0 < k < 2\sqrt{(g/a)}$, (iii) for $k = 2\sqrt{(g/a)}$ and (iv) for $2\sqrt{(g/a)} < k$. (Take $g/a = 1$.)

(b) Repeat the above exercise, but with the exact Equation (8) of §5 replacing Equation (7).

(See Arrowsmith and Place (1982) pp. 119–25 for a discussion of Equations (3) above with applications to car suspensions.)

As we pointed out in the previous section, equilibrium positions of autonomous systems can present real problems to a micro. If we are patient enough we can piece together a fairly good picture of how the integral curves fit together near the stationary point, but there will always be some small region inside which our system remains a mystery. In this section we show how one can fill in the resulting holes in the phase portrait by a fairly straightforward local analysis, and give a number of illustrations. The key to this local analysis is the theory of *linear* systems.

An autonomous system of the form

$$\left.\begin{array}{l} dx/dt = ax + by \\ dy/dt = cx + dy \end{array}\right\} \quad a, b, c, d \text{ constants} \tag{1}$$

is said to be a *linear system*; we have seen a number of examples before in Exercise 5.3 and in §6. We note that any linear system has a stationary point at the origin $(x, y) = (0, 0)$ and that conversely if $ad - bc \neq 0$ this is the only equilibrium position. The expression $ad - bc$ is the *determinant D* of the linear system, the sum $a + d$ is the *trace T* and these two quantities, or more precisely the quadratic *characteristic* equation

$$\lambda^2 - \lambda T + D = 0 \tag{2}$$

determine (with one, rather degenerate, exception) the way the integral curves of the linear system (1) fit together. In what follows we shall suppose that $D \neq 0$ so that $(0, 0)$ is the only stationary point of the system.

Given this we now describe the ten principal types of linear systems in the plane.

7.1 *Nodes and saddles*

Suppose that the quadratic equation, Equation (2), has real distinct roots, so that $T^2 - 4D > 0$ or equivalently $(a - d)^2 + 4bc > 0$. If the two roots of Equation (2) have the same sign, i.e. $D > 0$, then the system is said to have a *node* at $(0, 0)$, if the roots have opposite sign, $D < 0$, we have a *saddle*. As typical examples consider the simple equations

$$dx/dt = \mu x, \quad dy/dt = \eta y \tag{3}$$

for real μ, η. Here one easily checks that $x(t) = re^{\mu t}$, $y(t) = se^{\eta t}$ are solutions for any constants r and s; of course μ and η are also the roots of the corresponding characteristic equation (2). Taking $\mu = 2$, $\eta = 1$ (resp. $\mu = -2$, $\eta = -1$) yields respectively the *unstable* and *stable* nodes depicted in Fig. 16(a) and (b). At an unstable node the trajectories all move away from the stationary point; at a stable node they all move in towards the origin. (Stability here has a quite different meaning from its use in §6; there stability was a property of the whole phase portrait, while here it concerns a single stationary point.) Taking $\mu = 1$, $\eta = -1$ we obtain the saddle of Fig. 16(*c*). Note that the trajectories here lie on the curves $xy = $ constant; they move in towards the fixed point, pass through some point of closest approach, and then move away. Of course these pictures are easily obtained by using the explicit solutions given above. What is perhaps rather surprising is that the pictures are typical of *all* node and saddle points. That is, any pair of linear systems *both* yielding a stable node, an unstable node or a saddle give rise to equivalent phase portraits. In particular given *any* linear system for which the characteristic equation (2) has distinct real roots there is a two-way correspondence between its phase portrait and one of the portraits sketched in Fig. 16 with the correspondence taking trajectories to trajectories.

7.2 *Improper nodes and stars*
If Equation (2) has real coincident roots, so that $T^2 = 4D$ then there are four possible forms for the phase portrait. As typical examples consider the systems

$$\mathrm{d}x/\mathrm{d}t = \mu x, \quad \mathrm{d}y/\mathrm{d}t = \mu y \tag{4}$$

and

$$\mathrm{d}x/\mathrm{d}t = \mu x + y, \quad \mathrm{d}y/\mathrm{d}t = \mu y. \tag{5}$$

In case (4) one easily checks that $x(t) = r\mathrm{e}^{\mu t}$, $y(t) = s\mathrm{e}^{\mu t}$ are solutions for any constants r, s, so that the trajectories consist of the stationary point itself and half-lines through the origin. Taking $\mu = 1$ we have an *unstable star* (Fig. 17(*a*)), while $\mu = -1$ yields the *stable star* (Fig. 17(*b*)).

Fig. 16

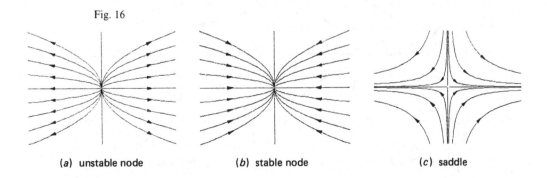

(*a*) unstable node   (*b*) stable node   (*c*) saddle

The system (5) is not quite as straightforward. One can check that $x(t) = (r + st)e^{\mu t}$, $y(t) = se^{\mu t}$ are solutions, for any r, s and the stationary point is an *improper node*. Taking $\mu = 1$ we have an unstable improper node (Fig. 17(c)), $\mu = -1$ yields the stable improper node (Fig. 17(d)).

7.3 *Foci and centres*
Finally we consider the case when the roots of the quadratic (2) are complex. There are three possible phase portraits in this case, and as in Section 7.1 the types are determined by the nature of the complex conjugate roots. As typical examples consider the systems

$$\mathrm{d}x/\mathrm{d}t = \alpha x - y, \quad \mathrm{d}y/\mathrm{d}t = x + \alpha y. \tag{6}$$

The corresponding quadratic equation is $\lambda^2 - 2\alpha\lambda + (1 + \alpha^2) = 0$ with roots $\alpha \pm i$, and one easily checks that $x(t) = re^{\alpha t}\cos(s + t)$, $y(t) = re^{\alpha t}\sin(s + t)$ are solutions for any r, s. If $\alpha > 0$, say $\alpha = 1$, we

Fig. 17

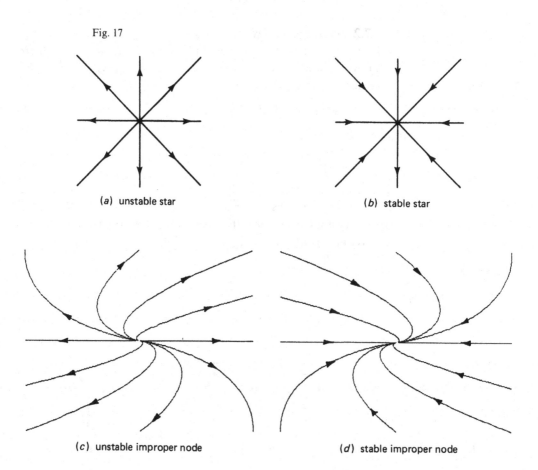

(a) unstable star

(b) stable star

(c) unstable improper node

(d) stable improper node

have the *unstable focus* illustrated in Fig. 18(*a*), if $\alpha < 0$, say $\alpha = -1$, we have a *stable focus*, as in Fig. 18(*b*), and if $\alpha = 0$ we have a *centre*, as in Fig. 18(*c*) where the trajectories are concentric circles with centre the origin. More generally for any linear system (1) for which Equation (2) has complex roots we have a phase portrait similar to those in Fig. 18(*a*), (*b*) and (*c*) if, respectively, the real parts of these complex roots are positive, zero, or negative.

7.4 *Exercise*
Check the plausibility of the assertions made in Sections 7.1–7.3 by sketching, on your micro, the phase portraits of various linear systems (1), computing the corresponding characteristic equation (2), and comparing with one of the standard phase portraits drawn above. Try for example the linear systems given by the following values for (a, b, c, d): $(0, \frac{1}{2}, 0, 2), (2, 1, 0, 1), (2, -1, 0, 2),$ $(2, -1, 1, 1), \ldots$.

(You will note that the correspondences between the phase portraits of these systems and those of our standard models are certainly not obtained by rigid motions of the phase planes. In particular centres generally have phase portraits made up of concentric *ellipses* not merely circles. In fact the correspondences are usually not even differentiable at the origin.)

7.5 *Exercise*
In Arrowsmith and Place (1982) pp. 125–31 there is a discussion of applications of linear autonomous systems to electrical circuit theory and economics. Look these up, and plot the corresponding phase portraits.

We return to our original problem of determining the nature of the trajectories near a stationary point of an autonomous system. Of

Fig. 18

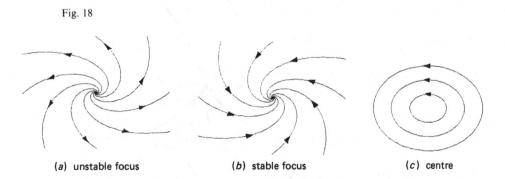

(*a*) unstable focus   (*b*) stable focus   (*c*) centre

course if this system is linear we now have a good idea of how these trajectories should all fit together; what if it is not linear? The basic idea in the (general) non-linear case is to find, at any stationary point, a linear system which best approximates the given system and then hope that near the stationary point in question the phase portraits of the approximating linear system and the original non-linear system are equivalent. This idea is best explained by means of some examples.

7.6 *Examples*

(*a*)   Consider the autonomous system

$$dx/dt = x - xy + y^3, \quad dy/dt = y + x^2.$$

This system clearly has a stationary point at $x = y = 0$. At this stationary point the linearized system is obtained by considering only the linear parts of the functions appearing on the right-hand side of the above equations. Thus we have the linearized system

$$dx/dt = x, \quad dy/dt = y$$

with trajectories $x = re^t$, $y = se^t$, any r and s, an unstable star. Our hope is that near $(0, 0)$ the trajectories of this star will resemble those of the original system. If you use one of our previous programs to draw the phase portrait of the original system you will find that this is indeed the case – compare Figs. 19 and 17.

(*b*)   Consider now the pair of DEs

$$dx/dt = \sin x, \quad dy/dt = 1 - e^y. \tag{7}$$

Again this system has a stationary point at $(0, 0)$, indeed stationary points at $(x, y) = (m\pi, 0)$, m any integer. The Taylor

Fig. 19

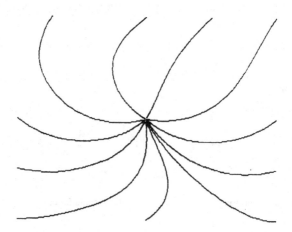

expansions of $\sin x$, $1 - e^y$ at $x = 0$, $y = 0$ start $\sin x = x - x^3/6 + \ldots$, $1 - e^y = -y - y^2/2 - \ldots$ and so the linearized system, *for the stationary point* $(0, 0)$, is

$$dx/dt = x, \quad dy/dt = -y.$$

You will easily check that we have here a saddle point, and sketching the phase portrait of the original system, using for example the Euler line method, we get a good agreement between the phase portraits of the non-linear and linearized system near the stationary point. See Fig. 20 where $-3.5 \leqslant x \leqslant 7$, $-3 \leqslant y \leqslant 3$.

(c) Finally we show how to find the linear part of an autonomous system near a stationary point which is *not* at the origin. Consider for example the stationary point $(\pi, 0)$ of the system $dx/dt = \sin x$, $dy/dt = 1 - e^y$ discussed in (b). The basic idea is to introduce new coordinates which vanish at the stationary point in question. So let $u = x + \pi$, $v = y$; $\sin x = \sin(u - \pi) = -\sin u$, $1 - e^y = 1 - e^v$, $dx/dt = du/dt$, $dy/dt = dv/dt$ and so we now consider the system

$$du/dt = -\sin u, \quad dv/dt = 1 - e^v$$

and are interested in the stationary point $u = v = 0$. Clearly the linearized system is now

$$du/dt = -u, \quad dv/dt = -v$$

a stable star, and we leave you to check that locally the phase portrait of Equations (7) near $(\pi, 0)$ does have the appearance of a stable star. (Actually in some sense the agreement is not

Fig. 20

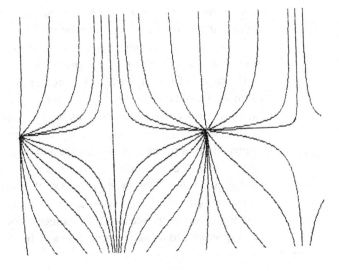

quite so good this time, the local two-way correspondence does more stretching and pushing in this case than in previous ones.)

Unfortunately this local analysis of stationary points does not always work, as you will see by doing the following.

7.7 *Exercise*

Show that the two systems

(a) $dx/dt = -y + x(x^2 + y^2)$, $dy/dt = x + y(x^2 + y^2)$

(b) $dx/dt = -y - x(x^2 + y^2)$, $dy/dt = x - y(x^2 + y^2)$

both have the same linearized system at the origin, but that their phase portraits are different.

A little thought will show that the result of Exercise 7.7 is not surprising. The linearized system at the origin for both (a) and (b) is the centre $dx/dt = -y$, $dy/dt = x$ and the phase portrait of this linear system consists of concentric circles, centred at (0, 0). Clearly this portrait is very sensitive to any change in the system: adding the non-linear terms given in (a) makes the trajectories spiral *away* from the origin, while the cubic terms in (b) result in a portrait with trajectories spiralling *towards* the origin. It turns out, however, that centres provide the only problems. (Since most linearized systems do *not* yield centres, i.e. $T = a + d \neq 0$ for most linear systems (1), these problems are not very significant.) We have the following result.

7.8 *Linearization Theorem*

Let the non-linear autonomous system

$$dx/dt = g(x, y), \quad dy/dt = h(x, y)$$

have a stationary point at the origin, say. If the corresponding linearized system has a single stationary point (also at (0, 0)), and is not a centre, then the phase portraits of the original system and the linearized system near (0, 0) are qualitatively equivalent.

The proof of the Linearization Theorem is far from easy, see for example Arnold (1983), pp. 119–25, but it *is* a plausible result. Thinking of the trajectories *near* (0, 0) as being obtained by the Euler line method we claim that consecutive segments making up our polygonal approximation to the trajectories are much the same for the original system and the linearized systems. For writing $g(x, y) = ax + by + g_1(x, y)$, $h(x, y) = cx + dy + h_1(x, y)$, where a, b, c, d are constants and $g_1(x, y)$, $h_1(x, y)$ are Taylor series consisting of quadratic and higher terms, we see that the changes in the x- and y-coordinates corresponding to some increment δt are, for the linearized system,

$$\delta x_1 = (ax + by)\,\delta t, \quad \delta y_1 = (cx + dy)\,\delta t$$

and for the original system

$$\delta x = \delta x_1 + g_1(x, y)\,\delta t, \quad \delta y = \delta y_1 + h_1(x, y)\,\delta t.$$

Since x, y are small the differences $\delta x - \delta x_1$, $\delta y - \delta y_1$, are small by comparison with δx_1 and δy_1, simply because g_1 and h_1 are made up of quadratic and higher terms in the small quantities x, y. Consequently $(x + \delta x_1, y + \delta y_1)$ is a good approximation to $(x + \delta x, y + \delta y)$. Of course this argument quite evidently does not work if $a = b = c = d = 0$ (!), and more subtly fails if the linear system is a centre (see Fig. 18(a), (b), (c)). However, if the linearized system is itself structurally stable it seems very plausible that it will furnish a good approximation to the original system near the stationary point.

7.9 *Exercise*
Use the Linearization Theorem to fill in the holes in your sketches of the autonomous systems of Exercise 5.3.

7.10 *Mathematical excursion*
We can obtain the solutions of the linear systems given above by the following plausible argument. Consider first the linear autonomous system in one variable $dx/dt = ax$. We know that this has solution $x = re^{at}$ for any r (compare Example 1.2). Consider now the linear system

$$\left.\begin{array}{l} dx/dt = ax + by \\ dy/dt = cx + dy \end{array}\right\} \tag{8}$$

and suppose, by analogy with the one variable case, that we have a solution $x = re^{\lambda t}$, $y = se^{\lambda t}$ from some real r and s. Differentiating and substituting into Equations (8) we obtain the pair of equations

$$\left.\begin{array}{l} \lambda r e^{\lambda t} = a r e^{\lambda t} + b s e^{\lambda t} \\ \lambda s e^{\lambda t} = c r e^{\lambda t} + d s e^{\lambda t} \end{array}\right\} \tag{9}$$

which, discarding the common non-zero factor of $e^{\lambda t}$, yields a pair of simultaneous equations

$$\left.\begin{array}{l} (a - \lambda)r + bs = 0 \\ cr + (d - \lambda)s = 0. \end{array}\right\} \tag{10}$$

Those of you who know a little about linear algebra and matrices may recognise these equations as the conditions that the vector (r, s) (more usually written in column form $\binom{r}{s}$) is an *eigenvector* of the matrix $A = \left[\begin{smallmatrix} a & b \\ c & d \end{smallmatrix}\right]$ with corresponding *eigenvalue* λ. Now Equations (10) above have a non-zero solution (r, s) if and only if the first equation is a multiple of the second, i.e. if the two lines in the (r, s)-plane through the origin determined by these two equations coincide. This clearly happens if and only if $(a - \lambda)(d - \lambda) - bc = 0$, and so λ is a root of the characteristic equation

$$\lambda^2 - (a + d)\lambda + (ad - bc) = 0,$$

or, in our earlier notation, $\lambda^2 - \lambda T + D = 0$. The ten cases discussed in Sections 7.1–7.3 largely correspond to the various possibilities for the roots of this equation. (The one exception is that stars and improper nodes both correspond to repeated real roots of the characteristic equation. In one sense this case is not very important anyway; *most* linear systems will result in characteristic equations which do not have repeated roots, i.e. for most values of a, b, c, d the quantity $(a - d)^2 + 4bc \neq 0$).

Suppose for simplicity that the roots of the characteristic equation λ_1, λ_2 are real and distinct. Let (r_1, s_1), (r_2, s_2) be corresponding eigenvectors, i.e. non-zero solutions of Equations (10). One easily checks that $(x(t), y(t)) = (r_1 e^{\lambda_1 t}, s_1 e^{\lambda_1 t})$ and $(x(t), y(t)) = (r_2 e^{\lambda_2 t}, s_2 e^{\lambda_2 t})$ are solutions of the linear system (8). In fact more is true: any *linear combination* of these solutions

$$\begin{aligned} (x(t), y(t)) &= c_1(r_1 e^{\lambda_1 t}, s_1 e^{\lambda_1 t}) + c_2(r_2 e^{\lambda_2 t}, s_2 e^{\lambda_2 t}) \\ &= (c_1 r_1 e^{\lambda_1 t} + c_2 r_2 e^{\lambda_2 t}, c_1 s_1 e^{\lambda_1 t} + c_2 s_2 e^{\lambda_2 t}) \end{aligned}$$

is also a solution for *any* constants c_1, c_2, as you can easily check. As c_1, c_2 vary we obtain all integral curves in this way.

If the roots of the characteristic equation are complex one has to argue more carefully, but again one can produce real solutions from the eigenvalues and eigenvectors (compare Arnold (1973) pp. 129–38). A less *ad hoc* construction of the solutions of linear autonomous systems uses the idea of exponential matrices, compare Arrowsmith and Place (1982) pp. 58–61 and Arnold (1973) pp. 97–115. (You might discover the idea yourself by thinking about the Euler line method as applied to linear systems.)

7.11 *Project: The Poincaré–Andronov–Hopf bifurcation*

As we remarked above stationary points whose linearized systems are centres are rather difficult to analyse. Such stationary points are, however, rare because the condition for a centre is that the trace of the linearized system should vanish. So in practice, for individual autonomous systems, centres cause no problems.

When considering *families* of autonomous systems the situation is rather different. For example the family of autonomous systems

$$\left. \begin{aligned} dx/dt &= \epsilon x - y - x(x^2 + y^2) \\ dy/dt &= x + \epsilon y - y(x^2 + y^2) \end{aligned} \right\} \tag{11}$$

depending on the parameter ϵ has a stationary point at the origin for each value of ϵ, and for $\epsilon = 0$ the linearized system clearly has a centre. In this one-parameter family this centre is *unavoidable*: in a one-parameter family of linearized systems one must expect the trace to occasionally vanish.

Sketch the phase portraits of the autonomous systems (11) corresponding to values of the parameter ϵ less than, equal to, and greater than 0.

(Hints: you might like to check first that for $\epsilon < 0$ the origin is a stable focus, for $\epsilon > 0$ an unstable focus. As ϵ passes from being negative to positive there is an associated birth of a closed trajectory or *limit cycle*: you can check that this is the circle $x^2 + y^2 = \epsilon$. For a direct analysis using polar coordinates see Arrowsmith and Place (1982) p. 211.)

The transition undergone by the system (11) as ϵ passes through 0 is called variously the Poincaré–Andronov or Hopf bifurcation, and such bifurcations arise naturally in many families of autonomous systems. For a discussion of this bifurcation, with an application to chemical systems, see Arrowsmith and Place (1982) pp. 212–16. For further information on this and other bifurcations see Arnold (1983) pp. 257–82 (the reader should be warned that this book, though rewarding, is rather advanced).

§8

A step into space: chaotic differential equations

We have spent most of this chapter considering plane autonomous systems. The fact that the trajectories lie in a plane seriously limits their behaviour. Any trajectories inside a limit cycle can certainly never escape outside for example. The point is that trajectories cannot cross in the plane.

Sometimes in applications one needs to consider not merely a pair of DEs determining two functions x and y but larger and more general systems. We shall be interested, in this section, in autonomous systems of the form

$$\mathrm{d}x/\mathrm{d}t = f(x, y, z), \quad \mathrm{d}y/\mathrm{d}t = g(x, y, z), \quad \mathrm{d}z/\mathrm{d}t = h(x, y, z). \quad (1)$$

As before we can consider these three equations as determining the velocity of a particle as a function of its position. The resulting trajectories, however, now spiral around three-dimensional space instead of the plane, and this extra degree of freedom can result in extraordinary complications as we shall see. Of course, it remains true that trajectories cannot cross, but they can move around one another, and intertwine.

If our autonomous system (1) is linear, i.e. the functions $f(x, y, z)$, $g(x, y, z)$, $h(x, y, z)$ are some linear combination of x, y and z, then one can describe the resulting phase portraits in much the same way as we did for linear systems in the plane, see Arnold (1973) pp. 139–41. As soon as we venture away from such linear DEs, however, we are into unknown territory – indeed the study of nonlinear autonomous systems is a very active current area of research. The particular system we shall consider is probably the most studied autonomous system of all time; these are the Lorenz DEs:

$$\left.\begin{array}{l} \mathrm{d}x/\mathrm{d}t = \sigma(y - x) \\ \mathrm{d}y/\mathrm{d}t = \rho x - y - xz \\ \mathrm{d}z/\mathrm{d}t = -\beta z + xy \end{array}\right\} \quad (2)$$

where σ, ρ and β are constants. These equations originally arose in a problem concerning meteorology in 1963, and although it was subsequently found that they were an inadequate model for the convection process considered, they do provide good examples of the incredibly rich structure and complicated behaviour possible with three-dimensional autonomous systems. We next present a program for sketching trajectories of this system. Of course these now lie in three-dimensional space so we need to project them onto some plane to get them onto our screen. In what follows we shall project to the (x, y)-plane, i.e. view the trajectories from the z-direction. Note the resulting *projection* of the trajectories will self-intersect and cross; the trajectories themselves do not. Here is the program.

8.1 *Program: Lorenz*
```
1Ø INPUT S, P, B
2Ø INPUT X, Y, Z, D, R, N
3Ø FOR I = 1 TO N
40 Calculate screen point (u, v) corresponding to (x, y)
5Ø Put a dot at screen point (u, v)
6Ø LETDX = S*(Y − X)*D:LETDY = (P*X − Y − X*Z)*D:
   LET DZ = (X*Y − B*Z)*D
7Ø LET X = X + DX: LET Y = Y + DY: LET Z = Z + DZ
8Ø NEXT I
```

First some remarks concerning the program: s, p, b are the constants σ, ρ, β appearing in Equations (2) above, while x, y, z give the initial position, the starting point, for the trajectory. The variable d is the increment δt of time, and r, which will appear in your line 4Ø specifies the window $-r \le x$, $y \le r$ considered. The variable n determines the number of points plotted out along the trajectory; you may prefer to omit it and line 3Ø, replace line 8Ø with 8Ø GOTO 4Ø and use the ESCAPE key when you hve seen enough points plotted. Line 6Ø merely implements the Euler line method, the changes δx, δy, δz in the x, y, z directions corresponding to the increment δt for the system (1) being given by

$$\delta x = f(x, y, z)\,\delta t, \quad \delta y = g(x, y, z)\,\delta t, \quad \delta z = h(x, y, z)\,\delta t.$$

The result of running this program with the values $(s, p, b) = (10, 28, \frac{8}{3})$, $(x, y, z) = (0.02, 0.01, 0.01)$, $(d, r, n) = (0.005, 30, 5000)$ is shown in Fig. 21.

From this strange picture it is clear that the behaviour of the trajectories of the Lorenz system is extraordinarily complicated and unpredictable. Also, quite small changes in our choice of initial point can lead to dramatic changes in the resulting trajectory. This is very entertaining but also worrying, for it means that small cumulative errors originating in the Euler line algorithm may well lead to a plotted trajectory which is totally different from the true trajectory sought. In other words one has to be very careful about the numerical algorithm used, and the choice of increment *d*. Indeed the Euler line algorithm is really an inadequate tool for studying the Lorenz equations and should be replaced by a more accurate method, such as a version of the Runge–Kutta procedure described in Exercise 5.3(*c*). (For more information on the Lorenz equation see Sparrow (1982).)

References V. I. Arnold *Ordinary Differential Equations*, MIT Press, Cambridge, Mass., 1973

V. I. Arnold *Geometrical Methods in the Theory of Ordinary Differential Equations*, Springer-Verlag, Berlin, 1983

D. K. Arrowsmith and C. M. Place *Ordinary Differential Equations*, Chapman and Hall, London, 1982

M. W. Hirsch and S. Smale *Differential Equations, Dynamical Systems and Linear Algebra*, Academic Press, London, 1974

I. G. Petrovski *Ordinary Differential Equations*, Dover, New York, 1966

C. Sparrow *The Lorenz Equations: Bifurcations, Chaos, and Strange Attractors*, Springer-Verlag, Berlin 1982

Fig. 21

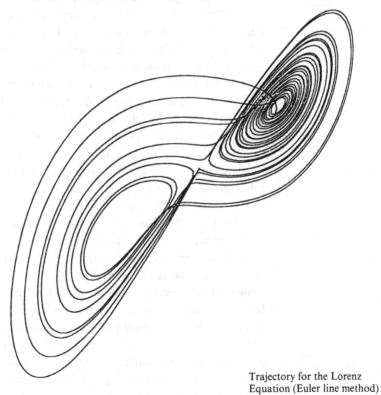

Trajectory for the Lorenz Equation (Euler line method)

8

Iteration of real functions

This chapter is devoted to the study of recurrence relations of the form

$$x_{n+1} = f(x_n), \quad n = 0, 1, 2, \ldots,$$

where f is some given real function and x_0 is a given initial value. Such recurrence relations, or iteration formulae, occur in many different areas of science and they have been studied by mathematicians for a very long time. The aim is to show that such a sequence is convergent, or tends to infinity, or behaves in some other regular or irregular manner. In recent years the study of iteration formulae has been pursued with increasing intensity, due largely to the easy availability of computers, and many unexpected aspects of their behaviour have been discovered. These can be illustrated very effectively using the graphical facilities of a micro.

Here is a plan of the chapter. After a brief introduction to iteration in §1 we give, in §2, simple programs generating iteration sequences, and in §3 a useful graphical interpretation of iteration, together with an implementation for the micro. The basic ideas of fixed points, periodic points, intervals of attraction and conjugate functions are introduced in the next four sections, together with the relevant programs. §8 then gives a complete discussion of the relatively simple cases of linear and Möbius sequences.

The bulk of the chapter is devoted to quadratic sequences discussed in §9. Quadratic functions, despite their disarmingly simple appearance, yield iteration sequences of amazing complexity (typical of large classes of functions) and we study their behaviour in great detail. The reader should be warned that quadratic iteration sequences have been the subject of much recent research, and are still far from being completely understood. *This section is an order of magnitude more demanding than any other material in the book.* We hope the extra effort is amply rewarded by an appreciation of some of the subtle and beautiful phenomena exposed here. The chapter is brought to a conclusion by a brief, but complete, discussion of exponential iterations.

§1
Introduction

Perhaps the simplest type of iteration sequence is

$$x_{n+1} = ax_n + b, \quad n = 0, 1, 2, \ldots, \tag{1}$$

where a and b are constants. A common example of such a sequence is the recurrence relation for compound interest

$$P_{n+1} = (1 + i/100) P_n, \quad n = 0, 1, 2, \ldots, \tag{2}$$

where P_n is the value after n years of an investment, assuming a constant rate of interest of $i\%$. Of course, in this special case the iteration formula (2) can be solved explicitly to give the compound interest formula

$$P_n = (1 + i/100)^n P_0, \quad n = 0, 1, 2, \ldots,$$

where P_0 is the sum initially invested. In fact the iteration formula (1), with $b \neq 0$, can also be solved explicitly, as we shall see later.

A somewhat more general version of Equation (1) is the iteration sequence

$$x_{n+1} = \frac{ax_n + b}{cx_n + d}, \quad n = 0, 1, 2, \ldots, \tag{3}$$

where a, b, c, d are constants. Such sequences arise, for example, in the study of continued fractions, which we met in Chapter 1, §5. Recall that the continued fraction expansion of the irrational number $\sqrt{2}$ is given by

$$\sqrt{2} = [1, 2, 2, \ldots]$$
$$= 1 + \cfrac{1}{2 + \cfrac{1}{2 + \ddots}}$$

If we let x_n denote the finite continued fraction

$$x_n = = [1, 2, 2, \ldots, 2],$$

in which the number 2 appears n times, then x_n is the nth 'convergent' of the continued fraction for $\sqrt{2}$ and we saw in Chapter 1, §5 that we must therefore have

$$\lim_{n \to \infty} x_n = \sqrt{2}.$$

An alternative approach to that of Chapter 1 is to obtain a recurrence relation for the sequence x_n, as follows:

$$x_1 = 1 + \frac{1}{2} = 1 + \frac{1}{1 + x_0} = \frac{x_0 + 2}{x_0 + 1},$$

$$x_2 = 1 + \frac{1}{2 + \frac{1}{2}} = 1 + \frac{1}{1 + x_1} = \frac{x_1 + 2}{x_1 + 1},$$

and so on. In general we have

$$x_{n+1} = \frac{x_n + 2}{x_n + 1}, \quad n = 0, 1, 2, \ldots. \tag{4}$$

This has the form of Equation (3) with $a = 1, b = 2, c = 1, d = 1$. The iteration formula (4) can now be used to prove that the sequence x_n tends to $\sqrt{2}$. Indeed, we show later that any iteration sequence of the form (3) can be solved to give an explicit formula for x_n. This enables us to describe precisely how such sequences behave.

Another example from mathematics is the Newton–Raphson method, described in Chapter 2, which is used to find approximate solutions to an equation of the form

$$g(x) = 0, \tag{5}$$

where g is a real function. If we take x_0 as an initial guess at a solution to Equation (5), then the sequence

$$x_{n+1} = x_n - g(x_n)/g'(x_n), \quad n = 0, 1, 2, \ldots, \tag{6}$$

converges very rapidly (under favourable conditions on g) to a solution of Equation (5). For example if

$$g(x) = x^2 - 2,$$

then the sequence (6) is given by

$$x_{n+1} = x_n - (x_n^2 - 2)/(2x_n), \quad n = 0, 1, 2, \ldots$$

i.e.

$$x_{n+1} = \frac{1}{2}(x_n + 2/x_n), \quad n = 0, 1, 2, \ldots.$$

Given an initial value $x_0 > 0$, this sequence converges rapidly to $\sqrt{2}$ (see Chapter 6, Section 2.3).

Next we look at an example from population dynamics. It is common for certain biological populations to increase in size when the population is small (assuming favourable conditions) but to decrease in size when the population is large (because of overcrowding or lack of food). If p_n denotes the population on the nth day, then we might find typical relationships between p_n and p_{n+1} as sketched in Fig. 1.

One possible model for the above behaviour, proposed as long ago as 1845 by P. Verhulst, is the iteration formula

$$p_{n+1} = \lambda p_n(1 - p_n/P), \quad n = 0, 1, 2, \ldots. \tag{7}$$

Here P is the maximum population size at which, for some unpleasant reason, the species dies out:

if $p_n = P$ then $p_{n+1} = 0$.

The number λ is a parameter which determines the rate of growth when the population is relatively small:

if p_n/P is small then $p_{n+1} \approx \lambda p_n$.

We can simplify Equation (7) slightly by writing $x_n = p_n/P$, for $n = 0, 1, 2, \ldots$, so that $0 \leq x_n \leq 1$. Since $p_n = Px_n$ and $p_{n+1} = Px_{n+1}$ we can rewrite Equation (7) as:

$$x_{n+1} = \lambda x_n(1 - x_n), \quad n = 0, 1, 2, \ldots . \tag{8}$$

The behaviour of the iteration sequence (8) depends on two factors: the initial term x_0, and the value of the parameter λ. This iteration formula is likely to model only very approximately the behaviour of an actual population. However, it is sufficiently simple to allow a detailed study which may shed some light on what happens in reality. One might expect that x_n would tend towards some limiting value, neither too small nor too large, which depends on the parameter λ. However, we shall see later in the chapter that, for some values of λ, the sequence x_n behaves in an exceedingly complex manner. In fact the family of iteration sequences of the form (8), despite its apparent simplicity, is still very far from being completely understood.

Our final example of an iteration formula is given by

$$x_{n+1} = a^{x_n}, \quad n = 0, 1, 2, \ldots, \tag{9}$$

where a is a positive constant. If the initial term $x_0 = 0$, then the first few terms of sequence (9) are

$$0, 1, a, a^a, a^{(a^a)}, \ldots .$$

Fig. 1

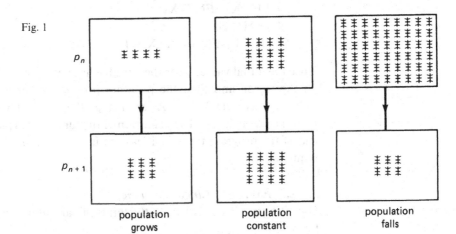

p_n

p_{n+1}

population
grows

population
constant

population
falls

This intriguing sequence has attracted the attention of many mathematicians from Euler in 1778 to the present, and it has some unexpected properties. If $a = 1$, then the sequence is clearly convergent with limit 1, but if $a = 2$, then the first few terms are

$$0, 1, 2, 4, 16, 65536, \ldots$$

and it seems clear that this sequence tends to infinity. You may like to guess how the sequence (9) behaves for values of a between 1 and 2. The answer will appear later in the chapter.

The behaviour of (9) for values of a between 0 and 1 is rather more complex, as we shall see also. In this range the sequence has a possible application in physics, since it has been proposed as a model for the behaviour of the lengths of collections of particles (called 'bunches') in a linear accelerator!

§2
Calculating iteration sequences

In this section we show you how to use your micro to calculate the successive terms of a given iteration sequence and we provide lots of exercises for you to try out. In later sections we shall attempt to explain the behaviour of these sequences.

Here is a program which simply calculates the terms of a given iteration sequence

$$x_{n+1} = f(x_n), \quad n = 0, 1, 2, \ldots,$$

and prints them on the screen. Here we have used the particular function $f(x) = x^2 - 1$.

2.1 *Program: Print iteration*
```
1Ø INPUT X
2Ø PRINT X
3Ø LET X = FN F(X)
4Ø GOTO 2Ø
5Ø DEF FNF(X) = X * X − 1
```

Once the initial value x_0 for the variable has been input, it is printed on the screen and then the program proceeds to give the values $x_1 = f(x_0)$, $x_2 = f(x_1)$, ... At each stage the value of x is printed, until the screen is full. The definition of the function f is placed at the end of the program to make it easy to find when modifications are required.

2.2 *Exercise: Linear sequences*
Uses Program 2.1 to calculate the terms of various sequences of the form

$$x_{n+1} = ax_n + b, \quad n = 0, 1, 2, \ldots,$$

by choosing values of the parameters a, b and initial term x_0. It will help to modify Program 2.1 as follows:

10 INPUT A, B, X

and

50 DEF FNF(X) = A * X + B

Try the following values for a, using $b = 1$ and $x_0 = 0$ in each case:

$$a = 0.5, 2, 0.9, 1, -1.$$

You should observe various different types of behaviour, such as convergence, tending to ∞, and alternating between two values. Then try the same five values of a, but vary the values of b and the initial term x_0. You should find that the type of behaviour of the sequence often depends on the value of a and not on the values of b and x_0.

2.3 *Exercise: Möbius sequences*

Use Program 2.1 to calculate the terms of various sequences of the form

$$x_{n+1} = \frac{ax_n + b}{cx_n + d}, \quad n = 0, 1, 2, \ldots,$$

by choosing values of the parameters a, b, c, d and initial term x_0. First modify Program 2.1 as follows:

10 INPUT A, B, C, D, X

and

50 DEF FNF(X) = (A * X + B)/(C * X + D)

Try the following values for a, b, c, d with $x_0 = 1$ in each case:

$$\begin{pmatrix} a \\ b \\ c \\ d \end{pmatrix} = \begin{pmatrix} 1 \\ 2 \\ 1 \\ 1 \end{pmatrix}, \begin{pmatrix} 2 \\ 1 \\ 1 \\ -2 \end{pmatrix}, \begin{pmatrix} 0 \\ 1 \\ 1 \\ 0 \end{pmatrix}, \begin{pmatrix} 3 \\ 2 \\ 4 \\ 3 \end{pmatrix}, \begin{pmatrix} 3 \\ 2 \\ 1 \\ 1 \end{pmatrix}, \begin{pmatrix} 3 \\ 2 \\ 1 \\ 2 \end{pmatrix}.$$

Then try the same six sets of values of a, b, c, d but vary the initial value x_0. Once again, you should find various types of behaviour, which are often independent of the choice of x_0.

2.4 *Exercise: Quadratic sequences*

Use Program 2.1 to calculate the terms of various sequences of the form

$$x_{n+1} = \lambda x_n(1 - x_n), \quad n = 0, 1, 2, \ldots,$$

by choosing values of the parameter λ and initial term x_0.

First modify Program 2.1 as follows:

    10 INPUT L, X

and

    50 DEF FNF(X) = L * X * (1 − X)

Try the following values of λ with $x_0 = 0.5$ in each case:

$$\lambda = 1, 2, 2.5, 3, 3.1, 3.2, 3.3, 3.8, 4.$$

Then try the same values for λ, but vary the initial value x_0.

Here you should find many different types of behaviour, which are often independent of the choice of x_0.

2.5 *Exercise: Exponential sequences*

Use Program 2.1 to calculate the terms of various sequences of the form

$$x_{n+1} = a^{x_n}, \quad n = 0, 1, 2, \ldots,$$

by choosing positive values of the parameter a and initial term x_0.

First modify Program 2.1 as follows

    10 INPUT A, X

and

Fig. 2

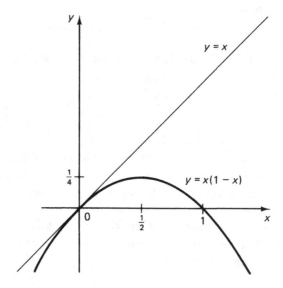

50 DEF FNF(X) = A↑X

Try the following values of a with $x_0 = 0$ in each case:

$$a = 1, a = 2, a = 1.5, a = \sqrt{2}, a = 0.5, a = 0.05.$$

Then try the same values for a, but vary the initial term x_0.

Once again you should find that the various types of behaviour are often independent of the choice of x_0.

§3
Graphical
iteration

We now try to explain some of the observations made in the experiments of the previous section. To do this it is helpful to introduce a graphical interpretation of the iteration process $x_{n+1} = f(x_n)$. Consider, for example, the iteration formula

$$x_{n+1} = x_n(1 - x_n), \quad n = 1, 2, \ldots,$$

where x_0 is given. In this case $f(x) = x(1 - x)$. You saw in Exercise 2.4 that

$$x_n \to 0, \quad \text{for } 0 \leqslant x_0 \leqslant 1,$$

and that

$$x_n \to -\infty, \quad \text{for } x_0 < 0 \quad \text{or} \quad x_0 > 1,$$

Here is a graphical explanation of these results. In Fig. 2 we plot the graphs $y = f(x) = x(1 - x)$ and $y = x$ on the same axes. The graph $y = x(1 - x)$ is a parabola which crosses the x-axis at $x = 0, 1$ and takes the maximum value $\frac{1}{4}$ at $x = \frac{1}{2}$. It meets $y = x$ at the single point $(0, 0)$ where $y = x$ is its tangent.

Now take an initial value x_0 which satisfies $0 < x_0 < 1$ and mark x_0 on the x-axis. The terms $x_1 = f(x_0)$, $x_2 = f(x_1)$, ... can then be constructed geometrically by drawing successively:

    a vertical line to meet the graph $y = f(x)$ at $(x_0, f(x_0)) = (x_0, x_1)$;

    a horizontal line to meet the graph $y = x$ at (x_1, x_1);

    a vertical line to meet the graph $y = f(x)$ at $(x_1, f(x_1)) = (x_1, x_2)$;

    a horizontal line to meet the graph $y = x$ at (x_2, x_2);

    and so on.

As you can see from Fig. 3 the resulting construction lines form a *staircase* which is trapped between $y = x$ and $y = x(1 - x)$, and descends towards 0. Because $y = x$ and $y = x(1 - x)$ meet only at $(0, 0)$ the staircase approaches arbitrarily close to this point. Hence $x_n \to 0$, as $n \to \infty$.

The behaviour of the sequence x_n for other initial values x_0 can be treated in a similar manner, as illustrated in Fig. 4.

From these diagrams we can read off an explanation of the behaviours of the various iteration sequences. It would clearly be a good idea to have a program to plot such diagrams. Our program will do the following:

(a) plot the graph $y = f(x)$, over a given interval $x_\ell \leqslant x \leqslant x_u$;
(b) plot the graph $y = x$, over the same interval;
(c) input the given initial value x_0;
(d) draw the successive vertical and horizontal lines to $y = f(x)$ and $y = x$, respectively.

We use various conventions introduced in Chapter 3, Curves:

XL – x lower
XU – x upper
VMAX – maximum vertical screen coordinate
XS – x scale factor.

In this chapter only, we use the following short forms:

(i) 'Put a dot at (x, y)' means 'convert (x, y) to screen coordinates (u, v) as in Section 1.7 of Chapter 1, and put a dot at (u, v)';

(ii) 'Draw a line to (x, y)' means 'convert (x, y) to screen coordinates (u, v) as in Section 1.7 of Chapter 1, and draw a line *from the current cursor position* to (u, v)'.

In the few cases where conversion to screen coordinates is *not* needed (e.g. Section 9.3 below) we write 'Put a dot at screen point (u, v)' or 'Draw a line to screen point (u, v)' to indicate this.

For simplicity, the plotting rectangle has been chosen to be a square with the graph $y = x$ forming one of the diagonals (thus

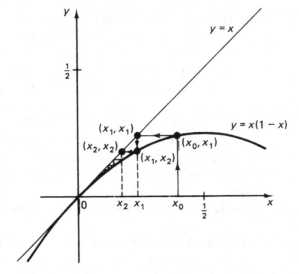

Fig. 3

Fig. 4

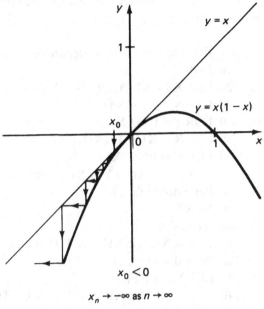

$x_0 < 0$

$x_n \to -\infty$ as $n \to \infty$

(a)

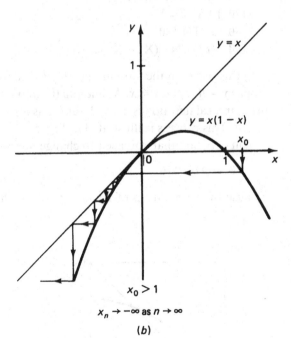

$x_0 > 1$

$x_n \to -\infty$ as $n \to \infty$

(b)

$y_\ell = x_\ell$ and $y_u = x_u$) and we have taken the number of plotted points to be $n = \frac{1}{2} v_{max}$.

3.1 *Program: Graphical iteration*

```
10  INPUT XL, XU
20  LET XS = VMAX/(XU − XL)
30  LET N = 0.5*VMAX
40  FOR I = 1 TO N
50  LET X = XL + I*(XU − XL)/N
60  LET Y = FN F(X)
70  IF XL < Y AND Y < XU THEN put a dot at (x, y)
80  Put a dot at (x, x)
90  NEXT I
100 INPUT X
110 IF X < XL OR XU < X THEN GOTO 100
120 Put a dot at (x, x)
130 LET Y = FNF(X)
140 IF Y < XL OR XU < Y THEN GOTO 100
150 Draw a line to (x, y)
160 Draw a line to (y, y)
170 LET X = Y
180 GOTO 130
190 DEF FN F(X) = X*X − 1
```

In this program the loop in lines 40–90 is devoted to plotting the graphs $y = f(x)$ and $y = x$. At line 100 the initial value x_0 is input and the graphical iteration is carried out for as long as it remains on the screen. This process is illustrated in Fig. 5.

You may find that you need to change line 180 to:

180 GOTO 120

because of the build up of rounding errors which can occur with

Fig. 5

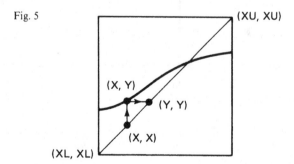

repeated use of the draw instruction on some micros. Of course, you may also wish to include the *x*- and *y*-axes.

Next we suggest that you repeat the exercises from Section 2, but this time use Program 3.1. In each case you will need to 'top and tail' the program in order to allow for the different functions and sets of parameter values. For example, to repeat the exercise on Möbius sequences make the following modifications:

> 5 INPUT A, B, C, D
> 19∅ DEF FNF(X) = (A * X + B)/(C * X + D)

You will also need to experiment with the location of the plotting square, given by x_ℓ and x_u.

While carrying out these exercises again, we urge you to try and answer the following question:

> *What special properties does the graph $y = f(x)$ have near a*
> *point c if c happens to be the limit of a sequence $x_{n+1} = f(x_n)$?*

Finally, here are some further functions for you to investigate using Program 3.1. Several of these functions will appear later in the chapter.

3.2 *Exercise*

Use Program 3.1 to investigate the behaviour of iteration sequences $x_{n+1} = f(x_n)$ with: (a) $f(x) = x^2 - 1$; (b) $f(x) = x^2 + x$; (c) $f(x) = x^3 + x$; (d) $f(x) = x^3 - 2x$; (e) $f(x) = 1 - x^2$; (f) $f(x) = x^2 + \frac{1}{4}$; (g) $f(x) = x(1 - x)$; (h) $f(x) = (\sqrt{2})^x$; (i) $f(x) = 1.5^x$; (j) $f(x) = (0.5)^x$; (k) $f(x) = \sin x$, where *x* is in radians.

§4

Fixed points

We hope that you discovered some answers to the question posed at the end of §3. Fig. 6 shows three of the plots which you should have obtained in cases when the sequence x_n appears to be convergent with limit *c*.

4.1 *The fixed point equation*

First of all you should have noticed that if the sequence x_n is convergent with limit *c*, then the graph $y = f(x)$ crosses $y = x$ at the point (c, c). Put another way, the function *f* takes the value *c* at the point *c*, i.e. $f(c) = c$. In this situation we say that *c* is a *fixed point* of the function *f*. In fact it can be proved that if *f* is a so called continuous function and a sequence of the form $x_{n+1} = f(x_n)$ is convergent with limit *c*, then *c* is a fixed point of *f*.

Roughly speaking, a *continuous function* is one whose graph can be drawn without lifting your pen from the paper. If the function *f* is continuous at a point *c*, then for any sequence x_n which tends to *c* as $n \to \infty$, we have

$$f(x_n) \to f(c), \quad \text{as } n \to \infty.$$

(see any Real Analysis textbook or Courant and Robbins (1947), Chapter 6).

Thus, if x_n is defined by the recurrence relation $x_{n+1} = f(x_n)$, then

$$c = \lim_{n \to \infty} x_{n+1} = \lim_{n \to \infty} f(x_n) = f(c),$$

and so c is indeed a fixed point of f.

Fig. 6

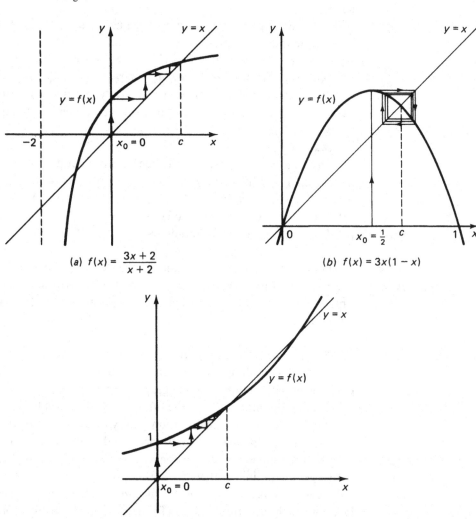

(a) $f(x) = \dfrac{3x + 2}{x + 2}$

(b) $f(x) = 3x(1 - x)$

(c) $f(x) = (\sqrt{2})^x$

All the functions f which are discussed in this chapter are continuous on the intervals where they are defined (you might argue that $f(x) = (3x + 2)/(x + 2)$ is not continuous at $x = -2$, but then this function is not actually defined at $x = -2$). Hence we can find the possible limits of our sequences of the form $x_{n+1} = f(x_n)$ by solving the fixed point equation:

$$f(x) = x.$$

4.2 *Exercise*
Find the fixed points of the functions in Fig. 6. What are the limits of the sequences x_n in Fig. 6? (You may assume that each of the three sequences *is* convergent.)

4.3 *The slope at a fixed point*
There is another important property of the graph $y = f(x)$ at a point c which is the limit of $x_{n+1} = f(x_n)$. The *slope* of the graph $y = f(x)$ at c is not too great. More precisely, you will find in the examples that if $x_n \to c$, then

$$|f'(c)| \leqslant 1.$$

This can be proved rather easily from the definition (Fig. 7).

$$f'(c) = \lim_{x \to c} \frac{f(x) - f(c)}{x - c}.$$

In fact, if $x_{n+1} = f(x_n)$ and $x_n \to c$, then we have $f(c) = c$ and so

$$f'(c) = \lim_{n \to \infty} \frac{f(x_n) - f(c)}{x_n - c}$$

$$= \lim_{n \to \infty} \frac{x_{n+1} - c}{x_n - c}.$$

Fig. 7

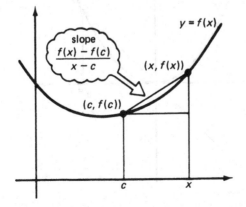

Now, if $|f'(c)| > 1$ then, for all sufficiently large values of n,

$$\left| \frac{x_{n+1} - c}{x_n - c} \right| > 1 \quad \text{and hence} \quad |x_{n+1} - c| > |x_n - c|,$$

and this contradicts the fact that $x_n \to c$. Hence $|f'(c)| \le 1$, as promised.

Sharp-eyed readers will have noticed that, in order for the above argument to work, the sequence x_n must converge to c *without ever taking the value c*. Otherwise the quotient

$$\frac{f(x_n) - f(c)}{x_n - c}$$

has zero denominator for some n. An example in which $x_n \to c$ but $|f'(c)| > 1$ is furnished by

$$x_{n+1} = f(x_n),$$

where $f(x) = x^2$ and $x_0 = 1$ (see Fig. 8). Here $x_n \to 1$, since $x_0 = x_1 = x_2 = \ldots = 1$, but $f'(1) = 2$, so that the condition $|f'(1)| \le 1$ does not hold.

4.4 *Exercise*
What are the derivatives of the functions in Fig. 6 at each of their fixed points?

4.5 *Classifying fixed points*
From our observation above it is clear that the size of the derivative of f at a fixed point c is closely related to the behaviour of a sequence

Fig. 8

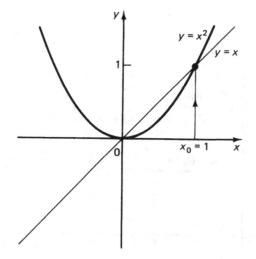

$x_{n+1} = f(x_n)$ near c. Therefore we distinguish between three types of fixed point.

A fixed point c of a function f is:

    attracting if $|f'(c)| < 1$;
    repelling if $|f'(c)| > 1$;
    indifferent if $|f'(c)| = 1$.

For example, the fixed points of the functions in Fig. 6 can be classified as in Fig. 9.

Fig. 9

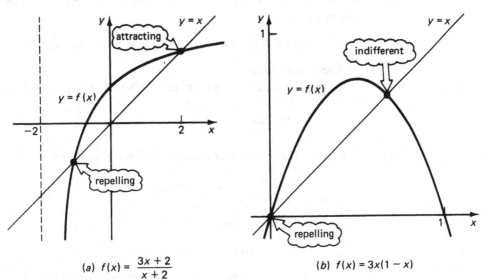

(a) $f(x) = \dfrac{3x + 2}{x + 2}$ (b) $f(x) = 3x(1 - x)$

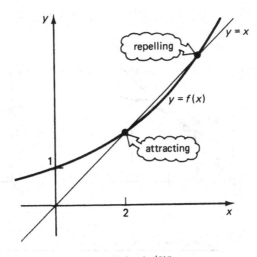

(c) $f(x) = (\sqrt{2})^x$

We saw in Section 4.3 that if c is a repelling fixed point then a sequence $x_{n+1} = f(x_n)$ cannot tend to c (unless it lands exactly on c) because if x_n is close to c, then

$$\left| \frac{x_{n+1} - c}{x_n - c} \right| = \left| \frac{f(x_n) - f(c)}{x_n - c} \right| \approx |f'(c)| > 1,$$

so that x_{n+1} is further from c than x_n. This explains the name 'repelling'.

On the other hand, if c is an attracting fixed point, then $x_{n+1} = f(x_n)$ must tend to c if some term of the sequence lands 'close enough' to c. (See Fig. 10.) To be more precise, there is a positive number δ such that

$$x_{n+1} = f(x_n) \to c \quad \text{as } n \to \infty, \text{ whenever } |x_0 - c| < \delta,$$

as illustrated in Fig. 11.

To prove this, choose a number r such that $|f'(c)| < r < 1$. Since

$$f'(c) = \lim_{x \to c} \frac{f(x) - f(c)}{x - c},$$

there is a positive number δ such that, for $0 < |x - c| < \delta$,

$$\left| \frac{f(x) - f(c)}{x - c} \right| \leq r \quad \text{and hence} \quad |f(x) - c| \leq r|x - c|, \quad (1)$$

since $f(c) = c$. Now suppose that $|x_0 - c| < \delta$. Then

$$|x_1 - c| = |f(x_0) - c| \leq r|x_0 - c|,$$

so that $|x_1 - c| < \delta$ also, and if we apply (1) repeatedly, then we obtain

$$|x_n - c| \leq r^n|x_0 - c|, \quad n = 1, 2, 3, \ldots. \quad (2)$$

Fig. 10

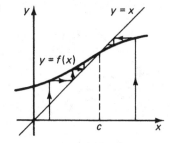

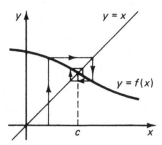

Fig. 11

$c - \delta \quad x_0 \quad x_1 \ x_2 \ x_3 \ x_4 \qquad c \qquad\qquad\qquad\qquad c + \delta$

Since $0 < r < 1$, the sequence $r^n \to 0$ as $n \to \infty$, and so we deduce that $x_n \to c$ as $n \to \infty$, as required.

Notice also that the smaller $|f'(c)|$ is, the smaller we can choose the number r (such that $|f'(c)| < r < 1$) and so, by (2), the faster does the sequence x_n converge to c. This convergence is, of course, especially fast if $f'(c) = 0$ and, for this reason, such points c are called *superattracting*.

4.6 *Exercise*

If g is a real function such that $g(c) = 0$, $g'(c) \neq 0$, show that the function $f(x) = x - g(x)/g'(x)$ has a superattracting fixed point at c. Relate this result to Equation (6) of §1.

The behaviour of a sequence $x_{n+1} = f(x_n)$ near an *indifferent* fixed point c, where $f'(c) = \pm 1$, is much more uncertain. You have already seen the example $f(x) = 3x(1 - x)$, where $c = \frac{2}{3}$ is a fixed point with $f'(c) = -1$. See Fig. 12. In this case the sequence $x_{n+1} = f(x_n)$, $x_0 = \frac{1}{2}$, *does* seem to converge (albeit rather slowly) to $c = \frac{2}{3}$. We shall look at this particular example in more detail in §9, and prove there that the sequence does indeed converge to $\frac{2}{3}$.

However, there are other examples of indifferent fixed points near which the behaviour is totally different. Two examples are given in Fig. 13. From these examples it is clear that each indifferent fixed point which we meet has to be treated on its own merits!

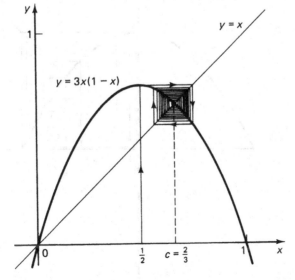

Fig. 12

Fig. 13

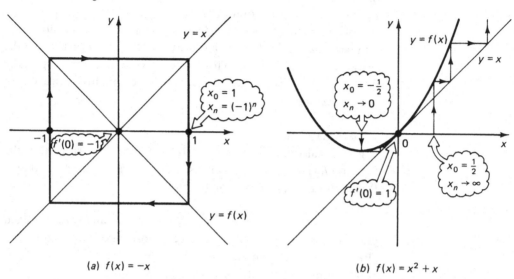

(a) $f(x) = -x$ (b) $f(x) = x^2 + x$

§5
Periodic points

If you attempted Exercise 3.2 (*e*), then you should have found examples of sequences $x_{n+1} = f(x_n)$ which appear to converge to a *pair* of limiting values rather than to a single limit. For example, graphical iteration of the sequence

$$x_{n+1} = f(x_n), \quad n = 0, 1, 2, \ldots, \tag{1}$$

where $f(x) = 1 - x^2$ and $x_0 = \frac{1}{2}$, yields the expanding cobweb of Fig. 14. In fact the even terms

Fig. 14

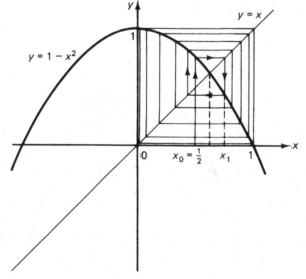

$$x_0, x_2, x_4, \ldots$$

appear to converge to the limit 0, whereas the odd terms

$$x_1, x_3, x_5, \ldots$$

appear to converge to the limit 1. What is happening here?

First of all it is clear that neither of the values 0, 1 is a fixed point of the function f (these are $\frac{1}{2}(-1 \pm \sqrt{5})$). Rather, we have

$$f(0) = 1 \quad \text{and} \quad f(1) = 0,$$

so that

$$f(f(0)) = 0 \quad \text{and} \quad f(f(1)) = 1.$$

So 0 and 1 are actually fixed points of the function

$$\begin{aligned} f(f(x)) &= 1 - (1 - x^2)^2 \\ &= 2x^2 - x^4. \end{aligned}$$

Furthermore

$$x_{n+2} = f(f(x_n)),$$

so that the even terms $x_0, x_2, x_4, \ldots$, and the odd terms $x_1, x_3, x_5, \ldots$, are obtained by iterating the composed function $f(f(x))$ starting from x_0 and x_1, respectively.

All this suggests that we should consider the graph $y = f(f(x))$ and attempt to understand sequences which are obtained by iterating this new composed function. As expected, the function $f(f(x))$ has

Fig. 15

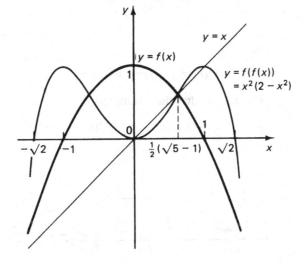

fixed points at 0 and 1, and also at $\frac{1}{2}(-1 \pm \sqrt{5})$, the original fixed points of the function $f(x)$. Furthermore we can see from Fig. 15 that if $0 < x_0 < \frac{1}{2}(\sqrt{5} - 1)$ then the even terms

$$x_{2n+2} = f(f(x_{2n})), \quad n = 0, 1, 2, \ldots,$$

do tend to 0. We can also see from Fig. 14 that if $0 < x_0 < \frac{1}{2}(\sqrt{5} - 1)$, then $\frac{1}{2}(\sqrt{5} - 1) < x_1 < 1$ and so the odd terms

$$x_{2n+3} = f(f(x_{2n+1})), \quad n = 0, 1, 2, \ldots,$$

do tend to 1.

Notice incidentally that $\frac{1}{2}(-1 \pm \sqrt{5})$ are repelling fixed points of $f(f(x))$, whereas 0 and 1 are attracting (in fact, superattracting), because

$$\frac{\mathrm{d}}{\mathrm{d}x} f(f(x)) = 4x(1 - x^2)$$

is equal to 0 at both $c = 0$ and $c = 1$.

Points, such as 0 and 1 in the above example, which are fixed points of higher iterates $f(f \ldots f(x) \ldots)$ of $f(x)$, are called *periodic points* of f. To discuss such points it is helpful to introduce a notation for the n-fold composition f^n obtained by applying f exactly n times:

$$f^2(x) = f(f(x)),$$
$$f^3(x) = f(f(f(x))),$$

etc. This notation should not be confused with the nth power of f, which is denoted by $(f(x))^n$ or with the nth derivative of f, which is denoted by $f^{(n)}(x)$.

A point c is called a *periodic point* of f with period p if

$$f^p(c) = c,$$

but

$$f^k(c) \neq c, \quad \text{for } 1 \leq k < p.$$

This means that the p numbers

$$c, f(c), f^2(c), \ldots, f^{p-1}(c),$$

Fig. 16

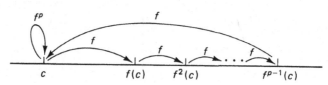

are all different and that $f^p(c) = c$. See Fig. 16. Alternatively, we say that these p numbers form a *p-cycle* of f. Thus a fixed point of f is actually a periodic point of f with period 1, (or a 1-cycle), whereas the numbers 0, 1 are periodic points of $f(x) = 1 - x^2$ with period 2 (or 0, 1 form a 2-cycle of f).

Determining the periodic points of a function f with period greater than 1 is usually more difficult than determining the fixed points of f. The formula for $f^p(x)$ is, for $p > 1$, rather complicated in general and the periodic point equation

$$f^p(x) = x$$

will typically have more and more solutions as p gets larger. Therefore, to understand the occurrence and nature of the periodic points it is useful to have a program available which plots the graph of the iterate f^p for a given $p \geqslant 1$ followed by cobweb/staircase diagrams as in Figs. 10–14. A simple modification of Program 3.1 is all that we require.

5.1 *Program: p-fold composites*

```
  5 INPUT P
 10 INPUT XL, XU
 20 LET XS = VMAX/(XU − XL)
 30 LET N = 0.5 * VMAX
 40 FOR I = 1 TO N
 50 LET X = XL + I*(XU − XL)/N
 60 GOSUB 190
 70 IF XL < Y AND Y < XU THEN put a dot at (x, y)
 80 Put a dot at (x, x)
 90 NEXT I
100 INPUT X
110 IF X < XL OR XU < X THEN GOTO 100
120 Put a dot at (x, x)
130 GOSUB 190
140 IF Y < XL OR XU < Y THEN GOTO 100
150 Draw a line to (x, y)
160 Draw a line to (y, y)
170 LET X = Y
180 GOTO 130
190 LET Y = X
200 FOR K = 1 TO P
210 LET Y = FNF(Y)
220 NEXT K
230 RETURN
```

240 DEF FNF(X) = X * X − 1

The program inputs the number p of iterates of f at line 5 and calculates the corresponding iterate of f in the subroutine at lines 190–230. This subroutine is called from lines 60 and 130. Note that the function f is, as usual, defined in the final line.

5.2 *Exercise*

Use Program 5.1 with $p = 2$ for each of the following functions $f(x)$ and investigate the existence of 2-cycles of f: (a) $f(x) = 1 - x^2$; (b) $f(x) = x^3 - 2x$; (c) $f(x) = \lambda x(1 - x)$, where $\lambda = 1 + \sqrt{5}$. You may like to modify Program 5.1 to deal with $y = f(x)$ and $y = f^p(x)$ simultaneously, thereby illustrating the connexion between p-cycles of f and fixed points of f^p.

The final exercise in this section deals with a function which has p-cycles for all $p \geqslant 1$. We shall study this function in greater detail later in the chapter.

5.3 *Exercise*

Use Program 5.1 to plot the graphs $y = f(x)$, $y = f^2(x)$, $y = f^3(x)$ and $y = f^4(x)$ for the function

$$f(x) = 4x(1 - x).$$

Can you explain why f has a p-cycle for each $p \geqslant 1$?

5.4 *Multiplier of a periodic point*

We remarked earlier that $f(x) = 1 - x^2$ has the 2-cycle 0, 1 and that

$$(f^2)'(0) = 0 = (f^2)'(1).$$

The fact that these two derivatives take *the same value* is in fact no accident. In general, if

$$c, f(c), f^2(c), \ldots, f^{n-1}(c)$$

form a p-cycle for f, then the derivative of f^p takes the same value at each point of the p-cycle. To see why this is, we apply the chain rule

$$\frac{\mathrm{d}}{\mathrm{d}x} f(g(x)) = f'(g(x))g'(x)$$

to the function $f^p(x)$. This gives

$$(f^p)'(x) = f'(f^{p-1}(x)) \ldots f'(f(x)) f'(x).$$

With $x = c$, we obtain

$$(f^p)'(c) = f'(f^{p-1}(c)) \ldots f'(f(c)) f'(c). \tag{2}$$

and with $x = f(c)$,

$$(f^p)'(f(c)) = f'(f^p(c)) \ldots f'(f^2(c)) f'(f(c)). \tag{3}$$

Since $f^p(c) = c$, we deduce from Equations (2) and (3) that $(f^p)'(f(c)) = (f^p)'(c)$. In the same way we obtain

$$(f^p)'(c) = (f^p)'(f(c)) = \ldots = (f^p)'(f^{p-1}(c)).$$

If c is a periodic point of f with period p, then we call $(f^p)'(c)$ the *multiplier* of c. Thus the multiplier of all points of the p-cycle $c, f(c)$, $\ldots, f^{p-1}(c)$ is the same. Just as for fixed points, we have the following classification of periodic points:

> c is *attracting* if $|(f^p)'(c)| < 1$;
> c is *repelling* if $|(f^p)'(c)| > 1$;
> c is *indifferent* if $|(f^p)'(c)| = 1$.

Also, if $(f^p)'(c) = 0$ then we often say that the periodic point is *superattracting*.

5.5 *Exercise*

(a) Use Program 5.1 to classify the 2-cycles which you found in Exercise 5.2

(b) Consider the function

$$f(x) = -\tfrac{5}{8}x^3 + \tfrac{3}{2}x^2 + \tfrac{1}{8}x - 1.$$

Use Program 5.1 to help determine an attracting p-cycle of f. Calculate the multiplier of this p-cycle

In §4 we found that if c is an attracting fixed point of f, then $x_{n+1} = f(x_n)$ tends to c if x_0 is close enough to c. Using the f^n notation, this result can be restated as follows:

If c is an attracting fixed point of f, then there is a positive number δ such that

$$f^n(x_0) \to c \quad \text{as } n \to \infty, \text{ whenever } |x_0 - c| < \delta.$$

By applying this result to the function f^p, we obtain a very similar statement for attracting p-cycles:

If c is an attracting periodic point of f with period p, then there is a positive number δ such that

$$(f^p)^n(x_0) = f^{pn}(x_0) \to c \quad \text{as } n \to \infty, \text{ whenever } |x_0 - c| < \delta. \tag{4}$$

It follows that if $|x_0 - c| < \delta$, then we also have

$$f^{pn+1}(x_0) = f(f^{pn}(x_0)) \to f(c) \quad \text{as } n \to \infty,$$
$$f^{pn+2}(x_0) = f^2(f^{pn}(x_0)) \to f^2(c) \quad \text{as } n \to \infty,$$
$$\vdots$$
$$f^{pn+p-1}(x_0) = f^{p-1}(f^{pn}(x_0)) \to f^{p-1}(c) \quad \text{as } n \to \infty,$$

so that the sequence $x_0, f(x_0), f^2(x_0), \ldots$ forms itself into p convergent subsequences with limits $c, f(c), \ldots, f^{p-1}(c)$, respectively. Thus we often say, rather loosely, that the sequence $f^n(x_0)$ converges to the p-cycle $c, f(c), \ldots, f^{p-1}(c)$. This convergence may be illustrated schematically in Fig. 17. The initial term x_0 lies close to c, $x_1 = f(x_0)$ lies close to $f(c)$, $x_2 = f^2(x_0)$ lies close to $f^2(c)$ and so on. Since $f^p(c) = c$, we find that $f^p(x_0)$ returns close to c. Indeed, by (4), the subsequence $x_0, f^p(x_0), f^{2p}(x_0), \ldots$ converges to c and, similarly, the subsequence $f(x_0), f^{p+1}(x_0), f^{2p+1}(x_0), \ldots$ converges to $f(c)$.

In Fig. 17 the letters $I_0, I_1, \ldots, I_{p-1}$ represent intervals surrounding $c, f(c), \ldots, f^{p-1}(c)$, respectively, having the property that

$$f^{pn}(x) \to f^k(c) \quad \text{as } n \to \infty, \text{ whenever } x \in I_k.$$

§6
Intervals of attraction

We saw in §4 that if c is an attracting fixed point of f, then there is an interval, I say, surrounding c such that if x lies in I then $f^n(x) \to c$ as $n \to \infty$. Thus we might call I an interval of attraction for c. Actually we reserve this name for the longest, or maximal, such interval; i.e. the *interval of attraction* of the fixed point c is the longest interval $I(c)$ surrounding c such that

$$f^n(x) \to c \quad \text{as } n \to \infty,$$

for all x in $I(c)$.

Notice that if $f(x)$ is a continuous function (as it always will be in this chapter) then $I(c)$ must be open (i.e. its end-points are not included). Indeed, if an end-point a of $I(c)$ were included then $f^n(a) \to c$ as $n \to \infty$, so that the sequence $f^n(a)$ would eventually lie inside $I(c)$. But this would imply, since f^n is continuous, that some small interval of points surrounding a would be mapped inside $I(c)$ by $f^n(x)$ and so we could extend $I(c)$ somewhat, contrary to our assumption that $I(c)$ is maximal.

Often it is easy to determine an interval of attraction explicitly by considering the relationship between $y = f(x)$ and $y = x$. For example if $f(x) = x^2$ and $c = 0$, then c is a (super)attracting fixed point of f with $I(0) = (-1, 1)$. See Fig. 18. It is usually straightforward to determine the interval of attraction if the function $f(x)$ is increasing and we can tell how many fixed points are present.

Fig. 17

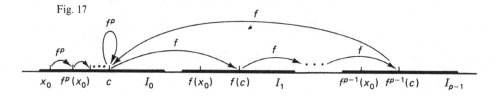

$x_0 \quad f^p(x_0) \quad c \quad I_0 \quad f(x_0) \quad f(c) \quad I_1 \quad f^{p-1}(x_0) \quad f^{p-1}(c) \quad I_{p-1}$

6.1 *Exercise*

Determine the attracting fixed points of the function

$$f(x) = \tfrac{1}{7}(x^3 + 6)$$

and find the interval of attraction of these fixed points.

However, it is not always so easy to determine the interval of attraction, especially if $f(x)$ is decreasing near the fixed point. Thus it is useful to have a program which determines the interval of attraction experimentally. To implement such a program we first choose a *target interval I* around the fixed point c, which is sufficiently short to be certain of lying entirely in $I(c)$. Then we consider a large number N of equally spaced initial points x and test each x in turn to see whether $x_{n+1} = f(x_n)$ does in fact land in the target interval I within a certain number M of iterations. In order that the program runs in a reasonable length of time the numbers N and M must not be chosen too large!

6.2 *Program: Interval of attraction*

```
 1Ø INPUT XL, XU
2Ø–9Ø As in Program 3.1
1ØØ INPUT X
11Ø FOR I = 1 TO 5Ø
12Ø LET X = FNF(X)
```

Fig. 18

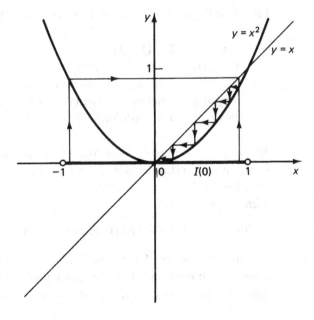

130 NEXT I
140 LET C = X: PRINT C
150 INPUT DELTA
160 FOR I = 1 TO N
170 LET X = XL + I*(XU − XL)/N
180 FOR J = 1 TO 20
190 LET X = FNF(X)
200 IF ABS(X − C) < DELTA THEN put a dot at (x, x_ℓ): draw
    a line to $(x, x_\ell + j(x_u − x_\ell)/50)$: GOTO 220
210 NEXT J
220 NEXT I
230 DEF FNF(X) = (X*X*X + 6)/7

Here lines 100–140 allow the user to input a value of x near the
proposed fixed point c and compute a value for c. Since it is essential
to obtain a reasonably accurate value for c, the number of iterations
at line 110 may need to be increased. Then at line 150 we input a
positive number δ which defines the target interval $I = (c − \delta, c + \delta)$.
Finally, for each initial value $x_0 = x$ used in the earlier plotting of
$y = f(x)$, it calculates M ($= 20$) terms of the sequence $x_n = f^n(x)$. At
line 200 the term x_n is tested to see whether it lies inside the target
interval and, if so, a vertical line segment is drawn, whose height
indicates how many iterations were required. Note that $x_\ell = y_\ell$ and
$x_u = y_u$ as in Program 3.1.

6.3 *Exercises*

(a) Use Program 6.2 to plot the intervals of attraction for:
    (i) $f(x) = (3x + 2)/(x + 2)$, $c = 2$, $\delta = 0.01$;
    (ii) $f(x) = 2.5x(1 − x)$, $c = 0.6$, $\delta = 0.01$;
    (iii) $f(x) = (\sqrt{2})^x$, $c = 2$, $\delta = 0.01$.

(b) Repeat (a) with various different values of δ.

(c) Try to use Program 6.2 when c is some indifferent fixed point.
    Why do you run into difficulties?

Warning   For some functions, such as $f(x) = (\sqrt{2})^x$, repeated
iteration with certain values of x can lead to numbers which are too
large for the computer to handle. In this case you may like to include
a line such as

195 IF ABS(X) > 50 THEN GOTO 220

so that such values of x are excluded from consideration and the
program can continue. The particular number 50 used in line 195
will of course depend on the function, the bounds x_ℓ, x_u, etc.

§7

Conjugate functions

If you attempted Exercise 3.2, then you may have noticed that certain iteration sequences display remarkably similar behaviour despite being defined by entirely different functions. Consider, for example, the sequences:

$$x_{n+1} = x_n(1 - x_n), \quad n = 0, 1, 2, \ldots, \tag{1}$$

where $x_0 = \frac{1}{2}$, and

$$x_{n+1} = x_n^2 + \frac{1}{4}, \quad n = 0, 1, 2, \ldots, \tag{2}$$

where $x_0 = 0$. See Fig. 19. It appears that Fig. 19(b) can be obtained from Fig. 19(a) by rotating about the origin through 180° and then translating $(0, 0)$ to $(\frac{1}{2}, \frac{1}{2})$ (or, what is equivalent, rotating about the point $(\frac{1}{4}, \frac{1}{4})$ through 180°). In fact this geometric effect is achieved by the change of variable:

$$x = -u + \tfrac{1}{2},$$

and if we write $x_n = -u_n + \frac{1}{2}$, $x_{n+1} = -u_{n+1} + \frac{1}{2}$, then Equation (1) becomes

$$-u_{n+1} + \tfrac{1}{2} = (-u_n + \tfrac{1}{2})(\tfrac{1}{2} + u_n)$$
$$= \tfrac{1}{4} - u_n^2,$$

i.e.

$$u_{n+1} = u_n^2 + \tfrac{1}{4},$$

which is precisely Equation (2). Notice also that $u_0 = -x_0 + \frac{1}{2} = 0$, so that the initial terms do correspond. It follows that any known information about sequence (1) can be applied to sequence (2), by using this change of variable.

Fig. 19

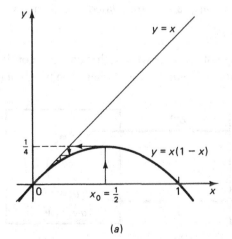

(a)

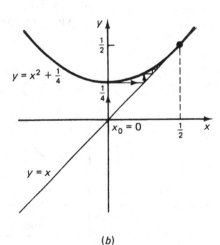

(b)

We can express this change of variable in function notation as follows. First write Equation (1) in the form

$$x_{n+1} = f(x_n), \quad n = 0, 1, 2, \ldots, \tag{3}$$

where $f(x) = x(1 - x)$ and $x_0 = \frac{1}{2}$. Then put $x = \phi(u)$, where

$$\phi(u) = -u + \tfrac{1}{2}. \tag{4}$$

Now Equation (3) can be written as

$$\phi(u_{n+1}) = f(\phi(u_n)), \quad n = 0, 1, 2, \ldots,$$

i.e.

$$\begin{aligned} u_{n+1} &= \phi^{-1}(f(\phi(u_n))) \\ &= g(u_n), \end{aligned}$$

where

$$g = \phi^{-1} \circ f \circ \phi. \tag{5}$$

Here ϕ^{-1} is the inverse function of ϕ. Schematically we have Fig. 20, in which $x_n = \phi(u_n)$, $x_{n+1} = \phi(u_{n+1})$. In our example

$$x = -u + \tfrac{1}{2} \quad \text{implies} \quad u = -x + \tfrac{1}{2},$$

so that the inverse of the function ϕ in (4) is

$$\phi^{-1}(x) = -x + \tfrac{1}{2}.$$

Hence, by Equation (5)

$$\begin{aligned} g(u) &= -f(\phi(u)) + \tfrac{1}{2} \\ &= -\phi(u)(1 - \phi(u)) + \tfrac{1}{2} \\ &= -(-u + \tfrac{1}{2})(\tfrac{1}{2} + u) + \tfrac{1}{2} \\ &= u^2 + \tfrac{1}{4}, \end{aligned}$$

as expected.

Whenever two functions f and g are related by a formula

$$g = \phi^{-1} \circ f \circ \phi.$$

in which ϕ is a 1–1 correspondence with both ϕ and ϕ^{-1} continuous, we say that f and g are *conjugate* to each other. The two functions f

Fig. 20

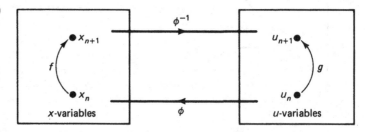

and *g* can then be considered equivalent, as far as iteration is concerned. Whatever behaviour is exhibited by a sequence

$$x_{n+1} = f(x_n), \quad n = 0, 1, 2, \ldots,$$

will also be exhibited by

$$u_{n+1} = g(u_n), \quad n = 0, 1, 2, \ldots,$$

where $u_0 = \phi^{-1}(x_0)$, and we say that the sequence u_n is *conjugate* to the sequence x_n.

In the following sections we shall see several examples where the consideration of a conjugate sequence greatly simplifies the understanding of a particular iteration sequence. Sometimes it is even possible to find a formula for x_n by finding a suitable conjugate sequence which can itself be solved explicitly. (See also Chapter 2, Section 6.10.)

7.1 *Exercises*

(a)   Find an explicit solution for the iteration sequence

$$x_{n+1} = x_n^2, \quad n = 0, 1, 2, \ldots,$$

with initial term x_0.

(b)   Consider the sequence

$$x_{n+1} = x_n^2 + 2x_n, \quad n = 0, 1, 2, \ldots,$$

with initial term x_0. By using the change of variables $x = u - 1$ show that

$$x_n = (x_0 - 1)^{2^n} + 1, \quad n = 0, 1, 2, \ldots.$$

7.2 *Exercise*

Suppose that f, g are conjugate functions with

$$g = \phi^{-1} \circ f \circ \phi.$$

Show that if c is a fixed point of f, then $\phi^{-1}(c)$ is a fixed point of g.

§8
Linear and Möbius sequences

In §2 and §3 you investigated the behaviour of various linear sequences of the form

$$x_{n+1} = ax_n + b, \quad n = 0, 1, 2, \ldots, \tag{1}$$

and you should have found that the behaviour of such sequences usually depends on the value of *a* or (if $a = 1$) on the value of *b*, rather than on the initial term x_0. For example, if $|a| < 1$, then the sequence (1) is always convergent. This can easily be explained graphically since, if $|a| < 1$ then:

(a) $y = ax + b$, crosses $y = x$ at a unique fixed point c of $f(x) = ax + b$, given by solving $ax + b = x$, which gives $c = -b/(a - 1)$;

(b) the derivative of f at this fixed point c is equal to a, and so the fixed point is attracting. See Fig. 21.

Actually we can do rather better than this. The method of conjugate functions can be used in this case to find an explicit formula for x_n. We make the change of variables

$$x = u - b/(a - 1), \quad a \neq 1,$$

which takes the fixed point $c = -b/(a - 1)$ of f to $u = 0$. Substitution in Equation (1) gives

$$u_{n+1} - \frac{b}{a - 1} = a\left(u_n - \frac{b}{a - 1}\right) + b, \quad n = 0, 1, 2, \ldots$$

which reduces after cancellation to

$$u_{n+1} = au_n, \quad n = 0, 1, 2, \ldots, \tag{2}$$

The explicit solution to (2) is

$$u_n = a^n u_0, \quad n = 0, 1, 2, \ldots,$$

which leads to

$$x_n + \frac{b}{a - 1} = a^n \left(x_0 + \frac{b}{a - 1}\right),$$

i.e.

$$x_n = a^n x_0 + b\left(\frac{a^n - 1}{a - 1}\right). \tag{3}$$

Fig. 21

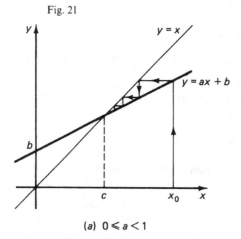

(a) $0 \leqslant a < 1$

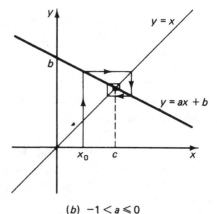

(b) $-1 < a \leqslant 0$

This explicit formula for x_n means that we need no help from the micro in order fully to explain the behaviour of sequences of the form (1). For example, it is clear that if $|a| < 1$, then $a^n \to 0$ as $n \to \infty$, and so

$$x_n \to -b/(a-1) \quad \text{as } n \to \infty.$$

8.1 *Exercises*

(a) Use Formula (3) to determine the behaviour of x_n if $|a| > 1$.

(b) If $a = 1$, then Formula (3) is not valid since $a - 1 = 0$. Determine an explicit formula for x_n in this case and deduce that $x_n \to \pm \infty$ as $n \to \infty$, if $b \neq 0$. Explain this behaviour graphically.

Before moving on to Möbius sequences, which are rather more complicated, we cannot resist including an application of Formula (3) to the solution of a variant of a puzzle which we met in Chapter 1.

8.2 *Exercise: Monkey puzzle*

(Compare Chapter 1, Exercise 2.2.) Five men and a monkey gather coconuts all day and then fall asleep. During the night each man wakes in turn and, after giving one coconut to the monkey, he removes and hides one fifth of the pile of coconuts for himself. In the morning the men divide the remainder equally among themselves leaving exactly one coconut, which again goes to the monkey. How many coconuts did they collect? (Hint: each man's nocturnal activity can be described mathematically as an application of the function

$$f(x) = \tfrac{4}{5}(x - 1),$$

to the number x of coconuts which they found.)

Remark For an account of the generalized problem with n men and m monkeys, each of which receives p coconuts, see Melzak (1973), p. 51.

In §2 and §3 you should also have investigated various Möbius sequences of the form

$$x_{n+1} = (ax_n + b)/(cx_n + d), \quad n = 0, 1, 2, \ldots, \tag{4}$$

where a, b, c, d are real numbers. Such a sequence reduces to a linear sequence if $c = 0$ and to a constant sequence if $ad - bc = 0$. Thus we assume that

$$c \neq 0 \quad \text{and} \quad ad - bc \neq 0.$$

You should have discovered that the behaviour of such sequences is again usually independent of the initial term x_0. For example, if

$$x_{n+1} = \frac{3x_n + 2}{x_n + 2}, \quad n = 0, 1, 2, \ldots,$$

then $x_n \to 2$ for almost all initial terms x_0. See Fig. 22. The only exceptions are $x_0 = -2$ where $f(x) = (3x + 2)/(x + 2)$ is not defined, and $x = -1$, which is a fixed point of f. How do we explain this behaviour?

You should also have found, in Exercise 2.3, examples of Möbius sequences which are divergent for every choice of initial term x_0. Can this be explained?

Once again it turns out that there is an explicit formula for x_n, which can be used to confirm the observations made earlier. We invite you to derive this somewhat more complicated formula in the following (extended) exercise.

8.3 Exercise
(a) Determine the fixed points of

$$f(x) = (ax + b)/(cx + d), \quad c \neq 0, \, ad - bc \neq 0.$$

Show that if

$$(a - d)^2 + 4bc > 0,$$

then f has two distinct fixed points, α, β say.
(b) By considering the product

$$(c\alpha + d)(c\beta + d)$$

Fig. 22

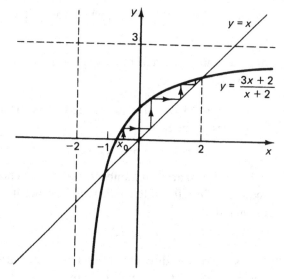

show that $c\alpha + d \neq 0$ and $c\beta + d \neq 0$.

(c) Use the facts that $\alpha = f(\alpha)$ and $\beta = f(\beta)$ to verify the equation

$$\frac{x_{n+1} - \alpha}{x_{n+1} - \beta} = \left(\frac{c\beta + d}{c\alpha + d}\right)\left(\frac{x_n - \alpha}{x_n - \beta}\right), \quad \text{if } x_n \neq \beta. \quad (5)$$

(d) Deduce from (c) that

$$\frac{x_n - \alpha}{x_n - \beta} = \left(\frac{c\beta + d}{c\alpha + d}\right)^n \left(\frac{x_0 - \alpha}{x_0 - \beta}\right), \quad n = 0, 1, 2, \ldots .$$

(e) Show that

$$f'(\alpha) = \frac{c\beta + d}{c\alpha + d} \quad \text{and} \quad f'(\beta) = \frac{c\alpha + d}{c\beta + d},$$

and deduce that if $|f'(\alpha)| < 1$, then

$$x_n \to \alpha \quad \text{as } n \to \infty,$$

for all real numbers x_0, apart from β and $-d/c$.

(f) Show that if

$$(a - d)^2 + 4bc = 0,$$

then

$$(a + d)^2 = 4(ad - bc)$$

and deduce that $f'(\alpha) = 1$. Show further that the change of variables

$$u = 1/(x - \alpha)$$

transforms the equation of part (c) into

$$u_{n+1} = u_n + 2c/(a + d).$$

Deduce that $u_n \to \pm \infty$ as $n \to \infty$, and hence that $x_n \to \alpha$ as $n \to \infty$, in this case.

(g) If

$$(a - d)^2 + 4bc < 0,$$

then f has no *real* fixed points and so x_n cannot be convergent. However, if α, β denote the *complex* fixed points of f, then Equation (5) is valid. Prove that

$$\left|\frac{c\beta + d}{c\alpha + d}\right| = 1$$

in this case, and hence describe the different possible ways in which x_n is divergent.

8.4 *Exercise*

Use the results of Exercise 8.3 to give a complete description of the behaviour of the Möbius sequences which were investigated in Exercise 2.3. Hence confirm that the continued fraction $[1, 2, 2, \ldots]$ converges to $\sqrt{2}$ (see §1).

§9
Quadratic sequences

The study of linear sequences and Möbius sequences in the previous section was rather straightforward because of the availability of explicit solutions. For quadratic sequences of the general form

$$x_{n+1} = ax_n^2 + bx_n + c, \quad n = 0, 1, 2, \ldots, \tag{1}$$

no explicit solution is available. There are some quadratic sequences for which an explicit solution can be found; for example the sequence

$$x_{n+1} = x_n^2, \quad n = 0, 1, 2, \ldots,$$

has the explicit solution

$$x_n = x_0^{2^n}, \quad n = 0, 1, 2, \ldots,$$

but usually other methods are required to determine the behaviour of a quadratic sequence.

In this section we shall focus attention on quadratic sequences of the form

$$x_{n+1} = \lambda x_n(1 - x_n), \quad n = 0, 1, 2, \ldots, \tag{2}$$

which arise in population dynamics, as we described in §1. See Fig. 23. Such sequences may seem much more special than (1), since there is only one parameter, namely λ, but in fact they are not all that special. Whenever the function $f(x) = ax^2 + bx + c$, which defines sequence (1), has a real fixed point, the sequence (1) is actually conjugate to a sequence of the form (2). This is the content of the following exercise.

9.1 *Exercise*

Suppose that $f(x) = ax^2 + bx + c, a \neq 0$, has the fixed point α and that $f'(\alpha) \neq 0$. Prove that the sequence (1) is conjugate to sequence (2) using the change of variable

$$x = -\left(\frac{2\alpha a + b}{a}\right)u + \alpha;$$

the corresponding value of λ is $\lambda = 2\alpha a + b = f'(\alpha)$.

9.2 *A systematic investigation*

In Exercise 2.4 you calculated the sequence

$$x_{n+1} = \lambda x_n(1 - x_n), \quad n = 0, 1, 2, \ldots,$$

for various values of the parameter λ in the range $0 \le \lambda \le 4$ and various initial values x_0. This range of values of λ is of particular interest because for $0 \le \lambda \le 4$ the function f_λ, defined by

$$f_\lambda(x) = \lambda x(1 - x)$$

maps the interval $[0, 1]$ into itself. Indeed you can readily check that f_λ takes its maximum value $\lambda/4$ at the point $x = \frac{1}{2}$ (Fig. 23).

You should have discovered that the behaviour of the sequence x_n varies very greatly depending on the value of λ, but for each fixed λ the behaviour is more or less independent of the initial term x_0. For example there are many values of λ for which the sequence is convergent and others for which it appears to converge to a p-cycle ($p > 1$). The time has now come for a systematic investigation of such sequences.

The program below takes a large number of values of λ between 0 and 4 and plots each of the corresponding sequences x_n (starting from $x_0 = \frac{1}{2}$) vertically above a horizontal λ-axis. In order to detect the eventual behaviour of x_n (where possible), only the terms x_{50}, x_{51}, ..., x_{100} are plotted. Thus if x_n is convergent, then a single point should be plotted and, more generally, if x_n converges to a p-cycle, then p points should be plotted.

9.3 *Program: Lambda plot*

```
1Ø LET N = Ø.25 ∗ VMAX
2Ø FOR I = 1 TO N
```

Fig. 23

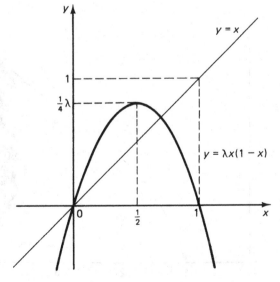

```
3Ø  LET L = 4*I/N
4Ø  LET X = Ø.5
5Ø  FOR J = 1 TO 1ØØ
6Ø  LET X = L*X*(1 – X)
7Ø  IF J > 49 THEN put a dot at screen point (4*I, VMAX*X)
8Ø  NEXT J
9Ø  NEXT I
```

Here VMAX denotes the maximum vertical screen coordinate and we have taken only $n = \frac{1}{4}v_{max}$ values of λ (denoted by the variable l) because the program is quite slow. After trying the program out, you may like to increase n.

Note: If your micro has the graphics origin at the top left of the screen, then, to get the picture the usual way up, you will need to use $(4*I, VMAX*(1 – X))$ in line 7Ø. Similar remarks hold for Programs 9.21 and 10.1.

The remarkable picture which emerges is shown in Fig. 24. We have added axes in order to measure where the different types of behaviour occur. The picture reveals the following:

> for $0 \leqslant \lambda \leqslant 1$, the sequence x_n is convergent with limit 0;
>
> for $1 < \lambda \leqslant 3$, the sequence x_n is convergent with non-zero limit;
>
> for $3 < \lambda \leqslant 3.45$ (approximately) the sequence converges to a 2-cycle;
>
> as λ increases beyond 3.45, the sequence x_n appears first to converge to a 4-cycle and then to behave in a rather chaotic manner.

Fig. 24

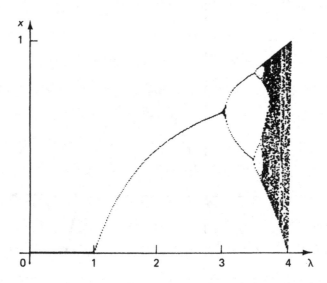

These observations suggest that we look in more detail at the range $3 \leq \lambda \leq 4$.

9.4 *Exercise*

(a)   Modify Program 9.3 so that λ varies from 3 to 4, by altering line 3∅:

  3∅ L = 3 + I/N.

(b)   Make a similar modification to look in detail at $3.5 \leq \lambda \leq 4$.

Fig. 25 is even more remarkable:
  for $3.45 \leq \lambda \leq 3.55$ (approximately) the sequence x_n converges to a 4-cycle;

Fig. 25

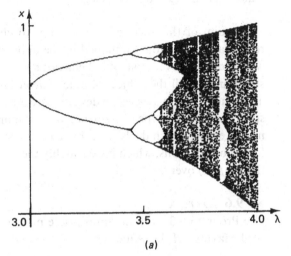

(a)

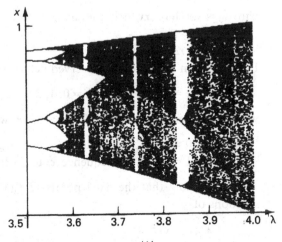

(b)

for $3.55 \leq \lambda \leq 3.57$ (approximately) the sequence x_n converges to an 8-cycle, and thereafter there appears to be a 16-cycle;

for λ close to 3.63 (approximately) the sequence x_n converges to a 6-cycle;

for λ close to 3.74 (approximately) the sequence x_n converges to a 5-cycle;

for λ close to 3.83 (approximately) the sequence x_n converges to a 3-cycle;

for other values of λ it appears that x_n is chaotic.

9.5 *Exercise*

Modify Program 9.3 so that λ lies in various narrow intervals between 3.5 and 4. Can you find another interval of values of λ in which x_n converges to a 4-cycle?

The aim of this section is to attempt to elucidate some of the remarkable behaviour contained in the above pictures. We should warn you, however, that this behaviour is not completely understood and is still the subject of much current research. In case you are wondering why it is worth devoting great effort to understanding such a specialised type of sequence we recommend that you try the next exercise, which deals with the iteration of an entirely different family of functions, which have roughly the same shape of graph as that of $f_\lambda(x)$ over $0 \leq x \leq 1$.

9.6 *Exercise*

Use Program 9.3, with an appropriate modification, to investigate the behaviour of the sequences

$$x_{n+1} = \lambda \sin(\pi x_n), \quad n = 0, 1, 2, \ldots, 0 \leq \lambda \leq 1,$$

with $x_0 = \frac{1}{2}$. (Here πx_n is in radians.)

9.7 *The range $0 \leq \lambda \leq 3$*

In this section we verify the observed behaviour of

$$x_{n+1} = \lambda x_n(1 - x_n), \quad n = 0, 1, 2, \ldots,$$

with $x_0 = \frac{1}{2}$, for λ in the range $0 \leq \lambda \leq 3$; i.e. we shall prove that:

for $0 \leq \lambda \leq 1$, the sequence x_n converges to 0;

for $1 < \lambda \leq 3$, the sequence x_n tends to a non-zero limit.

First we note that the fixed points of $f_\lambda(x) = \lambda x(1 - x)$ are the solutions of

$$\lambda x(1 - x) = x;$$

i.e.

$$x = 0 \quad \text{and} \quad x = 1 - 1/\lambda = c_\lambda,$$

say. Thus for $0 < \lambda \le 1$, the function f_λ has no fixed points between 0 and 1. Since $f_\lambda(0) = f_\lambda(1) = 0$, we deduce that the graph $y = f_\lambda(x)$ lies below $y = x$, for $0 < x < 1$, i.e.

$$0 < f_\lambda(x) < x, \quad \text{for } 0 < x < 1, 0 < \lambda \le 1.$$

It follows by graphical iteration that if we take *any* initial term x_0 with $0 < x_0 < 1$, then the sequence x_n converges to 0. See Fig. 26.

Next we consider the case $1 < \lambda \le 2$. For this range, the fixed point $c_\lambda = 1 - 1/\lambda$ of f_λ satisfies $0 < c_\lambda \le \frac{1}{2}$ and the graph of f_λ looks as in

Fig. 26

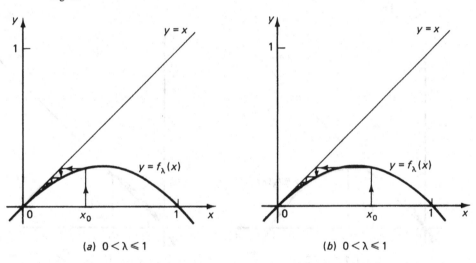

(a) $0 < \lambda \le 1$ (b) $0 < \lambda \le 1$

Fig. 27

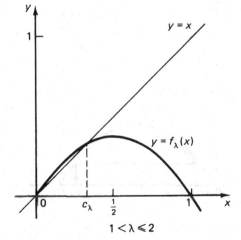

$1 < \lambda \le 2$

Fig. 27. Once again it is clear in this case that if $0 < x_0 < 1$, then x_n tends to $c_\lambda = 1 - 1/\lambda$. See Fig. 28.

Incidentally, this convergence shows that in Fig. 24 the part of the plot above the λ-interval $[1, 2]$ has the equation $x = 1 - 1/\lambda$. Since the part of the plot above the λ-interval $[2, 3]$ seems also to lie on the same curve, we expect that the sequence x_n (with $x_0 = \frac{1}{2}$) converges to c_λ for $2 < \lambda \le 3$ also.

In the range $2 < \lambda \le 3$ the fixed point $c_\lambda = 1 - 1/\lambda$ satisfies $\frac{1}{2} < c_\lambda \le \frac{2}{3}$ and so the graph $y = f_\lambda(x)$ is decreasing as it passes through c_λ. See Fig. 29. This suggests that the sequence $x_{n+1} = f_\lambda(x_n)$, $n = 0, 1, 2, \ldots$, $x_0 = \frac{1}{2}$, will yield a cobweb around c_λ, in other words

Fig. 28

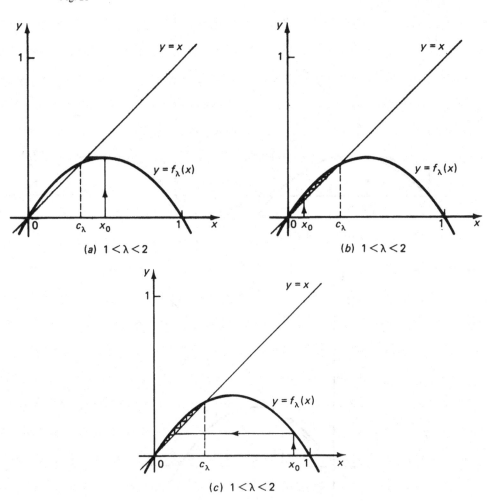

(a) $1 < \lambda < 2$

(b) $1 < \lambda < 2$

(c) $1 < \lambda < 2$

Fig. 29

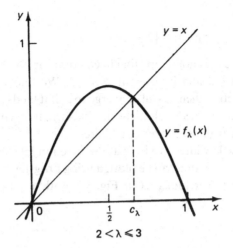

$$x_0 < x_2 < x_4 < \ldots < c_\lambda < \ldots < x_5 < x_3 < x_1.$$

See Fig. 30. Although the sequence x_n does appear to converge to c_λ, it is not clear how to *prove* this. The next few sections (up to Exercise 9.10) are devoted to the proof.

First note that

$$
\begin{aligned}
f_\lambda'(x)\big|_{c_\lambda} &= \lambda(1 - 2x)\big|_{c_\lambda} \\
&= \lambda(1 - 2(1 - 1/\lambda)) \\
&= 2 - \lambda,
\end{aligned}
$$

Fig. 30

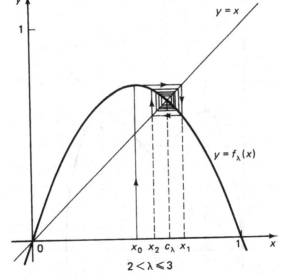

so that

$$|f'_\lambda(c_\lambda)| = |2 - \lambda|.$$

Hence c_λ is not a repelling fixed point for $2 < \lambda \leq 3$. It is attracting if $2 < \lambda < 3$ and indifferent if $\lambda = 3$. We know from §4 that if c_λ is attracting then x_n will converge to c_λ if it lands *close enough* to c_λ. But it is not immediately clear that this will happen if $x_0 = \frac{1}{2}$. Thus, some extra argument is required here.

The key idea is to look at the function $f_\lambda^2(x) = f_\lambda(f_\lambda(x))$. The graph of this function can be plotted using Program 5.1, with $p = 2$, and for $2 < \lambda \leq 3$ it looks as in Fig. 31. Both $y = f_\lambda(x)$ and $y = f_\lambda^2(x)$ are

Fig. 31

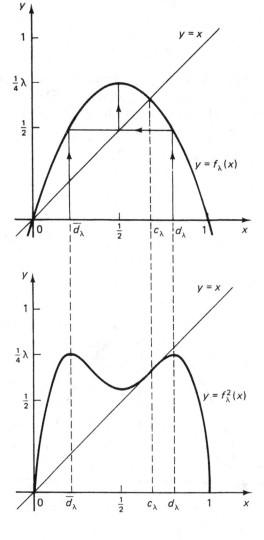

plotted in order to make comparisons. There are several key features of $y = f_\lambda^2(x)$, which we now ask you to verify.

9.8 *Exercises*
Let $f_\lambda(x) = \lambda x(1 - x)$ with $2 < \lambda \leqslant 3$.

(a) Prove that f_λ^2 is symmetric about the line $x = \frac{1}{2}$; i.e.

$$f_\lambda^2(\tfrac{1}{2} - x) = f_\lambda^2(\tfrac{1}{2} + x).$$

(b) Prove that f_λ^2 has a fixed point at c_λ, and that

$$(f_\lambda^2)'(c_\lambda) = (f_\lambda'(c_\lambda))^2.$$

(Hint: Use the chain rule.)

(c) Prove that f_λ^2 takes its maximum value $\lambda/4$ at d_λ and $1 - d_\lambda$, where $d_\lambda = \frac{1}{2} + \frac{1}{2}\sqrt{(1 - 2/\lambda)}$, so that $f_\lambda(d_\lambda) = \frac{1}{2}$.

(d) Prove that $c_\lambda < f_\lambda(\tfrac{1}{2}) < d_\lambda$ and deduce that

$$f_\lambda^2(\tfrac{1}{2}) > \tfrac{1}{2}.$$

(e) Prove that f_λ^2 is increasing for $\frac{1}{2} \leqslant x \leqslant d_\lambda$.

The final feature of $y = f_\lambda^2(x)$ which we require is that f_λ^2 has no fixed points in $(0, 1)$ other than c_λ. Put another way, the graph $y = f_\lambda^2(x)$ crosses $y = x$ only once for $0 < x < 1$. There are various ways to prove this fact, which seems so obvious from Fig. 31. The direct method is to write down the fixed point equation

$$f_\lambda^2(x) = x \tag{3}$$

and show that the only solutions are 0 and c_λ if $2 < \lambda \leqslant 3$. Although this is a quartic equation in x, all four roots can be found easily because we know that 0 and c_λ are solutions. We ask you to carry out this manipulation in the following exercise.

9.9 *Exercises*
(a) Prove that

$$f_\lambda^2(x) - x = (f_\lambda(x) - x)g_\lambda(x),$$

where

$$g_\lambda(x) = \lambda^2 x^2 - (\lambda^2 + \lambda)x + (\lambda + 1).$$

(Hint: Begin by writing

$$f_\lambda^2(x) - x = f_\lambda^2(x) - f_\lambda(x) + f_\lambda(x) - x.)$$

(b) Show that the solutions of $g_\lambda(x) = 0$ are

$$x = \frac{1}{2\lambda} (\lambda + 1 \pm \sqrt{((\lambda + 1)(\lambda - 3)))}$$

and deduce that f_λ^2 has no fixed points in $(0, 1)$, other than c_λ, if $2 < \lambda \leqslant 3$.

Having established that f_λ^2 has no fixed points in $(0, 1)$, apart from c_λ, it is now clear that

$$x < f_\lambda^2(x) < c_\lambda, \quad \text{for } \tfrac{1}{2} \leqslant x < c_\lambda,$$
$$x > f_\lambda^2(x) > c_\lambda, \quad \text{for } c_\lambda < x \leqslant d_\lambda.$$

See Fig. 32.

It follows that, for $\tfrac{1}{2} \leqslant x \leqslant d_\lambda$,

$$f_\lambda^{2n}(x) \to c_\lambda \quad \text{as } n \to \infty.$$

In particular the sequence $f_\lambda^{2n}(x_0)$, i.e. $x_0, x_2, x_4, \ldots$, converges to c_λ, as does $f_\lambda^{2n}(x_1)$, i.e. $x_1, x_3, x_5, \ldots$, (since $x_1 = f_\lambda(\tfrac{1}{2})$ lies in (c_λ, d_λ) by Exercise 9.8(*d*)). Thus we have shown that

$$x_n = f_\lambda^n(x_0), \quad n = 0, 1, 2, \ldots,$$

with $x_0 = \tfrac{1}{2}$, does indeed converge to $c_\lambda = 1 - 1/\lambda$ for $2 < \lambda \leqslant 3$.

It is natural to ask now whether $f_\lambda^n(x) \to c_\lambda$ for all initial terms x in $(0, 1)$ (if $x = 0$ or 1 then, of course, $f_\lambda^n(x) = 0$, for $n = 1, 2, \ldots$). We ask you to answer this question in the following exercise.

9.10 *Exercise*

Show that if $2 < \lambda \leqslant 3$ and $0 < x < 1$, then

$$f_\lambda^n(x) \to c_\lambda \quad \text{as } n \to \infty.$$

Fig. 32

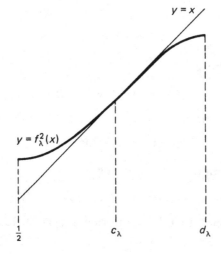

(Hint: Show that $f_\lambda^n(x)$ lies in $[\frac{1}{2}, d_\lambda]$ for some n depending on x.)

9.11 *What happens if $\lambda > 3$?*

Next we look in detail at what happens to the sequence $x_n = f_\lambda^n(\frac{1}{2})$ as λ increases beyond 3. In our earlier experiments we saw that for $3 < \lambda \leqslant 3.45$ (approx.) x_n converges to a 2-cycle. Why does this happen, and what is the significance of the number 3.45?

First let us see what the sequence x_n looks like (using Program 3.1) for a value of λ slightly greater than 3. See Fig. 33.

Once again we seem to have

$$x_0 < x_2 < x_4 < \ldots < c_\lambda < \ldots < x_5 < x_3 < x_1,$$

but this time the cobweb does not seem to close in on the fixed point c_λ. Let us see if the graph $y = f_\lambda^2(x)$ is any help (Program 5.1, with $p = 2$). Fig. 34 makes it much clearer what is happening. The function $f_\lambda^2(x)$ has acquired a new pair of fixed points, here labelled a_λ and b_λ. Indeed you have already found these two fixed points in Exercise 9.9(*b*), where you solved

$$f_\lambda^2(x) = x$$

to find the solutions 0, c_λ and $(1/2\lambda)\,(\lambda + 1 \pm \sqrt{((\lambda + 1)(\lambda - 3)))}$. The last two fixed points are real if $\lambda > 3$ and so we must have

$$a_\lambda = \frac{1}{2\lambda}\,[\lambda + 1 - \sqrt{((\lambda + 1)(\lambda - 3))}]$$

Fig. 33

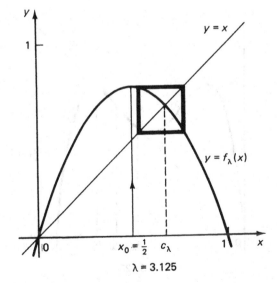

$\lambda = 3.125$

and

$$b_\lambda = \frac{1}{2\lambda} [\lambda + 1 + \sqrt{((\lambda + 1)(\lambda - 3))}].$$

(Notice that if $\lambda = 3$, then $a_\lambda = b_\lambda = c_\lambda = \frac{2}{3}$.)

In fact the numbers a_λ, b_λ form a 2-cycle of f_λ, i.e.

$$f_\lambda(a_\lambda) = b_\lambda \quad \text{and} \quad f_\lambda(b_\lambda) = a_\lambda.$$

This can be checked directly by substitution, or you can simply note that $f_\lambda(a_\lambda)$ is a fixed point of f_λ^2 and, since $f_\lambda(a_\lambda) \neq 0$, c_λ, then we must have $f_\lambda(a_\lambda) = b_\lambda$ and hence $f_\lambda(b_\lambda) = f_\lambda^2(a_\lambda) = a_\lambda$.

Since a_λ and b_λ form a 2-cycle of f_λ the slope of f_λ^2 at a_λ and at b_λ must be the same by the chain rule (see Section 5.4). So as λ increases the nature of the fixed points a_λ, b_λ of f_λ^2 remains the same. The actual value of the slope of f_λ^2 at these points (the *multiplier* of this 2-cycle) is given by:

$$\begin{aligned}
(f_\lambda^2)'(a_\lambda) &= f_\lambda'(f_\lambda(a_\lambda))f_\lambda'(a_\lambda) \\
&= f_\lambda'(b_\lambda)f_\lambda'(a_\lambda) \\
&= \lambda^2(1 - 2b_\lambda)(1 - 2a_\lambda) \\
&= \lambda^2(1 - 2(a_\lambda + b_\lambda) + 4a_\lambda b_\lambda) \\
&= \lambda^2 \left(1 - 2\left(\frac{\lambda + 1}{\lambda}\right) + 4\left(\frac{\lambda + 1}{\lambda^2}\right)\right) \\
&= -\lambda^2 + 2\lambda + 4,
\end{aligned}$$

using the formulae for a_λ and b_λ given above.

As expected, when $\lambda = 3$ we have $a_\lambda = c_\lambda = \frac{2}{3}$ so that the multiplier

Fig. 34

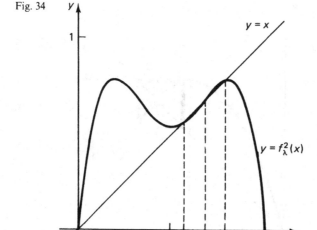

$\lambda = 3.125$

$(f_3^2)'(\frac{2}{3}) = 1$. However, as λ increases beyond 3 the multiplier $(f_\lambda^2)'(a_\lambda)$ decreases, so that a_λ, b_λ form an attracting 2-cycle. In the case illustrated above, $\lambda = 3.125$, you can see from the nature of the graph $y = f_\lambda^2(x)$ that $f_\lambda^{2n}(\frac{1}{2}) \to a_\lambda$ as $n \to \infty$, so that $f_\lambda^n(\frac{1}{2})$ does indeed converge to the 2-cycle a_λ, b_λ.

As λ increases, the multiplier reaches 0 when

$$(f_\lambda^2)'(a_\lambda) = -\lambda^2 + 2\lambda + 4 = 0$$

i.e. when $\lambda = 1 + \sqrt{5} \approx 3.236\,067\,98$. This is illustrated in Fig. 35. In this case $a_\lambda = \frac{1}{2}$ and the even subsequence

$$x_{2n} = f_\lambda^{2n}(\tfrac{1}{2}), \quad n = 0, 1, 2, \ldots, \lambda = 1 + \sqrt{5}$$

is identically equal to $\frac{1}{2}$, whereas the odd subsequence

$$x_{2n+1} = f_\lambda^{2n+1}(\tfrac{1}{2}), \quad n = 0, 1, 2, \ldots, \lambda = 1 + \sqrt{5}$$

is identically equal to $f_\lambda(\frac{1}{2}) = (1 + \sqrt{5})/4$.

It is not an accident that when the multiplier reaches 0, one of the points of the 2-cycle equals $\frac{1}{2}$. This happens because $\frac{1}{2}$ is the *only* point where $f_\lambda'(x)$ is equal to 0. Thus if

$$c, f_\lambda(c), \ldots, f_\lambda^{p-1}(c),$$

is *any* p-cycle of f_λ with multiplier equal to 0, then

$$0 = (f_\lambda^p)'(c) = f_\lambda'(f_\lambda^{p-1}(c)) \ldots f_\lambda'(f_\lambda(c))f_\lambda'(c),$$

and hence one of the terms of this product must vanish. The

Fig. 35

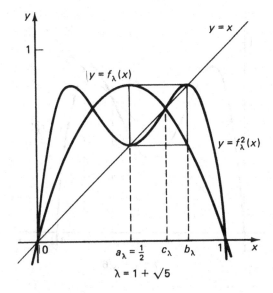

$\lambda = 1 + \sqrt{5}$

corresponding point of the p-cycle must then be $\frac{1}{2}$. This observation will be very important shortly.

As λ continues to increase the multiplier decreases to reach -1 when

$$(f_\lambda^2)'(a_\lambda) = -\lambda^2 + 2\lambda + 4 = -1,$$

i.e. when $\lambda = 1 + \sqrt{6} \approx 3.449\,489\,74$. See Fig. 36. The number 3.449 . . . should remind you of something. In our earlier experiment we found that $f_\lambda^n(\frac{1}{2})$ appears to converge to a 2-cycle for $3 < \lambda \leqslant 3.45$ (approx.). Now we have found that the 2-cycle a_λ, b_λ is attracting for $3 < \lambda < 1 + \sqrt{6}$, indifferent for $\lambda = 1 + \sqrt{6}$ and repelling for $\lambda > 1 + \sqrt{6}$. So we expect to be able to prove that $f_\lambda^n(\frac{1}{2})$ converges to this 2-cycle for $3 < \lambda \leqslant 1 + \sqrt{6}$. This can be done directly, but we shall omit the details because we are going to prove a more general result later. Instead let us investigate what happens as λ increases beyond $1 + \sqrt{6}$.

First recall that, as λ increases through the value 3, the fixed point c_λ of f_λ becomes repelling and an attracting 2-cycle a_λ, b_λ comes into being. Does the same phenomenon occur for f_λ^2 as λ increases through $1 + \sqrt{6}$? The graphs in Fig. 37 show $y = f_\lambda^2(x)$ and $y = f_\lambda^4(x)$ for $\lambda = 3.48$, which is slightly greater than $1 + \sqrt{6}$. Now a_λ and b_λ are repelling fixed points of $f_\lambda^2(x)$ (and hence of $f_\lambda^4(x)$), but we find that around both a_λ and b_λ there have appeared a pair of attracting fixed points of f^4. These form a pair of 2-cycles of f_λ^2 and all four form a 4-cycle of f_λ as illustrated in Fig. 38. This explains why the sequence $f_\lambda^n(\frac{1}{2})$ converges to a 4-cycle for λ slightly greater than

Fig. 36

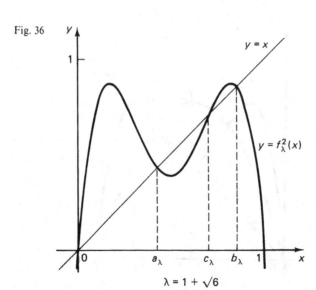

$$\lambda = 1 + \sqrt{6}$$

Fig. 37

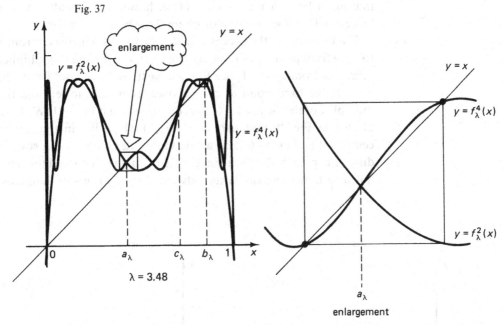

$\lambda = 3.48$

enlargement

$1 + \sqrt{6}$. Of course, we have not yet *proved* this convergence, but we have begun to understand why it occurs.

As λ continues to increase history repeats itself. The multiplier of the 4-cycle decreases from 1 when $\lambda = 1 + \sqrt{6}$ to 0 when $\lambda \approx 3.5$ and then to -1 when $\lambda \approx 3.54$. Beyond this an attracting 8-cycle of f_λ appears, followed later by an attracting 16-cycle, and so on. It would not be easy for us to prove here that this *period doubling bifurcation*, as it is called, does continue indefinitely, though we shall give some

Fig. 38

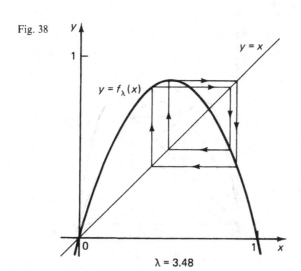

$\lambda = 3.48$

indication later in the chapter. Here, however, we shall consider more carefully the question of where these bifurcations occur.

The key steps in the process are as follows. As λ increases from 1 to 3 the fixed point c_λ of f_λ moves from left to right and its multiplier decreases from 1 to -1. See Fig. 39. Next, as λ increases from 3 to $1 + \sqrt{6}$, the fixed point a_λ of f_λ^2 moves from right to left and the multiplier of the 2-cycle a_λ, b_λ of f_λ decreases from 1 to -1. We have plotted in Fig. 40 that part of $y = f_\lambda^2(x)$ which lies in the square centred at $(\frac{1}{2}, \frac{1}{2})$ with (c_λ, c_λ) at the top right. Of course the scale is different in each diagram since c_λ is changing. You cannot have failed to notice the similarity between these two sets of diagrams.

Fig. 39

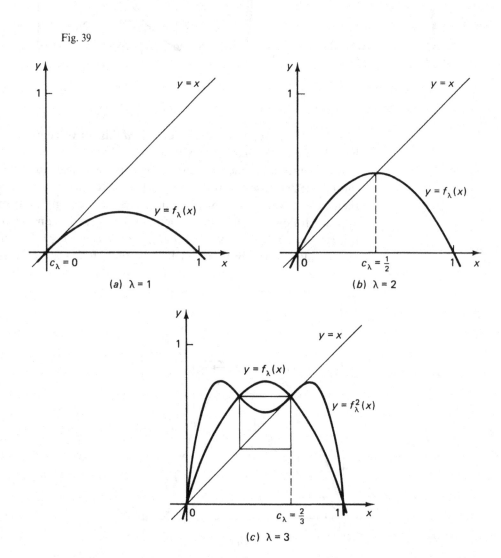

(a) $\lambda = 1$

(b) $\lambda = 2$

(c) $\lambda = 3$

Apart from being upside down, the graphs of f_λ^2 strongly resemble those of f_λ, with different values for λ of course.

In both Figs. 39(a) and 40(a), there is just one fixed point at a corner. As λ increases the 'hump' in the graph grows (in each case) so that a new attracting fixed point appears which, in Figs. 39(b) and 40(b), has multiplier 0 (and hence is actually at $\frac{1}{2}$). On further increasing λ, the new fixed point becomes indifferent in Figs. 39(c) and 40(c), and the process is ready to begin again (in the smaller square).

Let us denote by λ_n the value of λ at which the nth period doubling bifurcations take place. Thus $\lambda_1 = 3$, $\lambda_2 = 1 + \sqrt{6}$, and we also

Fig. 40

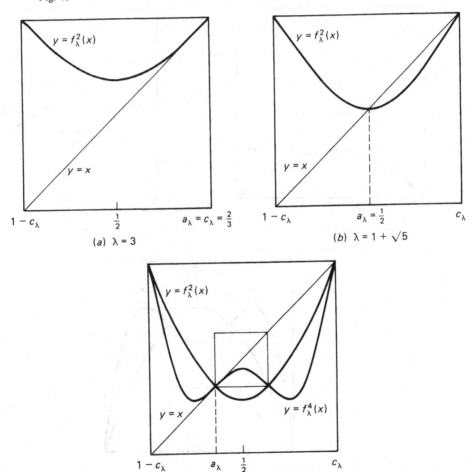

(a) $\lambda = 3$

(b) $\lambda = 1 + \sqrt{5}$

(c) $\lambda = 1 + \sqrt{6}$

define $\lambda_0 = 1$. Fig. 41 indicates the nth stage, where n is even. The function $f_{\lambda_n}^{2^n}$ has a fixed point a_n with multiplier 1. On increasing λ beyond λ_n, the hump grows, the fixed point moves to the right and the multiplier decreases, reaching 0 when the fixed point passes through $\frac{1}{2}$, and reaching -1 when λ reaches the next bifurcation point λ_{n+1}.

We have here denoted by μ_n the value of λ at which

$$f_{\mu_n}^{2^n}(\tfrac{1}{2}) = \tfrac{1}{2}. \tag{4}$$

For this value of λ, f_λ has a superattracting 2^n-cycle. Thus $\mu_0 = 2$ and $\mu_1 = 1 + \sqrt{5}$.

Fig. 41

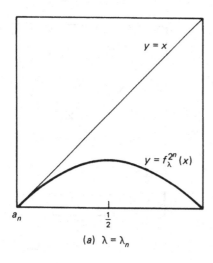

(a) $\lambda = \lambda_n$

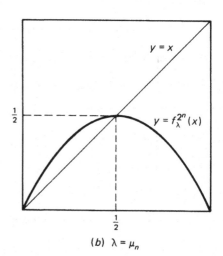

(b) $\lambda = \mu_n$

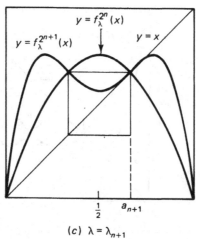

(c) $\lambda = \lambda_{n+1}$

Now it turns out, unfortunately, that it is in general rather difficult to compute accurately the values of λ_n at which the period doubling bifurcations occur, since λ_n satisfies the two equations

$$f_{\lambda_n}^{2^n}(a_n) = a_n \quad \text{and} \quad (f_{\lambda_n}^{2^n})'(a_n) = 1,$$

which contain the unknown fixed point a_n. On the other hand, the numbers μ_n lie among the solutions of Equation (4), which has no other unknowns. Of course, Equation (4) will have many solutions in general, but if we can obtain a rough estimate of where a given μ_n lies, then it should be possible to compute μ_n accurately by, for example, the bisection method (see Chapter 2). From Fig. 41, where n is even, we see that if a prospective value λ is too large, then

$$f_\lambda^{2^n}(\tfrac{1}{2}) > \tfrac{1}{2},$$

whereas if the prospective value λ is too small, then

$$f_\lambda^{2^n}(\tfrac{1}{2}) < \tfrac{1}{2}.$$

If n happens to be odd, then these inequalities are simply reversed.

The next program is designed to calculate the value μ_2 which satisfies

$$f_{\mu_2}^{4}(\tfrac{1}{2}) = \tfrac{1}{2},$$

by using the bisection method. Here $n = 2$ is even so the graph $y = f_{\mu_2}^{4}(x)$ is configured as in Fig. 41.

9.12 *Program: Mu two*

```
10 INPUT L, U
20 FOR I = 1 TO 30
30 LET M = 0.5*(L + U)
40 LET X = 0.5
50 FOR J = 1 TO 4
60 LET X = M*X*(1 − X)
70 NEXT J
80 IF X < 0.5 THEN LET L = M: GOTO 100
90 LET U = M
100 NEXT I
110 PRINT M
```

Here l and u represent the lower and upper guesses at the value of μ_2. Within the loop starting at line 20, the value M which is the average of the current lower and upper guesses, is tested as a solution μ to

$$f_\mu^{4}(\tfrac{1}{2}) = \tfrac{1}{2}.$$

If $f_\mu^4(\tfrac{1}{2})$ is found to be less than $\tfrac{1}{2}$, then μ must be too small and so we take $l = \mu$ as our new lower guess. If $f_\mu^4(\tfrac{1}{2})$ is greater than $\tfrac{1}{2}$, on the other hand, we take $u = \mu$ as our new upper guess. This bisection process is repeated 30 times giving μ_2 accurate to 2^{-30} (approx. 10^{-9}) times $u - l$.

9.13 Exercises

(a) Run Program 9.12 with various initial guesses for l and u, such as:

   (i) $l = 2,\ u = 4$; (ii) $l = 3,\ u = 4$.

You should find two solutions, one of which is μ_2. Why does the other solution appear?

(b) Use Program 5.1 to plot the graph $y = f_{\mu_2}^4(x)$ with the value of μ_2 found in (a); check that the graph passes through $(\tfrac{1}{2}, \tfrac{1}{2})$.

In Exercise 9.13, you should have found that $\mu_2 = 3.498\,561\,7$, and this has probably whetted your appetite to find μ_3, μ_4, ... Only minor modifications to Program 9.12 are required to find μ_3, namely:

 50 FOR J = 1 TO 8
 80 IF X > 0.5 THEN LET L = M: GOTO 100

The latter change is required because $8 = 2^3$ and 3 is odd, so that the graph $y = f_{\mu_3}^8(x)$ is in the 'upside down' position near $\tfrac{1}{2}$ and $f_\lambda^8(\tfrac{1}{2})$ is decreasing as λ increases through μ_3.

9.14 Exercise

(a) Run Program 9.12 with the above modifications and various initial guesses for l and u.

(b) Check whether you have found the correct value for μ_3 by plotting $y = f_{\mu_3}^8(x)$, using Program 5.1.

You should have found Exercise 9.14 more difficult than Exercise 9.13, because you need to make much more accurate guesses at the value of μ_3 to find the correct value $\mu_3 = 3.554\,640\,86$. To find μ_4, μ_5 and so on it seems a good idea to try and predict roughly where these values lie. The values so far are shown in Table 1. It looks as if the difference between the successive values of μ_n is decreasing by a factor of about 4 each time, i.e.

$$\frac{\mu_n - \mu_{n-1}}{\mu_{n-1} - \mu_{n-2}} \approx \tfrac{1}{4},$$

so that

$$\mu_n \approx \mu_{n-1} + \tfrac{1}{4}(\mu_{n-1} - \mu_{n-2}).$$

Table 1

n	μ_n	$\mu_n - \mu_{n-1}$
0	2	—
1	3.236 067 98	1.236 067 98
2	3.498 561 70	0.262 493 72
3	3.554 640 86	0.056 079 16

So it seems a good idea to take, for example,

$$\mu_{n-1} + 0.2(\mu_{n-1} - \mu_{n-2})$$

and

$$\mu_{n-1} + 0.3(\mu_{n-1} - \mu_{n-2})$$

as our lower and upper guesses for μ_n.

The following program calculates and prints μ_n for $n = 2, 3, 4, \ldots$ by using this idea. An array MU($\cdot$) is set up to store the values μ_0, μ_1, μ_2, $\ldots$ as they are calculated. We assume here that this array is labelled starting from 0; if your machine labels arrays starting from 1, then a minor change is required.

9.15 *Program: Period doubling*

```
10 DIM MU(20)
20 LET MU(0) = 2: LET MU(1) = 1 + SQR(5)
30 LET N = 1: LET K = 2: LET S = −1
40 LET N = N + 1: LET K = 2*K: LET S = −S
50 LET L = MU(N − 1) + 0.2*(MU(N − 1) − MU(N − 2))
60 LET U = MU(N − 1) + 0.3*(MU(N − 1) − MU(N − 2))
70 FOR I = 1 TO 30
80 LET M = 0.5*(L + U)
90 LET X = 0.5
100 FOR J = 1 TO K
110 LET X = M*X*(1 − X)
120 NEXT J
130 IF S*X < S*0.5 THEN LET L = M: GOTO 150
140 LET U = M
150 NEXT I
160 LET MU(N) = M: LET
        D = (MU(N − 1) − MU(N − 2))/(MU(N) − MU(N − 1))
170 PRINT M, D
180 GOTO 40
```

The variable n keeps track of the value μ_n being computed and the variable k is the number 2^n of iterations of f_λ required at the nth stage. The variable s is ± 1 depending on whether n is even or odd. At lines 4∅ and 5∅ the lower and upper guesses for μ_n are found and then the calculation of μ_n in lines 6∅–14∅ is very similar to lines 2∅–10∅ of Program 9.12. Next this value for μ_n is inserted in the array MU$(\cdot)$, the difference quotient

$$\delta_n = \frac{\mu_{n-1} - \mu_{n-2}}{\mu_n - \mu_{n-1}}$$

is computed and both μ_n and δ_n are printed. Finally the program returns to line 4∅ to begin calculating μ_{n+1}.

9.16 *Exercises*

(a)   Run Program 9.15. You should find that: (i) the sequence μ_n converges to a number $\mu_\infty = 3.569\,945\,6\ldots$; (ii) the values of δ_n settle down to about $4.669\ldots$ and then oscillate away from this value; (iii) each successive value of μ_n takes twice as long to calculate as the previous value, so the program is rather slow after the first few values.

(b)   (i) Try to decide how many digits of the ratios δ_n you can rely on (the number of digits will depend on n). Hence explain the observed oscillation in (a) (iii) above. (ii) The number 30 of bisections (see line 7∅) is unnecessarily large if $u - l$ is small. To speed up the program, try to replace 30 by a suitable number which *depends on* $u - l$.

9.17 *Universality*

The computations in Exercise 9.16 were carried out by a physicist called Mitchell Feigenbaum in 1976. The period doubling phenomenon was known earlier and similar computations had been done previously, but he seems to have been the first person to use the idea of *predicting* where the next μ_n would lie. In that way he encountered the number $4.669\ldots$, which determines the rate of convergence of the sequence μ_n. In fact Feigenbaum's approach to solving the equation

$$f_\lambda^{2^n}(\tfrac{1}{2}) = \tfrac{1}{2} \tag{5}$$

used the Newton–Raphson method (see Chapter 2) rather than bisection, which is a little more involved (see Exercise 9.19).

Some time later Feigenbaum performed the same experiment with the family of iterations

$$x_{n+1} = \lambda \sin(\pi x_n), \quad n = 0, 1, 2, \ldots, \tag{6}$$

for $0 \le \lambda \le 1$. This family experiences the same kind of period doubling bifurcations, as you should have found in Exercise 9.6. Here of course the values of μ_n are completely different (in fact they converge to $\mu_\infty = 0.865\,579\,2\ldots$). However, to his amazement, Feigenbaum found that the number δ which determines the rate of convergence of the μ_ns was once again $\delta = 4.669\ldots$! Indeed, when he performed these experiments with greater precision he found that

$$\delta = 4.669\,201\,609\,102\,9\ldots,$$

in each case.

As a result of these simple experiments it seemed that he had discovered a new universal constant associated with period doubling. The discovery has, not surprisingly, led to intense efforts by mathematicians and physicists to explain this universal behaviour and put its existence on a sound basis. A number of fundamental papers on this subject can be found in Cvitanović (1984).

9.18 *Exercise*
For the family (6) it is easy to see that $\mu_0 = \frac{1}{2}$. Adapt Program 9.12 to calculate μ_1 and then adapt Program 9.15 to calculate μ_n and δ_n for $n \ge 2$.

9.19 *Exercises*
Try to modify Program 9.15 to use Newton's method rather than bisection to solve Equation (5), using the following hints:
(*a*) take the value

$$\mu_{n-1} + \delta_{n-1}(\mu_{n-1} - \mu_{n-2})$$

as the initial guess when calculating μ_n;
(*b*) you can calculate

$$\frac{d}{d\lambda} f_\lambda^{2^n}(\tfrac{1}{2})$$

using an iteration formula for

$$\frac{d}{d\lambda} f_\lambda^k(\tfrac{1}{2}), \quad k = 0, 1, 2, \ldots,$$

which is obtained by differentiating the equation

$$f_\lambda^{k+1}(\tfrac{1}{2}) = \lambda f_\lambda^k(\tfrac{1}{2})(1 - f_\lambda^k(\tfrac{1}{2})), \quad k = 0, 1, 2, \ldots,$$

with respect to λ.

9.20 *A universal function*

In his attempt to explain the existence of the universal constant $\delta = 4.669\ldots$, Feigenbaum was led to look more closely at the graphs $y = f_{\mu_n}^{2^n}(x)$ near the point $x = \frac{1}{2}$. We saw earlier that these graphs resemble each other rather strongly, except for the change of scale and the fact that they are oriented differently for n odd or even. Feigenbaum had the idea of plotting these graphs on the same diagram, using the following observation about the period doubling process. In Fig. 42(a) $\lambda = \lambda_n$ and the period doubling bifurcation is about to occur. The indifferent fixed point is about to become repelling and an attracting 2-cycle for $f_\lambda^{2^{n-1}}$ is about to appear. In (b) this attracting 2-cycle of $f_\lambda^{2^{n-1}}$ has become superattracting, so that the points of the 2-cycle are $\frac{1}{2}$, a_n, where $a_n = f_{\mu_n}^{2^{n-1}}(\frac{1}{2})$. Once the value μ_n has been calculated it is a simple matter to determine a_n, and we can then plot the sequence of graphs $y = f_{\mu_n}^{2^n}(x)$, $a_n \leqslant x \leqslant \frac{1}{2}$, with their scales adjusted so that the fixed points at a_n and $\frac{1}{2}$ coincide. To be precise, we put $s_n = |a_n - \frac{1}{2}|$ and plot

$$y = \frac{|f_{\mu_n}^{2^n}(\frac{1}{2} + s_n x) - \frac{1}{2}|}{s_n}, \quad 0 \leqslant x \leqslant 1.$$

Thus the fixed point at $(\frac{1}{2}, \frac{1}{2})$ appears at $(0, 0)$ and the fixed point at (a_n, a_n) appears at $(1, 1)$.

The following program is a modification of Program 9.15 (which calculated the values of μ_n). Lines $3\emptyset$–$16\emptyset$ are not included as they are unchanged.

Fig. 42

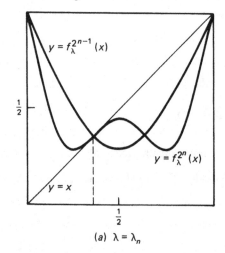

(a) $\lambda = \lambda_n$

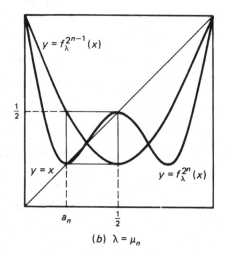

(b) $\lambda = \mu_n$

9.21 *Program: Universal function*
```
 1Ø DIM MU(2Ø): DIM S(2Ø)
 2Ø LET MU(Ø) = 2: LET MU(1) = 1 + SQR(5)
3Ø–16Ø As in Program 9.15
17Ø LET X = Ø.5
18Ø FOR I = 1 TO K/2
19Ø LET X = MU(N)*X*(1 − X)
2ØØ NEXT I
21Ø LET S(N) = ABS(X − Ø.5)
22Ø FOR I = 1 TO Ø.5*VMAX
23Ø LET X = Ø.5 + S(N)*I/(Ø.5*VMAX)
24Ø FOR J = 1 TO K
25Ø LET X = MU(N)*X*(1 − X)
26Ø NEXT J
27Ø LET Y = ABS(X − Ø.5)/S(N)
28Ø Put a dot at screen point (2*I, VMAX*Y)
29Ø NEXT I
3ØØ PRINT MU(N), S(N − 1)/S(N)
31Ø GOTO 4Ø
```

Lines 17Ø–2ØØ calculate the fixed point $a_n = f_{\mu_n}^{2^{n-1}}(\tfrac{1}{2})$ and the scale factor s_n is determined in line 21Ø. The loop from lines 22Ø–29Ø then plot the graph $y = f_{\mu_n}^{2^n}(x)$ with the scaling described earlier. As the program stands, the graph is not plotted for the case $n = 1$, but this can be achieved by adding the line

```
35 GOTO 17Ø
```

9.22 *Exercises*

(a) Run Program 9.21. You should find that the graphs appear to converge very rapidly to a function, $g(x)$ say, and that the ratio s_{n-1}/s_n converges to a number $\alpha = 2.502 \ldots$.

(b) Modify Program 9.21 to plot the corresponding graphs for the family of iterations

$$x_{n+1} = \lambda \sin(\pi x_n), \quad n = 0, 1, 2, \ldots,$$

$0 \leqslant \lambda \leqslant 1$. Compare the graphs of g and the values of α for each of these families.

Exercise 9.22 should convince you that these scaled iterated functions do indeed converge to a function $g(x)$ which does not depend on the particular family of iterates under consideration. For this reason, Feigenbaum called $g(x)$ a universal function! Moreover, the sequence of numbers s_n, which define the scalings of the graphs

$y = f_{\mu_n}^{2^n}(x)$, $a_n \leqslant x \leqslant \frac{1}{2}$, appears to tend to zero at a universal geo-metric rate, that is

$$\lim_{n \to \infty} \frac{S_{n-1}}{S_n} = \alpha = 2.502 \ldots .$$

It is a considerable understatement to say that these extraordinary properties are hard to explain. As we have stated, they are currently the object of intense study by mathematicians and physicists.

For example, there is much interest in the behaviour of $f_{\mu_\infty}(x)$ under iteration. Here $\mu_\infty = \lim_{n \to \infty} \mu_n = 3.569\,945\,6 \ldots$. The next exercise suggests one way that you could investigate this function.

9.23 Exercises

(a)   Use Program 3.1 to investigate the behaviour of sequences of the form $f_{\mu_\infty}^n(x)$, where $0 < x < 1$.

(b)   Try modifying Program 3.1 so that it only begins to plot and draw line segments after, say, 100 iterations. What do you observe? Does the result depend on the initial value x?

(c)   Further modify Program 3.1 so that you can zoom in more closely on the pattern of plotted line segments (you will have to deal with the possibility that some plotted points are off-screen). What do you observe?

In Exercise 9.23 you should have found that the sequences $f_{\mu_\infty}^n(x)$, where $0 < x < 1$, behave in a similar manner for large values of n, independently of the initial point x. They all settle down into a similar pattern. In fact, there is a subset E of the interval $[0, 1]$, which contains infinitely many points, to which the sequences $f_{\mu_\infty}^n(x)$ are attracted; for this reason E is called an *attractor*. As you should have found in Exercise 9.23(c), the closer you look at the set E, the more complicated it appears, which is why sets like E are sometimes called 'strange' attractors.

9.24 Attracting cycles for λ near 4

In Exercise 9.4 you plotted the sequences $x_n = f_\lambda^n(\frac{1}{2})$ for a large number of values of λ between 0 and 4, and it became apparent that even for $\lambda > \mu_\infty$ there are intervals of values of λ for which x_n converges to a p-cycle for some positive integer p. In this section we search for intervals of this type, which we call a *period p window*, and we try to describe where these intervals appear.

First, we remind you of a fundamental observation about attrac-ting p-cycles. If λ is a parameter value such that

$$f_\lambda^p(\tfrac{1}{2}) = \tfrac{1}{2}, \tag{7}$$

for some positive integer p, then there is a least integer q such that $f_\lambda^q(\tfrac{1}{2}) = \tfrac{1}{2}$ (it is easy to see that q must be a divisor of p). By the chain rule,

$$(f_\lambda^q)'(\tfrac{1}{2}) = f_\lambda'(f_\lambda^{q-1}(\tfrac{1}{2})) \ldots f_\lambda'(f_\lambda(\tfrac{1}{2}))f_\lambda'(\tfrac{1}{2})$$
$$= 0,$$

because $f_\lambda'(\tfrac{1}{2}) = 0$. Hence the numbers

$$\tfrac{1}{2}, f_\lambda(\tfrac{1}{2}), \ldots, f_\lambda^{q-1}(\tfrac{1}{2}),$$

form a superattracting q-cycle for f_λ. On the other hand, if the numbers

$$c, f_\lambda(c), \ldots, f_\lambda^{p-1}(c),$$

form a superattracting p-cycle for some c in $(0, 1)$, then the number $\tfrac{1}{2}$ must lie amongst these p numbers.

Fig. 43

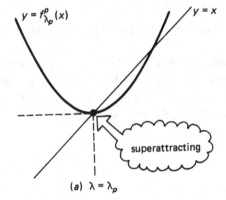

(a) $\lambda = \lambda_p$

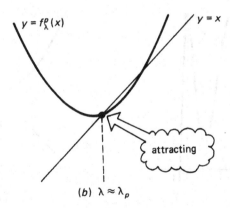

(b) $\lambda \approx \lambda_p$

This observation means that in searching for superattracting p-cycles of f_λ, $0 < \lambda < 4$, we can confine our attention to the solutions of Equation (7). Once such a superattracting p-cycle has been found, for some λ_p say, we can be sure that for nearby values of λ the function f_λ will have an attracting p-cycle. Indeed, if λ varies only slightly, then the graph $y = f_\lambda^p(x)$ will vary only slightly also and the fixed point of f_λ^p will remain attracting. See Fig. 43.

In Exercise 9.4 one of the main observations was that for $\lambda \approx 3.83$ the sequence $x_n = f_\lambda^n(\frac{1}{2})$ appears to converge to a 3-cycle. Let us now investigate this observation using Program 5.1. See Fig. 44. Notice first that f_λ^3 is symmetric with respect to $x = \frac{1}{2}$ because f_λ is, and that f_λ^3 has a local minimum at $\frac{1}{2}$. Altogether f_λ^3 has eight fixed points, three of which (labelled a, b, c) are attracting. In fact by looking at $y = f_\lambda(x)$ for $\lambda = 3.83$ (see Fig. 45) you can see that these three form a 3-cycle, which shows that $(f_\lambda^3)'(a) = (f_\lambda^3)'(b) = (f_\lambda^3)'(c)$. How can we use these pictures to give a method of computing the nearby value of λ such that

$$f_\lambda^3(\tfrac{1}{2}) = \tfrac{1}{2}? \tag{8}$$

For this value of λ, the graph $y = f_\lambda^3(x)$ should resemble Fig. 46 near $\frac{1}{2}$.

As you can see in Fig. 44, the local minimum of $f_\lambda^3(x)$ at $x = \frac{1}{2}$ lies just above $y = x$ for $\lambda = 3.83$. Some experimenting with Program 5.1 should convince you that as λ increases the local minimum at $\frac{1}{2}$ decreases. Thus, for values of λ near 3.83,

Fig. 44

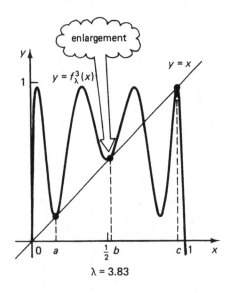

$\lambda = 3.83$

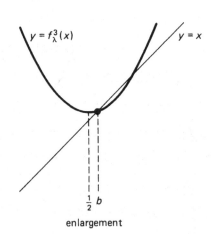

enlargement

$$f_\lambda^3(\tfrac{1}{2}) < \tfrac{1}{2} \Rightarrow \lambda \text{ too large}$$
$$f_\lambda^3(\tfrac{1}{2}) > \tfrac{1}{2} \Rightarrow \lambda \text{ too small.}$$

These inequalities provide a strategy for solving Equation (8), which is similar to that in Program 9.12. Can you explain the difference?

9.25 *Program: Superattracting 3-cycle*

```
10  INPUT L, U
20  FOR I = 1 TO 30
30  LET M = 0.5*(L + U)
40  LET X = 0.5
50  FOR J = 1 TO 3
60  LET X = M*X*(1 - X)
```

Fig. 45

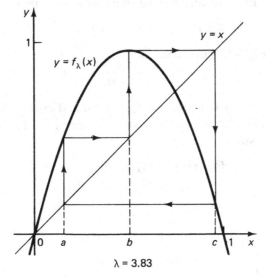

$\lambda = 3.83$

Fig. 46

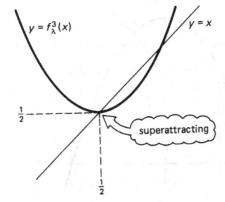

70 NEXT J
80 IF X < 0.5 THEN LET U = M: GOTO 100
90 LET L = M
100 NEXT I
110 PRINT M

9.26 *Exercise*

Run Program 9.25 with various initial guesses for *l* and *u*. Check your answers for λ by plotting $y = f_\lambda^3(x)$ near $\frac{1}{2}$ in each case. How many solutions for λ can you find?

You should find in Exercise 9.26 that there seems to be only one value of λ such that $f_\lambda^3(\frac{1}{2}) = \frac{1}{2}$ and that this value is 3.831 874 1. The following argument shows that there is exactly one such value of λ.
First we introduce the number a_λ such that

$$0 < a_\lambda < \tfrac{1}{2} \quad \text{and} \quad f_\lambda(a_\lambda) = \tfrac{1}{2}.$$

(Fig. 47.) These conditions imply that

$$a_\lambda = \tfrac{1}{2} - \tfrac{1}{2}\sqrt{(1 - 2/\lambda)}.$$

It is easy to check that $f_\lambda^3(\frac{1}{2}) = \frac{1}{2}$ if and only if $f_\lambda^3(a_\lambda) = a_\lambda$ and so we have to show that there is exactly one value of λ such that $f_\lambda^3(a_\lambda) = a_\lambda$.
Now

$$f_\lambda^3(a_\lambda) = f_\lambda^2(f_\lambda(a_\lambda)) = f_\lambda^2(\tfrac{1}{2}),$$

and

Fig. 47

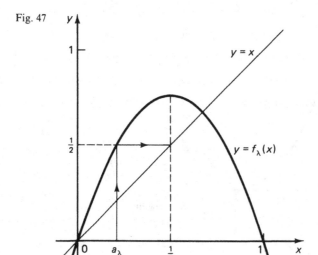

$$(f_\lambda^3)'(a_\lambda) = (f_\lambda^2)'(f_\lambda(a_\lambda))f_\lambda'(a_\lambda)$$
$$= (f_\lambda^2)'(\tfrac{1}{2})f_\lambda'(a_\lambda)$$
$$= 0.$$

It is a matter of calculus to check that if $\lambda > 3$, then the graph $y = f_\lambda^2(x)$ has a minimum at $x = \tfrac{1}{2}$ and, moreover, that the height $f_\lambda^2(\tfrac{1}{2})$ is decreasing for $3 < \lambda \leq 4$, with $f_4^2(\tfrac{1}{2}) = 0$. See e.g. Fig. 31. Hence $y = f_\lambda^3(x)$ has a local minimum at a_λ (indeed $(f_\lambda^3)'$ is negative to the left of a_λ and positive to the right) and the height of this local minimum is decreasing as λ increases. Since $a_4 \neq 0$ and $f_4^3(a_4) = 0$, we deduce that this local minimum coincides with the line $y = x$ at some unique point. Hence there is a unique λ such that

$$f_\lambda^3(a_\lambda) = a_\lambda,$$

as required.

Having found this unique superattracting 3-cycle of f_λ at $\lambda = 3.8318741$, it is natural to investigate the fixed point behaviour of f_λ nearby. Using Program 9.3 in the interval $3.82 \leq \lambda \leq 3.86$ we obtain Fig. 48. The period doubling phenomenon has appeared again! As λ increases beyond 3.83 there comes a point where the attracting 3-cycle of f_λ^3 is indifferent, as in Fig. 49. On further increasing λ this 3-cycle becomes repelling but a new attracting 6-cycle appears, with a new pair of attracting fixed points of f_λ^6 lying on either side of each of the old repelling fixed points of f_λ^3. As λ increases further, history repeats itself with the appearance of an

Fig. 48

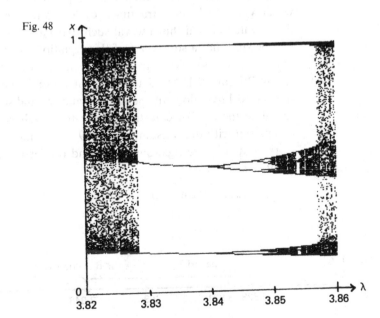

Fig. 49

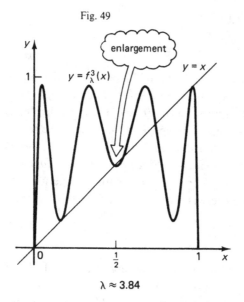

$\lambda \approx 3.84$

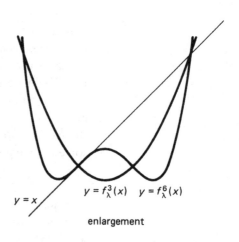

attracting 12-cycle, 24-cycle and so on. See Fig. 50. There are various investigations which you may like to carry out here.

9.27 *Exercises*

(a) At the left-hand end-point of the period 3 window the corresponding 3-cycle of f_λ has multiplier 1. Verify numerically that this value of λ is in fact $1 + \sqrt{8} = 3.828\,427\,12\ldots$. Can you prove that $\lambda = 1 + \sqrt{8}$?

(b) Adapt Program 9.12 to calculate the point in the period 6 window at which the attracting 6-cycle has multiplier 0; i.e. find a value of λ in this interval such that $f_\lambda^6(\tfrac{1}{2}) = \tfrac{1}{2}$. Why can you be sure that a solution λ of this equation, with $\lambda > 3.84$, does not give rise to an attracting 2-cycle or 3-cycle?

(c) Adapt Program 9.15 to calculate the corresponding points λ in the period 12 window, the period 24 window, and so on. Also calculate the rate of convergence for these values of λ and compare it with the constant $\delta = 4.669\ldots$ found earlier.

(d) Carry out the investigations in (b) and (c) for the family of iterations

$$x_{n+1} = \lambda \sin(\pi x_n), \quad n = 0, 1, 2, \ldots, 0 \leqslant \lambda \leqslant 1.$$

Fig. 50

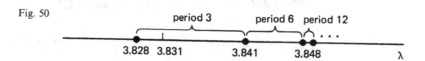

Although the period 3 window is the most conspicuous window for $\lambda > 3.56 \ldots$, we hope that you found many others in Exercise 9.5. We now focus attention upon a family of such windows which get closer and closer to $\lambda = 4$. You found in Exercise 9.5 that there is a period 4 window near $\lambda = 3.96$. Indeed the graph $y = f_\lambda^4(x)$ for $\lambda = 3.96$ shows that we are likely to find a value of λ nearby for which $f_\lambda^4(\frac{1}{2}) = \frac{1}{2}$. See Fig. 51. The corresponding superattracting 4-cycle will look as in Fig. 52. Once again it can be seen that for values of λ near 3.96

Fig. 51

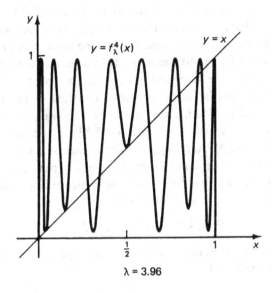

$\lambda = 3.96$

Fig. 52

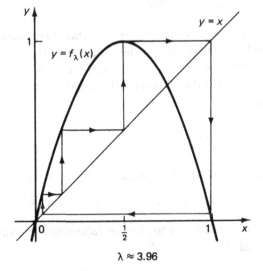

$\lambda \approx 3.96$

$$f_\lambda^4(\tfrac{1}{2}) > \tfrac{1}{2} \Rightarrow \lambda \text{ too small}$$
$$f_\lambda^4(\tfrac{1}{2}) < \tfrac{1}{2} \Rightarrow \lambda \text{ too large}.$$

Hence a simple modification of Program 9.25 allows the determination of λ for this superattracting 4-cycle.

9.28 *Exercise*

Modify Program 9.25 to determine the value of λ near 3.96 such that $f_\lambda^4(\tfrac{1}{2}) = \tfrac{1}{2}$. Use Program 9.15 to verify that your value of λ is correct (you may need to zoom in to the point $(\tfrac{1}{2}, \tfrac{1}{2})$).

You should have found in Exercise 9.28 that for $\lambda = 3.96027\ldots$ we have a superattracting 4-cycle and you will, by now, find it unsurprising that next door to the corresponding period 4 window we find a period 8 window, then a period 16 window and so on. Nor will you be surprised to hear that a repeat of Exercise 9.27 would turn up the same universal constant δ associated with period doubling. Rather than dwell on this, we pursue the new family of windows associated with $\lambda = 3.83 \ldots$ (period 3) and $\lambda = 3.96 \ldots$ (period 4). Actually these form part of a longer sequence starting with $\lambda = 2$ (period 1) and $\lambda = 1 + \sqrt{5}$ (period 2). It seems likely that we can go on to find an infinite sequence of λ values, which we call ν_p, $p = 1, 2, \ldots$, such that $\lim_{p \to \infty} \nu_p = 4$,

$$f_{\nu_p}^p(\tfrac{1}{2}) = \tfrac{1}{2}, \quad \text{for } p = 1, 2, 3, \ldots,$$

and each ν_p has a corresponding superattracting p-cycle. So far we have found

$$\nu_1 = 1, \qquad \nu_2 = 1 + \sqrt{5}, \qquad \nu_3 = 3.8318741\ldots \qquad \text{and}$$
$$\nu_4 = 3.9602701\ldots.$$

To calculate further values it is once again desirable to be able to predict where a given ν_p lies in terms of the previous values. Let us consider the rate of convergence of ν_p to 4, based on what we know so far. See Table 2. It seems reasonable from the table to guess that the ratio

$$\frac{4 - \nu_{p-1}}{4 - \nu_p} \tag{9}$$

will lie somewhere between 2 and 5, and hence that

$$4 - 0.5(4 - \nu_{p-1}) \leq \nu_p \leq 4 - 0.2(4 - \nu_{p-1}).$$

These estimates are used in the following program which determines ν_p and the quotients (9).

Table 2

p	ν_p	$4 - \nu_p$
1	2	2
2	3.236 068	0.763 932
3	3.831 874 1	0.168 125 9
4	3.960 270 1	0.039 729 9

9.29 *Program: Nu sequence*

```
10 DIM NU(20)
20 LET NU(1) = 2: LET NU(2) = 1 + SQR(5)
30 LET P = 2
40 LET P = P + 1
50 LET L = 4 − 0.5 * (4 − NU(P − 1))
60 LET U = 4 − 0.2 * (4 − NU(P − 1))
70 FOR I = 1 TO 30
80 LET M = 0.5 * (L + U)
90 LET X = 0.5
100 FOR J = 1 TO P
110 LET X = M * X * (1 − X)
120 NEXT J
130 IF X < 0.5 THEN LET U = M: GOTO 150
140 LET L = M
150 NEXT I
160 LET NU(P) = M
170 LET D = (4 − NU(P − 1))/(4 − NU(P))
180 PRINT M, D
190 GOTO 40
```

9.30 *Exercise*

Run Program 9.29. Check that the values you find for ν_3 and ν_4 agree with those found earlier and check that the values you find for ν_p, $p > 4$, do indeed give superattracting p-cycles for $f_{\nu_p}(x)$. What value do you think the sequence (9) is converging to?

In this exercise you may have been surprised to find that the difference quotients $(4 - \nu_{p-1})/(4 - \nu_p)$ do not seem to converge to $\delta = 4.669 \ldots$. But this is not so surprising since the sequence ν_p does not arise through the process of period doubling. In fact it is possible

to determine this limit theoretically. Before reading on you may like
to repeat Exercise 9.30 with the family

$$x_{n+1} = \lambda \sin(\pi x_n), \quad n = 0, 1, 2, \ldots,$$

$0 \leq \lambda \leq 1$. Recall that the corresponding values of ν_1 and ν_2 were
found earlier to be $\nu_1 = 0.5$ and $\nu_2 = 0.777\,733\,77$. Can you guess the
limit of the quotient corresponding to (9) in this case?

In fact, it can be proved that, for the quadratic family,

$$\lim_{p \to \infty} \left(\frac{4 - \nu_{p-1}}{4 - \nu_p} \right) = \frac{d}{dx} 4x(1-x) \bigg|_{x=0} = 4.$$

For the sine family, on the other hand, we have

$$\lim_{p \to \infty} \left(\frac{1 - \nu_{p-1}}{1 - \nu_p} \right) = \frac{d}{dx} \sin(\pi x) \bigg|_{x=0} = \pi.$$

So the rate of convergence in this case is very far from being
universal!

9.31 *Other attracting cycles for* $\lambda_\infty < \lambda < 4$

You will recall from Exercise 9.5 that there are periodic windows, for
$\lambda_\infty < \lambda < 4$, other than the ones associated with the sequence ν_p,
$p \geq 3$. For example, if λ is close to 3.63 there is a period 6 window
and if λ is close to 3.74 a period 5 window. To give you some idea of
how many windows are present, consider the following simple
observation: suppose that f_λ has a superattracting $(p-1)$-cycle and
f_μ has a superattracting $(p-2)$-cycle, so that

$$f_\lambda^{p-1}(\tfrac{1}{2}) = \tfrac{1}{2} \quad \text{and} \quad f_\mu^{p-2}(\tfrac{1}{2}) = \tfrac{1}{2}.$$

Suppose also that $\lambda > 2$ and $\mu > \mu_2 (= 1 + \sqrt{5})$, so that

$$f_\lambda(\tfrac{1}{2}) > \tfrac{1}{2} \quad \text{and} \quad f_\mu^2(\tfrac{1}{2}) < \tfrac{1}{2}.$$

Then

$$f_\lambda^p(\tfrac{1}{2}) = f_\lambda(\tfrac{1}{2}) > \tfrac{1}{2} \quad \text{and} \quad f_\mu^p(\tfrac{1}{2}) = f_\mu^2(\tfrac{1}{2}) < \tfrac{1}{2}.$$

Hence there is some ν lying between λ and μ such that $f_\nu^p(\tfrac{1}{2}) = \tfrac{1}{2}$, and
it follows that f_ν has a superattracting q-cycle, where q is some divisor
of p. Now we know already about the superattracting cycles in
Fig. 53. It follows that between 3.498 5 ... (the 4-cycle) and
3.813 8 ... (the 3-cycle) there must be a period 5 window and hence
also a period 6 window and a period 7 window, arranged in this
order:

$$4, 6, 7, 5, 3.$$

9.32 *Exercises*

(a)   Use Program 9.3 to determine the above period 7 window accurately.

(b)   Show that the above sequence can be extended to

$$4, 6, 8, 9, 7, 5, 3.$$

Use Program 9.3 to determine the period 8 window and the period 9 window.

The above method of proving the existence of new periodic windows does not by any means exhaust the list of windows which can be found. The only way to approach this problem systematically is to try and find *all* possible solutions to the equation

$$f_\lambda^p(\tfrac{1}{2}) = \tfrac{1}{2},$$

for $p = 1, 2, 3, \ldots .$ One way to do this would be to first plot the graph

$$y = f_\lambda^p(\tfrac{1}{2}) - \tfrac{1}{2}, \quad 3.5 \leqslant \lambda \leqslant 4,$$

for each integer p, in order to detect the approximate locations of zeros and then apply the method of bisection or Newton's method. In case you wish to attempt this project we provide in Table 3 a list of all the superattracting p-cycles up to period $p = 7$.

9.33 *The kneading sequence*

The list of superattracting p-cycles in Table 3 was taken from a paper published in 1973 by three authors Metropolis, Stein and Stein, (see Cvitanović (1984)). These authors also computed the corresponding superattracting p-cycles for the family:

$$x_{n+1} = \lambda \sin(\pi x_n), \quad n = 0, 1, 2, \ldots,$$

where $0 \leqslant \lambda \leqslant 1$. They found that these p-cycles appear in exactly the same order for each family and proposed an explanation for this 'universal' phenomenon, based on the kneading sequence, so called because it describes the way in which a function f mixes the interval $[0, 1]$ when f is applied repeatedly.

If λ is a parameter value such that f_λ has a superattracting p-cycle,

Fig. 53

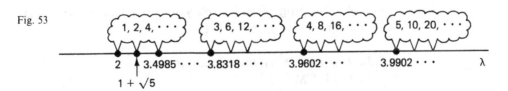

1, 2, 4, · · ·   3, 6, 12, · · ·   4, 8, 16, · · ·   5, 10, 20, · · ·

2   3.4985 · · · 3.8318 · · ·   3.9602 · · ·   3.9902 · · · λ

$1 + \sqrt{5}$

Table 3

Period	λ	Period	λ
1	2	7	3.922 193 4
2	3.236 068 0	6	3.937 536 4
4	3.498 561 7	7	3.951 032 2
6	3.627 557 5	4	3.960 270 1
7	3.701 769 2	7	3.968 976 9
5	3.738 914 9	6	3.977 766 4
7	3.774 214 2	7	3.984 747 6
3	3.831 874 1	5	3.990 267 0
6	3.844 568 8	7	3.994 537 8
7	3.886 045 9	6	3.997 583 1
5	3.905 706 5	7	3.999 397 1

then the *kneading sequence* $k(\lambda)$ of f_λ is a sequence, each of whose terms is R (for 'right'), L (for 'left') or C (for 'centre' or 'critical'). The sequence is obtained by noting where the points $f_\lambda^n(\frac{1}{2})$ fall on the interval $[0, 1]$. To be precise, the nth term $k_n(\lambda)$ of the kneading sequence is given by

$$k_n(\lambda) = \begin{cases} R & \text{if } f_\lambda^n(\tfrac{1}{2}) > \tfrac{1}{2}, \\ L & \text{if } f_\lambda^n(\tfrac{1}{2}) < \tfrac{1}{2}, \\ C & \text{if } f_\lambda^n(\tfrac{1}{2}) = \tfrac{1}{2}. \end{cases}$$

For example,

$$k(2) = (CCC\ldots), \quad k(1 + \sqrt{5}) = (RCRCRC\ldots).$$

In fact the kneading sequence can be defined for any f_λ, but if f_λ has a superattracting p-cycle and $\lambda > 2$ then the kneading sequence is of the form

$$k(f) = (XXX\ldots)$$

where X denotes a sequence of symbols, starting with R and finishing with C, which repeats indefinitely. We write this in abbreviated form

$$k(f) = (R\ldots C).$$

The following program will enable you to determine the kneading sequence of any given f_λ, $0 \leqslant \lambda \leqslant 4$.

9.34 *Program: Kneading sequence*
```
10 INPUT M
```

```
2Ø  LET X = Ø.5
3Ø  LET X = M*X*(1 − X)
4Ø  IF ABS(X − Ø.5) < Ø.ØØØ1 THEN PRINT "C": STOP
5Ø  IF X > Ø.5 THEN PRINT "R": GOTO 3Ø
6Ø  PRINT "L": GOTO 3Ø
```

At line 4Ø the program tests whether a term of the sequence is equal to $\frac{1}{2}$. The permitted error 0.0001 used there may need to be varied in certain cases, for example with a long superattracting cycle where rounding errors displace the term $\frac{1}{2}$ slightly.

9.35 *Exercise*
Determine the kneading sequences of those f_λ which have super-attracting p-cycles for $p \leqslant 7$.

Metropolis, Stein and Stein computed the kneading sequences for these superattracting p-cycles in their 1973 paper and also computed the kneading sequences of the corresponding p-cycles for the sine family $x_{n+1} = \lambda \sin(\pi x_n)$. By now you won't be surprised to hear that the kneading sequences were identical in each case. The iteration behaviour of these two families is essentially the same, although they are defined by completely different functions. It was these observations which motivated Feigenbaum to perform his numerical computations on these two iteration families, which led to the universal constant $\delta = 4.669 \ldots$. What more dramatic example of the power of computers to influence mathematics can be imagined?

The kneading sequence has been the object of very detailed study. Although each λ with a superattracting p-cycle has a kneading sequence of the form $(R \ldots C)$, it is not true that for each sequence of this form there is a corresponding λ with a superattracting p-cycle. For example, there is no λ with a superattracting 3-cycle having kneading sequence (RRC). Indeed, no kneading sequence of the form $(RR \ldots C)$ can ever occur (why?).

A much more elaborate restriction on kneading sequences can be given, however. This uses a strange kind of *order* on sequences of Ls, Rs and Cs, which we define as follows, using the natural order on the symbols L, R and C:

$$L < C < R.$$

Suppose that

$$a = (a_1 a_2 a_3 \ldots) \quad \text{and} \quad b = (b_1 b_2 b_3 \ldots)$$

are two sequences of Ls, Rs and Cs, and that

$$a_1 = b_1, a_2 = b_2, \ldots, a_{n-1} = b_{n-1} \quad \text{BUT} \quad a_n \neq b_n;$$

then we say that

$$a < b$$

if either

      (i) there is an even number of Rs in $a_1, \ldots, a_{n-1}$ and $a_n < b_n$; or

      (ii) there is an odd number of Rs in $a_1, \ldots, a_{n-1}$ and $a_n > b_n$.

For example,

$$(RLRC \ldots) < (RLRRC \ldots),$$

because the common leading sequence RLR contains an even number of Rs and the next pair of symbols are $C < R$. On the other hand

$$(RLRRC \ldots) < (RLLLC \ldots)$$

because the common leading sequence RL contains an odd number of Rs and then $R > L$.

Using this order, we can show that all kneading sequences $k(\lambda)$ have the property that:

$$k(\lambda) \text{ is greater than each of the terminal sequences of } k(\lambda), \quad (10)$$

(a terminal sequence of $k(\lambda)$ is obtained by deleting from $k(\lambda)$ one of its leading sequences). For example, the sequence $(RLRRC)$, which is the kneading sequence of the superattracting 5-cycle at $\lambda = 3.738\,914\,9$, satisfies

$$(RLRRC) > (LRRC),$$
$$(RLRRC) > (RRC),$$
$$(RLRRC) > (RC),$$
$$(RLRRC) > (C).$$

On the other hand $(RLRLLC)$ does not enjoy this property, as you can easily check, so it is not a periodic kneading sequence.

The proof of property (10) is based on two simple remarks about the functions f_λ:

Remark 1. The largest value of $f_\lambda^n(\tfrac{1}{2})$, $n = 1, 2, 3, \ldots$, is $f_\lambda(\tfrac{1}{2}) = \lambda/4$.

Remark 2. If $0 \le x < y < \tfrac{1}{2}$, then $f_\lambda(x) < f_\lambda(y)$, and if $\tfrac{1}{2} < x < y \le 1$, then $f_\lambda(x) > f_\lambda(y)$.

Suppose then that the kneading sequence

$$k(\lambda) = (a_1 \, a_2 \ldots C)$$

has a terminal sequence

$$k^{(n)}(\lambda) = (a_{n+1} \, a_{n+2} \ldots C),$$

and that their common leading sequence has length $m - 1$, i.e.

$$a_{n+1} = a_1, \qquad a_{n+2} = a_2, \qquad \ldots, \qquad a_{n+m-1} = a_{m-1} \quad \text{BUT}$$
$$a_{n+m} \neq a_m.$$

Since $a_{n+1} = a_1 = R$, we have $\frac{1}{2} < f_\lambda^{n+1}(\frac{1}{2}) < f_\lambda(\frac{1}{2})$ by Remark 1. Thus, on applying Remark 2 repeatedly, we find that:

if there is an even number of Rs in $a_1, a_2, \ldots, a_{m-1}$, then $f_\lambda^{n+m}(\frac{1}{2}) < f_\lambda^m(\frac{1}{2})$ so that $a_{n+m} < a_m$ and hence $k^{(n)}(\lambda) < k(\lambda)$;

if there is an odd number of Rs in $a_1, a_2, \ldots, a_{m-1}$, then $f_\lambda^{n+m}(\frac{1}{2}) > f_\lambda^m(\frac{1}{2})$ so that $a_{n+m} > a_m$ and hence $k^{(n)}(\lambda) < k(\lambda)$.

With greater difficulty it can be shown that if a periodic sequence of the form $(R \ldots C)$ does have the above property (10), then it *is* the kneading sequence of some superattracting cycle. Furthermore it is conjectured that the superattracting cycles of f_λ appear in the interval $[0, 4]$ in an order which corresponds precisely to the order given by their periodic kneading sequences, and that this applies to the family $x_{n+1} = \lambda \sin(\pi x_n)$ also.

9.36 *Exercises*

(a) Write a program to test the order of two given sequences with terms 'R', 'L' or 'C'. Use your program to confirm that the superattracting cycles of f_λ with period ≤ 7 do appear in an order which corresponds to the order of their kneading sequences.

(b) Modify your program to test whether a given sequence with terms 'R', 'L' or 'C' has property (10). Use your program to show that all such periodic sequences of length at most 7 do correspond to superattracting cycles of f_λ.

9.37 *A general convergence result*

This is a short theoretical section which illustrates some of the methods which are available to prove convergence results about iteration sequences. To be precise we shall prove the following result.

> *Theorem: If $f_\lambda(x) = \lambda x(1 - x)$ has an attracting p-cycle for some integer p, then the sequence $f_\lambda^n(\frac{1}{2})$, $n = 1, 2, \ldots$, must converge to this p-cycle.*

This result explains why we concentrated so much on the behaviour of the sequence $f_\lambda^n(\frac{1}{2})$ earlier on. One consequence of the theorem is that $f_\lambda(x) = \lambda x(1 - x)$ can have *at most one* attracting p-cycle. The theorem will also hold for other families of iteration sequences, such as that associated with $g_\lambda(x) = \lambda \sin(\pi x)$, as will be clear from the proof.

It is essential, for the following argument to work, that the initial term of our iteration sequence is $\frac{1}{2}$, the point which divides the function $f_\lambda(x)$ into its increasing and decreasing parts. It can be proved that if f_λ has an attracting p-cycle, then $f_\lambda^n(x)$ converges to this p-cycle for *most* x in $[0, 1]$, but this is considerably harder.

Suppose then that f_λ has an attracting p-cycle $c, f_\lambda(c), \ldots, f_\lambda^{p-1}(c)$. We know from Section 5.4 that there is an open interval I_0 containing c such that, for x in I_0,

$$f_\lambda^{pn}(x) \to c \quad \text{as } n \to \infty.$$

Similarly, for each $k = 1, 2, \ldots, p - 1$, there is an open interval I_k containing $f_\lambda^k(c)$ such that, for x in I_k,

$$f_\lambda^{pn}(x) \to f^k(c) \quad \text{as } n \to \infty.$$

We may assume that each $I_0, I_1, \ldots, I_{p-1}$ is a maximal open interval with this property and we aim to prove that the number $\frac{1}{2}$ lies in one of these intervals. Clearly each of the intervals $I_0, I_1, \ldots, I_{p-1}$ lies inside $(0, 1)$ because neither $f_\lambda^n(0)$ nor $f_\lambda^n(1)$ tends to the p-cycle. Since each of the intervals is maximal, we have

$$f_\lambda(I_0) \subseteq I_1, f_\lambda(I_1) \subseteq I_2, \ldots, f_\lambda(I_{p-1}) \subseteq I_0.$$

Suppose now that $\frac{1}{2}$ does *not* lie in any of the intervals $I_0, I_1, \ldots, I_{p-1}$. We shall try to obtain a contradiction from this. Because $\frac{1}{2}$ is the only point where $f_\lambda'(x)$ equals 0, the function $f_\lambda(x)$ must be monotonic (either increasing or decreasing) on each of the intervals $I_0, I_1, \ldots, I_{p-1}$ and so the composite function must be monotonic on I_0. Furthermore $f_\lambda^p(I_0) \subseteq I_0$ and the end-points of I_0 are not mapped into I_0 by f_λ^p (otherwise I_0 could be enlarged somewhat). Hence f_λ^p must map each of the end-points of I_0 to an end-point of I_0.

Thus, if f_λ^p is increasing on I_0, then f_λ^p has a fixed point at each end of I_0, in addition to the attracting fixed point at c in I_0. See Fig. 54. Moreover $(f_\lambda^p)'(x) \neq 0$ in I_0, since $f_\lambda'(x) \neq 0$ in $I_0, I_1, \ldots, I_{p-1}$.

Fig. 54

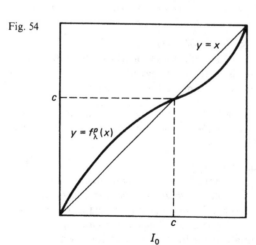

$$I_0$$

On the other hand, if f_λ^p is decreasing on I_0 then f_λ^p must interchange the end-points of I_0. But then $f_\lambda^{2p}(x)$ will have a fixed point at each end of I_0, in addition to the attracting fixed point at c in I_0. See Fig. 55. Here, once again, $(f_\lambda^{2p})'(x) \neq 0$ in I_0.

Thinking back to all the graphs of $y = f_\lambda^n(x)$ you have seen, it may well occur to you that this kind of configuration, in which an attracting fixed point is 'trapped' between two other fixed points, has never occurred (unless $(f_\lambda^n)'(x) = 0$ for some x in the interval). This leads us to formulate a conjecture which, if true, would prove our theorem.

Fig. 55

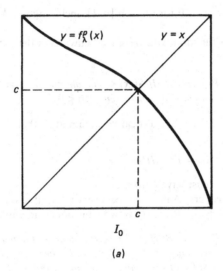

$y = f_\lambda^p(x)$ $y = x$

c

c

I_0

(a)

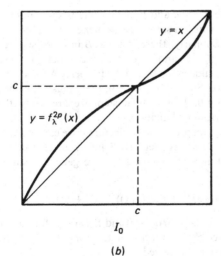

$y = x$

c

$y = f_\lambda^{2p}(x)$

c

I_0

(b)

Conjecture: If $f_\lambda^n(x)$ has fixed points at a and b and an attracting fixed point at c in (a, b), then $(f_\lambda^n)'(x)$ must equal 0 at some x in (a, b).

To prove this conjecture we are going to introduce a rather unexpected analytic expression. In the late 1970s it was realised that a notion from complex analysis called the Schwarzian derivative was useful in real iteration theory. This *Schwarzian derivative* is defined as follows:

$$Sf(x) = \frac{f'''(x)}{f'(x)} - \frac{3}{2}\left(\frac{f''(x)}{f'(x)}\right)^2,$$

provided that $f'(x) \neq 0$. You can easily check that for $f_\lambda(x) = \lambda x(1 - x)$:

$$Sf_\lambda(x) = -6/(1 - 2x)^2,$$

and so $Sf_\lambda(x) < 0$ for all x in $[0, 1]$, including $x = \frac{1}{2}$ if we allow the value $-\infty$.

Now a function with negative Schwarzian derivative has the following property.

Property A: If $Sf(x) < 0$ on an interval I and $f'(x)$ has a local minimum at a in I, then $f'(a) < 0$.

Indeed if $f'(x)$ has a local minimum at a, then $f''(a) = 0$ and $f'''(a) \geq 0$. Hence

$$Sf(a) = f'''(a)/f'(a) < 0,$$

so that we must have $f'(a) < 0$.

Now Property A may not seem very relevant to our conjecture. But it can be used to prove Property B, which is of considerable relevance.

Property B: If $f(x)$ has fixed points at a and b and an attracting fixed point at c in (a, b) and, furthermore $Sf(x) < 0$ in (a, b), then $f'(x)$ must equal 0 at some x in (a, b).

Because $f(a) = a$ and $f(c) = c$, there is some number α in (a, c) such that $f'(\alpha) = 1$. This is a simple consequence of the Mean Value Theorem in real analysis. Similarly, there is some β in (c, b) such that $f'(\beta) = 1$. Because $f'(\alpha) = f'(\beta) = 1$ and $f'(c) < 1$, the function $f'(x)$ must have a local minimum value in (α, β) and, by Property A, this local minimum value must be negative. Since $f'(\alpha) = 1 > 0$, there must be some point x in (α, β) such that $f'(x) = 0$. In this final step, we are using the Intermediate Value Theorem from real analysis.

Thus we can prove the conjecture if we can show that the functions $f_\lambda^n(x)$, $n = 1, 2, \ldots$, all have negative Schwarzian derivative. We know already that $Sf_\lambda(x) < 0$ and we deduce the more general result from the composition formula

$$S(g \circ f)(x) = Sg(f(x))f'(x)^2 + Sf(x). \tag{11}$$

This tells us that if $Sf(x) < 0$ and $Sg(x) < 0$, for all x, then $S(g \circ f)(x) < 0$ for all x. Hence $Sf_\lambda^n(x) < 0$ for all x, for $n = 1, 2, \ldots$; thus our conjecture and theorem are both proved.

9.38 *Exercise*

Use the chain rule $(g \circ f)'(x) = g'(f(x))f'(x)$ to prove the formula (11).

9.39 *Exercise*

Verify that the family of functions $g_\lambda(x) = \lambda \sin(\pi x)$ all have negative Schwarzian derivative, and hence formulate a version of the theorem for this family.

9.40 *Chaos*

Because of the apparent lack of structure in the iterates of $f_\lambda(x)$ for $\lambda_\infty < \lambda < 4$ (see Fig. 24), this interval is often referred to as the chaotic interval. However, we have seen that the interval $(\lambda_\infty, 4)$ contains many periodic windows in which, by the theorem of the previous section, the sequence $f_\lambda^n(\tfrac{1}{2})$ converges to an attracting cycle. For some other values of λ, the behaviour of the sequence $f_\lambda^n(x)$, for most x in $[0, 1]$, can genuinely be described as chaotic. Consider, for example, the case $\lambda = 4$.

The function $f_4(x)$ maps $[0, 1]$ onto itself exactly. See Fig. 56. This means that the sequence $f_4^n(\tfrac{1}{2})$, $n = 1, 2, \ldots$, is actually rather simple, namely $1, 0, 0, \ldots$. Since 0 is a repelling fixed point, we may conclude that the function $f_4(x)$ has no attracting p-cycles. In fact the iterates $f_4^n(x)$, for most values of x in $[0, 1]$, are very badly behaved as you can easily discover by running Program 3.1 with this function. Starting from almost any value of x in $[0, 1]$ (including $x = \tfrac{1}{2}$ if your micro is poor at arithmetic!) you will find that the sequence $f_4^n(x)$, $n = 1, 2, \ldots$, appears to visit every part of $[0, 1]$ not once but

Fig. 56

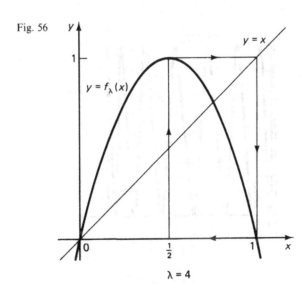

$\lambda = 4$

arbitrarily many times. This sequence could actually be used to generate 'random numbers'.

There are various mathematical ways to describe the chaotic behaviour of an iteration sequence such as $f_4^n(x)$. We shall focus on just one here, which is called 'sensitive dependence on initial conditions'. Roughly speaking a function f from an interval I to itself has sensitive dependence on initial conditions if in each subinterval

Fig. 57

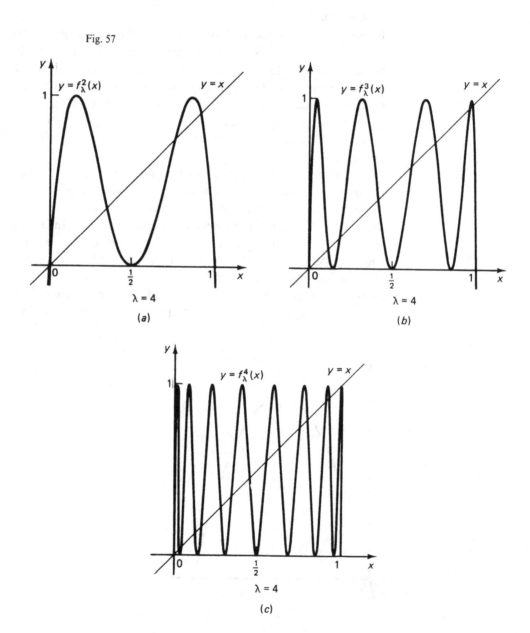

of I (no matter how short) there are points x, y which do not remain close together under the iteration of f. If f has this property, then it is clear that numerical computation of the sequence will be completely unreliable since small errors in a given calculation are capable of extreme magnification after a number of iterations.

It is easy to check that the function $f_4(x)$ appears to have sensitive dependence on initial conditions (try choosing x, y close together in $[0, 1]$ and computing several iterates of each). To see why $f_4(x)$ has this property, plot the graphs $y = f_4^2(x)$, $y = f_4^3(x)$, $y = f_4^4(x)$, . . ., using Program 5.1. See Fig. 57. The graph $y = f_4^n(x)$ consists of 2^{n-1} humps, each of which reaches from the x-axis to the line $y = 1$. (Can you explain this? It helps to consider $f_4^n(x) = f_4^{n-1}(f_4(x))$.) Also it appears that the points x in $[0, 1]$ such that $f_4^n(x) = 0$, for some n, form a 'dense' subset of $[0, 1]$, i.e. we can find such points in any given subinterval I of $[0, 1]$. Let us assume that such an interval I contains points a, b such that $f_4^n(a) = 0$ and $f_4^n(b) = 0$. Then there must be some c in (a, b) such that $f_4^n(c) = 1$. Hence in any subinterval I of $[0, 1]$ there are points a, c such that $|f_4^n(a) - f_4^n(c)| = 1$, so that f_4 does have sensitive dependence on initial conditions.

But how do we show that the points x where $f_4^n(x) = 0$, for some n, form a dense subset of $[0, 1]$? One way to prove this involves the remarkable fact that the function $f_4(x)$ is conjugate to a somewhat simpler function. Consider the change of variable:

$$u_n = (2/\pi) \sin^{-1}(\sqrt{x_n}).$$

Since $x_n = \sin^2(\pi u_n/2)$ the sequence

$$x_{n+1} = 4x_n(1 - x_n)$$

is conjugate to

$$\sin^2(\pi u_{n+1}/2) = 4 \sin^2(\pi u_n/2)(1 - \sin^2(\pi u_n/2))$$
$$= 4 \sin^2(\pi u_n/2) \cos^2(\pi u_n/2)$$
$$= \sin^2(\pi u_n),$$

by a half-angle formula. Using the graph $v = \sin^2(\pi u)$ (Fig. 58) it can be seen that

$$\frac{u_{n+1}}{2} = \begin{cases} u_n, & \text{if } 0 \leq u_n \leq \tfrac{1}{2}, \\ 1 - u_n, & \text{if } \tfrac{1}{2} < u_n \leq 1. \end{cases}$$

Hence the sequence u_n is obtained by iterating the so called tent map (Fig. 59).

$$T(u) = \begin{cases} 2u, & 0 \leq u \leq \tfrac{1}{2} \\ 2(1 - u), & \tfrac{1}{2} < u \leq 1. \end{cases}$$

Fig. 58

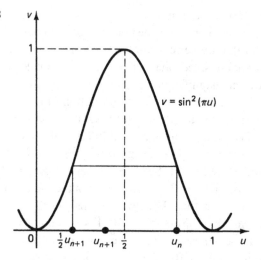

$$v = \sin^2(\pi u)$$

$$\tfrac{1}{2}u_{n+1} \quad u_{n+1} \quad \tfrac{1}{2} \qquad u_n \qquad 1 \qquad u$$

Put another way the function $f_4(x)$ is conjugate to $T(u)$ using the 1–1 correspondence $u = \phi(x) = (2/\pi)\sin^{-1}(\sqrt{x})$:

$$f_4(x) = \phi^{-1}(T(\phi(x))).$$

Now the graphs $v = T^n(u)$ are easy to describe (Fig. 60). The graph $v = T^n(u)$ has 2^{n-1} humps and the points u where $T^n(u) = 0$ are precisely those points of the form $p/2^{n-1}$, for $p = 0, 1, \ldots, 2^{n-1}$. Thus the points u where $T^n(u) = 0$, for some n, form the set of all rationals in $[0, 1]$ with a power of 2 in the denominator, and this set is certainly dense in $[0, 1]$. Now the points x where $f_4^n(x) = 0$, for some n, correspond to these points u under the 1–1 correspondence $u = (2/\pi)\sin^{-1}(\sqrt{x})$, and so they too must form a dense subset of

Fig. 59

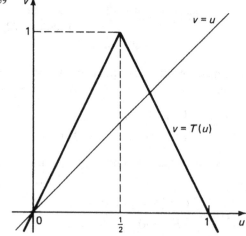

$$v = u$$

$$v = T(u)$$

[0, 1], as we claimed. This completes the proof that $f_4(x)$ does indeed have sensitive dependence on initial conditions.

It is natural to ask whether there are any other functions f_λ, for $0 < \lambda < 4$, which have sensitive dependence on initial conditions. One of the key features which causes f_4 to display this behaviour is that f_4 maps the interval [0, 1] onto itself and covers itself essentially

Fig. 60

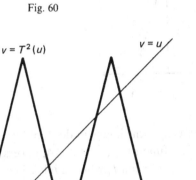

(a)

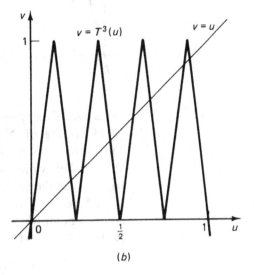

(b)

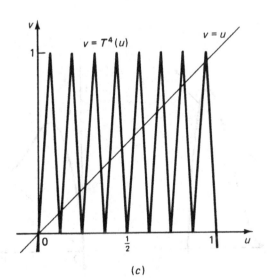

(c)

Fig. 61

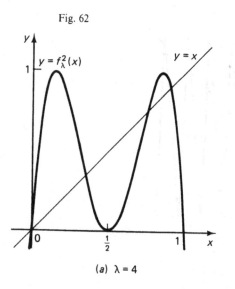

twice over. Every point in $[0, 1)$ is the image under f_4 of two points in $[0, 1]$. See Fig. 61. No other function f_λ, $0 < \lambda < 4$, covers $[0, 1]$ in this manner, but there are other such f_λ whose higher iterates have the same behaviour on certain subintervals of $[0, 1]$. For example, let us consider the behaviour of $y = f_\lambda^2(x)$ as λ decreases from 4 to $1 + \sqrt{5}$. (Fig. 62.) As λ decreases the value $f_\lambda^2(\tfrac{1}{2})$ increases and there comes a point when $f_\lambda^2(x)$ maps a certain symmetric subinterval of $[0, 1]$ onto itself. (Fig. 63.) In this position we have

$$f_\lambda^2(\tfrac{1}{2}) = 1 - c_\lambda,$$

Fig. 62

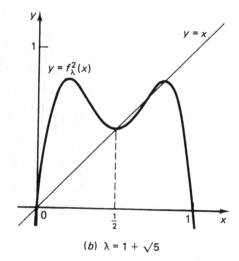

(a) $\lambda = 4$

(b) $\lambda = 1 + \sqrt{5}$

i.e.

$$f_\lambda^2(\tfrac{1}{2}) + c_\lambda = 1.$$

Substituting $f_\lambda^2(\tfrac{1}{2}) = \tfrac{1}{4}\lambda^2(1 - \lambda/4)$ and $c_\lambda = 1 - 1/\lambda$, we obtain

$$\frac{\lambda^2}{4}\left(1 - \frac{\lambda}{4}\right) + 1 - \frac{1}{\lambda} = 1,$$

which is the quartic equation

$$\lambda^4 - 4\lambda^3 + 16 = 0.$$

Noting that $\lambda - 2$ is a factor (why should we expect this?), this quartic reduces to

$$\lambda^3 - 2\lambda^2 - 4\lambda - 8 = 0.$$

9.41 *Exercises*

(a) Solve the above cubic equation, using the method of bisection or the Newton–Raphson method, to find the solution $\lambda = 3.678\,573\,5\ldots$ (and check where λ lies in Fig. 25(b)).

(b) Use Program 5.1 to check that $y = f_\lambda^2(x)$ has the desired form for this value of λ. What happens if you plot $f_\lambda^{2n}(x)$, for $n = 1, 2, \ldots$, where x is in $[0, 1]$?

You should have discovered in Exercise 9.41 that the function $f_\lambda^2(x)$, with $\lambda = 3.678\,573\,5\ldots$ does seem to have sensitive dependence on initial conditions (and so f_λ does also). The proof of this is rather similar to that for $f_4(x)$, but this time we do not have a

Fig. 63

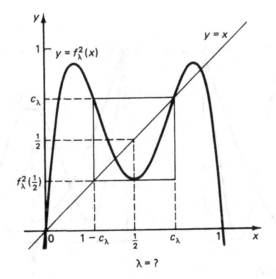

$\lambda = ?$

convenient change of variable to hand. (A more sophisticated argument is required which once again uses the fact that the functions f_λ have negative Schwarzian derivative! Compare 9.37.) Rather than go into the technicalities of this proof, we shall explain how to find a whole sequence of values of λ for which $f_\lambda(x)$ has sensitive dependence on initial conditions.

This sequence of values of λ arises in a manner which is reminiscent of the period doubling phenomenon discussed earlier. Consider what happens to the graphs $y = f_\lambda^2(x)$ and $y = f_\lambda^4(x)$ as λ decreases below $\lambda = 3.678\,573\,5\ldots$. (In Fig. 64 we have plotted only the central square with (c_λ, c_λ) in the top right-hand corner. As λ decreases the central hump of $y = f_\lambda^4(x)$ descends and at some point $f_\lambda^4(x)$ maps a certain symmetric subinterval exactly onto itself. By considering $f_\lambda^8(x), f_\lambda^{16}(x)$ and so on, one can see that this process will continue indefinitely to give a sequence Λ_n of values of λ such that each f_{Λ_n} has sensitive dependence on initial conditions:

$$\Lambda_0 = 4, \quad \Lambda_1 = 3.678\ldots, \quad \Lambda_2, \Lambda_3, \ldots.$$

But how do we calculate these points Λ_n?

Referring again to Fig. 64, it can be seen that

$$f_\lambda^4(\tfrac{1}{2}) - \tfrac{1}{2} = \tfrac{1}{2} - c,$$

i.e.

$$1 - f_\lambda^4(\tfrac{1}{2}) = c,$$

Fig. 64

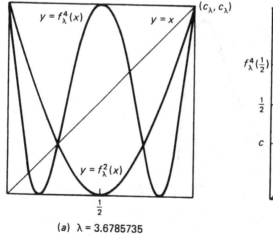

(a) $\lambda = 3.6785735$

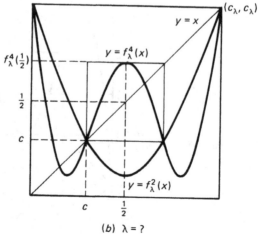

(b) $\lambda = ?$

where c is the nearest fixed point of $f_\lambda^2(x)$. This gives us a test for a prospective value for λ. To be precise, if λ is too great then

$$f_\lambda^4(\tfrac{1}{2}) - \tfrac{1}{2} > \tfrac{1}{2} - c,$$

i.e.

$$d = 1 - f_\lambda^4(\tfrac{1}{2}) < c.$$

Computing $f_\lambda^2(d)$ in this case, we find that

$$f_\lambda^2(d) > d.$$

On the other hand, if λ is too small, then

$$d = 1 - f_\lambda^4(\tfrac{1}{2}) > c,$$

so that

$$f_\lambda^2(d) < d.$$

In summary, our strategy for applying the method of bisection is:

$$f_\lambda^2(d) > d \quad \Rightarrow \quad \lambda \text{ too large;}$$
$$f_\lambda^2(d) < d \quad \Rightarrow \quad \lambda \text{ too small.}$$

The next program implements this strategy.

9.42 *Program: Lambda two*
```
10 INPUT L, U
20 FOR I = 1 TO 30
30 LET M = 0.5*(L + U)
40 LET X = 0.5
50 FOR J = 1 TO 4
60 LET X = M*X*(1 – X)
70 NEXT J
80 LET Y = 1 – X
90 FOR J = 1 TO 2
100 LET Y = M*Y*(1 – Y)
110 NEXT J
120 IF Y > (1 – X) THEN LET U = M: GOTO 140
130 LET L = M
140 NEXT I
150 PRINT M
```

9.43 *Exercise*
Run Program 9.42 with various choices of U and L to determine Λ_2. Use Program 5.1 to check that the graph $y = f_{\Lambda_2}^4(x)$ has the correct form with your value of Λ_2. What happens if you plot the sequence $f_{\Lambda_2}^{4n}(x)$, $n = 1, 2, \ldots$, for various choices of initial term x?

You should discover in Exercise 9.43 that $f^4_{A_2}(x)$ does have sensitive dependence on initial conditions (so that $f_{A_2}(x)$ does also) for $A_2 = 3.592\,572\,18 \ldots$. By now you should be itching to know more values of the sequence A_n and we hope that you have a good idea how to modify Program 9.42 in order to calculate these (use Program 9.15 as a model). Once again you will have to predict where A_n lies by using the values of A_{n-1} and A_{n-2}. Also, don't forget to take account of the different orientation of $f^{2^n}_\lambda(x)$, depending on whether n is even or odd.

9.44 Exercises

(a)   Write a program to compute the sequence A_n, for $n = 2, 3, 4, \ldots$. Hence find experimental values for:

$$\lim_{n \to \infty} A_n \quad \text{and} \quad \lim_{n \to \infty} \frac{A_{n-2} - A_{n-1}}{A_{n-1} - A_n}.$$

(b)   Adapt your program to compute the analogous quantities for the family $x_{n+1} = \lambda \sin(\pi x_n)$, $n = 1, 2, \ldots$.

This final exercise on quadratic sequences should convince you (if you were not already convinced) that there are good reasons for mathematicians and physicists to devote so much effort to studying such an apparently simple family of iteration sequences and, moreover, what a useful tool is the micro in such investigations.

§10 Exponential sequences

If you have read §9 Quadratic sequences, then you cannot fail to have been surprised at how complicated the behaviour of such apparently simple sequences can be. In this section we look at the so called exponential sequences defined by the iteration formula

$$x_{n+1} = a^{x_n}, \quad n = 0, 1, 2, \ldots, \tag{1}$$

where a is a positive real number. We shall sometimes use the notation $f_a(x) = a^x$, and we often take $x_0 = 0$, as the initial term of (1), so that the sequence is

$$0, 1, a, a^a, a^{a^a}, \ldots.$$

It is natural to ask whether the behaviour of the sequences (1) is more or less complicated than that of the quadratic sequences. On the one hand exponential functions are somewhat more tricky to deal with than quadratics, but on the other hand exponential functions have graphs which are either increasing or decreasing (depending on a).

In §2 and §3, you investigated the behaviour of several exponential sequences and we hope that you found several different types of behaviour. For example there are many values of a and x_0 for which the sequence is convergent and others for which it is divergent. A systematic investigation is clearly required.

The program below takes a large number of values of a, between 0 and 2, and plots each of the corresponding sequences x_n vertically above a horizontal a-axis, taking $x_0 = 0$ in each case. In order to detect the eventual behaviour of x_n (where possible), only the terms $x_{50}, x_{51}, \ldots, x_{100}$ are plotted. Thus if x_n is convergent, then a single point should be plotted and, more generally, if x_n converges to a p-cycle, then p points should be plotted.

10.1 *Program: a plot*

```
10 LET N = 0.25 * VMAX
20 FOR I = 1 TO N
30 LET A = 2 * I/N
40 LET X = 0
50 FOR J = 1 TO 100
60 LET X = A↑X
70 IF J > 49 THEN put a dot at screen point (4*I,
       VMAX*X/4)
80 NEXT J
90 NEXT I
```

Here VMAX denotes as usual the maximum vertical screen coordinate and we have taken $n = \frac{1}{4}v_{max}$ values of a. In plotting the points x_n (in line 70) it has been assumed that $0 < x_n < 4$; you will find that this holds most of the time, although for some values of a the terms x_n become too large for the computer to handle. Fig. 65 is the picture which emerges. As you can see, we've added axes in order to measure

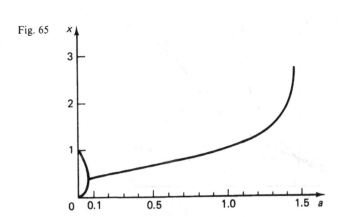

Fig. 65

where the different types of behaviour occur. The picture reveals the following:

> for $0 < a < 0.1$ (approx.) the sequence x_n converges to a 2-cycle;
> for $0.1 < a < 1.4$ (approx.) the sequence x_n is convergent;
> for $1.4 < a < 2$ (approx.) the sequence x_n becomes too large for the computer to handle.

These observations suggest that the behaviour of the exponential sequences (1) is going to be much easier to classify than were the quadratic sequences. However, there is something of a mystery over these numbers 0.1 and 1.4 (approx.) at which the behaviour of x_n changes. What exactly are these values?

In order to explain these observations, we consider the two cases $a > 1$ and $0 < a < 1$ separately (the case $a = 1$ is rather trivial, because if $a = 1$, then $x_n = 1$ for $n = 1, 2, \ldots$). This is because we are going to use the graphical iteration technique from §3 and the graphs $y = a^x$ are rather different for the two cases.

10.2 *The range $a > 1$*

For $a > 1$, the function $f_a(x) = a^x$ is increasing and convex (i.e. $f_a''(x) > 0$, for $x > 0$). Fig. 66 shows the graphs $y = a^x$ for a range of values of a, such that $a \geqslant 1$. As a increases from $a = 1$, the graph $y = a^x$ at first cuts the graph $y = x$ at two points, so that the function $f_a(x) = a^x$ has two fixed points. However, beyond a certain value of a (where f_a has exactly one fixed point) the graph $y = a^x$ does not meet $y = x$. Use of Program 3.1 shows that it is these differing relationships between $y = a^x$ and $y = x$ which determine the different behaviour of the sequence x_n. In both cases x_n is an increasing sequence, but the presence of a fixed point forces x_n to be convergent and its absence allows x_n to tend to infinity (Fig. 67).

Fig. 66

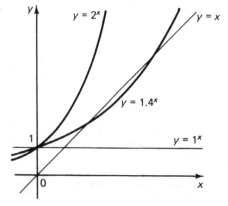

$y = 2^x$

$y = x$

$y = 1.4^x$

$y = 1^x$

Fig. 67

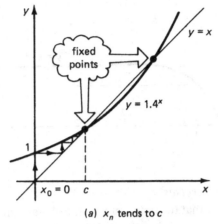

(a) x_n tends to c

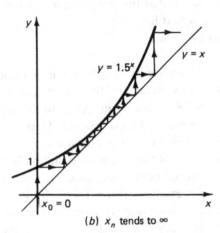

(b) x_n tends to ∞

Thus there is a number, $a_{\max}$ say, such that

$$x_n \text{ is convergent}, \quad \text{for } 1 < a \leqslant a_{\max}$$
$$x_n \to \infty, \qquad\qquad \text{for } a > a_{\max}.$$

To discover the value of $a_{\max}$, let us take b to denote the lower fixed point of $f_a(x) = a^x$, whenever such a fixed point exists. Thus

$$a^b = b \quad \text{and so} \quad a = b^{1/b},$$

since b is clearly positive.

Now, we are trying to find the largest value of a for which f_a has such a fixed point. Hence, we are trying to find the maximum value of $b^{1/b}$, for $b > 0$. Thus we need to consider the graph $y = x^{1/x}$, which is plotted in Fig. 68. This graph has several interesting features, which we ask you to verify in the next exercise.

Fig. 68

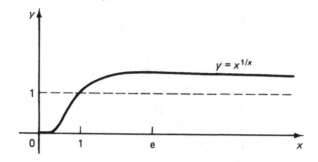

10.3 *Exercises*

(a)   Show that the function $x^{1/x}$, $x > 0$, has a single stationary point at $x = e$ and that this point is a maximum.

(b)   Show that $\lim_{x \to 0} x^{1/x} = 0$.

(c)   Show that $\lim_{x \to \infty} x^{1/x} = 1$.

According to Exercise 10.3(a), the maximum value of $b^{1/b}$, for $b > 0$, is $e^{1/e}$ and this must be the exact value of a_{max}. In fact, $e^{1/e} = 1.444\,667\,8\,\ldots$ is certainly close to the approximate value for a_{max} which we read off from Fig. 65. Thus, we have succeeded in classifying the behaviour of x_n, for $a \geqslant 1$.

We finally remark that if a is only slightly larger than $a_{max} = e^{1/e}$, then the corresponding sequence x_n displays quite unusual behaviour. For example, if $a = 1.5$, then the first ten terms of the sequence x_n are comparatively small and the sequence appears to be converging. However, by the thirteenth term the numbers involved are already too large for the micro to handle! The explanation is that, although the graph $y = 1.5^x$ does not meet $y = x$, the gap

Fig. 69

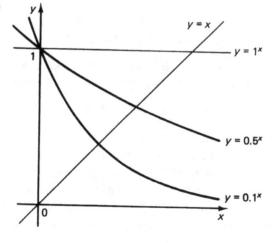

between these graphs is rather narrow and the sequence x_n must squeeze through this gap before accelerating off to infinity.

10.4 *The range* $0 < a < 1$

For $0 < a < 1$, the function $f_a(x) = a^x$ is decreasing and convex. Fig. 69 shows the graph $y = a^x$ for various values of a such that $0 < a < 1$.

For each value of a in this range, the function $f_a(x) = a^x$ has a unique fixed point, which we shall call b. Thus

$$a^b = b \quad \text{and so} \quad a = b^{1/b},$$

once again.

If we use Program 3.1 to view the sequence x_n graphically then we obtain a cobweb diagram, for each $0 < a < 1$ (Fig. 70). Thus the sequence x_n satisfies

$$x_0 < x_2 < x_4 < \ldots < b < \ldots < x_5 < x_3 < x_1. \tag{2}$$

10.5 *Exercise*

Prove that the inequalities (2) hold. (Hint: First note that $x_0 < x_2 < x_1$ and then apply the decreasing function $f_a(x) = a^x$ repeatedly.)

In Fig. 70 it appears that $x_n \to b$ as $n \to \infty$. However, we recall from our investigation with Program 10.1 that, for values of a below

Fig. 70

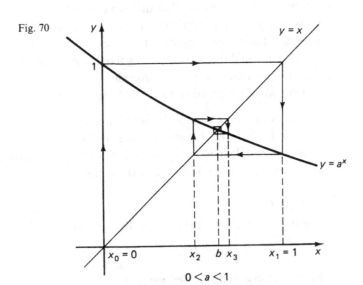

$0 < a < 1$

about 0.1, the sequence x_n appears to converge to a 2-cycle. This suggests that we should consider the function $f_a^2(x) = a^{a^x}$, which has the advantage of being increasing. We note that the odd and even subsequences of x_n can be defined as follows:

$$x_{2n+2} = f_a^2(x_{2n}), \quad n = 0, 1, 2, \ldots,$$

where $x_0 = 0$ and

$$x_{2n+3} = f_a^2(x_{2n+1}), \quad n = 0, 1, 2, \ldots,$$

where $x_1 = 1$. Also note that if $x_{2n} \to c$ as $n \to \infty$, then c must be a fixed point of $f_a^2(x) = a^{a^x}$, and we also have

$$x_{2n+1} = f_a(x_{2n}) \to f_a(c) \quad \text{as } n \to \infty.$$

Putting $d = f_a(c)$, we observe that c, d form a 2-cycle of f_a.

We can use Program 5.1 (with $p = 2$) to plot $y = a^{a^x}$, and it turns out that just two possibilities can occur. Either $f_a^2(x) = a^{a^x}$ has one fixed point, namely b, or $f_a^2(x) = a^{a^x}$ has three fixed points. In the latter case, the fixed points consist of b and a 2-cycle c, d of f_a. See Fig. 71. In (a) both the odd and even subsequences of x_n converge to b, whereas in (b) the sequence x_n converges to the 2-cycle c, d. These are the two kinds of behaviour which we detected with Program 10.1 and we aim to show that there is a number $a_{\min}$ such that

$$x_n \to b \text{ as } n \to \infty, \qquad \text{for } a_{\min} \leqslant a < 1,$$
$$x_n \to 2\text{-cycle as } n \to \infty, \quad \text{for } 0 < a < a_{\min}.$$

From Fig. 71, it appears that the two cases can be distinguished by considering the slope of $f_a^2(x) = a^{a^x}$ at the fixed point b. It is certainly true that if this slope exceeds 1, then the sequence x_n cannot tend to b because b would then be a repelling fixed point. The only possibility, therefore, is that x_n tends to a 2-cycle.

Thus we are reduced to two problems:

(a) For which values of a is it true that $(f_a^2)'(b) > 1$?
(b) If $(f_a^2)'(b) \leqslant 1$, can we prove that $x_n \to b$?

The first problem is easily solved by simply evaluating $(f_a^2)'(b)$, which we ask you to do in the next exercise.

10.6 *Exercise*

For $0 < a < 1$, let b satisfy $a^b = b$. Prove that

$$(f_a^2)'(b) = (\ln b)^2.$$

From Exercise 10.6, we deduce that

$$(f_a^2)'(b) \leqslant 1 \Leftrightarrow (\ln b)^2 \leqslant 1$$
$$\Leftrightarrow 1/e \leqslant b < 1 \quad \text{(since } b < 1)$$
$$\Leftrightarrow (1/e)^3 \leqslant a < 1,$$

since $x^{1/x}$ is a strictly increasing function for $0 < x < 1$.

This indicates that $a_{\min} = (1/e)^e = 0.065\,988\ldots$, which is certainly close to the approximate value in Fig. 65. To complete the classification, we need to show that if $(1/e)^e \leqslant a < 1$, then the sequence $x_n \to b$ as $n \to \infty$. This looks obvious from Fig. 71(a), but we have to exclude the possibility that the graph $y = a^{a^x}$ crosses $y = x$

Fig. 71

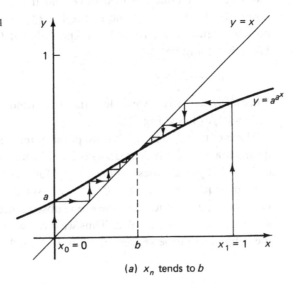

(a) x_n tends to b

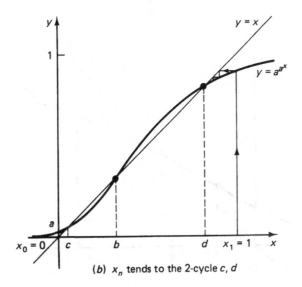

(b) x_n tends to the 2-cycle c, d

at points other than b. To do this we first observe that the graph $y = a^{a^x}$ has only one point of inflexion for $0 < a < 1$, i.e. only one point where $(f_a^2)''(x) = 0$.

10.7 *Exercises*

Suppose that $0 < a < 1$.

(a) Show that $f_a^2(x) = a^{a^x}$ has one point of inflexion t, and that $a^t = -1/\ln a$.

(b) Deduce that $a^{a^t} = 1/e$.

Exercise 10.7 enables us to deduce that if $(1/e)^e \leqslant a < 1$, then the point of inflexion t must lie to the left of the fixed point b (or is possibly equal to b). Indeed, we know that if $(1/e)^e \leqslant a < 1$, then $1/e \leqslant b < 1$ and so

$$a^{a^t} = 1/e \leqslant b = a^{a^b}.$$

Since a^{a^x} is increasing, we deduce that $t \leqslant b$ (and $t = b$ only if $b = 1/e$, i.e. $a = (1/e)^e$). See Fig. 72.

The fact that $f_a^2(x) = a^{a^x}$ has no point of inflexion to the right of b means that $(f_a^2)'(x)$ is decreasing for $x > b$ and since $(f_a^2)'(b) \leqslant 1$, we deduce that $y = a^{a^x}$ does not meet $y = x$ for $x > b$. It follows that the odd subsequence x_{2n+1}, $n = 0, 1, 2, \ldots$, starting from $x_1 = 1$, converges to b, and hence that the even subsequence $x_{2n+2} = f_a(x_{2n+1})$, $n = 0, 1, 2, \ldots$, does so also. Thus we have succeeded in classifying the behaviour of the sequences x_n for $0 < a < 1$.

Fig. 72

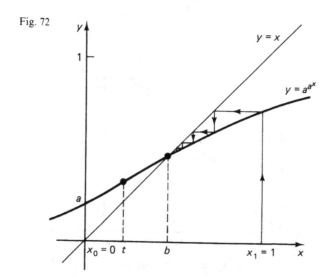

10.8 *The whole picture*

We have seen that it is possible to give a complete classification of the types of behaviour of the exponential sequence (1). This classification can be summarized in Fig. 73. It is worth remarking, finally, that since $x_n \to b$ as $n \to \infty$ for $(1/e)^e \leqslant a \leqslant e^{1/e}$ and since we have $a = b^{1/b}$, it is possible to describe part of Fig. 65 more precisely. Indeed the part of this plot which lies above the range $(1/e)^e \leqslant a \leqslant e^{1/e}$ must be part of the graph $y = x^{1/x}$ turned on its side. It is rather more difficult to describe the part of this plot which lies above the range $0 < a < (1/e)^e$ more precisely!

§11
Beyond real iteration sequences

We hope that this chapter has convinced you that the study of iteration sequences is of great interest and benefits enormously from the use of a micro. Indeed the advent of the micro has gone some way towards turning this area of mathematics into an experimental science! In this chapter, unfortunately, we had space to deal only with the iteration of real functions. However, many problems from physics, biology or economics deal with the iteration of functions from a higher dimensional space to itself, and the study of these is, as you can imagine, even more complicated.

One particularly nice family of functions to iterate are the functions of a complex variable, which are typically given by a formula such as

$$f(z) = z^2 + \sin z,$$

where z is a complex variable. By splitting the complex numbers into their real and imaginary parts, it is easy to plot, on a micro, a complex iteration sequence such as

$$z_{n+1} = z_n^2 + \sin z_n, \quad n = 0, 1, 2, \ldots,$$

and thus to begin the study and classification of such sequences.

Complex iteration sequences have been studied since the beginning of this century but there has been enormous growth in this area in the last ten years or so. This is partly because some of the computer pictures associated with such sequences are of great beauty and intricacy, falling into the category of computer art! You can read about this in Peitgen and Saupe (1988) and in Devaney (1986).

Fig. 73

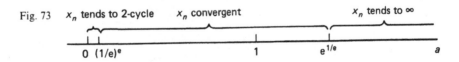

References

R. Courant and H. Robbins *What is Mathematics?*, Oxford University Press, Oxford, 4th Edn, 1947: (Paperback 1978)

P. Cvitanović (ed.) *Universality in Chaos*, Adam Hilger, 1984

R. L. Devaney *An Introduction to Chaotic Dynamical Systems*, Addison-Wesley, Reading, Mass., 1986

Z. A. Melzak *A Companion to Concrete Mathematics*, Volume I, Wiley-Interscience, Chichester, 1973

H. O. Peitgen and D. Saupe *The Science of Fractal Images*, Springer-Verlag, Berlin, 1988.

Index

The symbol → after a sub-heading indicates that the item is indexed in its own right elsewhere. Bold face numbers refer to major references or definitions.

Abelson, H. 85, 139, 244
addition, multiple precision 161
Ahlfors, L. V. 83
Alway factorization 184
Apostol, T. 113, 139, 244, 269, 280
arch
    of cycloid 134
    height of 53
Archimedes 63, 281
    spiral **118**
    and π 253f, 270
        program 256
        variant method 257
arclength 113
arithmetic–geometric mean 270
    program 271
arithmetic, multiple precision 160*ff*
Arnold, V. I. 304, 312, 314, 315, 317
Arrowsmith, D. K. 305, 309, 314, 315, 317
aspect ratio **87**, 88
astroid **69**
    picture 70
asymptotes
    avoiding 137*ff*
attracting, see fixed point; periodic point
attraction, interval of **342***ff*
    program 343
attractor 378
    strange 378
autonomous system **294**ff
    conservative **298**
    family of 314
    first integral **298**
    linear system →
    linearization 310*ff*
        not at origin **311**
    Lorenz 315
        program 316
    non-linear 310*f*
        saddle point **311**
        star **310**, **311**
    program 296
    stationary points **295**, 301*ff*

bacteria 282
Bertrand's postulate 146
Besicovich, A. S. 116
bifurcation
    period doubling 367
    Poincaré–Andronov–Hopf **314**
binomial theorem 30
biorhythms 5
Birkhoff, G. 40, 46, 83
bisection, method of **46***ff*, 371, 389, 403
    program for 47, 405
Borwein, J. M. and P. B. 273, 279, 280
Boyer, C. B. 46, 63, 83
brachistochrone 114
Brassett, S. 127, 139, 245
Brent, R. P. 270
    Program for π 272
Brouncker, Lord 23
Bruce, J. W. 105, 120, 124, 127, 131, 139, 187, 193, 204, 205, 206, 209, 219, 244
Brun's theorem 147
Budden, F. J. 31, 39
Bürgi, J. 273

Car suspensions 305
cardioid **116**
    evolute 116
Carmichael number **180**
Cartesian oval **218***ff*
    bounded 222
    inflexion on 223, 225
    physical interpretation 219
    pictures 226
    plotting 220*ff*
    polar equation 220
    theory of 223*f*
Cassinian curve **219**
Cauchy, A.-L.
    theorem on roots of polynomials 82
caustic **196***ff*
    of circle 197, 199, 203
    coffee-cup 196, 197
    cusps on 205
    of ellipse 200, 203